Russia Faces NATO Expansion

Russia Faces NATO Expansion

Bearing Gifts or Bearing Arms?

J. L. BLACK

ROWMAN & LITTLEFIELD PUBLISHERS, INC.
Lanham • Boulder • New York • Oxford

ROWMAN & LITTLEFIELD PUBLISHERS, INC.

Published in the United States of America
by Rowman & Littlefield Publishers, Inc.
4720 Boston Way, Lanham, Maryland 20706
http://www.rowmanlittlefield.com

12 Hid's Copse Road
Cumnor Hill, Oxford OX2 9JJ, England

British Library Cataloguing in Publication Information Available

Library of Congress Cataloging-in-Publication Data

Black, J. L. (Joseph Laurence), 1937–
    Russia faces NATO expansion : bearing gifts or bearing arms? /
J. L. Black.
        p.   cm.
    Includes bibliographical references and index.
    ISBN 0-8476-9866-1 (cloth)
    1. Russia (Federation) — Military policy.   2. North Atlantic Treaty
Organization.   I. Title.
    UA770.B577 2000
    355'.033047—dc21
                                                            99-41681
                                                            CIP

Printed in the United States of America

♾TMThe paper used in this publication meets the minimum requirements of American
National Standard for Information Sciences—Permanence of Paper for Printed Library
Materials, ANSI/NISO Z39.48–1992.

Contents

List of Acronyms and Special Terms   vii

Preface   ix

Acknowledgments   xi

Introduction   1

SECTION I: THE HISTORY

1. Herein Lies the Tale   5

    1.1. A Long-festering Issue   7

    1.2. 1997—Down to the Wire   22

    1.3. Albright Comes to Town   29

    1.4. Summit at Helsinki   36

    1.5. Toward the Russia-NATO Founding Act   38

    1.6. "May Days": A Modern Time of Troubles   45

       a. The Founding Act, 27 May 1997   52

       b. Second Thoughts   54

       c. Yeltsin's "Reward"   58

       d. Madrid Summit, 8–9 July 1997   59

    1.7. Manifestations of the Debate   64

       a. The *Drang nach Osten* Analogy   64

       b. "Friends" in the West   68

       c. "Friends" in East and East Central Europe   72

    1.8. Restructuring Relations with NATO   75

    1.9. A New Cold War ?   94

    1.10. 1999: The Anniversary Year   106

SECTION II: RIPPLE EFFECTS

Introduction	117
2. Groping for New Strategic Partners	119
2.1. China	130
2.2. Iran-Iraq	133
a. Iran	133
b. Iraq	138
2.3. "Double Standards": Yugoslavia and the Serbs	143
3. NATO and Russian National Security Questions: Resurrecting Old Demons	156
3.1. Military Reform	164
4. Ukraine Enigma	175
5. The Baltic States: Drawing a "Red Line" in the Sand	202
6. The Commonwealth of Independent States: Return of the "Great Game"?	221
Conclusions	237
Russian Newspapers, News Agencies, and Other Sources	243
Further Reading	245
Name Index	253
Subject and Place Index	258
About the Author	263

Acronyms and Special Terms

CFE	Conventional Armed Forces in Europe
CIS	Commonwealth of Independent States
CJPS	Combined Joint Planning Staff
CPRF	Communist Party of the Russian Federation
CSCE	Conference on Security and Cooperation in Europe
EAPC	Euro-Atlantic Partnership Council
EBRD	European Bank for Reconstruction and Development
EPAC	Euro-Atlantic Partnership Council
ESDI	European Security and Defence Identity
EU	European Union
Federal Assembly	Russian Parliament
Federation Council	Russian Parliament, Upper House
GATT	General Agreement on Tariffs and Trade
GDR	German Democratic Republic
IFOR	Implementation Force
IMEMO	Institute of International Economics and International Relations
IMF	International Monetary Fund
INF	Intermediate-range Nuclear Forces
ISKRAN	Institute of the USA and Canada
LDPR	Liberal Democratic Party of Russia
NAC	North Atlantic Council
NACC	North Atlantic Cooperation Council
NATO	North Atlantic Treaty Organization
NDR	Our Home is Russia
OSCE	Organization for Security and Cooperation in Europe
PfP	Partnership for Peace
PJC	[Russia-NATO] Permanent Joint Committee

SFOR	Stabilization Force
SHAPE	Supreme Headquarters Allied Powers Europe
START II, III	Strategic Arms Reduction Treaty
State Duma	Russian Parliament, Lower House
UN	United Nations
UNPROFOR	UN Protection Force
WEU	West European Union
WTO	World Trade Organization

Preface

The format of this book is somewhat unusual in that it is divided simply into two parts rather than into multiple chapters. The first part provides an historical continuum in which to set the question of NATO's recent enlargement. The second part looks to specific dimensions of the problem from the Russian perspective. I hope that this approach will provide a straightforward framework within which readers may evaluate the wide-ranging implications of NATO policy for Russia.

Footnotes, rather than endnotes, are used here because the eye-catching titles of Russian newspaper pieces, by far the bulk of my references, are themselves part of the story. Their impact on the tale would diminish considerably if left obscured in endnotes. Because a few mainstream Russian newspapers were not readily available, readers sometimes will find references to items from the press but with no Russian-language title. In such cases, the text originated with translations provided by the Foreign Broadcast Information Service (FBIS). These are noted. References to government press releases or news agency files (ITAR-TASS, Interfax, RIA-Novosti, and so on), are placed in the text, in brackets.

Acknowledgments

Several people helped gather research material for this project. In 1997 Jennifer Anderson regularly forwarded press clippings from Ukraine. At Carleton University, Centre for Research on Canadian-Russian Relations (CRCR) researchers Yana Kuzmin, Anatolii Znamanskii, and Vitalyy Rabotnik helped check the Russian and Ukrainian press holdings in Carleton University's library. I am grateful to Robert V. Daniels, Professor Emeritus of History at the University of Vermont, who was kind enough to read a first draft of this book and offer useful suggestions about it.

Special thanks to Joseph Black and Lisa Celovsky, both of the University of Tennessee English Department, for short notice help with proofreading and indexing.

I am much indebted as well to the North Atlantic Treaty Organization for a NATO Research Fellowship, 1997–1999, which helped make it possible for me to discuss this subject with informed people in Moscow and England. I am also grateful to the Donner Canadian Foundation, whose financial support for the Centre for Research on Canadian-Russian Relations enables it to subscribe to important resource materials and tools.

Introduction

It is always instructive to see ourselves as others see us. When NATO's plans for expansion eastward are viewed from the Russian perspective, for example, the reflected image is one that many in the West would not recognize. But common sense tells us that it would be a serious tactical misjudgment to ignore the implications of the Russian understanding of what NATO intends.[1] That understanding mirrors, and is shaped by, interpretations carried in the Russian media, pronouncements from officials and politicians in Moscow, debate within and between political parties and public organizations, and public opinion surveys. Historical consciousness plays an important role in the Russian perception of NATO behavior, and the point of this book is to determine the nature and meaning of that perception.

Public opinion on foreign affairs in Russia may be more difficult to gauge than it is in other countries. Moreover, the everyday struggle to make ends meet has so dominated peoples' lives in Russia that a discourse between voters and their representatives on issues of foreign policy is precluded. The press is "free" in post-Soviet Russia, but it is often dominated by special interests. Between elections there are few public forums in which the people can truly be heard, and habit helps isolate citizens from their government. Single and simple issues, therefore, have more resonance in Russian society than complex ones. But a complex matter like NATO expansion can easily be, and often is, made into a single and simple issue. Thus, the unusual unity of opinion about NATO's movement towards Russia's borders, and the political value-add it represents to politicians and certain interest groups in Russia is not surprising.

NATO expansion is a central concern to ordinary Russian citizens when it is

---

[1] It is the habit of NATO, and consequently Western journalists, to speak of NATO "enlargement." Russians continue to use the word "expansion" (*rasshirenie*), which is what I will use without intending to lead the witness.

1

seen as a cause, or potential cause, of the social and economic disarray within their community. As former USSR president Gorbachev put it directly to the U.S. Congress in April 1997, history recorded what happened when a defeated Germany was humiliated after World War I. A humiliated nation has a long memory, and Russia will make a comeback, he said with considerable foundation. This historical message and analogy appeared regularly in Russia during 1997–98, from all sides of the political spectrum.

The purpose of this book is not to pass judgement on NATO's decision to admit new members from East and East Central Europe; rather it represents an effort to understand what expansion means, and will mean, to Russians. Longtime American commentator on Russia and Eastern Europe, Zbigniew Brzezinski, said early in 1997 that a minority of Russians were adamantly opposed to NATO's expansion, another minority feels that expansion might even benefit Russia, whereas the majority "don't give a damn" about it.[2] This conclusion was rendered as if it had weighty significance. To be sure, public opinion polls consistently had shown that NATO expansion was not yet a big issue for the general Russian population. But the polls often lacked useful context. For a case in point, one need only turn to data compiled in 1996 suggesting that most Russians did not then feel threatened by NATO, yet nearly 40 percent of the respondents saw the United States as a potential threat.[3] Apathy on the part of the Russian "public" was not a good reason to discount the strong antipathy to NATO expansion in all of Russia's political parties, its popularly elected State Duma, and most of its mass media.

The admission to NATO of countries from the defunct Warsaw Treaty Organization has strategic, economic and political implications that Russian politicians and planners must factor into their deliberations. Addressing an American audience, Russian liberal Aleksei Arbatov said in August 1997 that the indifference shown by the Russian public to NATO was very misleading. The ordinary

---

[2]Zbigniew Brzezinski in an interview with Don Newman, Ottawa, CBC TV News program "Politics," 7 April 1997.

[3]See Richard Rose, "Do Russians Want to Fight?" *ACE: Analysis of Current Events* 9, No. 7 (July 1997): 1, 4–5. Results of a later public opinion survey, signed to press on 6 June 1997, showed that conditions of daily life ranked far ahead of foreign policy matters in order of importance. More than 75 percent believed that there was no external "threat" to Russia; the United States headed the list of those who believed that there was a threat (13 percent). Nevertheless, about 30 percent of the respondents were "concerned" about NATO's plans to expand eastward. See Yelena Bashkirova, "Rossiia i vneshnie ugrozy" [Russia and External Threats], *Nezavisimoe voennoe obozrenie,* No. 20 (7–13 June 1997).

Russian "who is at all interested in foreign affairs" is deeply concerned, Arbatov insisted.[4] The new NATO has been, indeed, a central part of the political discussion in Russia and will shape Russia's strategic and public attitudes towards its neighbors for some time to come.

Brzezinski and others shrugged off Moscow's objections to NATO expansion by insisting that they represented opinions held exclusively by the "foreign policy elite," who want their country to maintain its traditional sphere of influence.[5] This approach to understanding the depth of Russian hostility to NATO's expansion doesn't stand up very well against the centuries-old Russian expectation that Europe will attempt to isolate it; or to a growing perception among Russians that their current problems are due in part to practices forced on them from abroad. It is ironic, in fact, that Brzezinski said elsewhere (see section 2.2 of this work), and almost at the same time, that the U.S. administration's "strident" attempts to isolate Iran is driving that country into the arms of Russia. Apparently he did not see, or did not worry so much, that it may have been NATO expansion that prompted Russia to seek closer association with Iran and other countries sharing potential isolation.

The aim of the research represented here was to determine how deep-rooted Russia's antipathy to NATO enlargement eastward is, what form it takes in the mass media, and what the consequences of prevailing attitudes towards expansion are likely to be for Moscow's foreign policy-making. For that reason, the sources used for this study are almost entirely in the Russian language.

---

[4]Alexei Arbatov, "As NATO Grows, Start 2 Shudders," *New York Times* OP-ED (26 Aug 1997). This point was made as well by Susan Eisenhower, chair of the Center for Political and Strategic Studies in Washington, in "The Bear at Bay," *The Spectator* (12 July 1997): 14–15, and by Peter M. Roberts, former Canadian ambassador to the USSR, in "Let's Go Even Further Than de Gaulle Did—and Bid Adieu to NATO Entirely," *The Globe and Mail* (19 July 1997).

[5]Speaking to the United States Institute of Peace's European Security Working Group, 5 March 1997, Brzezinski said that "Russian opposition to NATO enlargement rests entirely with the Moscow-based foreign policy elite and does not include the Russian public. . . ." See "Managing NATO Enlargement," United States Institute of Peace. *Special Report* (April 1997).

The opinion that Russia's anti–NATO expansion stance was a monopoly of the political elite was repeated by Dimitrii Trenin, Carnegie Endowment for International Peace, Moscow, at a seminar, "NATO Enlargement—the Outstanding Issues," sponsored by the Canadian Council for International Peace and Security, Ottawa, 24 April 1997.

This book is purposely chronological, for it is in the sequence of events and commentary related to them that one can best measure the intensity of the feelings toward NATO held by Russia's officials and public. The bulk of the study encompasses Yevgenii Primakov's tenure as foreign minister, and reveals many of the convictions that he carried with him when he was appointed prime minister in the autumn of 1998.

Section I

The History

1. HEREIN LIES THE TALE

Russian suspicions of NATO's motives in taking in new members from Eastern Europe are part of a long historical tradition.

Since 1812, when Napoleon's huge international army burned Moscow, there has been a resilient assumption in Russia that unless it was in their greater interest to do otherwise the European powers will naturally combine to keep Russia weak and isolated from Europe. This belief was confirmed in the minds of Russia's nationalists during the Crimean War (1853–56) and by European attempts to mitigate the effects of Russia's regular defeats of Turkey during the 19th century. Slavophile resentment of Western cultural inroads and ideological confrontation between Panslavists and Pan-Germans were constant features of Russian-European relationships after 1848.

A uniquely Russian outlook was canonized in the writing of Nikolai Danilevskii (1822–85), whose systematic exposition of Panslavism, *Rossiia i Evropa* (Russia and Europe), was published first in 1869 and reissued many times in that century. Danilevskii wrote that Russia's historical mission was to unite all Slavs and form a new type of civilization with its capital in Constantinople, eclipsing and replacing the currently reigning Germano-Roman, or European civilization. The book became obligatory reading in Russia's military academies. It is no coincidence that the first Russian reprint of Danilevskii's political essay in Russia since 1890 appeared in 1998.[6]

---

[6]Originally a series of periodical articles published in 1869, the book appeared first in 1871 as *Rossiia i Evropa, vzgliad na kul'turnye i politicheskie otnosheniia slavianskogo mira k germano-romanskomu* [Russia and Europe, Views on Cultural and Political Relations of the Slavic World to the German-Romanic World] (St. Petersburg, 1871). The latest printing is N. Ya. Danilevskii, *Gore pobediteliam. Politicheskie stat'i* [Sorrow of the Victors: Political Essays] (Moscow, 1998).

The notion that Russia is surrounded by enemies poised to take advantage of any weakness was recast in the USSR as "capitalist encirclement" and rationalized with Lenin's assumption that the world was divided into two immutably hostile camps, capitalist and socialist. Even the theory of peaceful coexistence, as it was reformulated during Nikita Khrushchev's regime in the 1950s, was regarded as a temporary stage in the ongoing struggle between different economic and social systems represented by "East" and "West."[7] Thus, a traditional Muscovite xenophobia was given a philosophical basis by Danilevskii and a formulaic character by Marxism-Leninism.

During the final years of the Soviet Union, the presumption that Western countries will collude to isolate Russia took on new life with the reunification of the two Germanies in 1990. Mikhail S. Gorbachev, who was at first strongly opposed to reunification, and German Chancellor Helmut Kohl were central figures in the process that led to unification. Russian government releases at the time were optimistic about the consequences of reunification, whereas a very large part of the Russian press (then only recently freed from close government stricture), public organizations and the public itself were openly hostile to and nervous about a united Germany. Their fears were compounded as NATO's domain was extended eastward to include the territory of the former GDR. During 1990–91, the USSR was shunted to the periphery of the international scene, and the Warsaw Pact disappeared. The Soviet Union itself was overwhelmed by regional conflicts, fierce political and constitutional battles, economic collapse, real and imagined threats of coups d'état and, finally, complete disintegration.[8] NATO loomed larger and, to many Russians who were confused about what was happening to them as citizens of a Great Power, more menacingly. Born and educated in an actively socializing Soviet Union, many Russian citizens are still naturally receptive to visions of Western plots to undermine both the quality of their life and the security of their state.

Blame cast on foreign intrigue in the late 1980s by extremist groups, such as *Pamiat* (Memory) and *Soyuz* (Unity), attracted believers even among liberal, democratic movements and associations. NATO was one of the several targets for the anger and fear that came to dominate the Soviet and then Russian perception of

---

[7]For Khrushchev's version of peaceful coexistence, see his "Doklad Pervogo sekretaria TsK KPSS tovarishcha N.S. Khrushcheva" [Report of the First Secretary of the CPSU CC, Comrade N.S. Khrushchev], *Pravda* (15 Feb 1956) and Yu. B. Borisov, *O mirnom sosushchestvovanii i sotrudnichestve dvukh sistem* [On Peaceful Coexistence and Cooperation of Two Systems] (Moscow, 1956).

[8]There is a huge body of literature on this subject. For a documentary narrative of the USSR's fate in 1991, see J.L. Black, *Into the Dustbin of History: The USSR from Coup to Commonwealth, August–December 1991* (Gulf Breeze, FL, 1993).

what was happening to them.[9] Gorbachev's worries, it seems, were eased by promises from the American, French and German governments that NATO would expand no further to the east. Perhaps he was lulled by the fact that *Time* magazine chose him as the "Man of the Decade" for the first January issue, 1990, and in an accompanying essay editor-at-large Strobe Talbott mused that "[i]t is about time to think seriously about eventually retiring the North Atlantic Treaty Organization."[10]

1.1. A Long-Festering Issue

In terms of international status, the Russian Federation (RF) inherited everything from the USSR except its territorial integrity, secure borders and a sense of being an impregnable power. The huge "buffer" territory acquired by force of arms by St. Petersburg and Moscow over a period of 150 years disappeared in a flash. This had happened once before, in 1918–21, when Russia's territorial losses were almost as extensive as the paring down of the Soviet empire in 1991. In the years following the collapse in 1921, however, the self-styled internationalist and class-focussed Bolsheviks regained what Russia had "lost," with barbaric cruelty, cunning diplomacy and remarkable tenacity, usually driven by a relationship with Germany. Between 1989 and 1991, the Soviet Union was divested of more territory than Russia had lost 70 years earlier. Its East and East Central European "allies" and 14 former USSR republics had all declared themselves independent of Russian control by the end of 1991. This time the chance that Russia might regain an empire was very slight. Each of the new or reconstituted states, and Russia, had then to work out and consolidate new international alignments, and for the most part are still doing so. From the point of view of Russian strategists their borders were left more naked than they had been since the late eighteenth century, making the attitude of NATO a central issue for Moscow during the entire decade.

---

[9]See, for example, "Otvety M.S. Gorbacheva na voprosy korrespondenta Pravdy" [Gorbachev's Answers to Questions from a Pravda Correspondent], *Pravda* (21 Feb 1990); "Zaiavlenie vsesoiuznogo soveta veteranov voiny" [Statement of the All-Soviet Council of War Veterans], *Krasnaia zvezda* (3 March 1990); Aleksandr Bovin, "Mnenie politicheskogo obozrevatelia. Evropa, Germaniia, My . . ." [Opinion of a Political Observer: Europe, Germany, and Us . . .], *Izvestiia* (23 March 1990); A. Krivopalov, "Olivkovaia vetv' NATO" [NATO's Olive Branch], *Izvestiia* (7 July 1990).

Pamiat was a rabidly anti-semitic, anti-communist fascistic movement with a nation-wide following in the late 1980s; *Soyuz* was a nationalistic and Soviet patriotic bloc in the USSR Congress of People's Deputies, led by Col. Viktor Alksnis.

[10]See Talbott, "Rethinking the Red Menace," *Time* (1 Jan 1990): 38–44. Talbott also said that NATO was now only a "stopgap" until a more effective security system could be arranged for Europe. Gorbachev's portrait graced the cover of that issue.

Just as the USSR faded out of sight—if not out of mind—in the fall of 1991, NATO was reexamining its raison d'être. In November 1991, at the Rome Summit, the Alliance approved a new strategic concept, which was marked by a shift from the primacy of collective defense and a decision to take on more diverse tasks—among them intra-state conflicts. The concept emphasized the danger of instability on NATO's periphery and the proliferation of weapons of mass destruction. Territorial disputes, ethnic conflict, and economic crises also were among the potential unsettling forces NATO decided to monitor. It was at the Rome Summit that the Alliance created an institutional mechanism for dealing with members of the rapidly disintegrating Warsaw Treaty Organization, the North Atlantic Cooperation Council (NACC).

During the early years of Boris Yeltsin's regime as president of an independent Russia, his government maintained a strongly Western and reformist orientation. Foreign Minister Andrei Kozyrev pushed integration with the West against growing pressure from nationalistic and Communist forces.[11] Eventually the government was forced to retreat: nationalists prevailed in the Duma elections of 1993 and Communists moved to the forefront in 1995. Even on those occasions, however, NATO expansion was one subject on which the Russian government and the opposition could usually agree. When, in June 1992, NATO decided to move "out of zone" to support the CSCE (now OSCE) and the United Nations in peacekeeping and conflict management missions, Moscow was decidedly unhappy about it. Kozyrev already had insisted in April that there could "be no question of NATO participation" in peacekeeping activities, for operations of that sort lay entirely within the domain of the United Nations Security Council. He had, quite unwittingly, touched upon what was to become the sharpest point of departure between Moscow and NATO seven years later. In 1993, Kozyrev advised against the admission of former Warsaw Pact countries to NATO in the *NATO Review.*[12]

Later that year the first detailed Russian response to NATO expansion was published. Prepared by the Foreign Intelligence Service (FIS), the report emphasized the psychological storm expansion would cause in Russia, where NATO had long

---

[11]Kozyrev summed up his opinion on NATO expansion more than a year after he had been dismissed from his post. See Kozyrev, "A Treaty of Cooperation and Partnership with NATO Is Needed," *New Times* (March 1997): 44–45. "Whether we like it or not, NATO expansion will inevitably take place," he said, adding that it need not be such a serious problem if only the Russian state would adjust to it sensibly.

[12]Kozyrev, "The New Russia and the Atlantic Alliance," *NATO Review* (February 1993): 3–6; "Andrei Kozyrev: 'Soiuz Rossii plokhoe vneshnepoliticheskoe nasledstvo'" [Kozyrev: The Union Left Russia with a Bad Foreign Policy Heritage], *Nezavisimaia gazeta* (1 April 1992).

been regarded as a dangerously aggressive enemy. From the strategic perspective, the danger of new members making further inroads against Russia was highlighted. Romania might make a grab for Moldova, for instance, and the Baltic states could follow the Visegrad group (Hungary, Poland, Czech Republic, Slovakia) into the Alliance, creating an insurmountable barrier between Russia and the rest of Europe. NATO enlargement was already perceived, therefore, as the creation of a buffer zone in reverse, a means to isolate the new Russia from continental Europe. The FIS report was announced with some fanfare. Prior commentary could be found in the Russian media and the presentation itself was made at a large press conference, on 26 November, with an introductory and strongly supportive statement offered by the FIS director—Yevgenii Primakov.[13]

In early 1994, the unrelenting character of NATO's plans to recruit new members began to trigger responses at the highest level in Russia. In February of that year, Yeltsin felt so threatened by the possibility of NATO expanding without consulting Russia that he emphasized his country's opposition to it in his annual message to the Federal Assembly, and in a separate television address to the nation.[14] The presidential statement was much stronger than an earlier recommendation by Kozyrev that Russia work with NATO's North Atlantic Cooperation Council "to strengthen mutual trust and developing cooperation" as an alternative to a "faster expansion of NATO."[15] The leader of the Communist Party of the Russian Federation (CPRF), Gennadii Zyuganov, had staked his claim as a leading opponent of NATO expansion earlier in January, calling it part of an "attempt by certain circles of NATO . . . to keep Russia at bay."[16] All three declarations mirrored a common feeling of vulnerability.

Interestingly, in 1994 there was a feeling within military circles that Russia might eventually join NATO itself. At that time the geography of the external threat to Russia had shifted to the South, making an East-West accommodation especially important. But even then NATO membership was regarded as something well into

---

[13]"Opravdano li rasshirenie NATO? Osoboe mnenie Sluzhby vneshnei razvedki Rossii" [Is NATO Expansion Justified? Special Opinion of the Foreign Intelligence Service of Russia], *Nezavisimaia gazeta* (26 Nov 1993).

[14]"Poslanie Prezidenta Rossiiskoi Federatsii Federal'nomu Sobraniiu. Ob ukreplenii Rossiiskogo gosudarstva (Osnovnye napravleniia vnutrennei i vneshnei politiki)" [Address of the RF President to the Federal Assembly: On Strengthening the Russian State (Basic Directions of Foreign and Domestic Policy)], *Rossiiskaia gazeta* (25 Feb 1994). The address to the nation was delivered on 24 February over Ostankino TV.

[15]*Krasnaia zvezda* (14 Jan 1994), FBIS-SOV, No. 010.

[16]Zyuganov, "Silovoi risunok Rossii" [Russia's Pattern of Strength], *Sovetskaia Rossiia* (6 Jan 1994). Zyuganov was writing about the new military doctrine, adopted in November 1993.

the future, and only after Russia's entry into the European Union. There was another point of view. In the absence of a tighter East-West link-up, the "semi-isolation of Russia from the West could lead to a search for solid allies in the East, but it would be done not on an equal footing, but from a position of weakness," one military strategist wrote.[17] This judgment, which turned out to be a prophetic one, rang of Russia's deep-rooted fear of isolation and encirclement.

It was in 1994 as well that Russia joined NATO's Partnership for Peace Program (PfP),[18] but reluctantly and only after most former USSR republics and Warsaw Pact member states had done so. The PfP, which was first discussed in October 1993, was endorsed at a meeting of NATO heads of state in Brussels, January 10–11 that year, to "transform" relations between the Alliance and participating states. Its expressed purpose was, in part, to prevent Russia from being isolated, a possibility that had taken on ominous overtones after the radical nationalist Vladimir Zhirinovskii's success in the Duma elections of December 1993. The PfP projected active participation in the "evolutionary process of the expansion of NATO" by intensifying political and military cooperation and coordinating field exercises. Great expectations were generated by the announcement of this program, which promised wide ranging joint activities and military-technical development for its members. Russia had no real option but to join, losing, as it were, a tiny piece of its zealously guarded autonomy of choice in foreign policy. Some Moscow observers saw the PfP as a NATO vehicle for undermining the CIS.[19] Kozyrev put a positive spin on the PfP, implying to a Russian audience that pressure from his government persuaded NATO to take this step "instead of immediate extension . . . to the borders of the CIS."[20] On the other

---

[17]Dr. V. Larionov, Major-General (Ret.), "Europe and Russia on the Break of the Centuries," Center for National Security Problems and International Relations, Moscow, *Monthly Bulletin* (January 1994): 4.

[18]"Protokol," *Diplomaticheskii vestnik,* No. 13–14 (July 1994): 30–31. See also Michael Mihalka, "European-Russian Security and NATO's Partnership for Peace," *RFE/RL Research Report* 3, No. 33 (1994): 34–40.

[19]See, e.g., Viacheslav Nikonov, " 'Partnerstvo vo imia mira': Povestka dnia dlia Federal'nogo sobraniia" ["Partners for Peace": Agenda for the Federal Assembly], *Nezavisimaia gazeta* (7 April 1994); "Partnerstvo vo imia mira: Ramochnyi dokument" [Partners for Peace: Framed Document], *Nezavisimaia gazeta* (9 April 1994). For the Partnership for Peace Invitation, see Appendix XI, *NATO Handbook* (1995): 265–68.

[20]"Andrei Kozyrev: ne partiinye, a natsional'nye interesy dolzhny ob'edinit' diplomatov s parlamentariiami" [Andrei Kozyrev: Not Parties, but National Interests Must Unite Diplomats and Parliamentarians], *Rossiiskaia gazeta* (2 Feb 1994). The communist press, however, strongly protested NATO threats to circumvent the UN Security Council in Bosnia. See Yevgenii Popov, "NATO igraet s bombami" [NATO Plays with Bombs], *Sovetskaia Rossiia* (10 Feb 1994).

hand, Vladimir Lukin spoke for many when he complained, "we have been betrayed."[21] As chairman of the Duma's International Affairs Committee and a founder of the liberal Yabloko party, Lukin's opinions were considered moderate and influential. It was clear that Russian analysts saw the PfP as an infringement on their sphere of influence, one sign of which was Russia's refusal in November to sign documents creating military links between it and NATO. Bitter, confused and often ill-informed debate raged in the Russian mass media. Yet another intervention by Brzezinski caused even Kozyrev to go to press and call for a strengthened partnership between Russia and the United States; that is, a partnership of equals.[22] Believing Brzezinski to be an influential Cold Warrior and a spokesman for insider circles in the United States, the Russian media seized upon his opinions as especially threatening. His controversial book, *The Grand Chessboard: American Primacy and Its Geostrategy* (1997), was treated in Moscow as a blueprint for American world hegemony. Moreover, Brzezinski pitched the "Eurasian chessboard" as the arena for a new "Great Game" and urged that the area be drawn into the Western orbit. An apparent lack of decisiveness on the part of the Russian government exacerbated the new strategic gamemanship, allowing fears that exist to this day to take firm hold.[23]

The PfP debate raged throughout the spring: Political scientist Vladislav Chernov cautioned that candidates for NATO membership were almost all using the "potential threat from Russia" to rationalize their candidacy, and therefore the "motive force of the PfP consists mainly of the anti-Russian sentiments of our former friends and allies"; historian Jakov Pliaus warned that an expanded NATO plus the PfP would make that organization stronger than the UN; journalist Dmitrii

[21]Lukin, "Chto stroitsia v Evrope: novyi dom ili staryi zabor?" [What Is Being Built in Europe: A New Home or an Old Fence?], *Izvestiia* (12 May 1995).

[22]Kozyrev, "Rossiia i SShA: Partnerstvo ne prezhdevremenno, a zapazdyvaet" [Russia and the USA: Partnership Is Not Premature, but Overdue], *Izvestiia* (11 March 1994). He was responding to Brzezinski's "The Premature Partnership," *Foreign Affairs* 73, No. 2 (March/April 1994).

[23]See, for example, Dimitrii Gornostaev, "Dve storony 'partnerstva vo imia mira'. Kozyrev i Kostikov govorili o raznykh veshchakh" [Two Sides of "Partnerships for Peace": Kozyrev and Kostikov Talked about Different Things], *Nezavisimaia gazeta* (5 April 1994); "Dva politicheskikh poliusa vozglavili E. Gaydar i V. Zhirinovskii" [Two Political Poles Headed by Gaydar and Zhirinovskii], *Rossiiskaia gazeta* (5 April 1994); Aleksandr Sychev, "Rossiia vse-taki prisoedinitsia k program NATO, no ona nuzhdaetsia v dorabotke" [Russia Nevertheless Joins with the NATO Program, but It Needs to Be Worked Out], *Izvestiia* (6 April 1994).

Gornostaev, and Yeltsin, insisted that Russian membership in the PfP must not take precedence over a special agreement between Russia and NATO itself.[24]

When the influential non-government Council for Foreign and Defense Policy issued its widely-discussed theses on "Strategy for Russia" in May 1994, the danger of Russia's international position being undermined by NATO expansion held a prominent place in them. Among the recourses recommended by the Council was a mutually beneficial process of reintegrating parts of the former USSR. Ukraine was singled out as especially important to Russia. The "possibility of NATO's expansion without Russia's participation" makes it essential that Russia "seek alternative ways to ensure its security and political interests in Europe."[25] In December, at a meeting in Budapest of the Conference on Security and Cooperation in Europe (CSCE), Yeltsin and U.S. President Clinton disagreed on the question of former Warsaw Pact countries having memberships in NATO. Separate meetings between Kozyrev and U.S. Defense Secretary Warren Christopher, and U.S. Vice President Al Gore, Yeltsin, and Russian Prime Minister Viktor Chernomyrdin, in Moscow, eased the tension. But only temporarily.

The issue festered for a long time, increasing in intensity during 1995.[26] Yeltsin once more targeted NATO in his annual address to the Federal Assembly, accusing "the West" of wanting to expand the Alliance to protect Eastern Europe from "Moscow's evil intentions." "We have no evil intentions," he exclaimed, adding that Russia's devotion to democratic values is "irreversible." Without meaning to do so, he thereby encapsulated exactly the perceptual dilemma confronting both East and West. Later in the spring Foreign Minister Kozyrev offered an ambiguous statement on the adoption by the NATO Council of Russia's particular PfP program and a special document, Area of Broad and Profound Dialogue and Cooperation between Russia and NATO. The Council was meeting in Noordwijk, 31 May 1995. Kozyrev pointed out that, while these signs of deepening dialogue were welcomed, his government much preferred a pan-European security system—a Europe without dividing lines. NATO expansion "does not meet either the interest of Russia's national

---

[24]"Yel'tsin o partnerstvo v NATO" [Yeltsin on Partnership in NATO], *Nezavisimaia gazeta* (7 April 1994); Gornostaev, "Dve storony . . . ," *op cit.;* Pliaus, "Vyzovy vremen i 'partnerstvo vo imia mira'" [Challenges of the Time and Partnership for Peace], *Nezavisimaia gazeta* (20 April 1994); Vladislav Chernov, "Moskva dolzhna khorosho podumat', prezhde chem otvechat' na predlozhenie NATO" [Moscow Should Think Carefully before Responding to NATO's Proposal], *Nezavisimaia gazeta* (23 Feb 1994).

[25]"Strategiia dlia Rossii (2). Tezisy Soveta po vneshnei i oboronnoi politike" [Strategy for Russia (2): Theses of the Council for Foreign and Defense Policy], *Nezavisimaia gazeta* (27 May 1994).

[26]For a summary, see Aleksei Pushkov, "Russia and NATO: Dangerous Games in a Verbal Mist," *Moscow News* (7 April 1995).

security or the interest of European security as a whole."[27] As Russian journalists called for Moscow's position to be made clearer in light of a "thick information mist" about NATO emanating from the West, the Russian president made firm his country's stand against expansion in a speech to the UN General Assembly in October.[28]

Elections to the State Duma dominated the Russian political scene in the latter half of 1995 and NATO was an easy target for bitter diatribes from all sides. The Communist Party, co-opting Russian nationalism, included condemnation of NATO expansion in all of its major public pronouncements on foreign policy, and its election platform. So did the Power to the People! movement, headed by former Soviet premier Nikolai Ryzhkov, whose bloc promised to "take energetic measures against Russia's further isolation, its encirclement by military blocs, and NATO's eastward expansion."[29] The CPRF gained over 22 percent of the votes cast in the December elections, taking 157 of the 450 seats. Power to the People! earned only nine seats, but the new State Duma took on a strongly anti-NATO bias.

Grumbling against NATO was heard frequently also during the presidential election campaigning of 1996, when Zyuganov again made it part of his platform. "We are opposed to sabre rattling, to the arrogant appropriation by certain states of the function of international gendarme, against the eastward expansion of NATO. But it is well known that you cannot plead successfully for peace on a bent knee," he proclaimed in a section of the platform that called for military reform and a voluntary re-union of Russia, Ukraine, Belarus and Kazakhstan.[30]

---

[27]Kozyrev's statement at Noordwijk can be found on the NATO Website, NATO Ministerial Communiques, Russia. For Yeltsin's annual address (16 Feb 1995), see *Rossiiskaia gazeta* (17 Feb 1995), reprinted in *REDA 1995,* Vol. 1.

[28]Yeltsin's speech at the UN General Assembly was part of the 50th Jubilee Session. It was carried live on Russian TV (22 Oct 1995). See REDA 1995, Vol. 1, 254–55. For examples of the angry journalist belief that the West was putting something over on Russia while Yeltsin slept, see Grigorii Karasin, "Yasnost' argumentov i tuman otvetov" [Clarity of Argument and Obscurity of Reply], *Rossiiskie vesti* (5 Oct 1995), and Yu. Ivanenko, "Chirak ugrozhaet Rossii. Pochemu v Kremle etogo ne zamezhaiut?" [Chirac Threatens Russia: Why Does the Kremlin Not Recognize This?], *Sovetskaia Rossiia* (23 Sept 1995).

[29]"'VLAST'-NARODY!' Predvybornaia platforma izbiratel'nogo ob'edineniia" [POWER to the PEOPLE! Election Platform of the Electoral Bloc Association], *Pravda* (12 Sept 1995); for the communist position, see "Vo imiu Otechestva, v interesakh naroda. Doklad predsedatelia TsIK KPRF Gennadiia Zyuganova" [In the Name of the Fatherland, in the interests of the People: Report of the Chairman of the CPRF CC Gennadii Zyuganov], *Sovetskaia Rossiia* (24 Jan 1995).

[30]"Rossiia, Rodina, Narod! Predvybornaia platforma kandidata na post prezidenta Rossiiskoi Federatsii Ziuganova Gennadiia Andreevicha" [Russia, Fatherland, People! Pre-election Platform of Candidate for the Post of President of the RF, G.A. Zyuganov], *Sovetskaia Rossiia* (19 March 1996).

It is difficult to judge how this direct appeal to national consciousness played in the presidential election campaign, for there were many other matters at stake. But it is worth remembering that Zyuganov polled over 24 million votes in the first round (16 June), which was very close to Yeltsin's 26 million. After he secured the support of Aleksandr Lebed by giving him a (short-lived, as it happened) plum job, Yeltsin's support rose to 40 million. In a two-person run-off, 30 million cast their vote for Zyuganov, so Yeltsin's victory wasn't exactly the "smashing" one that Western media made it out to be.[31] Lebed, who campaigned on a nationalist platform, had warned in 1995 that NATO expansion would lead to World War III.[32]

Yeltsin survived the presidential election in 1996, but by that time Kozyrev was long gone. He had been replaced in January 1996 by Primakov, who preferred multipolarism to integration with the West, opposed the American tendency to use NATO as a vehicle for world domination, and was willing to look for new strategic partners for Moscow. Almost all of Russia's political leaders had, since 1993, come to believe that NATO expansion eastward posed a risk to their country. They foresaw an expanded NATO gathering in anti-Russian populations and isolating Russia from European security issues; and they were concerned that NATO would so greatly increase its fighting capacity that Russia would be vulnerable militarily for the first time since 1941. Russia's leadership felt threatened as well because NATO expansion lent credence to nationalist and Communist charges that it was selling out Russia's national interests to the West. From the psychological standpoint, all political groups in Russia claimed that their country had been stabbed in the back, or kicked when it was down, by a NATO that had promised not to do precisely what it was now doing.

The proposed expansion was not the only subject on which Russia and NATO were sharply divided in 1996. The anomaly of Russian peacekeepers joining with NATO in Bosnia was exposed when Leontii Shevtsov, deputy to NATO's Supreme Commander in Europe for Operation IFOR (George Joulwan), met and conversed with Serbian war criminals Radovan Karadzic and Ratko Mladic. It was difficult, *Izvestiia* wrote at the time, for Russians to reconcile their sympathy with the Serbs and their association with NATO in the region.

---

[31]In the first round, of 11 candidates, Yeltsin received 35.28 percent of the vote; Zyuganov 32.03; and Lebed, 14.52. Slightly less than 70 percent of eligible voters turned out for the second round, and nearly 4 million of those opposed both candidates. See *Rossiiskaia gazeta* (22 June, 10 July 1996).

[32]See "Lebed Predicts NATO Expansion Will Unleash 'World War III'," FBIS-SOV, No. 071 (13 April 1995). Interviewed by Prague's *Lidove noviny* (12 April 1995), Lebed said that NATO is a "major threat" to Russia and that war would result if the Czech Republic or Poland were admitted to the alliance.

A few days later, in his first meeting with the State Duma's Committee on International Affairs, Primakov, recently named foreign minister, said that the greatest "irritant" in Russia's relations with the West was NATO expansion eastward.[33] Former director of the Academy of Science's Institute of Oriental Studies and Institute of World Economics and International Relations (IMEMO), and adviser to Gorbachev on the Middle East, Primakov's most recent post had been as head of the FIS. Thus, he brought a wealth of experience to his new post, and strong feelings about NATO. Indeed, he told an interviewer that NATO expansion was "counter-productive" and would "create a new geopolitical situation for Russia."[34] Primakov had a long record of resisting American foreign policy almost everywhere. A journalist with murky links to the KGB before he moved into the academic arena, the new foreign minister had also been instrumental in elucidating the ideology of Gorbachev's foreign policy. More specifically, in 1987 he set out the philosophy of "new thinking" in *Pravda*, with the following basic tenets: precedence of political over military measures of deterrence; the principle of reasonable sufficiency as a means of military defense, and confirmation of the Soviet rejection of first strike with nuclear weapons; the universality of security issues; and an end to USSR-U.S. confrontation in seeking solutions to regional conflict. The only obstacle to widespread adoption of such principles, he thought at that time, was an American compulsion to do battle against all socialist principles.[35]

As head of IMEMO in 1987, Primakov had been a vocal advocate of close Soviet-India connections as a step towards a multipolar world. Within two years, he was adviser to Gorbachev on foreign policy, and delivering reports directly to the Politburo on matters as diverse as the tax system, and on his own

---

[33]Maksim Yusin, "Deputatam obeshchana velikaia derzhava" [Deputies are Promised Great Power], *Izvestiia* (10 Feb 1996); Boris Vinogradov, "Pervaia koshko mezhdu mirotvortsami iz Rossii i NATO v Bosnii uzhe probezhala [The First Cat Has already Run between Russian and NATO Peacekeepers in Bosnia], *Izvestiia* (3 Feb 1996).

[34]"Primakov's First Move: the CIS. On NATO Expansion," *Moscow News,* No. 2 (19–25 Jan 1996), 13. At least one Russian writer did not trust Primakov's motives. Konstantin Borovoi later wrote that the foreign minister was really playing "old, imperial games," pressuring the West into buying Russia off by exaggerating the consequences of NATO expansion. See Borovoi, "NATO is Coming!" *New Times* (March 1997), 50.

[35]Yevgenii Primakov, "Novaia filosofia vneshnei politiki" [A New Foreign Policy Philosophy], *Pravda* (10 July 1987). "Reasonable sufficiency" was the new defensive military doctrine adopted at the 27 CPSU Congress in 1986. A recent Russian biography of Primakov is very sketchy (even in 400 pages) about his alleged KGB and intelligence background. see L.M. Mlechin, *Yevgenii Primakov: istoriia odnoi kar'ery* [Yevgenii Primakov: History of One Career] (Moscow: Tsentrpoligraf, 1999).

meetings with officials in East Germany and France.[36] In March 1991, Gorbachev nominated Primakov to the new USSR Security Council, a seat he won only after a second round of voting in the Supreme Soviet. At that time, opinion polls ranked him among the twenty political and public people in whom Soviet citizens had some confidence.[37] Two years later, representing Russia's FIS, he predicted that a decision by NATO to expand its membership eastward would cause Moscow to institute "counter measures" and heighten anti-Western feelings in Russia.[38]

As foreign minister, Primakov's opinions changed very little. When NATO Secretary General Javier Solana met with Russian politicians and academicians at the Institute of Europe, Russian Academy of Sciences, Moscow, in March 1996, Primakov informed *Krasnaia zvezda* that NATO enlargement was not yet a foregone conclusion, implying at the same time that Russia could "prevent the NATO military infrastructure from approaching our territory." Solana was ironic about Primakov's claim, saying "let Mr. Primakov try to convince Czechs, Poles and Hungarians not to join. If he succeeds, we won't grow."[39] In fact, the NATO leader was greeted with widespread skepticism in Moscow. Former Warsaw Pact countries now will have a "nuclear umbrella" over their territories, one mainstream newspaper complained. Another paper referred to Solana as a "boa constrictor in the name of NATO" and used the term *Drang nach Osten* to describe Kohl's al-

---

[36]See, e.g, "V Politburo TsK KPSS" [In the Politburo of the CPSU Central Committee], *Pravda* (25 March 1989, 24 Nov 1989). For his comments on India and multipolarism, see Primakov, "Krupnyi shag vpered. Razmyshleniia posle vizita M.S. Gorbacheva v Indiiu" [A Major Step Forward: Some Thoughts of M.S. Gorbachev's Visit to India], *Pravda* (5 Jan 1987).

[37]Aleksei Levinson, "Komu my doveriaem" [In Whom Do We Have Confidence], *Izvestiia* (15 March 1991); on the new Security Council, A. Stepovoi, S. Chugarev, "Formiruetsia Soviet bezopasnosti SSSR" [The USSR Security Council Is Formed], *Izvestiia* (8 March 1991). Most of Primakov's colleagues on the USSR Security Council in 1991 were leaders of the August 1991 failed coup against Gorbachev. After the coup Gorbachev appointed Primakov to a new USSR Security Council and made him director of the re-organized Federal Intelligence Service.

[38]On this generally, see Suzanne Crow, "Russian Views on an Eastward Expansion of NATO," RFE/RL *Research Report* 2, No. 41 (1993): 21–24, and "Russia Asserts Its Strategic Agenda," RFE/RL *Research Report* 2, No. 50 (1993): 1–8.

[39]K. Eggert, "V Briussele ne budet vozrazhat', esli Rossiia ugovorit Vostochniui Evropu ne vstupat' v NATO" [There Will Be No Growth in Brussels if Russia Tells Eastern Europe Not to Join NATO], *Izvestiia* (23 March 1996).

leged broken promises of 1990.[40] The term, meaning the German "Drive to the East," has particularly ominous overtones for Russians. Its origins can be traced to the days of Charlemagne in the ninth century and it took a permanent place in Russian cultural and military history when Alexander Nevskii defeated the Teutonic Knights 400 years later. More recently, *Drang nach Osten* evokes vivid memories of German expansion into and occupation of the USSR in 1941.

Reminders of Kohl's alleged perfidy were still being circulated by worried government leaders when the G-7 summit was convened in Moscow, 19–20 April. Dazzled, perhaps, by the effusiveness of G-7 leaders and their obvious preference for him in the upcoming presidential election, Yeltsin let it be known that there would be "no forcing of NATO expansion for some time yet" and that it was even possible that Russia might gain a veto over additional NATO membership.[41] Such optimism was belied within a week, however, as the Russian president made an official visit to China, and appeared to be working on a contingency plan. It was said often in Russia that he was acting as an emissary of the G-7 during his stay in Beijing, but the fact that a major consequence of the visit was a five-state military "confidence-building" agreement (Russia, China, Kazakhstan, Kyrgyzstan, and Tajikistan) suggests that Russia's own strategic interests had pride of place. The Russian military press, for example, emphasized that Moscow and Beijing were making a strategic choice, in part to counter plans being "hatched" for NATO expansion eastward.[42] The China connection was to grow stronger in 1997 and 1998.

Already in June 1996 NATO leaders were called liars because of promises broken in 1990–91, when they were alleged to have said that former members of the

---

[40]Yevgenii Popov, "Zachem gensek Solana priezzhal v Moskvu? Ulybka udava po imeni 'NATO'" [Why Did Gensec Solana Come to Moscow? Smile of the Boa Constrictor Whose Name is NATO], *Sovetskaia Rossiia* (23 March 1996); Tamara Zamyatina, Nikolai Kalintsev, "Vstrechaiutsia kak-to dva genseka—KPRF i NATO . . ." [The Meeting of Two GenSecs Has Taken Place—CPRF and NATO], *Rossiiskaia gazeta* (23 March 1996). Primakov, "Vneshniaia politika Rossii dolzhna byt' mnogovektornoi" [Russian Foreign Policy Must Be Multi-Vectored], *Krasnaia zvezda* (2 April 1996).

[41]Yevgenii Bai, Vladimir Mikhaev, "Vse ostalis' dovol'ny vstrechei v Moskve, dogovorivshis' razreshit' raznoglasiia v rabochem poriadke" [Everyone Is Satisfied with the Meeting in Moscow, Having Agreed to Resolve Differences by Work Procedures], *Izvestiia* (23 April 1996).

[42]See Vladimir Kuzar, "Rossiia i Kitai delaiut vybor" [Russia and China Make a Choice}, *Krasnaia zvezda* (30 April 1996). See also another piece by Kuzar, "Rossiia-Kitai: partnerstvo, obrashchennoe v XXI vek" [Russia-China: A Partnership Formed for the 21st Century] *Krasnaia zvezda* (25 April 1996), and Vladimir Mikheev, "Boris Yel'tsin vypolnil v Kitae osoboe zadanie 'semerki'" [Boris Yeltsin Fulfilled Special Task of the "Seven" in China], *Izvestiia* (26 April 1996).

Warsaw Pact would never be allowed to join NATO. "How can we believe them now when they say that NATO is no threat to Russia," was a standard refrain. Questions about the logic of celebrating the elimination of medium-range missiles, when "tactical missiles with nuclear warheads" could now be moved close to the Russian borders, were being asked.[43] NATO's enthusiasm about admitting former Warsaw Pact countries was represented in the Russian mass media as a sign that the West generally, and the United States particularly, were opportunistically taking advantage of Moscow's weakness. One writer for *Nezavisimaia gazeta,* for example, listed at length all of the reasons why Eastern European countries were ineligible for NATO membership—using NATO's own criteria for admission.[44] He assumed that NATO's willingness to bend its own rules was driven entirely by its desire to contain Russia.

Ameliorating suggestions to what was verging on a national crisis were offered in October by the director of Moscow's Institute for the United States and Canada (ISKRAN), S.M. Rogov. Reprinted in ISKRAN's monthly publication *SShA* [USA] from the Minsk journal *Belarus i Mir* [Belarus and the World] (June 1996), Rogov's essay explained why the Russian Federation was opposed to NATO expansion: isolation from the new European security system. Of several constructive approaches the Western countries could take towards Russia, he recommended above all that Russia-NATO relations be institutionalized. Brzezinski later referred to Rogov's essay as Moscow's "voice of reason."[45]

By October, however, the first of many State Duma resolutions against expansion was adopted; in this case, warning that a larger NATO would undermine the validity of the CFE Treaty. Russia's preference for "elevating" the roles of the UN and the Organization for Security and Cooperation in Europe (OSCE, having replaced the CSCE) in European security was laid out. Vladimir Zhirinovskii told delegates to a November plenum of his aggressively nationalist Liberal Democratic Party of Russia (LDPR) that part of their party's strategy would be to move

---

[43]See, e.g., Anatolii Repin, "Rol' vedomogo—ne dlia nas. Yevgenii Primakov o printsipial'nykh napravleniiakh vneshnei politiki Rossii" [The Role of Follower Is Not for Us: Yevgenii Primakov on the Principal Directions of Russian Foreign Policy], *Trud* (25 June 1996).

[44]Dmitrii Gornostaev, "Trebovaniia k kandidatam NATO" [Demands on NATO Candidates], *Nezavisimaia gazeta* (5 July 1996).

[45]Brzezinski, "Voice of Reason from Moscow," *Washington Post* (17 Oct 1996); Rogov, "Rossiia i NATO" [Russia and NATO], *SShA,* No. 10 (October 1996): 3–8. Brzezinski's response was translated and printed in *ibid.,* 9–10. For less encouraging commentary, see "NATO rasshiritsia k 1996 godu" [NATO Is Expanding in 1996], *Krasnaia zvezda* (22 Oct 1996).

Russian troops towards any area of the Russian border that was approached by NATO forces, as a rightful "defense against aggression."[46]

That the hard nationalist vote was lurking out there, making certain that the NATO issue would remain prominent, was revealed by an extraordinary outburst in November. Reacting mainly to the appointment of Boris A. Berezovskii to the Security Council, a piece in the radical communist *Zavtra* [Tomorrow] dredged up all the old anti-semitic, Russian xenophobic battle cries: " . . . Russia, raped, with her eyes put out, deprived of the Caucasus and the Volga area, thrown under the caterpillar treads of NATO, . . . and turning into a slave market for European and Chechen merchants . . . . will have to take the AK's and once again assemble our Native Land." This appeal sounded remarkably like statements uttered by *Pamiat* members in the late 1980s.[47]

Hostility towards NATO enlargement was by no means a monopoly of fringe groups or communists. In late 1996 the Institute of International Economic and Political Studies, Russian Academy of Sciences, published a monograph, *Russian National Security and the Expansion of NATO* (*Scientific Report*).[48] Prepared by well-known historian V.I. Dashichev, this report located NATO's policy of enlargement in a continuum made up of "tragic" divisions of Europe into "two competing groups of states" since the formation of a Triple Entente in 1903. Each time of division led to war. Germany had been the fulcrum around which coalitions had been arranged (for and against), and the current situation was said to be no different. Russia had been duped in 1990, Dashichev wrote, when it was led to believe that, with the unification of Germany, there would be no further movement of NATO military infrastructure eastward. This belief was echoed by Gorbachev in

---

[46]Zhirinovskii, "Doklad na noiabr'skom Plenume TsK LDPR" (26 November 1996), 11. Reprinted as "*My, kak partii, sostoialis!*" by the LDPR, Moscow, 1997 (in 200,000 copies, the party claimed). "Obrashchenie Gosudarstvennoi Dumy. V sviazi s planami rasshireniia NATO" [Address to the State Duma: In Connection with the Plans for NATO Enlargement], *Rossiiskaia gazeta* (12 Nov 1996).

[47]*Zavtra,* No. 48 (Nov 1996). It had just been discovered that Berezovskii carried dual citizenship, of Russia and Israel. *Zavtra* is a communist newspaper, but its extreme nationalist viewpoint often goes beyond public positions taken by the CPRF.

[48]V.I. Dashichev, *Natsional'naia bezopasnost' Rossii i ekspansiia NATO (Nauchnyi doklad)* (Moscow: IMEPI RAN, 1996). Dashichev had covered some of this ground already in his "Evropeiskaia tragediia" [European Tragedy], *Nezavisimaia gazeta* (10 October 1995), and, with O.T. Bogomolov, "Moskva glazami Berlina" [Moscow in the Eyes of Berlin], *Nezavisimaia gazeta* (4 Feb 1996). More than 25 years ago Dashichev was the author of a two-volume study, *Bankrotstvo strategii Germanskogo fashizma* [The Bankrupt Strategy of German Fascism] (Moscow: Nauka, 1973), covering the years 1939–45.

his memoirs and repeated often later.[49] The current crisis is entirely the responsibility of an American desire for global hegemony, Dashichev continued, and will force Russia to reformulate its current military and foreign policy concepts and practice. This could mean a return to the arms race, a new confrontation between Russia and the West, especially the United States, renewed isolation of Russia on the international arena, and a sharp re-alignment of countries in Europe.[50]

The resilience of Dashichev's accusation about German duplicity was corroborated by statements delivered to a Finnish-Russian Roundtable in December 1996. The theme of the gathering was the future of Northern Europe and it was attended by some 100 delegates from northern countries. Boris Piadyshov, editor-in-chief of *Mezhdunarodnaia zhizn'* [International Affairs], organ of the RF Ministry of Foreign Affairs, told the audience that Russia's role in the future of Northern Europe would be shaped by the degree to which "NATO's military infrastructure looms over Russia's borders." He reminded them of an observation made by French President François Mitterrand in 1990 that NATO expansion "to the east was inadmissable, and that this would create a serious danger for the Soviet Union."[51] Further discussion at the Roundtable, especially in regard to the Baltic Sea, revealed a consensus that Russia had reason to worry.

Almost simultaneously with the appearance of Dashichev's monograph, secretary of the RF Defense Council Yurii Baturin told a panel of military experts that Russia's military doctrine needed revision. Among his reasons for requesting change in a doctrine that had been set as recently as 1993 was his belief that Russia's geopolitical position had altered considerably since that time. "NATO's plans to expand eastward remain a danger to Russia's security," Baturin warned, adding that even a revised doctrine would have to be transitional because of uncertainty in the international sphere.[52]

---

[49] See M. Gorbachev, *Zhizn' i reformy* Bk. 2 (Moscow, 1995): 167.

[50]Dashichev, *Natsional'naia bezopasnost' Rossii*, 13–18, 37–48. Dashichev cited *Engaging Russia: A Report to the Trilateral Commission* (New York: The Trilateral Commission, 1995), 8, as one of the few Western documents to recognize the problems NATO expansion eastward posed for Russia.

[51]"The Future of Northern Europe," *International Affairs* (Moscow), 43, No. 3 (1997): 127–38.

[52]Interfax (5 Nov 1996), and "Nuzhna novaia voennaia doktrina" [A New Military Doctrine Is Necessary], *Krasnaia zvezda* (2 Nov 1996). For Russia's military doctrine, printed in 1993, see "Osnovnye polozheniia voennoi doktriny Rossiiskoi Federatsii" [Basic Positions of the Russian Federation Military Doctrine], *Izvestiia* (8 Oct 1993), and Anatolii Stasovskii, "Voennaia doktrina Rossii: novoe ponimanie bezopasnosti strany" [Military Doctrine of Russia: New Understanding of the Country's Security], *Krasnaia zvezda* (18 Oct 1993), translated in *REDA 1993,* Vol. 1, 292–295.

It is worth mentioning as well that at that same time Primakov offered his most forthright observation on NATO policy to date. Speaking on Russian foreign policy at a strategic studies center in Egypt, he said,

> we do not want the old bloc divisions to be replaced with new ones that would divide the world into two parts. That is why Russia is against NATO expansion. . . . We have taken a negative position on this and we will stick to it. Of course, this does not mean that we can veto new admissions to NATO. . . . But we have the right to protect our national interests, and if NATO advances to our territory, we will take adequate measures in terms of military construction and will try to remedy the geo-political situation . . . in order to find new partners and allies (ITAR-TASS, 30 Oct 1996).

Even Grigorii Yavlinskii, head of Yabloko, the most pro-Western and "liberal" of Russia's major political parties, warned that NATO expansion would cause a "political earthquake" in his country, making it possible for "clowns" like Zhirinovskii to assert themselves.[53]

Prime Minister Chernomyrdin made Russia's position on NATO expansion unequivocal at the OSCE summit in Lisbon in early December, 1996: the approach of NATO's military infrastructure to Russia's borders will create new dividing lines in Europe and convince Russia that its security lies with a renewed integration in the CIS. The OSCE issued a Declaration on the European Security Model, which decried all notions of spheres of influence in Europe and agreed that the CFE should be adjusted to fit new circumstances, and that a European Security Charter should be drawn up. The OSCE pronouncement was preceded by a NATO decision (June 1996) to establish within itself the European Security and Defense Identity (ESDI), with strong support from Germany and France. Russia monitored these developments very closely and, in the case of the OSCE, claimed that, with the help of Jacques Chirac, it had been Primakov who had persuaded the meeting to provide new guarantees in connection with the eastern expansion of NATO.[54] Moscow's foreign minister followed this up at a NATO meeting in Brussels with a strong affirmation of Russia's status as a Great

---

[53]Yavlinskii's remarks were made in Budapest and quoted in *Magyar Nemzet* (14 Dec 1996), FBIS-SOV, No. 243.

[54]Nikolai Paklin, "Miach u vorot Vashingtona" [The Ball Is in Washington's Court], *Rossiiskaia gazeta* (5 Dec 1996). For Chernomyrdin's statement in Lisbon, see Interfax (2 Dec 1996).

Power and spoke very distrustfully of NATO protestations that nuclear weapons would not be deployed on the eastern territories.[55]

The year ended with vindication for Russian opponents of NATO expansion from an unexpected source. In a statement delivered on 5 December 1996, Jack Matlock, former American Ambassador to Moscow, said that NATO expansion was a strategy based on a misunderstanding of the Russian mentality. Moreover, Gorbachev was correct when he claimed that when Russia agreed to German reunification it had been led to believe by the United States and Western Germany that NATO would expand no further eastward. The assertion, "I was a witness to that, and we deceived Russia. Why then should they believe us now?" was attributed to Matlock again and again in the Soviet press.[56]

1.2. 1997—Down to the Wire

In January 1997 badly deteriorating conditions in the Russian Armed Forces prompted Minister of Defense Igor Rodionov and Chief of the General Staff Viktor Samsonov to cite NATO's projected expansion to bolster repeated calls for better funding from the government. The implications of NATO enlargement began to shape conversations over the long-promised military reform as well.[57] Their case was both political and practical and, although mostly ignored by the Defense Council and Finance Ministry, met with a receptive public opinion. The communist press charged that NATO's brain trust was perpetuating the West's dominant position in the world and keeping Russia permanently in a position as "loser" of the Cold War. America wants to squeeze Russia out of Europe, they said,

---

[55]Vasilii Safronchuk, "K itogam briussel'skoi vstrechi NATO. Ubaiukivaiut . . ." [Results of the NATO Brussels Meeting: They Are Trying to Lull Us . . .], *Sovetskaia Rossiia* (15 Dec 1996). Primakov, "Nasha vneshniaia politika ne mozhet byt' politikoi vtororazriadnogo gosudarstva" [Our Foreign Policy Cannot Be a Policy of a Second Rate State], *Rossiiskaia gazeta* (17 Dec 1996); see also Nikolai Paklin, "Sindrom NATO" [The NATO Syndrome], *Rossiiskaia gazeta* (14 Dec 1996).

[56]See, e.g., Dmitrii Gornostaev, " 'My obmanuli russkikh'. Na Zapade nachinaiut osoznavat' vozmozhnost' negativnykh posledstvii rasshireniia NATO" ['We Deceived the Russians': The Possibility of Negative Results of NATO Expansion Are Starting to Be Realized in the West], *Nezavisimaia gazeta* (22 Jan 1997). Matlock repeated this himself in an OP-ED written for the *New York Times* during the crisis in Kosovo in 1999: "The One Place NATO Could Turn for Help" (20 April 1999).

[57]See, e.g., Aleksandr Ruchkin, "Reforma v armii. Ot kakoi pechki tantsevat' " [The Reform in the Army: Where to Start?], *Rossiiskaia gazeta* (17 Jan 1997).

but other NATO members realize that Russian security needs should be recognized. Zhirinovskii and Duma deputy Maj. Gen. Nikolai Stoliarov recommended that Russia rearm itself.[58]

Yeltsin already had taken steps to counter NATO's plans. On 5 January, one day after meeting with Helmut Kohl in Moscow, he sat down with his foreign policy and military advisors and worked out retaliatory measures.[59] Kohl was portrayed in Russian government releases as someone who "understands the 'great psychological problem' that Russia has with NATO's expansion," but commentators were not impressed. The German Chancellor's statements were little more than a "smoke screen," said Yevgenii Popov in the leading communist paper, *Sovetskaia Rossiia*.[60] Just two days later Primakov told ITAR-TASS journalists that Russia was adamantly opposed to NATO's expansion plans and that Russia would defend its national interests.[61] A Solana visit to Moscow later in January gave the Russian government media further opportunity to blame Washington for NATO's aggressive moves to the east and to express Chernomyrdin's "categorical" opposition to expansion on the grounds that the Alliance was primarily a military one.[62]

A more compelling picture of the damage that NATO might be inflicting on Russia was drawn by Grigorii Yavlinskii. Speaking to a large audience of journalists and politicians in Prague on 13 January, the Yabloko leader predicted that the absorption by NATO of former Warsaw Pact countries would prove to be a mistake, for it would distract Russia from the natural convergence of its interests with

---

[58]See generally, Konstantin Kovalev, "Patriot. Pis'ma iz N'iu Iorka" [Patriot: Letters from New York], *Sovetskaia Rossiia* (4 Jan 1997). This same issue carried an unusually long article on the German threat to Moscow in 1941. See also "Drug Gel'mut nam pomozhet!" [Friend Helmut (Kohl) Will Help Us!], *Sovetskaia Rossiia* (6 Jan 1997). For the hardline recommendations by Zhirinovskii and Stoliarov, see Interfax (13, 14 Jan 1997).

[59]See "Vyrabotat' otvetnye deistviia na plany rasshireniia NATO" [To Work Out Retaliatory Actions to Plans for NATO Expansion], *Rossiiskie vesti* (9 Jan 1997), where Yurii Nikolaev described Yeltsin's hurried action and enumerated the numbers of fighter-bombers, tanks, airfields, and communications and supply infrastructure that Poland, the Czech republic and Hungary would add to NATO's arsenal.

[60]"Kohl Discusses NATO in Moscow," Interfax (4 Jan 1997). Popov, "Zavidovskie posidelki" [Zavidovo Gathering], *Sovetskaia Rossiia* (6 Jan 1997).

[61]ITAR-TASS (8 Jan 1997). See also "God Yevgeniia Primakova" [The Year of Yevgenii Primakov] (an interview), *Rossiiskaia gazeta* (10 Jan 1997).

[62]See, e.g., "Nezavidnaia missiia Kh. Solany" [Unenviable Mission of Solana], *Rossiiskaia gazeta* (21 Jan 1997).

those of Europe. The psychological effects of NATO's action could too easily evoke a nationalist "hysteria" reminiscent of Germany in the 1920s. The industrial-military complex would take advantage of the situation to demand more subsidies and the General Staff would keep planning as if a threat from Europe was its planning priority, when, in Yavlinskii's opinion, the greater danger still lay to the south. Moreover, Russian strategists could be persuaded to look elsewhere to establish a new military bloc of their own—with Belarus and Ukraine as its key components. Whereas Yavlinskii's comments did not impress his Czech listeners very much, they foretold the coming mood in Moscow accurately.[63]

An audience closer to home heard similar opinions from Anatolii Chubais, at that time chief of the Russian Presidential Staff and often a target of Yavlinskii's political venom. By January 1997, Yeltsin having been ill and mostly away from the office for nearly seven months, it was assumed by many that Chubais was actually running the government. Yeltsin's health was so great a concern that the State Duma voted 229–63 on 22 January to remove him. The vote was not binding and was withdrawn shortly thereafter on technical grounds, but the level of anxiety over the lack of leadership in Moscow was made clear. The absence of a strong hand at the center made NATO expansion appear more threatening and kick-started the latent assumption that the West would take advantage of Russia's temporary weakness.

In a long interview with *Trud* [Labor], where he explained both his role and the government's plans to accelerate the reform process, Chubais was asked about NATO expansion and the proposed Russia-Belarus union. His response rang with traditional Russian fears of encirclement: "It is well known that there are plans for a type of cordon sanitaire around Russia, stretching from Azerbaijan to the Baltic. To separate Russia from the civilized world and isolate it." Western opposition (e.g., U.S. "Republican politicians") to the Russian-Belarus union and proponents of NATO expansion share "a very poor understanding of what this means for Russia." Coming as they did from a young reformer in government, such opinions reveal how deeply entrenched Russia's concerns were. Chubais did not reject NATO completely, rather he insisted that a "real treaty with NATO" and carefully thought-out pre-expansion mutual commitments would provide a solution to the dilemma.[64] The requirements demanded by Chubais were to be met five

---

[63]Grigorii Yavlinskii, "The NATO Distraction," *Transition* 3, No. 5 (21 March 1997): 32–35.

[64] *Trud* (21 Jan 1997), FBIS-SOV, No. 016. A much more conciliatory essay prepared by Dmitrii Trenin, of the Carnegie Fund, provided some optimism that Russia and NATO could work out a mutually beneficial modus vivendi, but even he made it clear that the path would not be an easy one. See Trenin, et al., "Rossiia i NATO: kontrakt na budushchee" [Russia and NATO: Contract for the Future], *Nezavisimoe voennoe obozrenie,* No. 1 (11–18 Jan 1997).

months later. By that time, however, opposition to NATO expansion was far better organized and tied much more closely to the machinery of political campaigning in Russia. In short, the rules of the debate had changed, passing the moderates by.

Essays published in *Nezavisimaia gazeta* during the last two weeks of January typified Russian opinion about NATO and the Kremlin. On the 14th, for example, Viktor Kuvaldin asked readers not to demonize NATO while ignoring the reality of Russia's circumstances. Calling on the Russian government to direct its energies towards making the CSCE the primary vehicle for security in Europe, he cautioned that ranting against NATO would merely make the Alliance more formidable. The very next day, Dmitrii Gornostaev predicted greater tension between Moscow and Washington now that foreign policy management fell to Madeleine Albright and Primakov, both unbending when it came to their respective national interests. Subsequent articles claimed that Helmut Kohl was a "hostage" to Yeltsin's health, supporting the Russian president while keeping him at arm's length from NATO. If Yeltsin was forced out of office because of illness, then cooperation from Germany might diminish dramatically. Other reports included misgivings about "secret" meetings between the Polish president and NATO, objections to perceived Ukraine's deviousness in relationship to NATO, and condemnation of growing American aggressiveness in the matter of NATO enlargement. Finally, there were hints about a "secret" meeting between Primakov and Solana near Moscow and, on the 21st, a front page proclamation that "NATO Will Insist on a Charter and Russia Will Insist on an Agreement." Included in the speculation about Primakov's negotiations with Solana were data from an opinion poll showing that 50 percent of the respondents opposed former Soviet republics joining NATO, and 41 percent opposed the admission of any former Warsaw Treaty country.[65]

---

[65]Yuliia Petrovskaia, Dmitrii Gornostaev, "Zakrytaia vstrecha v podmoskov'e" [Closed Meeting Near Moscow], *Nezavisimaia gazeta* (21 Jan 1998); Petrovskaia, "NATO budet nastaivat' na khartii, a Rossiia na soglashenii" [NATO Will Insist on a Charter and Russia Will Insist on an Agreement], (22 Jan 1998); Gornostaev, "Tainaia beseda Kvatsnevskogo . . ." [Secret Conversations of Kwazniewskii], (18 Jan 1998); Aleksei Pushkov, "Ni mira, ni voiny v otnosheniiakh s al'iansom" [Neither War Nor Peace in Relations with the Alliance], (17 Jan 1998); an interview with Udovenko, Ukrainian foreign minister, "Vzlety i padeniia otnoshenii Moskvy i Kieva" [The Highs and Lows of the Relations between Moscow and Kiev], (17 Jan 1998); Viktor Sokolov, "Zalozhnik Rossiiskikh sobytii" [Hostage to Events in Russia (Kohl)], (15 Jan 1998); Gornostaev, "Moskva i Vashington pered novym krizisom" [Moscow and Washington Face a New Crisis], (15 Jan 1998); Viktor Kuvaldin, "Skazat 'A'—Evropeiskomu zapadu i vostoku nyzhno vosstanavlivat' rodstvennye otnosheniia sviazi" [Say 'Ah'—West and East Europe Need to Restore Their Relative Relationship], (14 Jan 1998).

All of these articles referred to growing anti-Western sentiments in Russia and connected them to NATO expansion, thereby discounting the idea that Russia's public had little interest in NATO. Vladimir Razuvaev dealt with this issue explicitly by dividing Russian commentators on NATO into categories: advocates who approved expansion as a means to bring stability to East and Central Europe, opponents who saw enlargement as a threat to Russia, "illusionists" who mooted the possibility of Russia joining NATO, and "realists" who said that expansion would happen anyway and that Russians should make the best of it. Generally, however, Razuvaev believed that, in varying degrees, all Russians were fearful of NATO.[66]

A more focussed campaign against NATO's plans to expand began to take shape in early February during the annual World Economic Forum at Davos, Switzerland. Although delegates to the huge international gathering were not there to hear Russia's complaints, Chernomyrdin and Chubais (representing and, clearly, speaking for Yeltsin) played for the audience at home. They spoke very aggressively against NATO expansion and were widely praised for the efforts in the Russian media. They and A.N. Shokhin (then representing the Russian Unity and Accord Party) were credited with bringing to the Forum's attention the specter of Russia having to rearm at the expense of its economic reforms.[67] Back in Moscow, Duma deputy Sergei A. Glotov called for the resumption of the production of missiles in Russia, and an Anti-NATO Expansion (soon shortened simply to Anti-NATO) faction was organized among the deputies. Introducing the group, nationalist Sergei N. Baburin insinuated that, if threatened, Russia might rescind the old Soviet commitment against the first use of nuclear weapons.[68] Glotov, also an organizer of the Anti-NATO group, holds the rank of Lieutenant Colonel and is a former instructor at the Krasnodar military-

---

[66]Razuvaev, "V Rossii vsegda budut opasat'sia NATO" [In Russia NATO Will Always Be Feared], *Nezavisimaia gazeta* (24 Jan 1997).

[67]See, for example, "Davos: nuzhna dobraia volia partnerov" [Davos: One Needs the Goodwill of Partners], *Rossiiskaia gazeta* (4 Feb 1997). A Chubais news conference at Davos, in English to "slow-witted" Western journalists, was praised especially in *Komsomol'skaia pravda* (5 Feb 1997). See also Dmitrii Gornostaev, "Chubais predupredil zapad o posledstviiakh rasshireniia NATO" [Chubais Warned the West about the Consequences of NATO Expansion], *Nezavisimaia gazeta* (5 Feb 1998).

[68]*Literaturnaia gazeta,* No. 5 (5 Feb 1997), 1, FBIS-SOV, No. 043. On the founding of the Anti-NATO group, see "Dumtsi formiruiut 'antinato'" [Duma Members Form an 'Anti-NATO' Group], *Nezavisimaia gazeta* (31 Jan 1997), and ITAR-TASS (27 Jan 1997). An Anti-NATO Club was established in Ukraine by the Ukrainian Civil Congress on 21 February, organized by Aleksandr Bazilyuk. See Interfax-Ukraine (21 Feb 1997).

engineering school for missile troops. At the time of its creation, the Anti-NATO Association consisted of 100 deputies. It more than doubled its membership in very short order.

While Moscow heated up about NATO, President Clinton's administration worked out its second term foreign policy. It was hoped that differences with Russia over NATO could be resolved, but Yeltsin's renewed bouts with heart disease and pneumonia slowed progress in U.S.-Russian relations. In anticipation of visits to Russia by Javier Solana and Madeleine Albright, anti-NATO forces in Moscow declared the ratification of START II a weapon of protest in February. State Duma Defense Committee chairman, Lev Rokhlin, warned on the 8th that ratification was possible but only after all of its implications for Russia's security were investigated. Speaking to reporters in London, Rokhlin blamed NATO's "broken promises" not to move into former Warsaw Pact territory for the distrustful mood in Moscow's parliament. He said that Russia's "bitter experience" compelled the State Duma to demand documented assurances from NATO before any decision on START II could be made (ITAR-TASS, 8 Feb). A week later the opposition majority in the Duma announced that it would, in fact, block ratification of START II, and the People's Patriotic Union of Russia bloc (including the CPRF, Agrarians and Power to the People!) circulated a resolution that it would not ratify if NATO moved east.[69]

The weeks before U.S. Secretary of State Madeleine Albright's visit to Moscow in February 1997 saw a flood of commentary hostile to NATO in the Russian press. The angry rhetoric sounded familiar to former sovietologists. Every Western commentator of some importance who spoke against NATO expansion was quoted at length in the Russian press. This practice, reminiscent of the old Soviet habit of portraying a ground swell of informed Western support for its position while ignoring the detail of Western contrary opinion, continued well after the Albright visit.[70] In the meantime, proponents of enlargement were depicted in the old "ruling circles" format; visits to Transcaucasia and Moldova by Solana were regarded with great suspicion; Clinton was said to be intransigent because of his

---

[69]See *Sovetskaia Rossiia* (17 Feb, 24 March 1997). The statement, signed by Zyuganov, was sent to Yeltsin, government and parliamentary leaders, and to the diplomatic missions in Moscow from NATO countries (Interfax, 15 Feb 1997).

[70]See, e.g., Edgar Cheporov, "Vo chto oboidetsia SShA rasshirenie NATO," *Rossiiskaia gazeta* (26 Feb 1997), where Ted Carpenter, head of the Cato Institute in Washington, is quoted as saying that Russia has good reason to feel threatened by NATO expansion.

own domestic difficulties; and the alleged broken promises related to German re-unification were referred to constantly.[71]

There were, to be sure, a few writers in the Russian press who attempted to moderate the furore over NATO, such as Oleg Moroz who pointed out in February 1997 that former Warsaw Pact members have good reason still to be afraid of Russia. His central point was that Russia's leadership needs an enemy to take the people's minds away from their many other problems. Dmitrii Trenin, of the Carnegie Institute's Moscow office, said much the same thing, noting that a compromise with NATO could benefit Russia and that enlargement was dangerous only if Russia stayed poor.[72] One of very few Russian advocates of NATO expansion, Konstantin Borovoi, blamed Primakov directly for changed attitudes of Russians towards NATO. In 1994, he said, only 18 percent of Russians had any interest in NATO, but in 1997 some 80 percent care about it. This was because, in contrast to Kozyrev, Primakov brought the old Soviet attitude back to the ministry of foreign affairs; that is, negative and defensive.[73] But Borovoi's opinions were drowned out in a cacophony of nationalistic outcry.

A roundtable organized by the Novosti Political Club in Moscow in early February concluded that a unique consensus had emerged in Russia against NATO's plans, and that even Russian democracy might take on an anti-Western character as a result of them. ISKRAN's Rogov, whom Brzezinski had called Moscow's

---

[71]See, e.g., Dmitrii Gornostaev, A. Reitov, "Klinton ne gotov predostavit' garantii" [Clinton Is Not Prepared to Provide Guarantees], *Nezavisimaia gazeta* (11 Feb 1997); Vladimir Katin, "GenSek NATO v stolitsakh SNG" [General Secretary of NATO Visits CIS Capitals], *Nezavisimaia gazeta* (11 Feb 1997); Tat'iana Koshkareva, "NATO i budushchii khoziain Kremlia" [NATO and the Future Master of the Kremlin], (Chernomyrdin), *Nezavisimaia gazeta* (11 Feb 1997); Andrei Riabov, "Novye Rossiiskie mify" [New Russian Myths], *Nezavisimaia gazeta* (13 Feb 1997); Yevgenii Grigor'ev, "Diplomatiia tseitnota" [Diplomacy of Time-Problem], *Nezavisimaia gazeta* (18 Feb 1997).

[72]Trenin, "Transformatsiia Rossiiskoi vneshnei politiki" [The Transformation of Russian Foreign Policy], *Nezavisimaia gazeta* (5 Feb 1997); Moroz, " Kremlin Politicians Are Trying by Might and Main to Frighten Those Who Are Mortally Afraid of Us," *Literaturnaia gazeta*, No. 5 (5 February 1997), 1, 9, FBIS-SOV, No. 043. Moroz acknowledged Soviet and Russian aggression against their neighbors and elsewhere, including the conflict in Chechnya, which he called "insane." He ridiculed Primakov and Lebed and blamed pressure from the "national-communist opposition" for the high degree of hostility against NATO's plans.

[73]Borovoi, "Ot Kozyreva k Primakovu—put' nazad" [From Kozyrev to Primakov, a Route Backwards], *Nezavisimaia gazeta* (6 Feb 1997). The likelihood of change to a more aggressive mode was noted by Yuliia Petrovskaia and others, see "Vneshniaia politika RF mozhet izmenit'sia" [The RF Foreign Policy Can Be Changed], *Nezavisimaia gazeta* (8 Feb 1997).

"voice of reason," now said that NATO expansion was harmful to Russia's national vital interests and should be vigorously opposed. Aleksei Arbatov, deputy chairman of the State Duma Defense Committee, cautioned the Novosti group that NATO expansion would give the communists a platform to ride back into power.[74] NATO's decision was the "West's greatest mistake since the Cold War," he complained. A few days later Col. Gen. Leonid Maiorov, deputy secretary of the RF Security Council, wrote that Russians could not possibly trust the West's promises as "the NATO military machine" moves inexorably towards their border. Head of the Duma's International Affairs Committee, Lukin, issued a statement with a similar point of view.[75] A consensus had been reached.

1.3. Albright Comes to Town

Two days before Yeltsin met with Albright, German Foreign Minister Klaus Kinkel visited Moscow and spoke with the RF president by telephone from Rodionov's office. Kinkel met as well with Prime Minister Chernomyrdin, Foreign Minister Primakov and Chubais.[76] Russian officials knew that the German government concurred with NATO policy, but the Russian public was left confused by ambiguous press accounts. Kinkel was said to have recognized that Russia should have a firm agreement with NATO before the Alliance's July summit and promised that his country would push for a general European security package. Italy's foreign minister, Lamberti Dini, showed up in Moscow the morning of Albright's arrival and also spoke to Yeltsin by phone, prompting more Russian reports to the effect that European countries were taking Russia's concerns seriously and that Russia's "firm" stance was the correct approach.[77] Interfax (22 Feb)

---

[74] *Trud* (13 Feb 1997). For Rogov's comments, see RIA Novosti (2 and 11 Feb 1997). The Novosti Roundtable proceedings were described a month later at length in the Hungarian press, *Budapest Nepszava* (11 March 1997), translated in FBIS-SOV, No. 070. Speakers at the roundtable included Rogov, Dimitrii Ryurikov, foreign political adviser to Yeltsin, Nikolai Afanas'evskii, deputy foreign minister, Aleksei Arbatov, and Col. Gen. Leonid Ivashov.

[75] Lukin, "Rossiia i NATO: vremia reshenii" [Russia and NATO: Decision Time], *Nezavisimaia gazeta* (13 Feb 1997); Maiorov, "Pochemu oni nervnichaiut" [Why They Are Nervous], *Rossiiskaia gazeta* (13 Feb 1997). This position was taken also by historian Sergei Kortunov, "Dogovor ne mozhet byt' platoi za rasshirenie" [An Agreement Cannot Be Payment for Expansion], *Nezavisimaia gazeta* (13 Feb 1997).

[76] Moscow NTY (18 Feb 1997), FBIS-SOV, No. 033. See also an interview with Primakov on NTV (16 Feb 1997), FBIS-SOV, No. 033.

[77] On Kinkel and Chubais, Interfax (18 Feb 1997); on Kinkel and Rodionov, ITAR-TASS and Interfax (19 Feb 1997); on Dini, Moscow Mayak Radio Network (19 Feb 1997), FBIS-SOV, No. 034. See also "Moskva kak magnit pritiagivaet zarubezhnykh viziterov" [Moscow Attracts Foreign Visitors Like a Magnet], *Nezavisimaia gazeta* (19 Feb 1997).

reported that Dini said that the Russian position that it should have a binding agreement with NATO prior to the July summit was sound.

Reports about these quick visits hinted at differences within NATO. France had already appeared as a potential maverick in the enlargement agenda,[78] so blame for the expansionist policy was cast directly on a renewed cold warrior United States. American critics of expansion, such as George Kennan and Michael Mandelbaum, were cited regularly in the Russian press. Prior to the Albright visit, it would certainly have seemed to Russian readers that firm resistance was the only possible stance. Subsequent reporting of the Primakov-Albright talks in the moderate and government media approved the correctness of this assumption. Albright accepted the notion of a mutually binding agreement, and Primakov "confirmed Russia's negative attitude to NATO enlargement"—or so the Russian foreign minister claimed (Interfax, 21, 24 Feb). He insisted that her statement that NATO did not intend to deploy nuclear weapons in Central or East European countries "must be recorded in the agreement." After two days of negotiation with Solana, Primakov went to Norway and at a news conference expressed "cautious optimism" about the talks in Brussels (ITAR-TASS, 24 Feb 1997). His credibility may have been suspect, however, because at that time the Russian press was filled with predictions of an impending shake-up of the entire cabinet.[79]

Primakov's visit to Norway evoked widespread Russian press commentary about the NATO question. On 27 February alone, *Izvestiia* said that a demilitarized zone between NATO and Russia was being discussed; *Rossiiskie vesti* described broad opposition to expansion in Slovakia and Hungary; and *Nezavisimaia gazeta* insisted that most Western "elites" opposed NATO expansion and only "adepts of the Cold War" justified the existence of NATO. As Primakov wound up his European tour in London, he said again that Russia's relations with NATO "must be enshrined in a legally binding document" because Russia does "not believe what the West says." Moreover, if NATO admits any former USSR republic, "all relations with NATO

---

[78] After a 3-hour meeting between Yeltsin and Jacques Chirac in Paris, a press release said that they held common positions on European security and NATO, "V sentiabre Zhe. Shirak snova sobiraetsia v Moskva" [Chirac Will Return to Moscow in September], *Rossiiskaia gazeta* (4 Feb 1997). See also Interfax (26 Nov 1996).

[79]See, e.g., "Skazhi mne, kto ne uidet iz pravitel'stva, i ya skazhu, kuda ono nas privedet!" [Tell Me Who Will Stay in the Government, and I Will Tell You Where This Government Will Lead Us!], *Rossiiskie vesti* (26 Feb 1997). The dismissal rumors were the result of a scolding said to have been delivered to Chernomyrdin and his cabinet for failing to resolve the non-payments crisis, and their inability to collect taxes. Chernomyrdin and Rodionov were picked by the media, wrongly as it turned out, as the most likely victims among ministers.

will end" and Russia may look to its East for partnerships.[80] These warnings were treated in the West as if they were face-saving idle threats.

ISKRAN got into the act again, but less optimistically than Rogov's intervention three months earlier. In "Some Reflections on NATO Expansion," Yu.N. Rakhmaninov vigorously objected to NATO's plans by employing an historical context, as Dashichev had done, and setting out clearly the problems enlargement would pose for Russia.[81] Rakhmaninov began his story in Prague, 13 October 1993, when without any prior consultation with Russia Clinton told the Visegrad group that the question of NATO expansion was not a matter of "if," rather it was "when."

By March, it was common in Russia to find analogies drawn between NATO expansion and the Cuban Missile Crisis. If Americans at that earlier time experienced "concern, suspicion, and apprehension," it is not surprising that a much weakened Russia felt that way in 1997, Vladimir Simonov wrote on 4 March, referring also to Matlock's 1996 statement, "Yes, we deceived Russia . . . "[82] It had become an article of faith that Western leaders had lied brazenly in 1990–91. Russia's demand for unequivocal assurances that NATO infrastructure (conventional forces, launch sites, staging airfields, and so on) not be moved closer to Russia's borders and that the projected Russia-NATO accord be ratified by parliaments in all 16 member-states was understandable.[83]

The communist and nationalist press objected to their own government's "weakness." The most prominent communist newspaper carried the message that Zyuganov took directly to a U.S.-Russia Business Forum on 20 February. In "Why Expand NATO?", Vladimir Kikilo suggested an alternative: a security guarantee for the countries of Eastern Europe endorsed by both the United States and Russia.[84]

---

[80]*Komsomol'skaia pravda* (4 March 1997), FBIS-SOV, No. 062.

[81] Rakhmaninov, "Nekotorye soobrazheniia o rasshirenii NATO," *SShA,* No. 2 (January 1997): 56–60.

[82]Simonov, "Kompromissy s NATO vozmozhny, no oni ne dolzhny zatragivat' zhiznennye interesy Rossii" [Compromises with NATO Are Possible, but They Should Not Affect the Vital Interests of Russia], *Rossiiskie vesti* (4 March 1997).

[83]See, e.g., Yuliia Petrovskaia, "NATO budet nastaivat' na khartii, a Rossiia na soglashenii" [NATO Will Insist on a Charter, and Russia Will Insist on an Agreement], *Nezavisimaia gazeta* (22 Jan 1997). By the end of March 12 countries had been formally accepted as candidates for discussion at the NATO meeting in Madrid in July: Poland, Hungary, the Czech Republic, Slovakia, Slovenia, Romania, Albania, Macedonia, Bulgaria, and the three Baltic states.

[84]Kikilo, "Zachem rasshiriat' NATO?" *Sovetskaia Rossiia* (22 Feb 1997). See also "Ne igrat' sud'boi Rossii" [Don't Play Games with Russia's Future], *Sovetskaia Rossiia* (27 Feb 1997), in which Zyuganov's comment to a Voice of America panel that NATO expansion was a "relapse to the Cold War" was printed.

NATO expansion would only encourage extremist forces within Russia and its neighbors, he wrote. On hearing the results of the Primakov-Albright talks, the State Duma's Anti-NATO Group (now called an Association) demanded that specific counter steps be taken. Included among the suggested measures were: active propa- gandization of the anti-expansion position to the "Russian and foreign public," the adoption by the Duma of a legislative framework to strengthen Russian national se- curity, cooperation with "executive authorities" to strengthen Russia in the interna- tional arena, and "deepening the integration of CIS states" with a new emphasis on defense. The Association's executive secretary, Glotov, claimed that deputy support in the Duma had grown to 243.[85]

A particularly harsh assault on NATO came in the form of a long open letter to Strobe Talbott, by then U.S. deputy secretary of state and adviser on Russia, in February.[86] Accusing Talbott of advocating an American version of "Deutschland über alles!", the piece resounded with accusations that the United States was im- posing its values on the rest of the world. NATO expansion was called a by- product of American "imperialism." Opening as a critique of a Talbott speech, the diatribe ended as a comparative analysis of the two (Lenin had called them "immutably hostile") social systems. The importance of the open letter lay not so much with its content as with the fact that it helped draw readers back into the larger "them vs. us" context that Albright had tried to dispel.

In his annual message to the Federal Assembly, delivered on 6 March 1997, Yeltsin reconfirmed Russia's antipathy towards NATO's eastward move, saying that it contradicted Russia's interests and caused a new split in Europe. Instead, Europe should be thinking of an effective security system that included Russia. This address was printed in all the major papers.[87]

---

[85]Moscow Radio Rossii Network (21 Feb 1997), FBIS-SOV, No. 036. Glotov was then a member of the State Duma's Committee on International Affairs, and of N.I. Ryzhkov's Power to the People! movement.

[86]Valentin Koptyug, "Vmesto zaveshchaniia. Dolzhna li Rossiia slepo vosprinimat' to, chego zhelaet ei Amerika" [In Place of a Will: Must Russia Blindly Accept Whatever Amer- ica Wishes], *Sovetskaia Rossiia* (27 Feb 1997). Since his 1990 suggestion that NATO be replaced by a more modern and effective security system for Europe, Talbott had become a leading exponent of NATO enlargement. See, e.g., Talbott, "Why NATO Should Grow," *The New York Review of Books* (10 Aug 1995), 27–30, and "A NATO Expansion Architect Makes His Case," *Christian Science Monitor* (27 Oct 1997).

[87]ITAR-TASS (5, 6 March 1997). Yeltsin, "Stranoi dolzhna upravliat' vlast', a ne ob- stoiatel'stva" [The Authorities Must Govern the Country, Not Circumstances], *Rossiiskaia gazeta* (7 March 1997). The speech was praised and summarized in *Izvestiia, Rossiiskie vesti, Trud* and other mainstream papers, each of which drew attention to the comments about NATO.

Yeltsin's speech raised the level of domestic campaigning on behalf of a hard government stand against the much-debated Russia-NATO accord. Primakov told the faculty of Russia's prestigious Diplomatic Academy that the forthcoming document must guarantee that NATO will not expand its military infrastructure onto the territory of its new members. Directing censure exclusively at the United States, which he admitted was now stronger than Russia, Primakov proclaimed that his country would never be "led" and that eventually it would regain strength. The "West" should bear this in mind. The core priority of Russia's foreign policy, he added, must be to draw together the former Soviet republics, above all Ukraine. This was an aggressive speech with an important strategic message, delivered to an influential audience (Interfax, 7 March).

Simultaneously, a joint statement issued by Yeltsin and Belarus President Alyaksandr Lukashenka on 7 March showed that opposition to NATO's plans was, indeed, a factor in negotiations about further integrating the two countries. The two presidents are "united in their unwillingness to accept NATO's plans to advance eastward," their communiqué said. Consequently, their foreign policies were to be linked more closely (ITAR-TASS, 7 March). The possibility of Belarusian missiles being rearmed to counter deployment of NATO forces in Poland was resurrected in the press release. Rumors about Turkish opposition to NATO expansion because of that country's close involvement with Russia on the Black Sea, and a hint in *Izvestiia* that NATO might even be planning to invite Russia to join NATO, made it appear to Russian readers that their country was gaining the upper hand.[88]

The hardline approach dominating Russian media reporting on the issue as the Yeltsin-Clinton summit drew nearer was in part pre-summit negotiating hype directed at both Russian and foreign (especially U.S.) audiences. Equally clear, however, was the general support for this type of stance. To cite but a few examples: two communist editors complained about government intrigues to undermine Rodionov at precisely the moment when Russia needed to gird up its Armed Forces against NATO expansion.[89] A NTV newscaster on the popular *Segodnya*

---

[88]On the report, from London, to the effect that a document was being prepared to invite Russia to join NATO and that the United States would make financial concessions if Russia yielded, see Vladimir Skosyrev, "Rossiia mozhet vstupit' v NATO" [Russia Can Join NATO], *Izvestiia* (7 March 1997). The potential for support from Turkey was raised first in March, see "Turtsiia vystupila protiv rasshireniia NATO" [Turkey Stood Up against NATO Expansion], *Nezavisimaia gazeta* (30 Jan 1997).

[89]V. Chikin, A. Prokhanov, "Ot patroticheskogo informbiuro[33] [From the Patristic Information Bureau], *Sovetskaia Rossiiskaia* (4 March 1997). Chikin is editor of *Sovetskaia Rossiia,* Prokhanov is editor of *Zavtra.*

[Today] program highlighted the dominant political positions in Russia on 10 March. Opening with encouraging commentary on the "positive environment" of talks between Solana and Primakov, Vladimir Lenskii noted that in Russia the question of NATO expansion had become a "tool of political struggle." Quoting representatives of the government (Chernomyrdin), the communists (Viktor I. Ilyukhin), the radical right (Zhirinovskii), and liberals (Aleksei Arbatov), he confirmed that an "absolute majority" of Russian politicians actively oppose NATO enlargement.[90] Lenskii's conclusions were not exaggerated. The notion that NATO's absorption of former Warsaw Pact countries was the "greatest mistake" of the post–Cold War period in international affairs had gained wide public credence in Russia by March. The State Duma issued a statement to this effect on 12 March, as did Yeltsin himself a few days later.[91]

A few liberals, such as Sergei Kovalev and Borovoi, still supported NATO as a democratic force; and Yegor Stroev, chairman of the Federation Council (the upper house of parliament), was one of the few Russian leaders openly seeking compromise at that time. The Council for Foreign and Defense Policy tried to ease the situation by proposing that Russia join NATO, thereby turning the Alliance into a European-wide security system rather than a military bloc. The Council's spokesman, Vyacheslav Nikonov, recognized that the probability of NATO welcoming Russia as a member was "almost nil," but a wider security arrangement was worthy of study.[92] These voices were lonely ones, as the Moroz and Trenin contributions had been earlier on. The general security question was raised often in Ministry of Defense publications, above all *Krasnaia zvezda* [Red Star], whose view was typified by a bold headline on 15 March "No Effective European Security System Can Be Created without Russia."[93]

---

[90]Moscow NTY (10 March 1997), FBIS-SOV, No. 070.

[91]See Antoninia Yefremova, "Byt' li Evrope bez transhei" [Will Europe Be Without Trenches?], *Rossiiskaia gazeta* (19 March 1997), where Yeltsin is quoted saying that the United States will make a "gross and serious error" if Russia's concerns are not mitigated. For an analysis of the Duma's position, "Stabil'nost' v Evrope mnogo stoit" [Stability in Europe Costs a Lot], *Rossiiskaia gazeta* (19 March 1997). See also the statement from the Russia and the World working groups of the Council for Foreign and Defense Policy, Moscow, "K pozitivnoi povestke dnia v Rossiisko-Amerikanskikh otnosheniiakh" [For a Positive Agenda in Russo-American Relations], *Nezavisimaia gazeta* (14 March 1997).

[92]Moscow Radio Rossii Network (13 March 1997), FBIS-SOV, No. 072.

[93]*Krasnaia zvezda* (15 March 1997). See also *Krasnaia zvezda* (19 March 1997), where it is said that Russia must have a "binding document," not merely a declaration, and that the British foreign minister, Portillo, agreed with Rodionov on this need.

Another voice was heard when the real Aleksandr Lebed began to stand up. In 1995–96 he had been a strident opponent of NATO expansion but later seemed to have fooled American and even Russian audiences into believing that he was a moderate on the issue. In March 1997, Lebed predicted that expansion would destabilize the Alliance itself by forcing it to resolve new regional conflicts and face up to its own internal contradictions. Labeling the expansion proposals products of Cold War thinking, Lebed charged that NATO would force Russia to rely on authoritarian politics—a style he was eminently suited to himself.[94] Lebed's new political party, the Russian People's Republican Party, was founded on the principle that Russia needs order above all else.

As Yeltsin prepared to leave for Helsinki, the Russian press treated the upcoming summit as one of extraordinary importance—the most important since World War II, according to a journalist for *Komsomol'skaia pravda* (20 March). Some were optimistic (e.g., *Nezavisimaia gazeta,* 20 March), others were pessimistic (e.g., *Izvestiia,* 20 March), or angry at the entire process (e.g., *Sovetskaia Rossiia,* 18, 20 March). A. Puzanovskii, Communist, deputy chair of parliament's Committee on Economic Policy, and professor of economics, wrote that an expanded NATO made a new Cold War inevitable and that it was driven entirely by American interests. The entire media urged the president to remain firm.[95] The State Duma addressed a resolution to Yeltsin at Helsinki, demanding that he "resist NATO

---

[94]Lebed, "'Novaia imperiia' nastupaet. Na starye grabli. Razmyshleniia po povodu rasshireniia NATO" [The 'New Empire' Steps on an Old Rake: Thoughts on NATO Expansion], *Izvestiia* (14 March 97). Lebed's statements were summarized in Interfax (13 March 1997). Read Lebed's *Za derzhavu obidno . . .* (Moscow: Moskovskaia pravda, 1995). For a Russian-language interview in which Lebed outlines his political ambitions, see *Novoe vremya,* No. 1 (January 1997). See also "Lebed Set to Co-operate with NATO," *Moscow News,* No. 40 (16–22 Oct 1996), 2.

For an especially gushing, but not untypical, U.S. press judgement on Lebed, see syndicated columnist Georgie Anne Geyer's "An Alexander Lebed–led Russia Holds Much promise," *Mobile Register* (28 Jan 1996). For a much less enthusiastic opinion, see J.L. Black, "Western Media Miss the Real Lebed Story," *Ottawa Citizen* (24 June 1996), A9.

[95]See, e.g., "Prezidentskii sammit budet trydnym" [The Presidential Summit Will Be Difficult], *Rossiiskie vesti* (19 March 1997); "Duel' dvukh patriotov" [The Duel of Two patriots], *Rossiiskie vesti* (19 March 1997); "Khel'sinki—peregovory budet tiazhelymi" [Helsinki, Negotiations Will Be Onerous], *Rossiiskaia gazeta* (20 March 1997).

expansion to the east," and at the same time began to discuss a draft resolution that would forbid Russia itself from ever joining NATO.[96]

1.4. Summit at Helsinki

Russia's media diagnosed the Yeltsin-Clinton talks for much of March, but no observer expected the U.S. president to yield on NATO's plan to expand eastward. Convinced that enlargement was primarily an American commitment to which other NATO members were more or less resigned, the Russian delegation at Helsinki hoped that Clinton would agree to a binding, legal accord between Russia and NATO. Ideally, this would include a commitment to keep NATO military infrastructure (above all, nuclear weapons) out of the new territories and some assurance that former USSR republics would not be accepted as members. Moscow's wishes were partly fulfilled by the ensuing Statement on European Security which called for a "document defining cooperation between Russia and NATO . . . constituting a firm commitment . . . adopted at the highest political level." In addition, it was agreed that NATO would transform itself and that the "new realities of Russia" would be reflected in the Russia-NATO relationship. The Statement confirmed that NATO did not "intend" to deploy nuclear weapons on the territory of its additional members (ITAR-TASS, 21 March 1997). Realistically, Yeltsin could not have expected more than that, but the apprehensions of wary nationalists were certainly not assuaged.

Yeltsin's enthusiastic claims of success rang hollow to most Russian commentators, though moderates accepted his assurances in a very general way and Yavlinskii called for closer dialogue with NATO.[97] Not surprisingly, nationalist and

---

[96]The draft resolution was introduced by the Anti-NATO group (ITAR-TASS, 20 March 1997), but it was dropped the next day (ITAR-TASS, 21 March 1997). For the Duma Address to Yeltsin, see "Protivostoiat' rasshireniu NATO na vostok" [To Resist the Expansion of NATO to the East], *Rossiiskaia gazeta* (20 March 1997). See Puzanovskii, "Rossiia i NATO: vozmozhna li novaia 'kholodnaia voina'? Zachem Amerike 'bol'shoe NATO'" [Russia and NATO: Is a New Cold War Possible? Why America Wants a "Greater NATO"], *Sovetskaia Rossiia* (18 March 1997).

[97]Moscow NTY (21 March 1997), *Segodnya,* reported in FBIS-SOV, No. 050. Antoninia Yefremova wrote in *Rossiiskaia gazeta* (24 March 1997) that Yeltsin had achieved the "maximum possible." The next day a feature item said that Yeltsin "did his best." See Yefremova, "Vstrecha v verkhakh: pozitivnyi kompromiss" [Summit Meeting: Positive Compromise], *Rossiiskaia gazeta* (25 March1997). *Trud* (25 March 1997), said that a "maximum compromise" had been reached, and even *Krasnaia zvezda* (25 March 1997) was encouraged by agreements on arms reductions. See also "Dolg prezidentov—dogovorit'sia!" [The Obligation of the Presidents Is to Reach an Agreement!], *Rossiiskie vesti* (22 March 1997).

communist public organizations reacted strongly against Yeltsin's assertions of accomplishment. G. N. Seleznev, chair of the Duma, and the Anti-NATO faction concluded that NATO's plans would revive the "psychological suspiciousness and hostility" that had undermined European stability for so long.[98] A senior adviser to the Belarusian president stepped into the debate, warning that his country would stand with Russia in taking "adequate measures" in response to Poland's membership in NATO. More ominously, Russia's deputy chief of staff said that Russia "must react to the new military threat somehow—and this is what any country would do!" NATO's eastward expansion is a "fatal mistake," General Valerii Manilov continued, because of the "purely emotional, subconscious" reaction it inevitably evoked among Russia's officer corps.[99]

An essay in *Novoe vremya* embodied the common feeling in Russia; that is, Russia "lost" at Helsinki.[100]

---

[98]For Seleznev's comments, see ITAR-TASS (22 March 1997), and for the Anti-NATO group ITAR-TASS (25 March 1997). Newspapers showing some optimism about Helsinki (see previous footnote) carried complaining pieces too. In "Komu nuzhna vtoraia 'kholodnaia voina'" [Who Needs a Second Cold War?] the usually moderate *Rossiiskie vesti* (21 March 1997) wrote that proponents of NATO expansion should remember the lessons of the Cold War. Aleksandr Rybkin, in "Chem nedovolen Shevardnadze" [What Dissatisfies Shevardnadze?], *Rossiiskaia gazeta* (25 March 1997) pointed to the presence of a NATO squadrons in the Black Sea and said that "NATO expansion already has become, in effect, an accomplished fact." Suspicion about Ukraine's intentions were common (see Kondrashov in *Izvestiia,* fn. 4, below, and Section 4). A mixed message also could be found in "Raznoglasiia ne iskliuchaiut sotrudnichestva" [Disagreements Don't Exclude Cooperation], *Rossiiskie vesti* (25 March 1997). *Zavtra,* of course, was aggressively hostile, see "Boi s teniu" [Battle with a Shadow], *Zavtra,* No. 9 (March 1997).

[99]General Manilov made these comments in response to questions from a reporter for Hamburg's *Die Woche* (21 March 1997). The Russian officer corps does not see NATO as an enemy, he said, but the Alliance's strategy and command system were still directed against Russia. Russia, in turn, may now be forced to increase its nuclear deterrence capabilities; tactical bombers from Poland could reach Smolensk and Kursk, he added. Manilov's remarks make a mockery of a truly astonishing assertion by Anne McElvoy, deputy editor of *The Spectator,* that Russia's Generals were not strongly opposed to NATO expansion. See McElvoy, "NATO: The true enemy is self-doubt," *Ottawa Citizen* (25 March 1997).

The Belarusian official was Mikhail Myasnikovich, head of the Presidential Administration, see Interfax (24 March 1997). For a more militant stance, see "NATO prët kak tank" [NATO Rushes Like a Tank], *Zavtra,* No. 10 (March 1997).

[100]N. Kuchin, Yu.Rusanova, "Russia and USA Made Concessions, but Did Not Retreat. Russia Made a Bigger Concession," *New Times* (April 1997), 50–52. It appeared earlier in *Novoe vremya* (30 March 1997). The authors noted as well that prior to the Helsinki meeting, the Russian media was filled with talk of an "Iranian card," or the advantages to Moscow of closer relationships with Iran, Iraq, Turkey and China.

1.5. Toward the Russia-NATO Founding Act

The fact that the premier of India and both the vice premier and foreign minister of China visited Moscow within days of the Helsinki summit drew many hints in the Russian press of eastern alliances lurking in the background. The idea was ridiculed by *Izvestiia,* but mainly because Russia was "too weak" to be regarded by China as a useful ally! The communist press urged that an alliance system be formed with India and China because Helsinki in effect isolated Russia from Europe (see section 2.2 of this work).[101]

Foreign policy adviser to the president, Dmitrii Ryurikov, provided a revealing interview to the press on the 27th. Putting a positive spin on his government's negotiations in Finland, he said they were successful because the "damage" caused by NATO's expansion was now "minimized." Pressed further, however, he admitted that the atmosphere at the Yeltsin-Clinton discussion was very tense and that the actual chance of a Russia-NATO document being signed was, at that time, only about "60–40" in favor. Ryurikov added that Russia would "revise" its position if "neighboring countries" were admitted to NATO.[102] Over the next two years, this particular warning was given so often that Moscow's officials eventually began talking of a "red line" on the map beyond which NATO must not go. That "line" of demarcation coincided with the borders of the former USSR.

Resigned to the inevitability of NATO enlargement, the Russian government could not allow the opposition to claim a monopoly on defending Russia against a new type of "iron curtain." Primakov bearded the lions in their dens, telling a press conference in Bonn after meeting with his counterpart, Klaus Kinkel, that the RF still thought NATO expansion was "the biggest mistake since the end of the Cold War" (ITAR-TASS, 29 March). We will make the best of a very bad policy, was the Russian stance. Primakov then carried this message to France, where

---

[101]Vasilii Safronchuk, "Trebuiutsia . . . molodye razoriteli" [What Is Needed Is . . . Young Wreckers], *Sovetskaia Rossiia* (29 March 1997). The article also pointed out that Russia might not be considered a "reliable" ally by either China or India, and that this situation must be redressed. See also Safronchuk, "Kliuch doveriia. Chto sumeli im otkryt' v rossiisko-kitaiskom sotrudnichestve" [The Key to Trust], *Sovetskaia Rossiia* (26 April 1997); Stanislav Kondrashov, "Soglasie o nesoglasii" [Agree on Disagreement], *Izvestiia* (27 March 1997).

[102] "Dmitrii Ryurikov: 'Nikakikh illiuzii nakanune sammita v Khel'sinki my ne pitali'" [We Harboured No Illusions on the Eve of the Summit in Helsinki], *Moskovskii komsomolets* (27 March 1997). State Duma deputy Boris Fedorov wrote in "Rossiia dolzhna vstupit' v NATO?" [Should Russia Join NATO?], *Rossiiskie vesti* (26 March 1997) that Russia should challenge the good faith of NATO members and especially the United States by applying for membership itself. He implied that Western politicians would soon reveal their "true" colors.

he spent a three-day official visit, 8–10 April. In that country he told reporters that NATO expansion must not bring the alliance's "military machine closer to our territory" and that no troops should be stationed beyond the borders of the present 16 member states. He said it again in Chisinau, Moldova, on 11 April.

Yeltsin won grudging approval from the Anti-NATO Association when it announced, on 2 April, that the president's stand against NATO's advance eastward was the correct one. Former USSR president Gorbachev chipped in, calling NATO's admission of former Warsaw Pact countries a "time bomb laid under Europe;" and a self-styled "Club of Realists" formed in Moscow agreed that, although NATO expansion was a grave error, Russia had little choice but to adapt and use the unpleasant reality to its own advantage. Both "sides" acknowledged that NATO expansion was the one issue on which Russians were unified.[103]

As the Baltic governments increased their efforts to make themselves acceptable to NATO, in April, and appeared to have some American senatorial backing (see Section 5), Russian media and politicians took a new approach. They insisted that NATO was being duped by Baltic applicants, who raised the specter of renewed Soviet-style aggression against them. The government paper, *Rossiiskaia gazeta,* complained that Baltic rhetoric drew an analogy between the Helsinki talks and appeasement of the 1930s, and insisted that the admission of eastern countries was going to cause more problems than benefits for NATO itself. In an interview with an Austrian reporter, Lebed (*Vienna Kurier,* 1 April) advised that the United States, France and Germany were going to have to pick up the tab for the new states. This too became a standard Russian refrain; that is, expansion was bad for NATO—and therefore would increase tension in unexpected ways.[104]

There followed a rush of press reports treating the Helsinki talks as "surrender" to American pressure and the Anti-NATO group of deputies resolved to make

---

[103]For the Club of Realists, see Svetlana Il'ina, "Ugroza NATO sposobna splotit' Rossian" [The Threat of NATO Enables Russians to Unite], *Nezavisimaia gazeta* (29 March 1997). Its position was published later as, *Rasshirenie NATO v Vostok: k miry ili voine?* [NATO Expansion to the East: Towards Peace or War?] (Moscow: Klub Realisty, 1998). By 1998, the Club was strongly against NATO expansion. Gorbachev's statement was made in Turkey, ITAR-TASS (2 April 1997), repeating a remark made to Americans in February (Interfax, 14 March 1997). On the Anti-NATO Commission (ITAR-TASS, 2 April 1997).

[104]See, for example, a piece by Nikolai Paklin, "Chem chrevata liubov' k NATO" [The Danger of Love for NATO], *Rossiiskaia gazeta* (2 April 1997). For harshly anti-Baltic pieces, Igor Maksimychev, "Privedet li dvoinaia moral' pribaltiiskikh politikov v NATO?" [Will the Two-Sided Morality of Baltic Politicians Lead to NATO?], *Rossiiskaia gazeta* (29 March 1997), and Lev Dorogushin, Arnold Park, "A byvalo moskvichi 'katali' na vykhodnye v Tallin" [Moscovites Used to Drive to Tallinn for the Weekend], *Rossiiskaia gazeta* (22 March 1997).

Victory Day (9 May) one of demonstrations explicitly against NATO enlargement.[105] Primakov confirmed Russia's antipathy to the expansion during meetings with Belarusian officials in Minsk, and even Yavlinskii cautioned against "the
absurdity of claims by some Russian politicians about the peaceful aims of the
North Atlantic alliance." NATO enlargement will cause the downfall of the Russian government, he told a press conference on 4 April: "a tank cannot be peaceful, even if you paint it pink, even if it is a tank for the sake of peace and stability
in Europe."[106] In making an early pitch for his own presidential candidacy, the
Yabloko leader illustrated the way in which NATO expansion would be made an
election issue in Russia.

Yavlinskii's viewpoint was understood by military personnel who might have
been thinking that Lebed, then a leading candidate to replace Yeltsin, was too
cautious on the issue. On 4 April first deputy chief of General Staff, Col. Gen.
Nikolai Pishchev, wrote that NATO expansion eastward was a sign that Russia
was a "vanquished state" and urged that the military reform currently under way
include a new military doctrine designed to strengthen Russia under new circumstances.[107] Russia lay under a "Sword of Damocles" not wanting to rearm,
but needing to in case economic chaos led to war. NATO expansion, he said, exacerbated Russia's dilemma. One writer raised eyebrows with a report on the
possibility of NATO headquarters also moving eastward—to Bonn in 1999
when Berlin becomes the capital of Germany. Ye. Bovkin mentioned this possibility in *Izvestiia,* attributing the suggestion to Solana himself. A few days later
the same paper proclaimed that Paris was as uneasy about NATO as Moscow
was, implying that Europe was quite divided on the issue of expansion.[108] At the

---

[105]Interfax (2 April 1997). See also *Komsomol'skaia pravda* (28 March–4 April 1997),
where Yeltsin is accused of "surrendering" at Helsinki.

[106]Interfax (4 April 1997). Yavlinskii was speaking at a news conference in St. Petersburg. He blamed the Russian government for the problem, saying that NATO's actions
were rooted in a mistrust of the current government's ability to curb the criminal element
in Russia. A few days later Yavlinskii told an audience at the University of Moscow that
NATO expansion did not pose a "military threat to Russia," adding that it did show that
Russian foreign policy over the last five years had been useless and that the West did not
believe that Russia soon would become a democracy, ITAR-TASS (6 May 1997).

[107]Pishchev, "Dal'nii pritsel NATO" [NATO's Long-Range Gunsight], *Nezavisimaia
gazeta* (4 April 1997). Coincidentally, Yeltsin's order to call up more than 214,000 con-
scripts appeared in the press on the same day.

[108]Yurii Kovalenko, "I Parizhu, i Moskve s NATO nelegko" [Both Paris and Moscow
Are Uneasy about NATO], *Izvestiia* (10 April 1997); Bovkin, "V NATO podumaiut o
pereezde v Bonn" [NATO will Think About a Move to Bonn], *Izvestiia* (8 April 1997).

end of the month Pishchev was back in press with a much longer explication under the "Threat" rubric, "NATO's Long Range Aim: Without Embarking On a War, Russia Could Find Itself in the Position of a Defeated State." His central point was that NATO, driven by the United States, seemed to be pushing the OSCE aside and taking for itself the role as "sole instrument for securing a unipolar system of interstate relations." Even without NATO troops on their territory, the new Eastern European members will pose a major threat as a bridgehead, forcing Russia, step by step, to make concessions.[109] Pishchev and others advocated using the OSCE as the basis for a European collective security system, making NATO redundant. This had been a Russian position since the late 1980s, when Gorbachev made the idea a central part of his campaign for a "common European home."[110]

In the meantime, Vladimir Dashichev, author of the 1996 Academy of Sciences booklet condemning NATO expansion, was back in the spotlight on 1 April 1997. This time he accused the Kremlin of behavior befitting only a defeated country. Again charging the United States with messianism, he drew parallels with appeasement and reminded readers of what had happened to a "trusting" Russia in 1941.[111] This harangue was the archetype of an increasingly aggressive portrayal of NATO's motives: the communist press began in April to depict NATO as an interventionist bloc, pointing to the predominance of its members in UN military deployments. Even the moderate press termed Western claims that Russian-Belarusian unity was evidence that NATO needed to expand hypocritical.[112] It was at this time as well that public opinion polls began to make it clear that Russian citizens had lost faith in the "Western democratic

---

[109]Pishchev, "Dal'nii pritsel NATO" [Long-Range Aim of NATO], *Nezavisimoe voennoe obozrenie*, No. 16 (26 April–16 May 1997).

[110]See, e.g., Gorbachev, "Za 'obshche evropeiskii dom', za novoe myshlenie" [For a "Common European Home," for New Thinking], *Pravda* (11 April 1987). This speech was delivered in Prague. See also V. Zhurkin, "Obshchii dom dlia Evropy. Razmyshleniia o tom, kak ego stroit'" [A Common Home for Europe. Thoughts on How to Create It], *Pravda* (17 May 1989), and Dmitrii Gornostaev, "OBSE kak tsentr Evropy" [The OSCE as the Center of Europe], *Nezavisimaia gazeta* (24 Dec 1997).

[111]Dashichev cited Newt Gingrach as proof that the United States was taken up with messianism, *Rabochaia tribuna* (1 April 1997). Similar, but less harsh, commentary was offered in an interview with Academician Maksimychev, *Komsomol'skaia pravda* (4–11 April 1997), and by the Federation Council's deputy speaker, V. Likhachev, "V Sovete Evropy my uzhe ne gosti" [We are No Longer Guests at the Council of Europe], *Rossiiskaia gazeta* (29 March 1997).

[112]See, e.g., Viacheslav Nikonov, "Chto nam delit'?" [What Divides Us?], *Rossiiskaia gazeta* (12 April 1997); V. Safronchuk, "Kulak NATO—nad Albaniei" [NATO Fist over Albania], *Sovetskaia Rossiia* (10 April 1997).

path" as a model for development. A "specific Russian" path was now greatly favored, if not yet defined.[113]

On 16 April, Gorbachev reminded the U.S. Congress that NATO was breaking promises made to him during the German re-unification process in 1990. The fact that the "promises" were not part of some written accord is irrelevant, Gorbachev maintained, for the expansion itself "crudely violates" the spirit of the Paris Charter. "I regard NATO expansion a blunder, and I shall not be convinced by assurances . . . that Russia should not worry," the former Soviet president said, while pointing out that Europe would be better off united at this time "when new centers of power appear in the Pacific."[114] The address to the U.S. Congress marked one of the rare moments in the 1990s that Gorbachev earned favorable press coverage in his homeland. Russian observers were well aware of division in Congress on enlargement and hoped that Gorbachev's continued popularity in the West might push some hesitant listeners towards the opposition ranks.[115]

The day after Gorbachev's speech in Washington, Yeltsin and Kohl announced in Baden-Baden that the Russia-NATO Charter would likely be made public on 27 May. The Russian president issued an especially strong statement at a concomitant ceremony (at which he was named "Man-of-the Year" for 1996 by the German mass media), telling German and Russian reporters that "it is the opinion of all of Russia" that advancing NATO towards the Russian border threatens to re-divide Europe. By that time, Russian officials were speaking stridently against NATO expansion all over Europe. On the 14th, for example, speaking for Primakov, Deputy Minister of Foreign Affairs Igor Ivanov told reporters in Madrid that Russia would "always" be opposed to NATO expansion.[116] It is worth bearing in mind here that Ivanov would become foreign minister a year and a half later, when Primakov moved into the prime minister's office. A change in NATO's military leadership at that time warrants note as well. On 1 April, General Wesley K. Clark was nominated by Pres-

---

[113]See, e.g., "Razocharovanie opasno ne menee, chem sotsial'nye volneniia" [Disappointment Is No Less Dangerous Than Social Agitation], *Rossiiskie vesti* (15 April 1997). The data showed that whereas in 1992 56 percent of respondents favored the Western model, by 1995 only 10 percent did so. The "specific Russian" path had moved up from 18 to 51.5 percent.

[114]ITAR-TASS (16 April 1997). For several perspectives on the alleged 1990 "promise," see Michael R. Gordon, "The Anatomy of a Misunderstanding," *New York Times* (25 May 1997), E3, and Dashichev, *Natsional'naia bezopasnost' Rossii i ekspansiia NATO,* 10–11.

[115]"O rasshirenii NATO eshche posporiat" [There Will Be Argument over NATO Expansion], *Rossiiskaia gazeta* (12 April 1997).

[116]For Ivanov's pronouncement, ITAR-TASS (14 April 1997); for Yeltsin's remark, ITAR-TASS (17 April 1997). See also the acerbic "Zapadnaia inakovost'" [The West Is Different], *Zavtra,* No. 14 (April 1997).

ident Clinton to take command of NATO and American forces in Europe. Clark, who would replace General Joulwan in July, speaks Russian and was the senior U.S. military officer in the Dayton negotiations on Bosnia.

Meanwhile, the most strident Russian opposition to expansion upgraded its organization in the Duma. The newly created 15-member Anti-NATO Commission immediately drafted a letter to Yeltsin demanding that he set out a national agenda for thwarting NATO expansion eastward. The Commission was, in fact, the Anti-NATO Association's leadership granted special Duma status by decree. Its letter, hailed in the Russian press, claimed that diplomatic means had failed and Russia was "facing its greatest threat" since the Second World War.[117] Almost simultaneously, 33 deputies announced the formation of a For Atlantic Dialogue group. Calling for a union of Russia and NATO, this body purposely countered the Commission and planned a fact-finding trip to NATO headquarters in Brussels. Its message seemed to be that Russia should make the best of a bad deal.[118]

Before very long, the For Atlantic Dialogue group of deputies was lost in the shuffle. Primary author of the Anti-NATO Commission's letter, Baburin, by this time also deputy chair of the Duma, complained elsewhere of increased NATO overflights of Kaliningrad and linked them to Poland's expected admission to NATO. The military took the "threat" to Kaliningrad seriously, and the Air Defense Troops of Russia's Ground Troops began to revise plans for combat readiness in the region.[119] But it was the political opposition that was most vocal and attracted the most public attention. On 24 April the State Duma adopted a resolution supporting the Anti-NATO Commission's recommendation that the annual victory rally on 9 May be directed against NATO.[120] Stating unequivocally

---

[117]The Anti-NATO Commission was established in the Duma on 17 April and a copy of the letter to Yeltsin was circulated that day by ITAR-TASS (17 April 1997). On the Anti-NATO Commission's founding, see " 'Anti-NATO' nachinaet deistvovat' " ["Anti-NATO" Begins to Act], *Rossiiskaia gazeta* (17 April 1997). On the front page of the same issue it was said that Madeleine Albright, in Prague, told the Czechs that all NATO members were equal and that there would be no second-class members. To Russian observers this could only mean that the former Warsaw Pact countries would have ready access to NATO military infrastructure, see "Olbreit ubaiukivaet" [Albright Lulls Them], *ibid.*

[118]Spokesman for the small group was Konstantin Borovoi. Most of its members were from Our Home is Russia (NDR), but it also included Yabloko supporters, several independents, and even one each from the LDPR and Agrarian parties. See Interfax (18 April 1997).

[119]Pointing out that some 500 modern air bases will pass into the hands of NATO when it is joined by former Warsaw Pact countries, Col. Gen. Boris Dukhov supervised a two-day conference in Smolensk to discuss new responsibilities of the Air Defense Troops at length, Interfax (21 April 1997); for Baburin's observations, Interfax (17 April 1997).

[120]The resolution was given status as a parliamentary "Address." Interfax (24 April 1997).

that NATO's action posed "the greatest military threat to our country over the last 50 years," the resolution was adopted 253–14. The "nays" came from a few members of the "government party," Our Home is Russia (NDR), the faction associated with prime minister Chernomyrdin. Thus Primakov's oft-repeated notion that NATO expansion was the "greatest mistake" since the Cold War was growing larger in the propaganda of expansion's opponents.

Moreover, at its 4th Congress (held in Moscow 19–20 April) the CPRF made opposition to NATO expansion part of its platform. The opening sentences of a "Statement" adopted by the Congress on the national security of the Russian Federation says it all: "The condition of national security in the Russian Federation has reached a critical level. A real danger that our people will lose their independence and freedom, turning the country into a semi-colony, has arisen. Abandoned face to face with NATO as it pushes eastward, with unprotected borders. . . . "[121] Stances taken up by the CPRF, the largest single party represented in the State Duma, tend to be treated as communist cliché in the Western media. Thus it is worth noting that NDR, the second largest party in the Duma, adopted a position on NATO similar to that of the communists. As "one of the leading world powers," Russia opposes any division of Europe into military blocs, NDR delegates said in a Political Resolution adopted on 19 April at their own 4th Congress. "The NATO expansion plans show that the 'divide and rule' principle is still alive and well . . . and that double standards apply," the Resolution concluded.[122] Obviously, the notion that Mother Russia was being threatened had become a very real part of political discourse in Russia. NATO expansion is one of the very few subjects on which the NDR and CPRF agree, though for somewhat different reasons. These political groups are far broader in the public support they command than the "foreign policy-making elite" referred to rather contemptuously by Brzezinski and others.

Yeltsin's preference was made clear in a letter to John Major, dated 29 April, in which he said that the OSCE should provide the security umbrella for Europe. With more members than NATO and not primarily a military alliance, the OSCE

---

[121]"Zaiavlenie IV S'ezda kommunisticheskoi partii Rossiiskoi Federatsii. O natsional'noi bezopasnosti Rossiiskoi Federatsii" [Statement of the IV Congress of the CPRF: On the National Security of the Russian Federation], *Pravda Rossii* (26 April 1997). See also Zyuganov's report to the Congress, Section 2, below.

[122]*Dom i Otechestvo* [Home and Fatherland] (5–11 May 1997). This NDR newspaper is a weekly insert in *Rossiiskaia gazeta.* See also, in the same issue, Yelena Kaliadina, "NATO uzhe v Moskve. Neozhidannyi gost'" [NATO Is Already in Moscow: An Unexpected Guest], on an American journalist touting for NATO in Moscow.

would not confirm "new dividing lines" in Europe. By the end of April, such statements seemed oddly out of touch with both the European and Russian moods.

1.6. "May Days": A Modern Time of Troubles

In early May the United States Institute of Peace circulated a Special Report on a seminar it had convened in March. Entitled, "Managing NATO Enlargement," the report summarized recommendations made to it by Brzezinski.[123] To ensure ratification of enlargement, he insisted, the United States should make it clear that countries failing to ratify are rejecting not only new members but also the United States itself! This veiled threat came as no surprise to the Russians, who had been portraying expansion as a policy forced on NATO by the United States.

As the clock wound down for the 27 May Russia-NATO charter signing ceremony, the argument intensified in Russia. The May Day annual socialist celebration in Moscow was muted in part by public indifference and in part by the NATO conundrum. Communists called Madeleine Albright's arrival in Moscow on 1 May "blasphemous." The timing of the meeting was doubly galling because she was there to impose "humiliating conditions" on Russia, *Sovetskaia Rossiia* fumed.

Both sides admitted that negotiations were difficult. Russia wanted limits placed on the military capacity of the expanded NATO, in effect relegating the new members to a secondary status in the Alliance. No specific decisions seemed to have been reached. Making the matter worse for nationalists in Russia, Chubais was then in Washington negotiating with the International Monetary Fund for a continuation of promised funding. He reminded reporters of an American pledge to facilitate his country's admission to the Paris Club and the World Trade Organization, and attributed this promise to Moscow's "tough stance on NATO's enlargement plans." Chubais told Al Gore that failure to sign a Russia-NATO agreement before the end of May would generate "extremist moods" in Russia.

But such sentiments already were emerging. "IMF's henchmen" Chubais (and Boris Nemtsov) were "selling Russia for dollars," a communist journalist intoned. Rather than hold the line, government officials contradicted by their very actions Primakov's consistent assertion that the Russian government would not cave in to

---

[123]"Managing NATO Enlargement," United States Institute of Peace, *Special Report* (April 1997).

[124]Vasililii Safronchuk, "Trebuiutsia . . . molodye razoriteli" [Wanted—Young Wreckers], *Sovetskaia Rossiia* (29 April 1997). For Chubais' statements in Washington, see Interfax (29 April 1997).

NATO's demands.[124] In fact, Primakov was interviewed in Madrid only two days after Albright departed Moscow and said yet again that "NATO is enlarging as a move against Russia." His central point was that expansion was merely a recreation of blocs and that it was primarily an American offensive. He, and Pishchev (in his 26 April feature), were unambiguous in their belief that Russia must reconsider its foreign policy and military doctrine if a fully satisfactory Russia-NATO charter was not signed.[125]

The Russian public was buffeted by confusing signals. During the Spanish royal visit to Moscow, on 6 May, Spain's foreign minister, Abel Matutes, told reporters that Russia had nothing to fear from NATO enlargement; but the fact that Solana was in Kiev almost simultaneously opening a NATO Information Center was unnerving to many Russian commentators. A note in *Izvestiia* to the effect that Primakov, by that time in the United States, had "yielded to Washington" and was no longer demanding a pledge that nuclear weapons not be sited in the new eastern member-states added to the consternation of nationalists. So did their perception that smaller new nations were now clamoring for membership, for example Croatia, the "enemy" of Russia's "friend" Yugoslavia.[126]

On the 7th, Yeltsin opened a RF Security Council session with an exhortation that it approve the draft concept of Russia's national security, still lying fallow after a year. NATO's "eastward expansion" was the context in which the security concept must now be discussed, he said. On that same day, *Rossiiskie vesti* carried a very long essay by Vladimir Kirichev, taking issue with Henry Kissinger, who had written recently in strong opposition to any consultative role for Russia in NATO's affairs. The specter of war was raised by *Sovetskaia Rossiia*, in "At Whom Will NATO Shoot?!" In this long piece, Nikola Zhivkovich set out a theoretical scenario for World War III, with Russia as the obvious target for destruction. *Zavtra* was even more aggressive in its prediction of war, suggesting the United States needed an enemy.[127]

---

[125]For Primakov's interview in Madrid, FBIS-SOV, No. 087. For his continued opposition to NATO expansion eastward, see an interview in *Novoe vremya,* No. 15 (20 April 1997).

[126]Vladimir Nadein, "Moskva ustupaet Vashingtonu i otkazyvaetsia ot svoikh uslovii rasshireniia NATO" [Moscow Yields to Washington and Gives up on Its Conditions for NATO Expansion], *Izvestiia* (6 May 1997), "Khorvatiia stremitsia v NATO" [Croatia Seeks Membership in NATO], *Krasnaia zvezda* (5 May 1997).

[127]"Snova v poiska vraga" [Again in Search of an Enemy], *Zavtra,* No. 18 (May 1997); Nikola Zhivkovich, "Uzhe pishut stsenarii tret'ei mirovoi . . . . V kogo vystrelit NATO?!" *Sovetskaia Rossiia* (7 May 1997); Kirichev, "Al'ians izzhil sebia" [The Alliance Became Obsolete], *Rossiiskie vesti* (7 May 1997). Kissinger's piece appeared in the *Washington Post*. On Yeltsin's remarks to the Security Council, Interfax (7 May 1997).

When Solana visited Moscow on 13 May for "final" talks with Primakov the Russian mass media was swept up in a flurry of speculation. Duma deputies sent a collective open appeal to NATO parliamentarians asking them to oppose the creation of a new "iron curtain," or a "Berlin Wall," in Europe. Enlarging NATO eastward will increase the danger of war, they said, raising at the same time the level of military expenditures in Europe and forcing Russia to shift funds away from economic reform.[128] Ye. Kozhokhin, director of the Russian Institute for Strategic Studies, wrote in *Argumenty i fakty* that whereas Primakov may be the ideal negotiator for the Russian side, he was negotiating the wrong thing. It would be better for Europeans not to rely on NATO alone for security; rather they should be advocating multiple security zones.[129] Lebed got into the act on several occasions, stating publicly that the entire effort on Moscow's part was worthless, NATO had made up its mind and was merely tossing a bone to help Moscow's leadership save face before the Russian public eye. In his turn, Rodionov insisted, in Washington, that there must still be a "deep transformation" of NATO before any real accommodation with Russia was possible (ITAR-TASS, 14 May 1997).[130]

All these words to the wise notwithstanding, on 14 May Primakov and Solana announced in Moscow, with fanfare, that a "tentative" Russia-NATO agreement had been reached. *Komsomol'skaia pravda* caught the puzzled Russian reaction exactly, saying that it came as a "bolt out of the blue."[131]

Without even seeing the document, the two sides in Russia's debate on NATO expansion quickly hardened their positions. On the 15th, *Nezavisimaia gazeta* called the settlement "a diplomatic success," *Sovetskaia Rossiia* called it treason, and *Rossiiskie vesti* saw it (by quoting Solana) as a victory for both sides. Officialdom waffled, calling the agreement a major accomplishment while qualifying it

---

[128]"K parlamentariiam gosudarstv-chlenov NATO" [To Parliamentarians in NATO Member-States], *Rossiiskaia gazeta* (13 May 1997).

[129]*Argumenty i fakty,* No. 20 (14 May 1997), FBIS-SOV, No. 134. Signed to press 13 May 1997.

[130]Rodionov, in fact, worked out a bilateral widening of U.S./RF military cooperation while he was in Washington. See also "Tri zvonka iz Moskvy" [Three Calls from Moscow], *Rossiiskie vesti* (14 May 1997); "NATO-Rossiia: eshche odna popytka k 'proryvu'" [NATO-Russia: One More Attempt at a "Break-Through"], *Krasnaia zvezda* (14 May 1997). For Lebed's remarks, Interfax (13 May 1997).

[131]*Komsomol'skaia pravda* (14 May 1997).

as much as possible.[132] Rodionov, for example, agreed with Primakov's statement that it was reflective of "complete mutual understanding" (Interfax, 14, 15 May), but then told reporters in Honolulu that the document did not solve the main problems (Interfax, 15 May). On arriving in Japan on the 16th, and without yet seeing the Primakov-Solana paper, Rodionov said that Russia still distrusted NATO (an "instrument of the Cold War") and only a final, legally binding document would alleviate the suspicion (ITAR-TASS, 16 May).

As a result of yet another government shakeup, Rodionov was out of a job by the 22nd, replaced by missile commander General Igor Sergeev. The foreign minister was still carrying the torch, however. After talks with new UN secretary general, Kofi Annan, Primakov made it clear that Russia saw NATO expansion as a "major mistake" (Interfax, 15 May). Interviewed on television, he too said that only a legally binding Founding Act would ease Russian suspicion of NATO. In its turn, the Duma demanded to see the full text of the draft agreement and was told only that it would get its chance sometime *before* the 27 May signing ceremony.

In the midst of all this speculation, Sergei Ivanov, correspondent for *Sovetskaia Rossiia,* interviewed three prominent academics in St. Petersburg. The printed version of these conversations took up an entire page, accompanied by a drawing of crushed and broken Russian Orthodox icons being passed by a marching horde of German troops, designed presumably to invoke the worst fears in readers. Dean of the Faculty of International Relations at the State University of St. Petersburg, K.K. Khudolea, Dean of the History Faculty, I.Ya. Frolianov, and the president of the Russian Geographical Society, S.B. Lavrov, provided detailed versions of the implications of "NATO advancement to the east." Khudolea saw Russia completely isolated, with no potential for truly long term partnerships anywhere but Belarus, and so recommended negotiation with NATO even though it would have to be from a position of weakness. The other two scholars were more aggressive. They dredged

---

[132]The Russian press was filled with commentary related to the document. The following is a cross-section, in which the three positions noted above predominate: "Akt Rossiia-NATO: mify i real'nosti" [The Russia-NATO Act: Myths and Realities], *Rossiiskie vesti* (23 May 1997); "V osnovopologaiushchem akte NATO obeshchaet izmenit'sia" [NATO Promises to Change in the Fundamental Act], *Izvestiia* (16 May 1997); "Dostignutye soglasheniia Vashingtone ponimaet inache, chem Moskva" [Washington Understands the Achieved Agreement Differently Than Moscow], *Izvestiia* (16 May 1998); "S rasshirennym al'iansom my gotovy sosushchestvovat', no na svoikh usloviiakh" [We Are Prepared to Co-Exist with the Expanded Alliance, but on Our Own Conditions], *Izvestiia* (16 May 1997); "NATO i Rossiia pochti dogovorilis'" [NATO and Russia Almost Come to an Agreement], *Krasnaia zvezda* (16 May 1997).

up memories of Germany's *Drang nach Osten,* made much of the prescience of Nikolai Danilevskii's 19th-century *Russia and the West,* and exhorted the Russian government to sign full union with Belarus as soon as possible. A "cordon sanitaire" was desperately needed, Lavrov insisted.[133]

The Russian press carried few details of the proposed Founding Act on Mutual Relations, Cooperation and Security between NATO and the Russian Federation. This was because no draft copy was made available, forcing Russian journalists to turn to the Western press where the Act's content was widely publicized. One bitter Russian commentator claimed that he had not even seen the Act's actual name other than in English.[134] Contrary opinions expressed by the chairmen of the Duma's Security and International Affairs committees were symptomatic of the division in parliament: Ilyukhin (CPRF) named the Primakov-Solana deal a "betrayal of Russia's interests"; and Lukin (Yabloko) said that the agreement was the "best that could be expected" while still worrying about the former Warsaw Pact infrastructure now available to NATO (Interfax, 15 May).

The intensity of Russian media anger increased proportionately to the perceived gloating in the West.[135] *Sovetskaia Rossiia* led the way in intensifying the debate, ridiculing Yeltsin and Clinton assumptions that the Act would ensure security. Russia will be able to veto nothing, it is a "pig in a poke," and expansion itself is a "stab in Russia's back," were the rhetorical refrains. NATO will be vastly stronger now, with the tanks, plans, artillery and airfields coming to it from former Warsaw Pact states, having "catastrophic military-strategic consequences" for Russia, was an especially serious charge. The usually pro-reform, but sensationalist and popular, *Moskovskii komsomolets* [Moscow Komsomolite], described the U.S. administration as gloating, and voiced strong mistrust of American intentions.[136] Lebed

---

[133]Ivanov, "KRESTONATO. Tri positsii: Leningradskie uchenye—o prodvizhenii NATO na vostok" [NATO-Cross: Three Positions: Leningrad Scholars on the Advance of NATO to the East], *Sovetskaia Rossiia* (15 May 1997).

[134]Safronchuk, "Illiuziia bezopasnosti" [An Illusion of Security], *Sovetskaia Rossiia* (17 May 1997).

[135]The NATO perspective on NATO expansion has been left out of this book purposely, for it is available everywhere; suffice it to say here that statements by Albright (15 May) linking the "victory" to doctrines set in place by Harry Truman, a *New York Times* (16 May) OP-Ed by German Social Democrat Friedbert Pfüger calling the agreement "appeasement" to Russia, a *Time* magazine (26 May) essay by Christopher Ogden describing the event as a "crushing capitulation for Russia," and many others were highlighted by Russian protagonists. George Kennan's repeated opposition to expansion was cited regularly as well.

[136]Melor Sturua, "NATO: ot Trumena cherez Yel'tsina do Klintona" [NATO from Truman, through Yeltsin to Clinton], *Moskovskii komsomolets* (17 May 1997); Safronchuk, "Illiuziia bezopasnosti," (17 May 1997), *op. cit.*

called the agreement "empty" in a televised news conference. President Clinton's 14 May explanation, "Russia will work closely with NATO, but not within NATO, giving Russia a voice in, but not a veto over NATO business," was cited with widely differing spins by both sides.[137]

The communist press vented its outrage on an almost daily basis. Sergei Ivanov was back on the 20th with the second part of his KRESTONATO invective, "Bloc and Blockade," encapsulating years of ideological hatreds and practical concerns in one dramatic outburst. Re-stating all the old antagonisms to NATO, NATO expansion and U.S. "hegemony" in lurid detail, Ivanov's message now was that NATO troops were likely to appear in the area of the former USSR and that this would be abetted by expediency-driven Caucasus (Georgia and Azerbaijan) and Central Asia (Uzbekistan) leadership. Detailed enumeration of troops and materiel that would accrue to NATO with the addition of Polish, Czech and Hungarian Armed Forces bolstered a somber picture painted by senior officers of Western political and military leaders poised to emasculate Russia once and for all.[138]

Zavtra was typically acrimonious, in a long essay by a French communist on how best to destroy Europe. Its subtitle, "To Badly Understand Russia is as Dangerous as Ignoring It," carried the lesson to be learned. NATO expansion is an American scheme to ensure its preponderance in Europe by destabilizing Central Europe and forestalling Russian growth by compelling it to spend more money on defense. Arguments offered in the mid-1990s by opponents of NATO expansion seemed here to have come full circle.[139]

Within a few days government officials were issuing strangely mixed messages related to, but without mentioning, issues raised by Ivanov. Interfax releases on 22 May summarized stern warnings from Yeltsin's press attaché against any NATO expansion onto former USSR territory; and an optimistic observation from a ministry of defense official claiming that the Founding Act "suspended" the possibility of NATO military infrastructure moving closer to Russia's borders. At an RIA-Novosti roundtable in Moscow, Yeltsin's spokesman, Sergei Yastrzhembskii, made it plain that memberships for former USSR republics were absolutely "unacceptable," adding that Western leaders were fully informed of that fact. Speaking for the

---

[137]See NATO Website, "Russia." Lebed's comment was made on Moscow NTV (20 May 1997), FBIS-SOV, No. 140.

[138]Ivanov, "KRESTONATO. Blok i Blokada" [NATO-Cross: Bloc and Blockade], *Sovetskaia Rossiia* (20 May 1997). This article was illustrated with the same group of Orthodox Christian icons as was his first piece on the 15th.

[139]Michel Schneider, "Kak razrushit' Evropu?" [How to Destroy Europe?], *Zavtra*, No. 20 (May 1997).

ministry of defense, Col. Gen. Leonid Ivashov, head of the department for international cooperation, told participants in the roundtable that the Act gave NATO the right to bring conventional forces on to the new territories only temporarily (for exercises) or in the case of a direct threat of aggression. Very few Russians (or East Europeans) took this meliorating explanation seriously.

Constantly insisting that it remained adamantly opposed to NATO expansion, the Russian government nevertheless issued communiqué after communiqué saying that it had wrung important concession on its main demands. But the Kremlin still seemed strangely reluctant to have the contents of the proposal made public. When Primakov finally brought the Founding Act to the Duma for discussion, the press was not admitted to the session and deputies did not get to see the actual document. The Duma now was promised only that the Act would be the subject of debate *after* its signing on the 27th.

Primakov described the document thoroughly, promising the deputies that Moscow would have a veto over any NATO decision that affected the interests of Russia (Interfax, 23 May). He credited the government, and therefore himself, with compelling NATO to make it explicit that the Act be binding and include a provision that NATO "will have no plans, intentions, or reasons" to deploy nuclear arms in the new territories. Since *Izvestiia* already had quoted these exact words from Madeleine Albright more than two weeks previously, some deputies wondered how meaningful the promise was and if Primakov had played a role in achieving it.[140] A flurry of comments showed that, while many deputies appreciated the discussion, few opinions were reversed. A *Moskovskii komsomolets* editorial said on the 23rd that the Act was something only a "feeble" country would sign. Zhirinovskii proclaimed that no agreement should have been signed, and invoked the image of 22 June 1941 as a consequence of Russia legitimizing NATO expansion (Interfax, 23 May). Ilyukhin set the stage for many future threats by observing that Russia could always opt out of the agreement if the West reneged on any of the "binding" provisions of the Act.

The Anti-NATO Commission was, of course, not persuaded. Its leader, Baburin, and deputy chair of the Duma International Affairs Committee, Aleksei Podberezkin, drafted a statement that the Act contradicted the Russian government's long standing position that it would not agree to the expansion of NATO (Interfax, 23 May).

[140]Vladimir Nadein, "Moskva ustupaet . . . ," *op. cit.;* Natal'ia Timakova, "Lokomotiv NATO obeshchal pritormozit' u granits Rossii" [The NATO Locomotive Promised to Put the Brakes on at the Russian Border], *Moskovskii komsomolets* (27 May 1997).

The run-up to the 27 May final agreement on a Russia-NATO Founding Act promised to leave a lot of scars on the Russian political landscape.[141]

a. The Founding Act, 27 May 1997

On 27 May, the day it was signed in Paris, ITAR-TASS finally circulated a copy of the Founding Act, and it was immediately printed in the Russian press.[142] Not many minds were changed, though Sergei Larionov was more sanguine in *Moskovskii komsomolets* than the article of the 23rd had been. Russia found true protection in this agreement, he said, for it had "teeth" and would be deposited with the general secretaries of the United Nations and OSCE.[143] Nikolai Paklin was less hopeful, but still far more accepting than he had been earlier. Russia will take part in important European decision-making, he said. The military threat is tempered and Russia has a chance to be a full member of a G-8, the Paris Club and the World Trade Organization; but Russia's "main condition," that former USSR republics not be admitted, was ignored.[144] Likewise, *Trud* saw the Act as a breakthrough for Russia's involvement in Europe. *Krasnaia zvezda* expressed the same general optimism—at first. *Moskovskii komsomolets* remarked that the euphoria accompanying the big event was overdone, but firmly endorsed the idea

---

[141]See, e.g., "Nastupit li za 13 maia v Moskve 27-e v Parizhe" [Will the Meeting in Moscow on the 13th Be the Setting for the 27th in Paris?], *Izvestiia* (12 May 1997); "Prikaz 'Nach Osten!' NATO ne dast" [NATO Will Not Give the "Nach Osten!" Order], *Rossiiskaia gazeta* (20 May 1997); "Voennoe sotrudnichestvo budet prodolzheno" [Military Cooperation Will Be Continued], *Krasnaia zvezda* (22 May 1997); "Po schetu pridetsia platit'" [Someone Will Need to Pay the Bill], *Krasnaia zvezda* (23 May 1997); "Novaia taktika Borisa Yel'tsina . . ." [Boris Yeltsin's New Tactics . . .], *Rossiiskie vesti* (27 May 1997); "Eliseiskii dvorets zhdet 'duaiena'" [The Elysian Palace Awaits the 'Doyenne'], *Rossiiskie vesti* (27 May 1997).

[142]The Founding Act ("Osnovopolagaiushchii Akt") was published in *Rossiiskaia gazeta* (28 May 1997) and in *Krasnaia zvezda* (29 May 1997); see also N.N. Afanas'evskii, "Osnovopolagaiushchii Akt Rossiia-NATO" [The Russia-NATO Founding Act], *Mezhdunarodnaia zhizn'*, No. 6 (1997), 8–12.

[143]Larionov, "My podpishem 'zubastyi' akt" [We Sign an Act with "Large Teeth"], *Moskovskii komsomolets* (27 May 1997).

[144]Nikolai Paklin, "Rossiia-NATO: balans interesov" [Russia-NATO: Balance of Interests], *Rossiiskaia gazeta* (27 May 1997). For other hopeful, if somewhat skeptical, commentary, see "Boris Yel'tsin: negativnye posledstviia rasshireniia NATO budut svedeny k minimumu" [Boris Yeltsin: The Negative Consequences of NATO Expansion Will Be Brought to a Minimum], *Rossiiskie vesti* (27 May 1997); "Novye obiazatel'stva pered Evropoi" [New Obligations Before Europe], *Rossiiskie vesti* (28 May 1997). See also "Vchera v Parizhe, podpisan osnovopologaiushchiia akt Rossiia-NATO" [The Founding Act Was Signed Yesterday in Paris], *Rossiiskaia gazeta* (28 May 1997).

that NATO would not deploy nuclear weapons on the territory of new members. "It is a good document," one of the paper's commentators said, adding that some prominent Europeans, such as the Czech Republic's Vlacav Havel, complained that Russia was given too much to say about NATO's admission policies.

As the rhetoric at the signing ceremony in Paris trickled through to Russian readers, misgivings began to emerge. Clinton's reference to the Marshall Plan set Russian teeth on edge, and Yeltsin's grandiose announcement that target assignment programs would be removed from Russian missiles aimed at NATO countries caused some amusement. In regards to Yeltsin, *Moskovskii komsomolets* wondered what he had been drinking. *Izvestiia* suggested that the proposal had a purpose: Yeltsin now had something to "revise" if NATO deploys unwanted nuclear or military infrastructure on the territory of the former Warsaw Pact countries.[145]

On the other hand, Sergei Rogov rushed to press with cautious support of the Founding Act. It had accomplished some of what earlier he had said was necessary. Russia's interests will be considered, at least "to a minimum extent," force will not be used when Russia and NATO have differences, and the "non-deployment of nuclear weapons" in Eastern Europe seems to be guaranteed. Moreover, the consultative Russia-NATO Permanent Joint Council (PJC) will give Russia a voice in European security issues. But the problems are not all solved, Rogov went on to say. The document may amount to very little if Russia cannot afford active participation, if the rest of Europe objects to Russian participation, and/or rivalries with the myriad other integrative organizations in Europe emerge.[146]

Rogov failed to forestall a wave of protest against the Founding Act. Even his deputy director at ISKRAN, V.A. Kremenyuk, found little to be thankful for in the Act. In his opinion, NATO's purpose in the first place was to provide a platform from which to extend its own "sphere of influence" into the Baltic countries and Ukraine. Evidence of NATO's aggressive character could be found in the way it usurped the OSCE prerogative in Bosnia. Kremenyuk attributed all this directly

---

[145]"Podpisi postavleny. NATO dvinulos' na vostok" [The Signatures Are Dried: NATO Moves on the East], *Izvestiia* (28 May 1997); Natalya Timakova and Alena Nevskaia, "Yel'tsin slomal protokol" [Yeltsin Broke Protocol], *Moskovskii komsomolets* (28 May 1997); Vyacheslav Prokof'ev in *Trud* (28 May 1997); "Cherez ternii—k kompromissu" [Through the Thorns to Compromise], *Krasnaia zvezda* (28 May 1997); "Novoi mirnoi Evrope, nerazdelennoi na bloki—byt'" [There Will Be a New Peaceful Europe, Not Divided into Blocs], *Krasnaia zvezda* (31 May).

[146]Rogov in *Literaturnaia gazeta,* No. 21 (28 May 1997), 9. Rogov, "My lishaem zapad svobody rukh" [We Tied the Hands of the West], *Izvestiia* (28 May 1997). See also "My zastavili strany NATO chest' zakonnye interesy Rossii" [We Forced the NATO Countries to Respect the Legal Interests of Russia], *Rossiiskie vesti* (31 May 1997).

to the foreign policy of Clinton's administration.[147] As the dust settled on the 27th, however, it was a long front-page feature in *Nezavisimaia gazeta* that reflected most accurately things to come. Andranik Migranyan equated the Founding Act in importance with agreements reached at the Vienna Congress, Versailles, Yalta and Potsdam, but cast Russia in the role of "defeated power." The Act symbolized Russia's "humiliation" and the *de jure* acceptance of NATO enlargement. Now, Migranyan admonished, the Alliance's eastward movement must be stopped at the borders of the former USSR. He was therefore one of the first journalists to voice aggressively the concept of what was later to be called a "red line" drawn on the map by officialdom in Moscow to signify territory into which NATO must not cross.[148]

b. Second Thoughts

Skeptical and unfavorable commentary began to gather momentum as the document itself was studied more carefully. Lebed roared in *Izvestiia* that "Russia was deceived," harshly criticizing the Yeltsin team for standing down in the face of Western pressure. Melor Sturua called the agreement a final "act of capitulation" in the Cold War, and cited Lebed's remark that it was a "Yalta without Russia."[149] The most vitriolic charge was led by the communist press, yet again. *Sovetskaia Rossiia* also called the Founding Act "capitulation," a new anti-Russian version of Yalta, and a document that rendered Russia helpless in the face of unified NATO. Promises of admission to high level integrative economic organizations were scorned by Vasilii Safronchuk as a means for the traditional "G-7" countries to widen their "sphere of colonial exploitation." *Pravda Rossii* headlined a biting attack on the perceived new assertive stance taken by Washington and predicted a sharp divergence of interests between the United States and Europe, with NATO a testing ground for opposing

---

[147]Kremenyuk, "Vneshniaia politika administratsii Klintona: na novyi srok so starym bagazhom" [The Clinton Administration's Foreign Policy: For a New Term with Old Baggage], *SShA,* No. 5 (May 1997): 20–32.

[148]Migranyan, "Oshibka ili net? Segodnia v Parizhe Boris Yel'tsin podpishet dogovor Rossiia-NATO. Moskva priznaet protsess rasshireniia NATO na vostok, no lish' do granits byvshego SSSR" [Mistake or Not? Today in Paris Boris Yeltsin Signs the Russia-NATO Act: Moscow Recognizes the Process of NATO Expansion, but Only to the Borders of the Former USSR], *Nezavisimaia gazeta* (27 May 1997). On the same front page there were platitudes from Solana and a caricature ridiculing Yeltsin's attempts to placate Russians, as NATO tanks passed them by on their way eastward.

[149]Sturua, "Porazhenie ili pobeda" [Defeat or Victory], *Moskovskie komsomolets* (29 May 1997); Lebed, "Rossii podbrosili dokhluiu koshku" [One Threw a Dead Cat at Russia], *Izvestiia* (27 May 1997).

Western perspectives. The Leninist image of a world divided into two immutably hostile camps resurfaced, if more subtly than in Cold War days. The panacea offered by Russia's communists was a world made up of balanced centers of power (multipolar) to forestall the hegemony of a single superpower. In this, at least, their view coincided with Primakov's most cherished pursuit.[150]

On the 29th, Zyuganov told Radio Rossii listeners that the Russia-NATO document represented "complete and unconditional surrender" and a betrayal of Russia's national interests. The president's own radio broadcast on the 30th was much less bleak, yet still not very enthusiastic. NATO's plans to expand eastward still threatened Russia's security, Yeltsin admitted, but its consequences now have been "minimized." He claimed to believe that NATO had pledged "not to deploy nuclear weapons . . . or to carry out any preparatory work to deploy them" in the new territories; nor would NATO build up its Armed Forces "near our borders." We now have nothing to fear, he concluded.[151] Whatever optimism there existed in the Russian media was quickly dispelled, however, as presidents of the three Baltic countries, plus Ukraine and Poland, met for strategic deliberations on 27–28 May (see Section 5).

Neither Yeltsin's ambiguous confidence, nor his interpretation of guarantees said to be in the document, were believed in Russia. Indeed, a rousing speech by Madeleine Albright on 5 June at Harvard, where the 50th anniversary of the Marshall Plan was being celebrated, was seen by many Russian observers as acknowledgment that the United States was seeking "global leadership." Expansion, Irina Zhinkina wrote in *Krasnaia zvezda,* was part of Washington's plan to preserve its preponderance in NATO. New members would serve as territories where the United States could broaden new combat systems, and so on, thereby extending its leadership to new frontiers. Andrei Grachev expressed graver doubts in the usually supportive *Novoe vremya,* chastising Clinton for behaving in Paris like a triumphant leader and going on to say that Russia had gained little by signing the document. Even confirmation that NATO did not plan to deploy nuclear

---

[150]Richard Ovinnikov, "Neuzheli ty slepa, starushka Evropa?" [Are You Really Blind, Old Woman Europe?], *Pravda Rossii* (27 May 1997); Safronchuk, "Budet li Rossii uiutno?" *Sovetskaia Rossiia* (29 May 1997). See also Aleksandr Trubitsyn, "Gvalt" [Uproar], in a special issue of *Narodnaia armiia* [People's Army], a supplement to *Sovetskaia Rossiia* (29 May 1997). And Konstantin Kovalev, " 'Streliate v krasnye zvezdy' " [Shoot in the Red Star], *Sovetskaia Rossiia* (29 May 1997), where the opinions on Russia and NATO in various New York groups are analyzed.

[151]Yeltsin's short speech was read over Ekho Moskvy (30 May 1997). A translation can be found in FBIS-SOV, No. 149, as can Zyuganov's commentary.

weapons in Eastern Europe is something that could change tomorrow, Grachev (and others) pointed out.[152]

There was more at stake here than American leadership in NATO, and the Russians quickly picked up on it. Following Clinton's lead, Albright's celebration of the long-term benefits accrued from the Marshall Plan carried an implicit reference to the potential cost of NATO expansion to the American taxpayer. "We must accept responsibility and lead," she said, knowing that NATO expansion still had to be ratified by legislatures responsible to taxpayers. Stress at home on America's "global leadership," now that the "Soviet threat" could no longer be waved as a rallying flag, was one of the few cards the U.S. Administration had left to play. Albright's remarks struck Russian commentators as explicit confirmation of the world vision represented in Brzezinski's "Grand Chessboard." Secretary of Defense William Cohen's abrupt pre-emption in early June of NATO discussion of how many new members—three—would be admitted provided further corroboration of Moscow's conviction that NATO policy was made in Washington. These were ominous notes for Russian analysts, who saw their country's chances of gaining equality with Europe/NATO fading and fretted that the "Russian threat" might again be employed to persuade legislators to ratify. Yavlinskii made this point for an American audience in early June.[153]

More or less at the same time, the CPRF decided to make the NATO issue a key weapon in its larger campaign to discredit Yeltsin's government. The Founding Act handed them a means with which to trigger frightening historical memories, focus blame-casting for Russia's domestic ills, and predict a bleak future unless changes to their liking were instituted. The communist hope, of course, was to raise the barrier that seemed to limit their popular support to a consistent 25 percent. In May–June the opinion polls revealed Aleksandr Nemtsov's emerging popularity, Lebed returned to the campaign mode and Moscow's mayor, Yurii Luzhkov, created a television network (Center TV) primarily to push his own can-

---

[152]Grachev, in *Novoe vremya* (8 June 1997): 28. In her speech Albright said that "no nation in the world need be left out of the global system we are constructing," *New York Times* (6 June 1997), A8, and this was picked up on by the Russian writer on strategic studies. Irina Zhinkina, "Transatlanticheskoe edinstvo i svoe liderstvo" [Transatlantic Unity and Its Leadership], *Krasnaia zvezda* (6 June 1997).

[153] Yavlinskii, "Shortsighted: By Supporting the Yeltsin Government You Are Alienating the Average Russian," *New York Times Magazine* (8 June 1997). See also Vissarion Sisnev, "It Was Easier for Truman: For Clinton the Signing of the Russia-NATO Agreement in Paris Is Just the Beginning of a Campaign Inside the United States for a New and Expensive European Policy," *Trud* (3 June 1997), FBIS-SOV, No. 105, and "Skol'ko stoit rasshirenie NATO?" [How Much Does NATO Expansion Cost?], *Izvestiia* (11 June 1997).

didacy for president. The communists were forced to become more politically aggressive, and NATO provided them with a cause.

A CPRF Central Committee Presidium Statement, "We Will Not Agree to a Shameful Role," encapsulated the party's new approach. Criticizing bitterly the "so-called young reformers" (Chubais and Nemtsov), the Statement warned that "consent to NATO expansion, reduction in the level of combat readiness of the nuclear forces, division of the Black Sea Fleet, and *de facto* recognition of the secession of Chechnya" would result in Russia losing its independence and prestige. A "creeping coup" launched by the "reformers" against the State Duma (Rybkin recently had advocated its dissolution) must be stopped by patriotic, mass demonstrations demanding Yeltsin's resignation.[154]

The communist press also resurrected the old image of a powerful foreign enemy, playing up the idea that the United States claimed "global leadership" at Russia's expense and quoting statements to that end by American leaders. Clinton-Albright rejoicing in memory of the Marshall Plan was described in Russia as gloating over the economic containment of the USSR. The American "side" was exploiting Europe via NATO once again to achieve world hegemony, whereas Russia and others would much prefer a multi-polar world balance. The Russian government itself was placed in a camp of "appeasers," and even the sacking of Rodionov was explained in this manner by a member of the Union of Russian Officers.[155]

The neo–Cold War images in the communist press of Western military and economic forces inexorably advancing towards Russia's borders were startling in their resemblance to Cominform imagery of the 1940s-1950s. Vasilii Safronchuk, the most vociferous opponent of NATO expansion among communist journalists, wrote that Russia received no real military guarantees from the Founding Act, and so was vulnerable to attack. His colleague, Vladimir

[154]"Zaiavlenie Prezidiuma TsK KPRF. 'Ne soglasimsia na postydnuiu rol'" [Statement of the Presidium of the CPRF CC, "We Will Not Agree to a Shameful Role"], *Sovetskaia Rossiia* (5 June 1997).

[155]Major-General Vitalii Lysov, "Ministr, kotoryi udoben . . . NATO" [The Minister Who Is Convenient for NATO], *Pravda Rossii* (3 June 1997). See also an extraordinary interview with V.A. Demin, a professor and economist with the Federal Security Service of Russia, who saw the U.S. special services becoming more active world wide, after the "capitulation of Russia," "Tainyi front tret'ei mirovoi. Ostalis' li bez raboty spetssluzhby SShA posle nashei kapituliatsii?" [The Secret Front of the Third World War: Did Our Capitulation Leave the USA's Secret Service Jobless?], *Sovetskaia Rossiia* (5 June 1997); and "Nevoennaia voina" [The Non-Military War], *Zavtra*, No. 24 (June 1997).

Gerasimov, insisted that Hungary, already host to American troops, would soon become an economic "colony" of the United States and a front line base for NATO military forces.[156]

The economic advantages to the proposed new members of NATO, including funds for housing, road, and airport construction, new and relatively wealthy consumers of goods and services, and so on, also drew the attention of Russia's media. Whereas commentators did not often begrudge East and East Central European countries such economic opportunity, it was obvious to readers that Russian windows of trade and other economic relations with Poland, Hungary and the Czech Republic would now begin to narrow. The "economic colony" image rang true even for non-communist observers of trends in the Visegrad group.[157]

The equation of NATO expansion with events of 1941 appeared with increasing frequency in the communist and nationalist press during the period after the Founding Act was signed in May and the Madrid Summit in July. Richard Ovinnikov, for example, prepared an essay for *Pravda Rossii* (24 June) under the heading "NATO: *Drang nach Osten?*", complete with photo of goose-stepping Wehrmacht troops. He claimed that Germany helped the United States direct NATO eastward, even while other members of the alliance were more interested in the southern tier and the Mediterranean. The new *Drang nach Osten* is but part of the continuum of Germany's historical ambition for "military-political hegemony" in Eastern Europe, Ovinnikov wrote: Poland, the Czech Republic, and Hungary first; Ukraine and the Baltic republics next. Appearing at a time when Russia was mourning the anniversary of Hitler's invasion of Russia, 22 June 1941, Ovinnikov's analogy would not be missed by Russian readers.[158]

c. Yeltsin's "Reward"

In return for signing the Founding Act, Yeltsin was invited to participate "fully" in the G-7 Denver meetings, which opened on 21 June. Called a Summit of the Eight (S-8) because Russia was not included in the economic decision-making

---

[156]Gerasimov, "'Vnebrachnoe sozhitel'stvo's NATO. Vengerskii variant natovskoi 'okkupatsii de-fakto' v rakurse istorii i geopolitiki" ["Natural Cohabitation" with NATO: The Hungarian Variant of NATO's "De-Facto" Occupation in Historical and Geopolitical Perspective], *Sovetskaia Rossiia* (10 June 1997); Safronchuk, "Maiskie 'pobedy' B. Yel'tsina" [The May "Victories" of B. Yeltsin], *Sovetskaia Rossiia* (7 June 1997).

[157]See, e.g., "Pol'sha vstupaet v NATO, a Frantsiia ostaetsia za bortom" [Poland Joins NATO, but France Is Left at the Gate], *Izvestiia* (7 June 1997).

[158]Ovinnikov, "Drang nach Osten? NATO Germaniiu tolkaiut na vostok" [Drang nach Osten? NATO Pushes Germany to the East], *Pravda Rossii* (24 June 1997).

process, the event was nonetheless a symbolic victory for the Russian president. It wasn't an easy one, for Japan balked at Russian membership until the last moment. Russia also had been promised, and was granted, full membership in the Paris Club of lender nations and, with much cautious qualification, entry into the World Trade Organization sometime in 1998.

The Russian press was mixed in its reaction to Yeltsin's prominent public role in Denver. Relishing the prestige that came with Russia's new status, government supporting media saw their country's status in the S-8 as a breakthrough to Western markets and investors. The opposition accused Yeltsin of toadying to the West. The entire media recognized that the invitation to Russia was a "reward" for signing the Founding Act, and all expressed some words of caution.[159] Lebed, no friend of the communists, nevertheless took up their tendency to draw parallels with German history in the 20th century. Granting that the Founding Act was a small "step" in the right direction, he accused NATO of callously risking civil conflict in Russia. By "endlessly trampling our country's dignity into the dirt," he told an interviewer in Denmark, NATO will cause "deformed" political parties to emerge in Russia as they did in Germany in the 1920s. Lebed voiced here what had become by that time the most widespread assumption in Russia about the meaning of NATO expansion: the West doesn't care what happens to us![160]

d. Madrid Summit, 8–9 July 1997

Not surprisingly, Yeltsin refused to attend the NATO summit in Madrid, at which Poland, the Czech Republic and Hungary were invited to prepare themselves for membership by 1999. Russia was represented by relatively low level personnel, Vice Premier Valerii Serov and Deputy Foreign Minister Nikolai N. Afanas'evskii. Belarus president Lukashenka also refused to participate, sending Viktor Sheiman, state secretary of the Belarusian Security Council, who told the Euro-Atlantic

---

[159]See, e.g., Andrei Kabannikov in *Komsomol'skaia pravda* (24 June 1997); Vasilii Safronchuk, "Zagnulas' li 'semerka' v 'vos'merku'?" [Did a "Seven" become an "Eight"?], *Sovetskaia Rossiia* (24 June 1997), and "Esli Ya vstanu . . . a ya tonu" [If I Arise . . . I am Sinking], *Zavtra*, No. 29 (July 1997). For a long essay outlining the "pros" and "cons" of S-8 membership for Russia, see Dmitrii Radyshevskii in *Moskovskie novosti,* No. 25 (22–29 June 1997).

[160]Lebed was interviewed in Copenhagen for *Det fri Aktuelt* (2 July 1997). Translated in FBIS-SOV, No. 184. Yet another Brzezinski treatment of the subject tended to confirm this opinion among Russian observers, for he made the "real possibility [though unlikely] that Russia will revert to past behavior" a central consideration of NATO expansion. See Brzezinski and Anthony Lake, "For a New World, a New NATO," *New York Times* OP-ED (30 June 1997).

Partnership Council (EAPC) that the NATO decision to expand eastward "has no solid ground and is a faulty one" (NATO Website, 9 July). This position echoed statements by the Russian delegates and a simultaneous comment from Primakov in Moscow that NATO expansion is "probably the worst [mistake] since the end of the Cold War" (Interfax, 8 July).

Russian diplomats conveyed this obligatory response everywhere they went. On 9 July, Aleksandr N. Shokhin, former minister of economics and at this time first vice speaker of the Duma and parliamentary leader of the NDR, told journalists in Canada that NATO "expansion is very dangerous for the balance of power between Eastern and Western Europe." Shokhin was in Ottawa to promote trade and investment, but could not avoid expressing his opinion of the Madrid summit. The Canadian press also quoted Russia's ambassador in Ottawa, Aleksandr Belonogov, that the expansion was a "big political mistake."[161] Rhetorical and expected as Russian commentary on Madrid clearly was, it was also true that a line had been officially crossed and the risk of NATO's policy generating strident Russian nationalism was now greater.

The summit and build-up to it were keynote topics for Russian newspapers, few of which had much good to say about them. *Izvestiia* presented a relatively moderate perspective shortly before the meetings were held, suggesting that a new "Russian mafia" at NATO, created by the Founding Act, could influence the Alliance's next set of decisions about new members. Konstantin Eggert claimed that few Russians believed that NATO was acting out a specifically anti-Russia agenda. It was nonetheless a military alliance, and the presence of hard core "anti-Russians" among the military personnel at Brussels was something to worry about. Yulia Petrovskaia noted in *Nezavisimaia gazeta* that even though there were "serious contradictions" within NATO the "frontal expansion" towards Russia's borders had gone ahead without any hesitation. Political divisions in NATO were ominous, rather than comforting, because they obviated negotiations about a new security system for Europe. *Rossiiskie vesti* found the statements emerging from NATO to be "vague" and representative of an unusually divided alliance. The paper left no doubt, however, that in its opinion the expansion of NATO was a policy initiative of the Clinton ad-

---

[161] *Ottawa Citizen* (14 July 1997). For Shokhin's observations, see *Ottawa Citizen* (10 July 1997). Shokhin was elected to the State Duma in 1993 as a member of the Russian Unity and Accord Party. He also is head of the organizational committee for a Russian-Canadian Financial Forum.

[162]Petrovskaia, "Madridskii sammit daet signal k frontal'nomu nastupleniiu NATO na granitsy Rossii" [The Madrid Summit Gives the Signal for a Frontal Invasion of NATO on the Russian Borders], *Nezavisimaia gazeta* (8 July 1997); Igor Sedykh, "Poletit li iz Madrida golub' mira?" [Will the Dove of Peace Fly from Madrid?], *Rossiiskie vesti* (8 July 1997); Eggert, "V NATO vstupiat vse, no po ocheredi" [Everyone Will Get into NATO, in Their Turn], *Izvestiia* (5 July 1997).

ministration, and that Washington would always have its way.[162] The opening day of the summit was dubbed the "day of Russia's national shame" by the communist press, where the Kremlin's "attempt to pose as a principled opponent of NATO expansion" was called "thoroughly hypocritical." Yeltsin and Kozyrev were entirely responsible for this turn of events, Vasilii Safronchuk claimed, tracing the "genuflection" of Russia to NATO directly to Yeltsin's statement in Poland in 1993.[163]

Communist observers still delighted in naming prominent American opponents of expansion, above all Jack Matlock and George Kennan, and detailing various projections about the potential cost of the venture to existing NATO members. They pointed out endlessly that the new members would bring both military infrastructure and weapons to NATO, skewing the existing CFE arrangement and simultaneously serving as important new markets for U.S. and other Western weapons suppliers. They and many non-communist commentators wrote angrily or with resignation about Russia's humiliation by the events concluded at Madrid, and the negative and lasting psychological impact these events were to have on the Russian political scene.[164] Georgi Arbatov, founding director and now honorary director of ISKRAN, told *Trud* that "the entire NATO enlargement affair is a serious error on the part of the United States and its most influential allies."[165] Seleznev urged the Polish Sejm, which was hosting a parliamentary session of the OSCE, not to allow NATO to become the main basis of security in Europe (ITAR-TASS, 8 July), and the next day reiterated an earlier Yeltsin statement that Russia would, indeed, revise the Founding Act if Baltic countries were admitted to NATO (ITAR-TASS, 9 July).[166] Another Russian delegate to the international gathering in Warsaw, deputy speaker of the Russian Federation Council, Oleg Korolev, said that the OSCE was the only security organization that could eliminate the lines of division in Europe (Interfax, 9 July). Ironically, Seleznev was elected deputy chairman of the OSCE parliamentary assembly by the gathering in Warsaw. Also meeting in Warsaw was an Alternative Forum of Non-governmental Organizations, claiming representatives from a wide variety of NGOs in Western and Eastern European countries, including

---

[163]Safronchuk, "Kolenopreklonenie v Madride . . . Den' pozora Rossii" [Genuflection in Madrid . . . Day of Russia's Shame], *Sovetskaia Rossiia* (8 July 1997).

[164]See an interview with Sergei Karaganov, deputy director of the Institute for European Studies and member of the RF Presidential Council, NTV (Moscow) (8 July 1997), FBIS-SOV, No. 189, and Gennadii Tarasov, director of the Information and Press Department of the RF Ministry of Foreign Affairs Mayak Radio Network (Moscow) (11 July 1997), FBIS-SOV, No. 190.

[165]Arbatov, in *Trud* (11 July 1997), FBIS-SOV, No. 191.

[166]On the OSCE session and Seleznev's remarks, see "Assambleia OBSE" [OSCE Assembly], *Sovetskaia Rossiia* (10 July 1997).

Poland and the Czech Republic. They demonstrated in front of the Sejm (Parliament) while the OSCE was meeting inside, and called upon European parliaments to reject the expansion of NATO and the European Union.[167]

Ukrainian president Kuchma's trip to Madrid to sign the final draft of the Charter on a Distinctive Partnership between NATO and Ukraine (9 July), with great celebration, irked Russian commentators.[168] The fact that the Charter incorporated the statement: "Ukraine welcomes the statement by NATO members that 'enlarging the Alliance will not require a change in NATO's current nuclear posture and, . . . NATO countries have no intention . . . to deploy nuclear weapons on the territory of new members, and do not foresee any future need to do so,'" was greeted with even more derision in Russia than it had been earlier. Much play was given to an apparently unilateral statement by Albright (in Ljubljana, 12 July) to the effect that there was "no stronger candidate" than Slovenia for the next round and similar remarks in Bucharest by Clinton about Romania's future chances.[169] The view from behind the Kremlin walls was of NATO aggrandizement accelerating exponentially.

On his return from Madrid, Serov encouraged further negotiations with NATO. Asked on television how Russia could persuade Romania, Slovenia and the Baltic states not to join NATO, he answered that Russia must demonstrate that it is not a threat by creating a system of "confidence and guarantees," making it unnecessary for those countries to join a military bloc.[170] His partner in Madrid, Afanas'evskii, agreed in an interview for *Rossiiskie vesti,* adding that the blandness of decisions made at Madrid reflected deep divisions within NATO itself. The deputy foreign minister expressed special concern over the possibility of Baltic membership and NATO's apparent attempt to bypass the OSCE as a potential security umbrella for Europe.[171]

Astonishingly, some (perhaps most) Western pundits seemed to have missed the

---

[167]"Protiv rasshireniia NATO" [Against the Expansion of NATO], *Sovetskaia Rossiia* (8 July 1997).

[168]The complete Charter was distributed by Interfax-Ukraine, in English, on 9 July 1997.

[169]See, e.g., Vladimir Lapskii, "Komu otkryli dveri v NATO" [To Whom Did NATO Open Its Doors], *Rossiiskaia gazeta* (10 July 1997); Nikita Shevtsov, "NATO rasshiriaetsia. Chto dal'she?" [NATO Is Expanding: What Next?], *Trud* (10 July 1997); and commentary by Anatolii Potapov in English on Voice of Russia World Service (Moscow) (9 July 1997). For Clinton's remarks in Bucharest, 11 July, to a crowd chanting "NA-TO! NA-TO!", see Alison Mitchell, "Clinton Makes Also-Ran Feel Like Winner," *New York Times* (12 July 1997).

[170]Valerii Serov interviewed by Lidiia Podolnaia, Mayak Radio Network, Moscow (11 July 1997). FBIS-SOV, No. 192. Serov was dismissed by Yeltsin in February 1998.

[171]Afanas'evskii, "Odnoznachno negativnoe" [Unambiguously Negative], *Rossiiskie vesti* (22 July 1997).

fermenting discontent in Russia altogether. On 22 July, for example, Michael Mc-Faul wrote in an OP-ED piece for the *New York Times* that, in spite of all the predictions that NATO expansion would strengthen nationalist and communist opposition forces in Russia, the invitations to Poland, Czech Republic and Hungary "came and went . . . without producing any visible reaction from Russia's opposition." He went on to say that this phenomenon was the consequence of the fact that Russia did not have a strong and constructive "loyal opposition."[172] McFaul was worried, rightly, that the absence of a parliamentary opposition could lead to dictatorships by Lebed or some more menacing force. He was quite wrong if he intended to imply that the notion of NATO expansion as a threat had dissipated in Russia. Almost every day, in fact, communist and nationalist columnists vented rage at one or the other activity of NATO, and at Yeltsin's failure to protect Russia's "interests" in the international arena. One harangue came from Professor Yurii Kachanovskii who worried about the debilitation of Russia's defense capacity in the 1990s. Calling Yeltsin's presidency a "regime of betrayal," Kachanovskii repeated the charge that the Act in no way guaranteed that NATO would not deploy nuclear weapons in the new territories. Other pieces reviled NATO actions against Serbian war criminals in Bosnia, urged the Armed Forces to organize themselves as General Rokhlin proposed (see section 3.1 of this work), accused Poles and Czechs of duplicity (or of being duped), and warned that they would be victims of high pressure Western arms dealers. Madeleine Albright, NATO leaders and Yeltsin were savagely caricatured, and cries of a new, United States sponsored "*Drang nach Osten*" rang throughout the "opposition" press.[173]

---

[172]McFaul, "Russia's Ominous Void," *New York Times* (22 July 1997).

[173]See, for example, Sergei Uvarov, "Pol'sha 'vliapalas'" v NATO . . ." [Poland Gets Itself Involved in NATO . . .], *Sovetskaia Rossiia* (15 July 1997). See also Yurii Kachanovskii, "Rezhim izmeny. Issledovaniia iurista" [The Regime of Betrayal: A Lawyer's Investigation], *Sovetskaia Rossiia* (10 July 1997); Safronchuk, "NATO razzhigaet konflikt mezhdu bosniiskimi serbami. Pervaia aktsiia posle Madrida" [NATO Stirs Up Conflict between Bosnian Serbs: The First Action after Madrid], *Soverskaia Rossiia* (10 July); "Poteriav armiiu, my poteriaem Rossiiu" [Having Lost the Army, We Will Lose Russia], *Ibid.* (12 July 1997); Yevgenii Ivanov, "Nachalas' okhota na serbov . . ." [The Hunt for Serbs Has Started], *Sovetskaia Rossiia* (12 July 1997); Safronchuk, "Obozrenie. NATO protiagivaet shchupal'tsa . . ." [Review: NATO Stretches out Its Tentacles], *Sovetskaia Rossiia* (15 July 1997); "Tsvetochnitsa Madlen" [The Flower Girl Madeleine (Albright)], *Sovetskaia Rossiia* (15 July 1997); Safronchuk, "Obozrenie. NATO prodolzhaet davit' na bosniiskikh serbov . . ." [Review: NATO Continues to Pressure Bosnian Serbs], *Sovetskaia Rossiia* (22 July 1997); Yevgenii Popov, "Pozitsiia. Tanki NATO okruzhili rezidentsiiu Radovana Karadzhicha" [Position: NATO Tanks Surrounded the Residence of Radovan Karadzhich], *Sovetskaia Rossiia* (22 July 1997).

1.7. Manifestations of the Debate

a. The Drang nach Osten *Analogy*

As we have seen, the charge that NATO's expansion eastward was a modern version of Nazi Germany's *Drang nach Osten* came back into general use in 1996
when the communist press caricatured Solana's assurances in the form of a smil-
ing boa constrictor. But the communists were not the only ones to draw on the
Hitler analogy. In February 1997, for example, the Russian Committee of War
Veterans petitioned all veterans of the "anti-Hitler coalition" to oppose NATO expansion eastward.[174] Later, Strobe Talbott was accused of acting as agent for a
"*Deutschland über alles!*" policy and in a number of cases feature articles about
NATO expansion were accompanied by drawings and old photos of jack-booted
Wehrmacht troops. That the government press was not averse to using the theme
was clear early in 1997 when Aleksei Chichkin remarked in a feature story that
one of the costs of NATO expansion would be a Russian compulsion to upgrade
its military against the new *Drang nach Osten.*[175] A few weeks after the Founding
Act was signed, for example, the historian Dashichev reminded readers of an earlier agreement that allowed an enemy to impose "slavery on our country" on 22
June 1941.[176] The conviction that the United States and Germany were conniv-
ing to acquire unchallenged supremacy over the world was common in both communist and nationalist writing.

As the sound and fury related directly to the Founding Act dwindled, such
charges were heard less often in Russia, but they did not go away. And, as we
shall see, they were to be resurrected with a vengeance in 1999. Although the
fait accompli endorsed by the Act diminished as a target by August 1997,
NATO itself reappeared as a potential enemy. An acidic two-part piece in the
extreme leftist *Zavtra* by General Viktor Filatov in which NATO's long stand-

---

[174]"K veteranam voiny stran antigitlerovskoi koalitsii" [To War Veterans in Countries
of the Anti-Hitler Coalition], *Rossiiskaia gazeta* (5 Feb 1997).

[175]Chichkin saw expansion as inevitable and noted that eastern Europe and all of the
western CIS countries would be drawn into NATO either as part of the PfP or as full members. See "Tsenu NATO sprosi i Evropy" [The Costs of NATO Demands of Europe],
Rossiiskaia gazeta (31 Jan 1997).

[176]Dashichev, in *Rabochaia tribuna* (1 April 1997). For the reference to Talbott, see
Richard Ovinnikov, "Drang nach Osten? NATO Germaniiu tolkaiut na vostok" [Drang
nach Osten? NATO Pushes Germany to the East], *Pravda Rossii* (24 June 1997). For earlier such references see, Yevgenii Popov, *Sovetskaia Rossiia* (23 March 1996), *op. cit.;*
Valentin Koptyug, *Sovetskaia Rossiia* (27 Feb 1997), *op. cit.;* and sections 1.5 and 1.6 of
this work.

ing "non-military" offensive, that is, its research activity, was lumped in with Hitler's demeaning opinion of Russians, was typical of the radical opposition. The West was assaulting Russia again with research funds and dollars, he wrote.[177] Filatov's outburst was characteristic of the old Leninist assumption that Russia was surrounded by enemies, a notion actually entrenched in the USSR's first constitution.[178] This theme emerged as a pillar of the communist argument that NATO was driven by the United States against Russia primarily to prevent the CIS from consolidating under Moscow's leadership. Writing in September 1997, Mikhail Postol said that the purpose of an agreement in May between the United States and NATO was to protect Europe from Moscow: "If we remember that from the first day of its formation, NATO was directed against Russia, although it was then called the Soviet Union, it is not difficult to see who the armed forces of the United States and NATO are directed against today." The essay was accompanied by a caricature of NATO in the shape of a crocodile (the United States) with a globe named Russia and the CIS in its teeth. No room was left for subtleties here.[179] The resilience of this point of view was such that it reappeared nearly a year later in *Nezavisimaia gazeta*.[180]

Some silver linings were found in 1997, even when the horror of the Second World War was recollected. One of these came from historian Sergei Lunev, who saw benefits for Russia in NATO's actions. Writing in *Obshchaia gazeta,* he too reminded readers of the Western "conspiracy" that culminated in Hitler's *Drang nach Osten,* adding that NATO expansion had at last provided Russians with a

[177] Filatov, " 'Zelenaia papka' Gitlera" [Hitler's 'Green File'], *Zavtra,* No's 31, 32 (August 1997). Journalist Vladimir Yurkov used the expression *Drang nach Osten* while describing NATO expansion eastward during an interview with Vladimir Petrovskii, UN Deputy General Secretary, European Division, in April 1997. Petrovskii ignored the analogy, but he was undoubtedly aware that the symbolism of NATO = Hitler-like threat was becoming common in Russia, "Vladimir F. Petrovskii: 'Sila silu lomit, ili chego ishchet NATO u rossiiskikh granits' " [Vladimir F. Petrovskii: "Power Overcomes Power, or What Is NATO Looking for Near the Russian Borders], *Rossiiskaia gazeta* (9 April 1997).

[178]See Constitution (Fundamental Law) of the Union of Soviet Socialist Republics, adopted on 6 July 1923 and ratified on 31 January 1924, Pt. I: Declaration: " . . . [the Union is established] into a common front against capitalist encirclement."

[179]Postol, "Krivoe vereteno" [The Crooked Spindle], *Sovetskaia Rossiia* (27 September 1997).

[180]Vladimir Mukhin, "Prichiny anti-Rossiiskoi pozitsii riada gosudarstv SNG" [Reasons for the Anti-Russian Attitude in Several CIS States], *Nezavisimaia gazeta* (24 July 1998).

long-missing unifying force. Furthermore, illusions about the West's "gentle-manly conduct" were now shattered, as declassified documents from the early 1990s showed that the West lied about the "impossibility" of further eastward expansion. Lunev advocated that Russia stop its rhetoric about NATO and take pragmatic, and opportunistic, advantage of growing splits between Europe and America, North and South.[181]

The inference that NATO's current activities resembled Germany's agenda for Russia in the 1930s and 1940s became standard fare in Moscow's political arena. In late October 1997, Safronchuk told readers that Yeltsin, Chubais, and company were doing to Russia what Hitler had hoped to do many years earlier, breaking it up into little pieces owned by the West. In the same long tract, but separately, he attributed similar plans to NATO and the United States. The communist press raised the Hitler image again in December, this time equating Yeltsin's entire economic reform program with the Führer's economic schemes for Eastern Europe. A photo of Yeltsin embracing Kohl enhanced the image.[182]

Reminiscences about Hitler and the Nazis still were evoked as NATO was debated in 1998, especially in the early spring after the Latvian government allowed former SS volunteer legion members to parade in Riga. At one international conference held in the Russian State Duma building, with delegates from 25 countries, Zyuganov told a large audience that "the logic according to which NATO expansion develops—is Hitlerite." He, Baburin and representatives of the Anti-NATO Commission underscored Russia's losses during World War II and drew scary comparisons between the newly combined military might of NATO and a much weakened Russia.[183] Second World War parallels were part of the communist approach during the early stages of the crisis in Kosovo as well, referring, for

[181]Lunev, "Nothing Brings People Together Like a Threat from the Outside. The Minuses of the North Atlantic Alliance's Expansion Have Been Counted, Time to Count the Pluses," *Obshchaia gazeta*, No. 39 (2–9 Oct 1997), FBIS-SOV, No. 280.

[182]"Byla u Gitlera ideia. 'Dzhornel of kommers end kommershlz' o rossiiskikh reformakh" [The Journal of Commerce and Commercials about Russian Reforms], *Sovetskaia Rossiia* (16 Dec 1997); Safronchuk, "Obozrenie. "Bredovye idei Gitlera v sovremennom ispolnenii" [[Review]: The Wild Ideas of Hitler in Contemporary Application], and "Spory v Severoatlanticheskom al'ianse i vokrug nego" [Arguments in the Atlantic Alliance and around It], *Sovetskaia Rossiia* (21 Oct 1997).

[183]Vladimir Gerasimov in *Pravda* (21 April 1998).

example, to "jackboots" in August 1998 when the German foreign minister took a strong stand against the Serbs.[184]

As the Kosovo situation brought the Russia-NATO relationship closer to the brink of dissolution, Russian and Ukrainian communists began using the term "new world order" as a synonym for a Nazi-like attempt by the United States, via NATO, to dominate the world. Ukrainian parliamentary deputies from the radical left Progressive Socialist Party, for example, quoted directly from Hitler's *Mein Kampf* to link Hitler, NATO, Israel, and the United States with a "common gangster goal—to destroy and rob." In an extraordinary vilification they charged the United States and NATO of planning to "establish a world empire of the white race, meaning the Anglo-Saxon race, exterminate and sterilize the rest of mankind, and destroy sovereignty of all states that will not submit." Their "Statement," issued after a conference on NATO in Moscow, happened to coincide with the CPRF's defense of Russian Duma deputy Albert Makashov's anti-semitic remarks in Moscow. The implication is that the radical left's hatred of NATO and Washington was converging in their minds with latent racism, and thoughts of clashes between "civilizations." Anti-NATO Commission head Baburin echoed this view at the same conference, equating NATO enlargement with German expansion in the 1930s.[185] Opinions such as these, which began to re-appear more and more often in the Russian mainstream media, came out in full force when NATO opened its bombing campaign against Yugoslavia in March 1999. The annual May celebration of Soviet victory over Germany, for example, saw an orgy of analogies drawn between

---

[184]See, e.g., Yevgenii Popov, "Kosovo: eshche odna psikhicheskaia ataka NATO na Serbov: Grokhochut sapogi . . ." [Kosovo: One More Psychic Attack by NATO Against Serbs: Jackboots Are Stamping . . .], *Sovetskaia Rossiia* (20 Aug 1998). See also Yurii Pankov, "Novye initsiativy FRG po Kosovo" [Germany's New Initiatives on Kosovo], *Krasnaia zvezda* (3 July 1998).

[185]Statement by the Ukrainian Progressive Socialist Party, "Zaiava fraktsii Progresivnoy sotsialistichnoy partiy Ukrayni, Sanktsii SShA proti Iraku ta inshikh krayn—zagroza miru i bezpetsi vsikh narodiv" [The U.S. Sanctions against Iraq and Other Countries Are a Threat to Peace and Security of Nations], *Holos Ukrayiny* (3 Nov 1998). The international conference in Moscow hosted, it claimed, representatives from 20 countries, and was titled exactly as the "Statement" was titled. Baburin, "Threat to European Security in Connection with NATO Enlargement (Balkan Events as Example)," *Vooruzhenie, Politika, Konversiia,* Nos. 5–6 (Dec 1998): 5–7, FBIS-SOV, No. 329. See also Yurii Morozov, Igor Nekipelyi, "Mirotvorcheskaia agressiia NATO. Sobytiia v Kosovo pozvoliaiut ekstrapolirovat' kharakter inostrannogo voennogo vtorzheniia na Severnyi Kavkaz" [NATO's Peacekeeping Aggression: Events in Kosovo Make it Possible to Extrapolate the Nature of Foreign Military Invasion of the North Caucasus], *Nezavisimoe voennoe obozrenie,* No. 42 (6–12 Nov 1998).

Nazi and NATO behavior. Swastikas and the NATO symbol were superimposed everywhere.[186]

b. *"Friends" in the West*

Highlighting opposition to NATO expansion from Western luminaries was a recurring tactic of anti-NATO writers in Russia, who believed that a surge of support for their cause was emerging in the United States. An overwhelming majority of Americans are opposed to expansion, Richard Ovinnikov wrote in *Pravda Rossii* [Russian Truth], a CPRF newspaper. Calling the public mood in the United States the "Achilles heel" of Washington's policy makers, he charged that "Hawks" were manipulating the process.[187] American opponents of NATO expansion were given great play in the communist press. Citing U.S. think-tanks such as the Cato Institute *Sovetskaia Rossiia* said on 11 March that the Russian people "are not deceived" by the "saccharine assurances" that NATO would not be directed against them.[188]

A later case in point was the reprinting in Russian of an open letter to President Clinton from 46 prominent American politicians, arms control specialists, scholars and diplomats. The letter, originally published in the *Washington Post* (August 1997), called NATO expansion "a policy error of historic proportions" and said that it would both weaken the Alliance and undermine European security. Expansion provides succour to the "undemocratic opposition" in Russia, will make it difficult to get START II and III adopted by the Duma (see section 3.1 of this work), and will re-align Europe between countries in NATO and those

---

[186]See, e.g., a full page publications of Nazi documents from 1938 accompanied by two photographs: one of Hitler, Göring, and Chamberlain at Munich in 1938; the other of Clinton and Solana whispering together at a table. "Novyi miunkhei" [New Munich], *Sovetskaia Rossiia* (6 May 1999), and Vadim Solov'ev, "Den' pobedy, kazalos', navsegda postavil tochku v istorii fashizma. Cherez 54 goda vse povtoraetsia vnov'" [The Day of Victory, It Seemed, Was the Stopping Point in the History of Fascism: After 54 Years Everything Is Starting Again], *Nezavisimoe voennoe obozrenie*, No. 17 (7–13 May 1999). In "Esli by Gitler pobedil . . . a pobedila SSSR Yel'tsin . . ." [If Hitler Had Won, but Yeltsin Has Vanquished the USSR], *Sovetskaia Rossiia* (8 May 1999), war veteran Aleksei Sanin called Yeltsin a puppet of NATO and a "5th columnist of American fascism." See also "Klinton—eto vtoroi Gitler. SShA i NATO—natsisty!" [Clinton Is the Second Hitler: The USA and NATO are Nazis!], *Sovetskaia Rossiia* (11 May 1999).

[187]Ovinnikov, "Akhilesova piata NATO. K rossiisko-amerikanskoi vstreche v verkhakh" [The Achilles Heel of NATO: Towards the Russo-American Summit], *Pravda Rossii* (11 March 1997).

[188]"'Rukopozhatie' NATO russkikh ne obmanet" [Russians Are Not Deceived by NATO's "Handshake"], *Sovetskaia Rossiia* (11 March 1997).

outside it, the group warned. These and other reasons to oppose NATO expansion were old arguments by the summer of 1997, but their resilience (and the names of their supporters) even after the Founding Act gave them additional credence.[189] Drawn as they were from a decidedly non-communist ideological base, it is interesting that the views contained in the U.S. open letter coincided almost exactly with opinions expressed by Zyuganov in a long interview for the Russian magazine *Patriot*.[190]

State Duma opponents of NATO expansion followed up on the U.S. letter by sending an open letter of their own to Clinton themselves under the heading "NATO Will Shatter Trust." Signed by the chairs of Duma committees on Security, Defense, Conversion, Legislation, Property and Privatization, Veterans' Affairs, Education and Science, Public Associations and Religious Affairs, Federation Affairs, Geopolitical Questions, CIS Affairs, Information Policy, Industry, Social Policy, and Self-Government, the letter was unusually representative of Russia's democratically elected parliamentarians. Communist hardliners such as A. Lukianov and V. Varennikov were among its authors, as was General Lev Rokhlin. The letter, published only in the communist press, restated the opinion that NATO expansion would jeopardize START II and START III and weaken

---

[189]"Oshibka istoricheskogo masshtaba. Otkrytoe pis'mo prezidentu Klintonu ot opponentov rasshireniia NATO" [A Mistake on an Historical Scale: Open Letter to President Clinton from Opponents of NATO Expansion], *Sovetskaia Rossiia* (28 Aug 1997). The letter was preceded by a day by a letter to Clinton from 20 Senators, representing both parties, asking for greater debate and "circumspection" on the idea of NATO expansion. Among the signatures on the second letter were those of former senators Bob Bradley, Sam Nunn, Gary Hart, Mark Hatfield, and Gordon Humphrey; former ambassadors Richard T. Davies, Arthur Hartman, and Jack Matlock; former secretary of defense Robert McNamara; professors Richard Pipes and Marshall Shulman; and think-tank heads Susan Eisenhower and Edward Lutwak. Eisenhower organized the letter.

A later statement urging the "enlargement" of NATO, in support of Clinton and signed by 133 senior U.S. foreign policy experts, was not reported in Russia. The list included former vice presidents (Quayle, Mondale), secretaries of state (Rogers, Kissinger, Vance, Haig, Baker, Schultz, and Christopher), plus a cross-section of former secretaries of defense and national security advisers. The statement was issued on 13 September by the New Atlantic Initiative, a group organized by the editor of the *National Review*. See David E. Sanger, "Top Ex-Aides Are Supporting a Wider NATO," *New York Times* (14 Sept 1997).

[190]"Soiuz vo blago Rossii" [Union for the Good of Russia], *Sovetskaia Rossiia* (7 Aug 1997). This piece was an abridged version of Zyuganov's interview for *Patriot*, where he said that NATO expansion would constantly stimulate patriotic growth, for it was the best example of the West's indifference to Russia's legitimate concerns.

the Atlantic Alliance itself. Western countries were accused of setting out on an "unfriendly and even confrontational" course against Russia.[191]

Historian Lunev again took a different tack: opposed to a resurrection of either the communist or a strongly nationalist approach to the question of NATO expansion, he wrote in October 1997 that if Russia could remain patient, opponents of expansion in the West eventually would win the day. They "will become much more numerous as soon as money from budgets in Western countries begins to vanish somewhere in Poland," he said.[192] Vasilii Safronchuk offered like opinions in *Sovetskaia Rossiia* (21 October 1997). Proponents of this line of reasoning could have taken heart from discussions on the future of Russian-American relations held at Moscow's Institute for the World Economy and International Affairs (IMEMO) in November for delegates from the U.S. Atlantic Council and the Institute's own scholars. A joint statement included opinions on which the two "sides" differed, and also demonstrated the great extent to which NATO enlargement dominated the sessions. There was unanimity in the belief that Russia and NATO must work closely together on matters of European security, and the statement noted as well that an offer of NATO membership to former Soviet republics would cause a "very serious reaction" in Russia.[193]

During the warmup for the congressional debate in the United States, with proponents and opponents taking pot shots at each other on American editorial pages, Russian commentators began to find their names appearing in the U.S. media. One long-standing U.S. journalist opponent of NATO expansion, Thomas L. Friedman, for example, saw the NATO question increasingly present in Moscow as U.S.-Russia relations deteriorated over the Iraq issue. Calling expansion a "brain-dead Clinton move that has put the most pro-American Russians on the defensive," Friedman described concerns over the U.S. presence on Russia's southern frontier, quoting especially the respected Sergei Rogov.[194] Russian writers were rankled by Madeleine Albright's claim to the Senate Foreign Relations Committee that failure to approve enlargement would lead to costly arms buildups and instability in Eastern Europe. Assertions by Committee Chairman Jesse Helms, and others, to the ef-

---

[191]"Otkrytoe pis'mo prezidentu SShA Uil'iamu Dzh. Klintonu. NATO rastopchet doverie" [Open Letter to the President of the USA William J. Clinton: NATO Will Shatter Trust], *Sovetskaia Rossiia* (16 Oct 1997).

[192]Lunev, *Obshchaia gazeta*, No. 39 (2–8 Oct 1997), *op. cit.*

[193]The meetings were held over 3–5 November 1997. The joint statement appeared in the IMEMO journal as "Rossiisko-amerikanskie otnosheniia na poroge novogo veka" [Russian-American Relations on the Threshold of a New Century], *Mirovaia ekonomika i mezhdunarodnye otnosheniia*, No. 5 (May 1998): 109–115.

[194] Friedman, "Backlash," *New York Times* (24 Nov 1997).

fect that Russia should not be appeased also figured prominently in the Moscow media. Albright's middle ground, which included the specific desire to "engage" Russia so that it would not feel isolated, while insisting that Moscow could in no way "dilute, delay or block NATO decisions," left Russian analysts frankly confused.

Russian opponents of NATO expansion were cheered somewhat in January 1998 when the formation in Washington of a Coalition Against the Expansion of NATO was announced. According to ITAR-TASS (27 Jan), the new group included both liberal and conservative public organizations and for the most part opposed NATO because expansion was not in the interest of the United States. Jonathan Dean, the leader of one group, was quoted saying that further expansion, which could include the Baltics, Ukraine or Azerbaijan, would lead to "confrontation with Russia."[195]

The names of well-known American opponents of NATO expansion cropped up in the Russian press regularly during the period late March to early May 1998 as the U.S. Senate postponed, debated and finally ratified the expansion process. In addition to statements by Jack Matlock, George Kennan's claim in February 1997 that the broadening of NATO was "the most fateful error in the entire post–Cold War era" appeared frequently. Editorials from the *New York Times* urging caution as the U.S. Senate debated expansion, and Kennan's remark to Thomas L. Friedman, "I think it [Senate ratification of NATO expansion] is the beginning of a new cold war," were prominently displayed in Russia.[196] So was the opinion of U.S. Senator Daniel Patrick Moynihan, who quoted Kennan while trying to persuade the Senate to postpone further NATO expansion for at least three more years.[197]

---

[195]The Russian military press picked this up with pleasure; see "V SShA sozdana 'Koalitsiia protiv rasshireniia NATO'," *Krasnaia zvezda* (28 Jan 1998).

[196]See, e.g., Yevgenii Umerenkov, who warned of a new Cold War in *Komsomol'skaia pravda* (6 May 1998), and Aleksei Pushkov, "Ten' ukhodit . . . na vostok?" [Does the Shadow Move to the East?], *Nezavisimaia gazeta* (6 May 1998). See also George F. Kennan, "A Fateful Error," *New York Times* (5 Feb 1997), and Thomas L. Friedman, "Now a Word From X," *New York Times* (2 May 1998).

For earlier commentary, see Stanislav Kondrashov, "Pokhozh li Klinton na kapitana 'Titanika'" [Is Clinton Like the Captain of the Titanic?], *Izvestiia* (11 March 1998), where Susan Eisenhower is quoted at length, and references to NYT editorials "What's the Rush on NATO?" (9 March 1998) and "NATO Myopia" (5 March 1998) are made. Melor Sturua, "Senat SShA otlozhil obsuzhdenie voprosa o rasshirenii NATO" [U.S. Senate Delayed Discussion of the Question of NATO Expansion], *Izvestiia* (24 March 1998), Yevgenii Byi, "Senat SShA gotovitsia postavit' tochku v debatakh o rasshirenii NATO" [U.S. Senate Is Preparing to Complete the Debate on NATO Expansion], *Izvestiia* (29 April 1998).

[197]See, e.g., Moynihan, "NATO Expansion and Nuclear War," *ACE: Analysis of Current Events* 10, No. 7/8 (July/Aug 1998): 5–6. Moynihan's position was picked up on by Marina Nestorova in "NATO-Rossiia: Razgovor lukavogo s ubogim" [NATO-Russia: Conversation of the Cunning with the Miserable], *Nezavisimaia gazeta* (2 July 1998).

c. "Friends" in East and East Central Europe

Problems faced by Poland, the Czech Republic and Hungary as they negotiated membership were highlighted in the Russian media as well: for example, Poland placed itself in an awkward situation by negotiating with Israel in August for the purchase of military hardware, when the United States hoped that the provisioner would be Boeing;[198] and the public reaction in early October, when NATO made it clear to the three countries that they would have to bear most of the cost of joining the Alliance themselves. This was especially the case with the Czech republic, where military expenditure was at 1.5 percent of GDP in 1997. In September, U.S. Assistant Defense Secretary Franklin D. Kramer told the Czech defense ministry that Prague was not spending enough on the military, and that the Czech population was at the time not sufficiently enthusiastic for NATO membership—raising the sorry image of poor countries having to upgrade military spending and "persuade" their citizens of the benefits of NATO. The Russian media played this situation up.[199]

The Russian press allotted considerable space to the question of cost of admission, and to the vagaries of the propaganda used to persuade the potential new members to join.[200] The Hungarian situation was described already in September 1997 as one in which the citizenry would lose much by joining NATO and, on 1 November, *Rossiiskaia gazeta* carried an article criticizing NATO for shifting the financial burden of admission to the East and East Central European countries.[201]

Of the three potential new members, only Hungary held a referendum on ad-

---

[198]On this matter, see Witold Ygulski, "Elbit Strikes Back," *Warsaw Voice*—News No. 13 (440)(30 March 1997). Elbit is the Israeli manufacturer of anti-tank rockets that Poland wishes to purchase.

[199]The matter had been raised, in fact, in the spring. See, e.g., Anatolii Kurganov, "Shtabisty provoronili sekrety" [Staff Yawned at the Secrets], *Rossiiskaia gazeta* (12 April 1997); the Ukrainian left picked this up as well. See, e.g., "Skil'ki komtuvatime NATO novobrantsiam"? [How Much Will NATO Cost Its New Members?], *Demokratychna Ukraina* (19 July 1997); " 'Difens Nius' o raskhodakh na rasshirenie NATO" ["Defense News" on the Cost of NATO Expansion], *Krasnaia zvezda* (18 Dec 1997).

[200]See, e.g., "Pol'sha: mezhdu Germaniei i Rossiei?" [Poland: Between Germany and Russia?], *Nezavisimaia gazeta* (20 Sept 1997); "Kandidaty v NATO poluchili osobyi status" [Candidates for NATO Have Received Special Status], *Nezavisimaia gazeta* (1 Oct 1997).

[201] Anatolii Kurganov, "Podschitali—proslezilis'. I prosleziatsia" [The Calculators Shed Some Tears. And Will Shed Tears], *Rossiiskaia gazeta* (1 Nov 1997). "Dan start peregovoram o prisoedinenii Vengrii k NATO' [Negotiations for Hungarian Admission to NATO Have Begun], *Nezavisimaia gazeta* (12 Sept 1997); "NATO ishchet sredstva na rasshirenie" [NATO Seeks Resources for Expansion], *Nezavisimaia gazeta* (3 Oct 1997).

mission to NATO. The voting took place on Sunday, 16 November 1997, and about 85 percent of the voters supported joining NATO. But the positive spin put on this event by proponents of NATO rang a little hollow in light of a turn-out of only 49.18 percent of the eligible voters. The fact that the government in Budapest campaigned extensively (and expensively) for a "yes" vote and the question was cleverly worded ("Do you agree that the Republic of Hungary should provide for the protection of the country by joining NATO?") helped ensure success. The Russian, and some Western media, interpreted the referendum results as a sign of a high level of indifference to NATO.[202] Speaking for the Anti-NATO deputies in the Russian State Duma, S.N. Baburin somewhat disingenuously told reporters that the turnout of eligible voters implied a Hungarian peoples' boycott of the referendum (Interfax, 17 Nov). A Russian ministry of foreign affairs official said more or less the same thing (Interfax, 17 Nov). The Russian press echoed these feelings and also remarked on the fact that the Czech government would not "dare" to conduct such a referendum.[203] Presumably, the reality lay somewhere between the positions taken by officialdom in Budapest and Moscow.

---

[202]An interview granted in Kiev by the Hungarian ambassador to Ukraine, Janos Kisfalvi, is a case in point. Asked about the referendum before it took place, Kisfalvi insisted that the majority of the Hungarian citizens "understands the necessity" of NATO membership, and suggested that neutrality would be much more expensive. The voting results tended to contradict his optimistic statements, see *Uryadovyy Kuryer* (6 Nov 1997). See also Jane Perlez, "Hungarians Approve NATO Membership," *New York Times* (17 Nov 1997), where the positive spin dominates and the turnout was said to be 51 percent. For an interview with the Hungarian Foreign Minister, Lazlo Kovacs, in Ottawa, see Mike Trickey, "Hungary Sees NATO as Way Out of Dark," *Ottawa Citizen* (5 Dec 1997).

The actual turnout was 49.24 percent of the 8,059,039 eligible voters, but about 5000 failed to turn in their ballot sheets. Final data came from the Embassy of the Republic of Hungary, Ottawa (25 Nov 1997). The Hungarian position was that the referendum results were decisive, especially in light of the law that makes it necessary for a winning side to have support from 25 percent of the eligible voters.

[203]See, e.g., "Chekhi sdali zaiavlenie v NATO" [Czechs Applied to Become a NATO Member], *Nezavisimaia gazeta* (14 November 1997); see also "Pozitsiia prezidenta Chekhii" [Position of the Czech President], *Krasnaia zvezda* (15 May 1997). On Hungary "Vengry idut v NATO cherez referendum" [Hungarians Enter NATO by Means of a Referendum], *Nezavisimaia gazeta* (12 November 1997); see also "Vengriia skazala 'da' chlenstvu v al'ianse" [Hungary Says "Yes" to Membership in the Alliance], *Nezavisimaia gazeta* (19 Nov 1997); "Budapest gotov k integratsii v NATO" [Budapest Is Ready for Integration with NATO], *Nezavisimaia gazeta* (18 Nov 1997); Natal'ia Prikhodko, "My stupaet v NATO ne potomy, chto boitsia Russikh" [We Join NATO, but Not Because We Fear Russia], *Nezavisimaia gazeta* (19 Nov 1997); "Vengriia uzhe pochti v NATO" [Hungary Is Almost a Member of NATO], *Krasnaia zvezda* (4 Dec 1997).

In April 1998, the Moscow press made much of a report from *Der Spiegel* to the effect that Hungarian, Czech and especially Polish secret services had continued to spy regularly on NATO. The charges immediately were denied by the accused governments.[204] Poland was denounced for hypocrisy by Moscow in May, in response to statements made by Bronislaw Gieremek in Helsinki. The Polish foreign minister called for troop reduction in Kaliningrad (see sections 2 and 5 of this work), prompting Russian foreign ministry officials to wonder aloud why he had made no such request during his Moscow visit in March (Interfax, 21 May). Because Poland was the current candidate most central to Russia's strategic interests, especially in light of its growing ties with Ukraine, Poland's negotiations with NATO were watched closely in Moscow. And Polish statements that there was nothing anti-Russian about their application to the Western alliance were believed far less than similar observations from Prague and Budapest. Russian analysts predicted that the Baltic states would be drawn quickly into the NATO orbit with strong support from Warsaw.[205]

Eastern European and Baltic acquiescence in NATO's Balkan activities was especially galling to Russian observers, who held in contempt Hungarian, Polish and Baltic offers to assist NATO first in Bosnia and later in Kosovo (see sections 2.3 and 5 of this work).[206] Observers in Moscow scorned NATO candidates for subjecting themselves to repeated "loyalty tests."[207] Underlying the bitter commentary in Russian reporting then, and later, was a sense that Eastern Europe was irretrievably lost.[208]

---

[204]See, e.g., PAP (6 April 1998), an English-language press release from Warsaw, and Valerii Masterov in *Moskovskie novosti* (25 April–3 May 1998). Vladimir Lapskii, "V NATO probralsia 'Agent 008'" ["Agent 008" Sneaked into NATO], *Rossiiskaia gazeta* (14 April 1998).

[205]See, e.g., "Pol'skie sokoly ne gotovy letat' v natovskom nebe" [Polish Falcons Are Not Prepared to Fly in NATO's Sky], *Izvestiia* (21 Nov 1998); Sergei Pinchuk, Anatolii Trinkov, "Varshava pochti v NATO" [Warsaw Is Almost in NATO], *Nezavisimaia gazeta* (28 Jan 1999).

[206]See, e.g., Sergei Merinov, "Balkanskii uzel. NATO i ego vernopoddanye" [Balkan Knot: NATO and Its Loyal Subjects], *Rossiiskaia gazeta* (9 Oct 1998), which especially criticized Poland, Romania and Lithuania.

[207]See, e.g., Vladimir Katin, "Proverka na loial'nost' NATO" [Checkup for Loyalty to NATO], *Nezavisimaia gazeta* (26 Dec 1998).

[208]The actual admission of Poland, the Czech Republic and Hungary to NATO in March 1999 evoked many more mournful, rather than angry, commentaries in the Russian press. See, e.g., Aleksandr Kuranov, "NATO popolniaetsia novobranuaets" [NATO has New Recruits], *Nezavisimaia gazeta* (13 March 1999); Gennadii Charodeev, "Vengriia, Pol'sha i Chekhiia uzhe v NATO" [Hungary, Poland and Czechia Are Already in NATO], *Izvestiia* (12 March 1999).

1.8. Restructuring Relations with NATO

Russia's government worked hard during the second half of 1997 to make the best of its new relationship with NATO, without appearing to give anything more away. On 27 August, Yeltsin appointed Primakov chairman of an RF Inter-Department Commission on Cooperation with NATO and the Implementation of the Founding Act. The foreign minister was given two months to prepare a draft statute on the commission and its composition, a project that was completed and approved by Yeltsin on 18 December.[209]

The likelihood of the Russia-NATO PJC working to give Russia a powerful influence on NATO was treated with considerable skepticism by Russian pundits. Aleksei Pushkov, member of the Council for Foreign and Defense Policy, for example, wrote in August that Russian views might now be taken into consideration but that on important issues NATO and the United States would still do what they wished. This, of course, is precisely what Clinton had said on 14 May. Pushkov warned that Russia would be co-opted to support NATO on some questions of mutual interest and ignored at other times at NATO's whim.[210] A month later, First Deputy Foreign Minister Igor Ivanov offered the official view, which, for the most part, reflected the idea that Russia was stuck with NATO expansion and must make the best of it. The purpose of the PJC would be to "minimize the process of NATO expansion" (Interfax, 17 Sept). This was not much of an endorsement.

When the first ministerial-level meeting of the PJC opened at the United Nations on 26 September, Primakov delivered two central points to the 16 NATO foreign ministers: 1) that Russia wanted "equality" in the body, and 2) that his country still did not approve of NATO expansion eastward. The stage had been set for this approach four days beforehand, when Yeltsin was quoted in the mainstream Russian press as being opposed to NATO expansion and saying that his country would prefer that the United States be less involved in Europe. The Russian president's notion that Europe should be in charge of its own security was given tacit

---

[209]The Statute of the Interdepartmental Commission of the Russian Federation for Interaction with NATO and the Implementation of the Founding Act on Mutual Relations, Cooperation, and Security between the Russian Federation and the North Atlantic Treaty Organization and the Composition of the Interdepartmental Commission was published by ITAR-TASS, 18 December 1997. See also Interfax (18 Dec 1997). In addition to Primakov as its chairman, the Commission included 16 highly-placed persons, among them the deputy directors of finance, the Federal Border Service, science and technologies, economics, communications and information, internal affairs, and civil defense, and V. Kvashnin, Chief of the General Staff of the Armed Forces.

[210]Pushkov, "Rossiia-NATO: Sovet, po poka neliubov'" [Russia-NATO: A Council, but in the Meantime Not Much Love], *Rossiiskaia gazeta* (13 Aug 1997).

support by France's Chirac, who was in Moscow at the time. Yeltsin promised to bring the matter up at a Council of Europe meeting scheduled for 9 October in Strasbourg.[211]

Interestingly, the Russian media reaction to the Kremlin's participation in the PJC was much more mixed than earlier commentary would have led one to expect. The military press urged the foreign ministry to take advantage of the new forum to push a Russian agenda, and also criticized Washington for setting obstacles in the way of Moscow's path back to Great Power status. *Zavtra* was cynically hostile, but other papers expressed unusual optimism about impending reintegration of Russia into European security affairs.[212]

Paradoxically, Russia's government now warned against too much optimism. Primakov's public assessment of the Council session was favorable, but grudgingly so. On the one hand, he noted that a list of major issues had been set out for future discussion and that consensus would be the PJC's aim. On the other hand, "we are protecting our interests" and have not in any way given the "green light to NATO enlargement" (ITAR-TASS, 26 Sept). Prime Minister Chernomyrdin confirmed this position a few days later at The Hague (ITAR-TASS, 1 Oct), where he said also that expansion created "new lines of division" in Europe. Primakov simultaneously told reporters in Ottawa the same thing (ITAR-TASS, 1 Oct), as did Defense Minister Sergeev on his return to Moscow from Maastricht, where he had been a guest at an informal meeting of NATO defense ministers (ITAR-TASS, 2 Oct). Sergeev and Chernomyrdin advised their audiences that NATO should reduce its military component and become more of a political organiza-

---

[211]See Nikolai Paklin, "Frantsuzskii sezon v Moskve" [French Season in Moscow], and Vladimir Lapskii, "Nam blizhe stalo li Parizha" [Did Paris Get Closer to Us?], *Rossiiskaia gazeta* (25 Sept 1997). According to ITAR-TASS (22 Sept 1997), Solana told reporters that good relations with Russia was a "priority" for NATO. See also "Primakov i Klinton vystupili v OON" [Primakov and Clinton Spoke at the UN], *Nezavisimaia gazeta* (24 Sept 1997).

[212]"U NATO i Rossii obshchie interesy" [NATO and Russia Have Common Interests], *Izvestiia* (24 Sept 1997); "Rossiia zanimaet opredeliaiushchee mesto v mire" [Russia Occupies a Definable Place in the World], *Nezavisimaia gazeta* (24 Sept 1997); "Rossiia rasshiriaet svoi kontakty s NATO" [Russia Expands Its Contacts with NATO], *Nezavisimaia gazeta* (30 Sept 1997); "Sotrudnichestvo Rossiia s NATO dolzhno stat' vazhnym elementom bezopasnosti v Evrope" [Russian Cooperation with NATO Should Become an Important Element of Security in Europe], *Krasnaia zvezda* (3 Oct 1997); "Chtoby verkhovodit' v mire, SShA gotovy okazat' davlenie na liuboe gosudarstvo, dopuskaiushchee raskhozhdenie s 'Amerikanskimi standartami'" [In Order to Rule in the World, the USA Is Prepared to Put Pressure on any State That Differs from the "American Standards'], *Krasnaia zvezda* (2 Oct 1997); "Iliuzii Mira" [Illusions of Peace], *Zavtra*, No. 38 (Sept 1997).

tion. All three officials recalled earlier warnings that any attempt to include the Baltic countries in NATO would force Russia to reconsider its relationship with the Alliance (see section 5 of this work).

When Yeltsin finally spoke, briefly, to the Council of Europe in Strasbourg the Russian press gave him some credit as a player in European affairs, but called his participation little more than a photo-op. The communist press ridiculed the president's performance, complaining that he failed to raise the issue of NATO expansion and that he knuckled under on the question of American participation in European security matters.[213] Chernomyrdin did his part, repeating to Austrian Chancellor Viktor Lima (in Moscow) that NATO expansion eastward was a "grave historic error" (Interfax, 29 Oct). The new Russian Chief of Staff, General Kvashnin, made the same point during meetings at NATO HQ in Brussels, on 23–24 October.

Chair of the International Affairs Committee of the Duma, Lukin, approved the Chernomyrdin-Primakov stance on NATO: oppose, but work to mitigate the effects of expansion. Responding to an interviewer for the ministry of foreign affairs' magazine *Mezhdunarodnaia zhizn'* [International Affairs] in October, Lukin said that the mainstream political establishment in Washington wanted Russia stable, but not strong. Accusing the United States of trying to separate Moscow and Kiev, isolating Russia from its natural allies, he nevertheless agreed that the Duma should ratify START II, mainly so that START III might come into force sooner.[214] Chernomyrdin's intervention reflected the pervading mood at a joint meeting of Russian, Ukrainian, Moldovan, and Belarusian members of anti-NATO parliamentary factions. Gathering in Moscow on 21 October, delegates claimed to represent 205 of 416 Ukrainian Supreme Soviet deputies, and 39 of 101 Belarusian National Assembly deputies.[215] The purpose of the conference was to coordinate the opposition to NATO expansion that, its many speakers insisted, was growing in the CIS countries. Leader of the Russian Anti-NATO Commission Baburin participated in a more specifically Russian event a few weeks later. Addressing the 4th Congress of Russian Nationalists, which met in St. Petersburg on 6 December, he called for a union of the some 20 parties and movements represented there to resist a variety of government policies (ITAR-TASS, 6 Dec).

---

[213]Safronchuk, "Obozrenie. Boris Yel'tsin otkryvaet Evropy . . ." [Review: Boris Yeltsin Discovers Europe], *Sovetskaia Rossiia* (14 Oct 1997).

[214] Lukin in *Mezhdunarodnaia zhizn'*, No. 10 (October 1997): 9–17.

[215]The conference was described in detail by Safronchuk, "Obshchestvennost' protiv rasshireniia NATO!" [Public Opinion Is against the Expansion of NATO!], *Sovetskaia Rossiia* (28 Oct 1997).

The Russian government, in its turn, continued to build bridges with NATO's infrastructure. A military representative was sent to Brussels in October (see section 3.1 of this work), and a permanent mission to NATO was opened on 15 November. The Cabinet posted a 36-person staff to Brussels, ordering the Russian Embassy and Trade Mission to house them (Interfax, 19 Nov). An Interdepartmental Commission for Cooperation with NATO, with Primakov serving as Chairman, was given formal structure on 17 December (Interfax, 18 Dec).

In November academicians had begun to examine the Russian-American relationship from the perspective of NATO expansion eastward as a "done deal." Writing in *SShA*, for example, V.A. Kremenyuk saw Russia and the United States poised for a mutually advantageous "new beginning." The one impediment to a very positive broadening of cooperation between the two countries would be an attempt by NATO to expand further eastward, especially if such expansion encroached upon former USSR republics.[216] Russian strategic studies specialists also began to project scenarios in which the Founding Act could be made to work to Russia's advantage. A long study in *Nezavisimoe voennoe obozrenie*, for example, outlined ways and means with which to solve the problem of a "growing imbalance of forces" between NATO and Russia. These included measures to ensure agreement on arms monitoring, with special emphasis on modernizing the Treaty on Conventional Armed Forces in Europe (CFE); the establishment of mechanisms for a broader and franker exchange of military information; far greater cooperation on defense industry planning and arms provision; and joint action in creating a European tactical ABM system. The West's "actual aims and intentions" would be tested, the authors of the report said, by the degree to which they agree to a formula limiting the numbers of combat aircraft and helicopters, and troop deployment, on the territory of new members. NATO's willingness to treat Russia as a strategic partner in defending its own southern borders, and the extent to which Russia is allowed to break into the U.S. and European monopoly on arms sales in Europe, would serve as other measurements of the Alliance's commitments to Russia. A "we will believe it when we see it" tone to the paper was lent credence by a Ministry of Defense statement issued a few days later. In regards to negotiations in Vienna on the CFE, Col. Gen. Leonid Ivashov said that there were serious differences in in-

---

[216]Kremenyuk, "Rossiisko-amerikanskie otnosheniia: Novoe nachalo?" [Russian-American Relations: A New Beginning?], *SShA*, No. 11 (Nov 1997).

terpreting the Founding Act promise not to place "substantial combat forces" on the territory of its new members.[217]

In addition to lobbying for more favorable military relations with NATO, Yeltsin revived the Soviet practice of attempting to divide NATO from within. On 30 November he and German Chancellor Kohl held informal talks at Yekaterinburg and, after Yeltsin telephoned France's President Chirac, they agreed to a three-country discussion in Russia sometime during the first half of 1998. It was the Russian hope that the meetings would initiate a relationship able to counterbalance American influence in Europe. After Kohl and Yeltsin met, however, the communist press mocked the Russian president's optimism, pointing out that nothing was said at the meeting about NATO expansion, Russian access to the European market, or Russian arms sales to Europe.[218]

It was in December 1997 that Primakov laid out the hopes that Russia had for NATO at that time, telling a meeting, in Brussels, of foreign ministers of the Euroatlantic Council that the Alliance should be primarily a peacekeeping organization (Interfax, 17 Dec). Cooperation with the OSCE, coordination of the Partnership for Peace program, and the avoidance of closed regional interest decisions were vital, he said, to the success of a new European security system. The Russia media reported Primakov's wish list, but doubted that his preference for the OSCE would appeal to Albright.[219] Secretary of State Albright had, in fact, preempted Primakov's presentation at Brussels. On 16 December, as the Alliance members signed agreements with Poland, the Czech Republic and Hungary, she appealed for a wider NATO strategy to deal with threats from nuclear, chemical, and biological weapons. These threats emanated from "the Middle East and

---

[217]ITAR-TASS (28 Nov 1997). According to Ivashov, the Russian view was that "substantial" meant a brigade, approximately 5,000–8,000 men, whereas NATO took it to mean a division, or 12,000–15,000. For the prior essay, Andrei Piontkovskii, Vitalii Tsygichko, "Rossiia i NATO posle Parizha i Madrida. Obshchee interesy dolzhny stat' fundamentom mira v Evrope" [Russia and NATO after Paris and Madrid: Common Interests Must Become the Foundation of Peace in Europe], *Nezavisimoe voennoe obozrenie*, No. 43 (21–27 Nov 1997). See also Vyacheslav Krasiukov, "NATO po vsemu svetu—utopiia ili real'nosti'?" [NATO in the Full Light—Utopia or Reality?], *Rossiiskaia gazeta* (21 Nov 1997).

[218]"'Lidery pokhlopyvaiut drug druga po plechu, no obshchego iazyka naiti ne mogut'" [The Leaders Slap Each Other on the Back, But They Cannot Find a Common Language], *Sovetskaia Rossiia* (2 Dec 1997).

[219]See, e.g., Dmitrii Gornostaev, "RF i NATO podpisali plan sovmestnykh deistvii" [The RF and NATO Signed a Plan for Combined Activities], *Nezavisimaia gazeta* (18 Dec 1997); "Novaia kartiia dlia Evropy" [A New Charter for Europe], *Nezavisimaia gazeta* (19 Dec 1997).

Eurasia." It was obvious that her reference was primarily to Iraq and Iran, but Russian diplomats immediately took offense (see section 2.2).

As the year wound down, the Kremlin's position on NATO was given doctrinal status in the National Security Concept, which was published on 26 December after two months of debate. The very long and somewhat rambling Concept found the greatest threats to Russian security in internal matters: the weakened economy, organized crime, regional separatism, corruption and a "spiritual malaise." But NATO's expansion to the East was perceived as the greatest external menace:

> Russia's influence on settling leading questions in international affairs which affect our state interest has decreased significantly. In these circumstances, the desire of a number of states to undermine Russia's positions in the political, economic and military spheres has increased. . . . The prospect of NATO expansion to the East is unacceptable to Russia because it represents a threat to its national security.

Russia rejected force as a means to resolve international disputes but warned that some "foreign states and international organizations" were deliberately interfering in the internal affairs of "Russia's peoples" and called this too a "potent threat" to the country. It was to NATO that the Concept returned, however, saying that expansion created a "threat of a new split in the continent which could be extremely dangerous." To defend itself against such hazards, the Concept concluded, Russia "reserves the right to use all the forces at its disposal, including nuclear weapons, if the unleashing of armed aggression results in a threat to the actual existence of the Russian Federation."[220]

As the year ended, military scholar Yu. P. Davidov warned that Russia's refusal to accept its powerlessness in regard to NATO undermined its chances of making the best of the Founding Act. He found problems as well with those who urged Russia to seek alliances with anti-Western regimes to build a new center of power based on the CIS, or to count on a split within NATO itself. Pledges to raise the price of expansion, by ending various disarmament negotiations, including

---

[220]"Kontseptsiia Natsional'noi bezopasnosti Rossiiskoi Federatsii" [Russian Federation National Security Concept], *Rossiiskaia gazeta* (26 Dec 1997); *Krasnaia zvezda* (27 Dec 1997). The Concept generated widespread discussion in Russia. It was debated in October (see Section 3), rendered in final draft on 17 December, and signed by Yeltsin on 23 December. The Anti-NATO group in the Duma was among its proponents, pointing out at a news conference that NATO expansion would bring a huge new military infrastructure (air fields, bases, barracks, warehouses, and communications systems) close to Russia's borders, ITAR-TASS (24 Dec 1997).

START II, strengthening ties with Cuba, increasing the size of the army, applying economic sanctions against Ukraine or the Baltic states, and so on, would also be counter-productive, he cautioned. Davidov made no recommendations; rather he analyzed several routes to follow. Charging his own government with using "hysterical propaganda" against NATO expansion, he favored instead a search for some "juncture of interests," or compromise, between Russia and NATO.[221] A similar position had been taken by Tatiana Parkhalina, who wrote that there was no alternative to a strategic partnership with the West. She and another commentator in IMEMO's main journal cautioned that there was need for reform in NATO itself. In the latter case, a conviction was expressed also that NATO must not allow itself to become a tool for U.S. world domination.[222] There was not much optimism in the Russian mass media that a "juncture of interests" would be found.[223]

Russia's foreign policy related to such scattered, but nonetheless connected, issues as NATO, Iraq, the United States, and the concept of a multipolar world, was outlined by Primakov in a long interview for *Nezavisimaia gazeta* on 30 December 1997. Throughout, he claimed to have a better understanding of Saddam Hussein, and also of Iran, than Western leaders. Moscow's insistence that the world is multipolar, and that Washington must be persuaded to accept that, ranked high among his priorities. He saw the Founding Act as a sign of progress, but made it clear that if a Baltic country was admitted to NATO the Act would be undone. In short, he summarized and confirmed things that he had been saying for many months, in a rather reactive way, in a sequence of firmly stated positions.[224]

---

[221]Davidov, " Rossiia i NATO: 'posle bala' " [Russia and NATO: "After the Ball"], *SShA,* No. 1 (Jan 1998): 3–18. Davidov, whose essay was signed to press on 6 December 1997, is an historian, a scientific associate of ISKRAN, and an academician with the RF Academy of Military Sciences. Brzezinski liked this piece; see Brzezinski, "On to Russia," *Washington Post* (5 March 1998).

[222]Kh.-I. Shpanger, "NATO na puti k pliuralisticheskomu soobshchestvu bezopasnosti?" [Is NATO on the Way to a Pluralistic Security Association?], *Mirovaia ekonomika i mezhdunarodnye otnosheniia,* No. 10 (Oct 1997): 29–35. Spanger called current reform pronouncements in NATO a "facade." Parkhalina, "O novoi arkhitekture bezopasnosti v Evrope" [On a New Architecture of Security in Europe], *Mirovaia ekonomika i mezhdunarodnye,* No. 12 (Dec 1997), 14–24.

[223]See, e.g., "Rasshirenie NATO vse idet svoim cheredom" [NATO Expansion Still Follows its Course], *Krasnaia zvezda* (18 Dec 1997); "NATO: novyi format, staroe soderzhimoe" [NATO: New Format, Old Content], *Krasnaia zvezda* (16 Dec 1997); "Kakaia Rossiia nuzhne Amerike" [What Russia Does America Need], *Nezavisimaia gazeta* (11 Dec 1997).

[224]Aleksei Pushkov, "Evgenii Primakov: 'Ya chustviiu doverie prezidenta'" [Yevgenii Primakov: "I Feel That I Have the Confidence of the President"], *Nezavisimaia gazeta* (30 Dec 1997).

No respite was offered in 1998 to anyone in Russia who might have been growing tired of the NATO question, and before the year was out Russia's government and parliament would find themselves poised to sever relationships with the Atlantic alliance over the Kosovo question (see section 2.3). In January, media reporting on the build-up to the signing, in Washington, of a U.S.-Baltic Charter (see section 5) kept the matter in the forefront of international news. Increasing apprehension that the United States might call for an air strike against Iraq also exacerbated public hostility towards NATO. Both potentials for crisis were linked in the Soviet press to Bill Clinton's domestic troubles and were interpreted as ways in which the American public's attention might be distracted from their president's libido. The military press, on the other hand, described the Pentagon's behavior as a natural outcome of its long-standing "imperialist" thinking and *Nezavisimaia gazeta* even warned that NATO's nuclear weaponry would soon be more threatening than ever to Russia.[225]

Ironically, the Baltic Charter coincided almost exactly with the anniversary of the founding of the State Duma's Anti-NATO Association, whose leaders announced on 21 January that their organization would cease to exist only when NATO gave up its plans for eastward expansion (ITAR-TASS, 21 Jan). Spokes-man Anatolii Greshnevikov informed reporters that the movement now included over 300 members, including some from the Federation Council. On the day of Greshnevikov's interview with TASS, the Voice of Russia World Service carried an English-language broadcast in which Eduard Sorokin took strong exception to Madeleine Albright's suggestion that NATO spread its influence far outside its European-Atlantic sphere. The Alliance's pressure on Central Asia and Transcaucasia through the PfP represents "creeping expansion," he said, seriously undermining the role of the UN and the OSCE in international security and conflict resolution. Sorokin concluded that Washington's insistence on widening NATO's influence was a way to keep the UN Security Council, where Russia wields a veto, out of play.[226] Thirteen months later Sorokin would have the right to say, "I told you so!" The Anti-NATO Commission came forward with a resolution that an active national plan against NATO expansion be formulated by the government. All 247 deputies present at that session (Friday, 23 January) supported the resolution. The mood of the Duma (even though it later rejected the resolution for "lack of clarity") was noted by Defense Minister Sergeev, who warned that NATO expansion was still the main obstacle against getting START II ratified (Interfax, 23 Jan).

---

[225]"Yadernoe oruzhie NATO ostalos' takim zhe groznym" [NATO's Nuclear Weapons Are Still a Threat], *Nezavisimaia gazeta* (17 Jan 1998); "Imperskoe myshlenie SShA" [The Imperial Thinking of the USA], *Krasnaia zvezda* (13 Jan 1998).
[226]Voice of Russia World Service (21 Jan 1998), FBIS-SOV, No. 022.

In fact, START II became an item again in late February when the *Nezavisimoe voennoe obozrenie* carried a long series of "pros" and "cons" to ratification. Aleksei Arbatov, deputy chairman of the Duma's Defense Committee, and Col. P.B. Romashkin, consultant to Yabloko, spoke in favor of ratification because Russia desperately needed START III. A.I. Podberezkin, deputy chairman of the Duma International Affairs Committee, and A.V. Surikov, director of data analysis in the Institute of Defense Research Center, Moscow, opposed ratification on the grounds that it would leave the United States with decisive superiority over Russia. The essays tended to be very technical, but their authors used NATO expansion to support their cases: ratify to ameliorate the danger posed by expansion; reject to stay strong in the face of expansion. A new variable was introduced in the "con" position, the China factor. A Russian-U.S. reduction in arms did not take into account the possible build up of nuclear forces in China, which could pose a far greater risk to Russia than to the United States, was a point emphasized by opponents of ratification. They called at the same time for funding priority to be given to the deteriorating Strategic Nuclear Forces (SNF) in Russia. Even they, however, asked only that ratification be delayed until the year 2000, until after Yeltsin's presidential term was up and the upgrading of Russia's SNF was complete.[227]

During an official visit to Germany at the end of January, Sergeev delivered an unusually blunt declaration against NATO expansion, telling a press conference in Rendsburg that the Alliance threatened only Russia and hinted that a deployment of a Russian-Belarusian military structure in Belarus was possible (Interfax, 29 Jan). In Bonn he said that the admission of Eastern European countries posed new problems for Russia and, while advocating compromise, made it clear that Russia had little choice but to re-think its strategic circumstances (ITAR-TASS, 28 Jan; RIA Novosti, 29 Jan). As it happened, Zyuganov was in Strasbourg at the same time as a member of a Russian delegation to the Parliamentary Assembly of the Council of Europe. His anti-expansion message, delivered also in Brussels, was much stronger than Sergeev's (ITAR-TASS, 28 Jan).

The possibility of conflict in Iraq caused many Russians to conclude that their country's opinion was still likely to be ignored when they differed from positions supported by the United States and its NATO allies. "Especially disturbing," said the communist press in mid-February, was "the willingness of the

---

[227]For these long and detailed essays, which were couched in strategic and military language rather than the usual political rhetoric, see Podberezkin and Surikov, "Dogovor, daiushchii preimushchestva SshA" [An Agreement That Gives Power to the USA]; Arbatov and Romashkin, "Ratifikatsii SNV-2 net al'ternativy" [There Is No Alternative to Ratification of START II], *Nezavisimoe voennoe obozrenie,* No. 7 (20–26 Feb 1998).

'candidate' members of NATO, the Poles, Hungarians, and Czechs, to demonstrate support for the military actions of the USA and England against Iraq." This opinion was echoed in the non-communist press.[228] A comment a few weeks later by John Lough, former NATO representative in Moscow, to the effect that deployment of nuclear weapons on the territory of new members of NATO could not be ruled out met with an angry response from the Russian ministry of foreign affairs (ITAR-TASS, 26 Feb). On that same day the usually conservative *Rossiiskaia gazeta* blasted the designated new NATO members for their "remarkable speed" in "smartly saluting the United States" on the Iraq question. Even Estonia offered to send troops, the author said with scorn. He concluded with a query: "how can one fail to fear NATO's eastward expansion" when prospective members are quicker than existing members to support America's "aggressive" policies?[229] In the meantime, Moscow tightened up its own formal association with NATO when Yeltsin appointed Sergei Kislyak ambassador to Belgium and permanent representative to NATO (Interfax, 27 Feb).[230] At home, however, Andrei Kokoshin, who had warned in 1996 that NATO expansion would force Russia to revise its foreign policy strategy (see section 2), replaced I.P. Rybkin as secretary of Russia's Security Council. Kokoshin soon had more friction to deal with.

Russia's journalists were especially angered by Albright's hardliner approach to Iraq, to the extent that a Friedman essay for the *New York Times*, "Madeleine's Folly" was translated and printed in full without comment in the Russian government's press. The essay quoted many U.S. opponents of NATO expansion, such as Jack Matlock.[231] The Iraq situation was made more ominous to Russian observers when violence broke out in Kosovo, and the United States first called for forceful action there. Concurrently, Ukraine appeared to be wavering about its potential as a NATO member. It was the escalating crisis in Kosovo that persuaded

---

[228]Safronchuk, "K visitu B. Yel'tsina v Italiiu" [On B. Yeltsin's Visit to Italy], *Sovetskaia Rossiia* (12 Feb 1998). See also Vladimir Lapskii, "Esli nazval'sia gruzdem . . ." [If It Is Called Cargo . . .], *Rossiiskaia gazeta* (14 Feb 1998).

[229]Anatolii Shapolev, "Pospeshish'—kogo nasmeshish'" [If You Hurry—Who Will Mock], *Rossiiskaia gazeta* (26 Feb 1998).

[230]Kislyak presented his credentials to Solana in Brussels on 18 March 1998, officially inaugurating Russia's permanent mission to NATO (ITAR-TASS, 18 March). On the same day, Moldovan, Romanian, Bulgarian, and Kazakh representatives opened their missions.

[231]See "Glupost' Madlen Olbrait" [The Folly of Madeleine Albright], *Rossiiskaia gazeta* (26 Feb 1998). The Russian word for "Folly" could just as easily be translated as "Stupidity," and undoubtedly was. Translated from Friedman, "Madeleine's Folly," *New York Times* (17 Feb 1998).

some Russian journalists that the Founding Act did little to prevent their country from becoming more and more isolated in matters of European security.[232]

This might explain Nemtsov's unusually harsh (for him) words about NATO expansion eastward during a tour of Germany: in Bonn he called expansion an "insanity" (ITAR-TASS, 4 March) and in Berlin he accused NATO of creating a second "iron curtain" in Europe (ITAR-TASS, 9 March). The Anti-NATO Commission rejoined the fray, complaining to Primakov on 10 March that the PJC was accomplishing nothing for Russia. The Commission pointed specifically to planned U.S.-NATO manoeuvres on the territory of Lithuania, Ukraine and Kazakhstan, asking how it was that they could take place near Russia's borders without consultation with Moscow.[233] A large scale European NATO military training exercise called Strong Resolve-98, the plan was decried by Col. Gen. Valerii Manilov, First Deputy Chief of the Russian Armed Forces, and others. Manilov objected that the exercises undermined the purpose of the Founding Act (Interfax, 13 March).[234] Vasilii Likhachev, parliamentarian responsible for foreign policy issues and international relations in the upper house, expressed anxiety that NATO was openly building up its "military might." He interpreted the training session as a sign that NATO "wants to dominate not only in Europe, but also in the world at large." Likhachev concluded that he hoped the Founding Act would ameliorate NATO's new impulse "to dictate . . . standards of behavior to the world." His tone suggested that he did not expect this to happen.[235]

Complaints such as these did not prevent Russia from cooperating with NATO on a wide front of activities. *Nezavisimoe voennoe obozrenie*, for example, published in full an address by U.S. Secretary of Defense William Cohen un-

---

[232]See, e.g., Maksim Yusin, "Kosovo: Rossiia okazalas' v izoliatsii" [Kosovo: Russia Finds Itself in Isolation], *Izvestiia* (11 March 1998).

[233]"Deputaty obespokoeny positsiei NATO" [Deputies Worried by NATO Stance], *Rossiiskaia gazeta* (7 March 1998).

[234]The purpose of the exercise was to test NATO's ability to defend against attacks on two fronts, in northern and southern Europe The northern part of the operation took place in Norway, the North Sea and Norwegian Sea; its southern dimension was a peacekeeping operation in Spain, Portugal and the Atlantic and Mediterranean Seas. Strong Resolve-98, involving 50,000 troops and officers from all NATO countries and 10 partner countries from East and East Central Europe, was set for 9–21 March.

For another strongly irritated Russian position see Vadim Markushin, "Neskol'ko zhe sil'noe 'sil'noe reshenie'?" [How Strong Is the "Strong Resolve"?], *Krasnaia zvezda* (18 March 1998).

[235]Voice of Russia World Service (19 March 1998). FBIS-SOV, No. 079. This was an English-language broadcast from Moscow; the interview was conducted by Vyacheslav Alekseev.

der the rubric "NATO Extends Stability to All of Europe." In addition to cross-fertilization under the auspices of the PJC, officials from Russia and NATO ministries of defense met in Moscow to discuss questions of military-related ecology.[236] In May, Russia agreed to participate in the Central Asian Battalion '98 (Tsentrazbat) exercises under the auspices of the PfP, joining troops from the United States, Turkey, Azerbaijan, Georgia, and the Central Asian countries of Kazakhstan, Uzbekistan and Kyrgyzstan. On 16 May it was announced that marines from the Russian Baltic Fleet would take part in a NATO manoeuvre scheduled for 18–29 May in Northern Denmark.[237] *Nezavisimaia gazeta* had noted with satisfaction in April, on its front page, that NATO was making a special effort to make Russia party to its endeavors. But, Vadim Solov'ev wrote, one should not take that to mean that Russia was going to have significant influence in the Alliance.[238] The military press was particularly gloomy in this regard.[239]

In April 1998, with the NATO expansion question clearly not laid to rest, parliamentarians from NATO and other countries joined their Russian counterparts in Moscow for a conference on "The New Security Architecture of Europe and NATO." Deputy chairman of the Duma's Security Committee, and member of the NDR, Sergei Boskholov greeted delegates with the hardened Duma position: "We are categorically against NATO expansion eastward. We are categorically against admission of the Baltic republics into the bloc." His outburst came in response to NATO's claim that a study by the Gallup Institute in Russia showed

---

[236]Vadim Markushin, "Vstrecha ekologov Rossii i NATO" [Meeting of Russian and NATO Ecologists], *Krasnaia zvezda* (2 April 1998); William Cohen, "'NATO rasprostraniaet stabil'nost' na vsiu evropu'" [NATO Extends Stability to All of Europe], *Nezavisimoe voennoe obozrenie,* No. 8 (27 Feb–5 March 1999).

[237]For the Baltic participation, see the report by Yuliia Zheglova, "Russian Marines to Participate in NATO Exercises," Voice of Russia World Service (16 May 1998). FBIS-SOV, No. 136.

[238]Vadim Solov'ev, "Moskva v ob'iat'iiakh NATO. Razrabatyvaetsia spetsial'naia programma vovlecheniia Rossii v Severoatlanticheskii soiuz" [Moscow is in the Embrace of NATO], *Nezavisimaia gazeta* (23 April 1998). See also Anatolii Kurganov, "Prodam tserkhvushku—vstupliu v NATO" [We Will Sell the Church—I will join NATO], *Rossiiskaia gazeta* (28 April 1998).

[239]See, e.g., Vladimir Kuzar, "Rasshirenie NATO—eto oshibka" [NATO Expansion Is a Mistake], *Krasnaia zvezda* (21 April 1998); Vadim Markushin, "NATO—eto uzhe ne voennyi blok" [NATO Is No Longer a Military Bloc], *Krasnaia zvezda* (23 April 1998).

that 48 percent of Russians supported NATO enlargement.[240] A NATO representative, Donald McConnell, director of the Alliance's political department, told an audience in St. Petersburg that the ties forged between NATO and Russia on the basis of the Founding Act are very important. They provide the basis for a new European security structure, which would be impossible without Russia's participation, he concluded in a report on the first year of relationships under the aegis of the Founding Act. McConnell's hopeful pronouncement passed almost unnoticed by the Russian media. The conference hosted representatives from 19 different countries and its delegates represented a wide variety of views. Duma speaker Seleznev spoke against NATO expansion towards Russia and called for a broader European security system than one represented by NATO. The Anti-NATO Commission's Baburin and Oleg Mironov both lashed out against the NATO position, as did Zyuganov and delegates from Greece and Yugoslavia. Parliamentarians from Germany, Norway and Romania took the opposite position. So the issue stirred lively debate in Moscow.[241]

In the meantime the Russian government had undergone a sweeping overhaul. On 23 March, Yeltsin, back from yet another short illness, fired his entire cabinet. Sergei Kiriyenko, 35-year-old oil and energy minister was picked to replace Chernomyrdin. Yeltsin accused his previous government of "stagnation" and practically compelled the State Duma to accept his new candidate. Confrontation between the Duma and the Presidency loomed, as Kiriyenko lost in each of the first two rounds of voting. But, on the third ballot, the communist-led offensive against the young candidate was undermined by the use of a secret ballot and the reluctance of deputies to fight the general election that another rejection would have necessitated.

New faces were brought into Cabinet, but continuity in foreign affairs was guaranteed by the immediate reappointment of Primakov and Sergeev. Political confrontation was not defused, however, for in May the State Duma initiated im-

---

[240]Interfax (2 April 1998). See also Vladimir Gerasimov in *Pravda* (21 April 1998), *op. cit.* Shortly thereafter, *Pravda* (28 March 1998) published and headlined a long interview with a former (and anonymous) British Ministry of Defense official in which Western rationalizations of the entry of former Warsaw Pact countries into NATO were challenged. The interview was conducted in London by Stanislav Menshikov, who concluded with the comment, "the West does not just want Russia to restructure on the basis of their model, but first and foremost [it wants Russia's] obedience and subordination."

[241]Interfax (3 April 1998). McConnell read from his report, "Russia and NATO: A Year after Paris." For Mironov's statement, see "Novaia arkhitektura bezopasnosti Evropy i NATO" [The New Architecture of European Security and NATO], *Krasnaia zvezda* (17 April 1998).

peachment procedures against Yeltsin, and conducted hearings on a 12-page indictment that included charges that he led a "state coup" against parliament in 1993.[242]
A wave of strikes by miners and teachers exacerbated criticism of the government,
undermining at the same time its credibility in questions of international affairs.

As more and more government spokesmen began to urge ratification of START
II in the spring of 1998, the Duma tightened up its resistance to the arms reduction agreement. A scheduled debate on ratification was postponed during the crisis over Kiriyenko's appointment. The close link between ratification and NATO
expansion had been explained anew to American think-tanks in March by
Yabloko's Aleksei Arbatov.[243] Humiliated by its inability to hold deputies in the final vote against Kiriyenko's appointment and concerned by the almost simultaneous appointment of "pro-NATO" Borys Tarasyuk as foreign minister of Ukraine,
even hard line oppositionists began to recognize the danger of losing everything
when their resistance was seen as intractable. Thus, a Duma report, issued in late
April, that did not oppose ratification so much as it urged the Russian government
to require certain concessions was received with some relief. The report, "START
II Treaty: Prospects for Ratification," recommended that Britain, France and China
be involved in the process and that "a European security system with Russia's participation, given NATO's eastward expansion," be created (Interfax, 29 April).

The U.S. Senate's ratification of NATO expansion a few days later sparked a
flurry of comments in the Russian media (see section 1.7.b), among them renewed
warnings about the potential in the second wave for a "serious and long term rift"
between Russia and NATO.[244] The sporadic Senate debate appeared headed for

---

[242]The first open Duma debate on impeachment procedures took place on 12 June,
nine days after *Sovetskaia Rossiia* (3 June 1998) carried a long list of Yeltsin's alleged
"crimes" against the state and people. Proponents claimed to have the signatures of 205
deputies in support of impeachment.

[243]Arbatov was the guest in Washington of the Center for Political and Strategic Stud-
ies, 21–27 March 1998. He gave interviews to the media, made a presentation before the
Washington Council on Foreign Relations, testified before the Senate Armed Services
Committee, and met with senators and congressmen. A summary of his opinions was dis-
tributed by the Canadian Council for International Peace and Security at a seminar,
"NATO Enlargement—The Way Ahead," Ottawa, 2 June 1998. See also Safronchuk,
"Obozrenie: Kiriyenko i NATO" [Overview: Kiriyenko and NATO], *Sovetskaia Rossiia*
(21 April 1998).

[244]See, e.g., Aleksei Pushkov, "Ten' ukhodit . . . na vostok?" [Does the Shadow Move
towards the East?], *Nezavisimaia gazeta* (6 May 1998), and his earlier "Dokumenty o
NATO peredany v senat SShA" [Documents about NATO Given to the U.S. Senate],
Izvestiia (17 Feb 1998), "NATO prodvinulos' k Moskve" [NATO Advanced towards
Moscow], *Izvestiia* (17 Feb 1998).

approval in February when the Foreign Relations Committee concluded its hearings. But the matter was lifted from the Senate calendar on 20 March as a result of domestic political squabbling. Final approval came only on 30 April (80–19), after a detailed and often emotional debate.

Watching the discussion in Washington closely, Yeltsin told his foreign ministry officials that Russia's goal was "multipolarity"; that is, a world in which no one country was in a position to dictate to the rest of the world. All signs of Moscow's decline as a major player in world affairs must be forestalled, he insisted, and again called on world leaders to utilize the UN, the OSCE, and the G-8 as vehicles for world stability. Interestingly, the speech was delivered on the same day (12 May) that *Sovetskaia Rossiia* carried a strident communist call for a Russian national liberation movement to resuscitate Russian patriotism. The Anti-NATO Commission's Glotov likewise noted that his and other groups supported the strengthening of the OSCE and UN military structures to counter a trend towards "a unipolar world" and U.S. hegemony.[245] As one might expect, Glotov's partner in the Anti-NATO Commission, Baburin, also appeared regularly in the Russian press ranting against NATO. But the extremists were not alone on the floor: more moderate observers such as Melor Sturua, an old time Soviet journalist turned visiting lecturer at the University of Wisconsin, inveighed against the folly represented by U.S. officials and journalists who assumed that Russians were indifferent to NATO expansion. Citing examples from *New York Times* editorials and Secretary of State Albright, he warned that Americans and NATO were dangerously misreading the mood in Russia.[246] This apparent consensus on world affairs was made more dramatic by the degree to which the political and ideological forces in Russian society normally are divided on everything else.[247]

By May, and thereafter for much of 1998, communists and nationalists exploited anger in the workplace (caused by the government's failure to pay wages or to sup-

---

[245]Glotov, "Evropa sama sebia obezopasit" [Europe Will Take Care of Its Own Security], *Rossiiskaia gazeta* (12 May 1998); Zyuganov, "Dukhom okrepnem v bor'be. Lefaia oppozitsiia posle aprel'skikh batalii v Dume" [We Will Strengthen Spiritually in Struggle: Left Opposition after the April Battles in the Duma], *Sovetskaia Rossiia* (12 May 1998); Yeltsin's speech was summarized at length by ITAR-TASS (12 May 1998).

[246]Sturua, "Molchalivoe pronatovskoe lobbi Rossii" [The Silent Pro-NATO Lobby in Russia], *Nezavisimaia gazeta* (14 May 1998). He referred specifically to pieces by Michael R. Gordon, "NATO Is Inching Closer, But Russians Don't Blink," *New York Times* (2 May 1998), and Thomas L. Friedman, "Ben & Jerry & NATO," *New York Times* (28 April 1998). On Baburin, see Viktoriia Ivanova, "Rasshirenie NATO bylo i ostaetsia nepriemlemym" [NATO Expansion Was and Remains Unacceptable], *Nezavisimaia gazeta* (15 May 1998).

[247]On this generally, see "Predpochtenie OBSE a ne NATO" [The Preference Is for OSCE, but Not NATO], *Rossiiskaia gazeta* (21 April 1998).

port adequately the unemployed and pensioners) to rail against the government. Yeltsin's obvious inability to resolve the country's economic ills and his "friend Bill's" sponsorship of NATO's "menacing" activity on the international arena were naturally volatile fuels to pour on this potential fire. On 19 May the Duma again decided to postpone a debate on START II previously set for 9 June, in spite of (or perhaps to spite) a plea from Yeltsin not to do so (Interfax, 19, 21 May).[248] Members of the parties headed by Zyuganov and Zhirinovskii continued to oppose ratification aggressively, prompting Yeltsin to take the matter to a meeting of the "Four" (Russia, Belarus, Kazakhstan, Kyrgyzstan). Strikes by Russia's coal miners and teachers forced START II off their agenda, however, and breathed new life into the movement to have Yeltsin impeached. In calling for Yeltsin to resign immediately, the CPRF linked the breakdown of Russia's social and economic fabric to foreign policy. Among the rallying slogans adopted by the Party were "Strengthen Russia Unity!", "No to Russia's Disarmament!", and "No to NATO Expansion!"[249] Virulent nationalist Col. Gen. Albert M. Makashov weighed in on the issue, providing readers of *Sovetskaia Rossiia* with a long list of reasons why START II should not be ratified.[250] Makashov, who gained nearly 3 million votes for president of Russia in 1991 and whom the Congress of People's Deputies appointed minister of defense during its struggle against Yeltsin in October 1993, proclaimed that ratification would help only the United States and could make Russia into little more than a colony. When, after the murder of General Lev Rokhlin in July, Makashov was elevated to a senior position

---

[248]Duma Chairman Seleznev, a proponent of ratification, pointed out that the government had not yet provided Duma with an economic feasibility study to show how the 1998 budget could provide funds for the implementation of START II if it was ratified. He, Stroev, head of the Federation Council, Kiriyenko and Yeltsin had met to discuss the matter on 20 May.

[249]"Zaiavlenie Piatogo (vneocherednogo) s'ezda Kommunisticheskoi partii Rossiiskoi Federatsii, O pozitsii partii v usloviiakh novogo obostreniia sotsial'no-ekonomicheskogo krizisa v strane" [Statement of the Fifth (Extraordinary) Congress of the Communist Party of the Russian Federation, On the Party's Position amidst the Latest Exacerbation of the Socio-economic Crisis in the Country], *Sovetskaia Rossiia* (26 May 1998). See also the 19 May People's Patriotic Union's resolution to pursue the impeachment of Yeltsin: "Prezidium NPSR postanovliaet" [Decision of the People's Patriotic Union of Russia Presidium], *Sovetskaia Rossiia* (21 May 1998), and Ivan Rodin, "V Dume nachali protseduru impichmenta prezidenta" [Procedures for the Impeachment of the President Begin in the Duma], *Nezavisimaia gazeta* (21 May 1998), where the link to NATO expansion is raised as well.

[250]For Makashov's litany, see "Petlia" [Noose], *Sovetskaia Rossiia* (26 May 1998). See also Nikolai Arinich, Viacheslav, "'Nevinnye khitrosti' generalov iz Pentagona i mudretsov iz piatoi kolonny v Rossii" [Innocent Cunning of Generals from the Pentagon and Sages from the Fifth Column in Russia], *Sovetskaia Rossiia* (4 June 1998), where the Duma was urged not to ratify START II, "this trap for our foreign policy."

with Russia's largest military political support movement (see section 3.1), his opposition to START II became more threatening to the government.

To make a very bad month even worse for Yeltsin, the U.S. Congress imposed sanctions against Russia for alleged arms deals with Iran (see section 2.2), outraging even the moderate press in Moscow. In a banner front page piece, for example, a writer for *Izvestiia* complained that Congress was "openly punishing Russia." He and others agreed that U.S. congressmen were merely ensuring successes on the part of Russia's communists and opponents of START II.[251] The Congress action came only a few days after President Clinton formally approved, in a public ceremony, the earlier Senate ratification of NATO expansion. In an accompanying address, Clinton spoke mainly of NATO as an organization for maintaining "our" security and "pursuing our vital interests," a theme that seemed to verify Russian opinion that NATO was a tool of U.S. global strategy.[252] This opinion was in the back of Duma speaker Seleznev's mind when he told a press conference on 2 June that any attempt to link the planned Clinton visit to Moscow to the debate on START II would "guarantee" its further postponement. "Russians have their pride, so when foreign presidents try to impose their dates and terms on us, we simply don't take it," he said (Interfax, 2 June). He repeated this message 10 days later at a forum of European parliament heads in Stockholm (ITAR-TASS, 12 June). Seleznev is a communist but nonetheless supports ratification of START II.

The Duma's delaying tactics notwithstanding, the Russian Security Council announced on 10 June that it had scheduled a special session of its own on START II, for 26 June. In its turn, the General Staff named 16 June (the day the Duma was supposed to open debate on the arms agreement) as the date for a conference on START II and invited Duma deputies to apply to attend. About 200 names were gathered (Interfax and ITAR-TASS, 10 June).[253]

The upsurge of interest in NATO expansion eastward flowed naturally

---

[251]Vladimir Mikheev, "Amerikanskii kongress vvodit sanktsii protiv Rossii" [American Congress Introduces Sanctions against Russia], *Izvestiia* (26 May 1998); see also *Komsomol'skaia pravda* (26 May 1998).

[252]See, e.g., Vladimir Kuzar', "NATO—instrument global'noi strategii SShA?" [Is NATO an Instrument of U.S. Global Strategy?], *Krasnaia zvezda* (22 May 1998). The White House ceremony in Washington took place on 21 May.

[253]The communist press re-opened its campaign against START II with an editorial, under the rubric of "From the Patriotic Informburo," on 2 June, that ended with a firm "No to the pro-American Treaty START II!" See "Ot patrioticheskogo informbiuro," *Sovetskaia Rossiia* (2 June 1998), signed by the editors of *Sovetskaia Rossiia* and *Zavtra*. The military press was mixed, but generally supportive of ratification; see, e.g., Vladimir Mariuzha, "SNV-2: vypolniv etot dogovor, Rossiia stanet sil'nee" [START II: Russia Will Be Stronger after It Fulfils This Agreement], *Krasnaia zvezda* (16 June 1998).

from a media tendency to look back at the first full year of the Founding Act. Preparing for expected fanfare, a spokesman for Yeltsin reminded a RIA-Novosti Roundtable on 22 May that his government was unequivocally opposed to NATO membership for any former USSR republic, saying again that any such action would force Moscow to revise the Founding Act. He noted that the West was fully aware of Moscow's position and hinted darkly that Russia had "a broad range of partners" other than NATO to which it could turn.[254] A Solana speech delivered on 27 May 1998, in which the previous year of Russia-NATO cooperation was described as one of great fulfilment, was reported in the Russian press, but with little enthusiasm.[255] Indeed, there were very few words of celebration and the general opinion resembled one carried in the *Nezavisimoe voennoe obozrenie* on 28 May. Its author, Vadim Solov'ev, said that Russians signed the Founding Act to gain certain guarantees: no nuclear weapons or substantial combat forces on the territory of new NATO members, and wide-ranging consultation between NATO and Russia. He was convinced, after a year, that no such guarantees were actually in place. Solov'ev acknowledged that much had been accomplished, even if inadvertently: Russia had a greater degree of military cooperation with European countries and NATO than it had had a year ago; regional security structures were now resisting NATO's dominant role on the continent, and Europe was aspiring to solve its own security problems. So changes for the better had taken place, even if they had not been planned at the time of the Founding Act.[256] Even uninspired optimism such as that shown by Solov'ev was rare. The overall disposition was better represented by a writer for *Izvestiia* who protested that even though Russians now had NATO forums in which to present their perspective, such as the Parliamentary Assembly, they were ignored or misunderstood.[257]

---

[254]This oft-repeated approach was delivered by Sergei Yastrzhembskii with unusual forcefulness. See Interfax, 22 May 1997.

[255]See, e.g., "Khav'er Solana ob otnosheniiakh Rossiia-NATO" [Javier Solana on Russia-NATO Relations], *Krasnaia zvezda* (27 May 1998); Leonid Ivanov, "Rossiia-NATO: tseli prodeklarirovany" [Russia-NATO: The Aims Are Proclaimed], *Nezavisimaia gazeta* (27 May 1998); Solana, "NATO i Rossiia—na poroge XXI veka" [NATO and Russia, on the Threshold of the 21st Century], *Izvestiia* (28 May 1998).

[256]Solov'ev, "Russia-NATO Founding Act Is One Year Old," *Nezavisimoe voennoe obozrenie* (29 May–4 June 1998), FBIS-SOV, No. 155. The piece was signed to press 28 May 1998.

[257]Vladimir Vernikov, "V Barselone my zaiavili i nashikh opaseniiakh, no i na Severoatlanticheskoi assamblee nas ne poniali" [We Expressed Our Fears in Barcelona, but the North Atlantic Assembly Did Not Understand Us], *Izvestiia* (28 May 1998). See also a later piece by Lt. Gen. Aleksandr Voronin, member of the Duma's Committee for Defense and Security, who wrote that Russia heard nothing new at the 44th session of the NATO Parliamentary Assembly in Barcelona and urged that the NATO organization implement the Founding Act, *Pravda* (20 June 1998).

It was obvious in the spring of 1997 that Russian authorities still hoped that NATO expansion might be derailed by one of its original 16 members. A meeting of the Russo-French Inter-Parliamentary Commission was opened by Seleznev with a statement that Russia was "still negative on the spread of NATO." His ambition was to persuade French parliamentarians not to ratify the new membership when it came to the French Assembly two days later. The head of Russia's parliament pulled no punches, calling the expansion a "historic mistake" and warning his audience that if the Baltic countries joined "our revision of relations with NATO will be inevitable."[258] The most revealing sign of Russia's feeling about the anniversary of the Founding Act, however, came on 15 June when the Duma passed a decree formally approving the activities of the Anti-NATO Commission. Urging the Commission to "continue the work it has started," the decree instructed its members to consult with Anti-NATO associations in the Ukrainian and Belarus legislatures and begin preparation for another conference on "The New Security Architecture of Europe and NATO" for 1999.[259] Statements issued by Russia's defense ministry called a NATO training exercise scheduled for the Black Sea in June, a "threat" to Russia's national security and implied that NATO had lied to Russia about its activity in Kosovo. Not much had changed since the Founding Act was signed.[260]

Interestingly, the crisis in Kosovo (see section 2.3) prompted Russian defense officials to seek closer involvement with NATO on matters related to European security. General Leonid Ivashov became a leading spokesman for what amounted to a new strategic direction. On several occasions he said that mutual suspicions had diminished since the PJC had begun to operate seriously. Russia's posting of a military envoy to NATO had helped make the PJC function and the position should not be left derelict because of Kosovo, he said, warning at the same time that forces who wished a return to the Cold War still existed (e.g., ITAR-TASS, 23 June). Public statements by NATO's Solana in July intimated that the Alliance

---

[258]ITAR-TASS (8 June 1998). The 4th Grand Russo-French Inter-Parliamentary Commission met in St. Petersburg on 8 June.

[259]"V Gosudarstvennoi Dume. Arkhitektura bezopasnosti" [In the State Duma: Architecture of Security], *Rossiiskaia gazeta* (16 June 1998). On 12 June Seleznev announced that the Anti-NATO Association included over 200 Duma deputies (ITAR-TASS, 12 June 1998).

[260]For the comment about Kosovo and a reiteration of Russia's strong opposition to NATO expansion eastward as a "serious threat to Russia" by chief of the Department of International Military Cooperation, Gen. Leonid Ivashov, see ITAR-TASS (19 June 1998); on the Black Sea Exercise, Cooperative Neighbor '98 (14–27 June), which included forces from the United States, Germany, the Netherlands, Turkey, Greece, Italy, Spain, Ukraine, Georgia, Romania and Bulgaria; see separate ITAR-TASS release (19 June 1998).

was aware of the need to strengthen ties with Russia. He too was encouraged by the degree of cooperation that had grown out of bilateral discussion at the PJC.[261]

1.9. A New Cold War?

Elsewhere, however, Ivashov had written that Russia's defense establishment was worried about NATO's "double standards" in the Kosovo affair. Ivashov continued to believe that favorable trends had taken place since the Founding Act, yet blamed the Alliance for playing "European policeman" at the expense of the UN. He cautioned that a new Cold War in Europe would inevitably follow if NATO undertook "strong-arm actions without support of the [UN] Security Council." Ivashov's position was strongly supported by contributors to *Krasnaia zvezda,* where he was lauded for saying that the real problem lay with the Alliance's tendency "to take for itself the right to act outside of international laws and the UN Security Council."[262] This was exactly the objection on every Russian commentator's lips four months later as NATO planes were poised for air strikes against Serbs.

Georgi Arbatov raised the possibility of a new Cold War as a result of indifference in the West to Russia's interests. Neither he nor Ivashov pretended that Russia was blameless in the state of affairs that saw a potentially good East-West relationship sliding out of their mutual grasps. They were convinced, though, that NATO's new aggressiveness had, as Arbatov put it, "an especially bad influence on the relationship of the Russian public to the West."[263]

Talk of a new Cold War from prominent and experienced analysts such as these were the result of soul-searching reevaluations of the directions in which Russia appeared to be heading in the troubled spring of 1998. In this regard, careful rethinking of Russia's strategic relationship with the West generally and the United

---

[261]Solana spoke to a press conference at the National Press Club in Washington, 16 July 1998. He was in the U.S. capital to discuss Russia-NATO relations with the U.S. Administration. ITAR-TASS (16 July 1998).

[262]Cited in Yurii Pankov, "Vremia sverit' pozitsii" [It Is Time to Collate Positions], *Krasnaia zvezda* (14 July 1998). For Ivashov's earlier statements, "NATO Double Standards Worry Moscow: Russian Defense Minister Advances Alternative Ways to Ensure International Security," *Nezavisimoe voennoe obozrenie* (26 June–2 July 1998), FBIS-SOV, No. 182. For a strongly supportive discussion of Ivashov's recommendations, see Pankov, "Rossiia- NATO: Shag vpered, dva shaga nazad" [Russia-NATO: One Step Forward, Two Steps Backward], *Krasnaia zvezda* (20 June 1998).

[263]Arbatov, "'Kholodnaia voina' snova mozhet stat' real'nost'iu" [A Cold War Can Again Become a Reality], *Nezavisimaia gazeta* (17 June 1998). Arbatov was addressing a meeting at ISKRAN, which was celebrating his 75th birthday.

States in particular had been initiated by two of Russia's leading political "liberals": Georgi Arbatov's son Aleksei and Grigorii Yavlinskii.

Yavlinskii wrote in *Foreign Affairs,* a journal aimed at the American foreign policy elite, on the enormous problems and idiosyncracies of Russia's "phony capitalism." Musing prophetically about the almost insurmountable problems faced by Russia's economic and political planners, he criticized Western leaders for their "two-faced" habit of praising developments under Yeltsin when they knew they were not working. Indeed, the "most important message of NATO expansion for Russians . . . is that political leaders of Western Europe and the United States do not believe that Russia can become a real Western-style democracy within the next decade or so."[264] Aleksei Arbatov's audience was Russian. In a very long two-part treatise on "The National Idea and National Security," he blamed the United States and NATO expansion for "an ever greater split in relations between Russia and the West." Like Ivashov and Georgi Arbatov, he urged Russia to look to Europe for its main political, economic and military partnerships, but condemned the United States for treating his country as a defeated power. NATO was the wellspring of what had gone wrong: "NATO's expansion to the east, [was] undoubtedly a turning point in relations between Russia and the West in the post Cold War period," he said, noting that NATO's policy had led to "broad agreement" in Russia that the Alliance had violated "accepted rules" under which the Cold War had ended.[265]

All the standard complaints of the previous year boiled over into what purported to be a long philosophical colloquy on the "Russian Idea," set in centuries of Russian history. Broken promises alleged to have been made to Russia when Germany was reunified were brought up again. The West was called "arrogant" and indifferent to Russia's interests; American leaders were willing to solve their domestic problems at Russia's expense. Duma resistance to ratifying START II, increased Russian anti-West nationalism, a reorientation towards China, Iran and India, and (partly because of the need for military expenditures) continued economic decline in Russia were among the dire consequences of NATO expansion raised once again by Arbatov.

Arbatov provided but one of the more thoughtful new (or resurrected) theses on Russia's future and its national ideals, only a few of which focus specifically on

---

[264]Yavlinskii, "Russia's Phony Capitalism," *Foreign Affairs* (May/June 1998), 67–79.

[265]Aleksei Arbatov, "Natsional'naia ideia i natsional'naia bezopasnost'" [The National Idea and National Security], *Mirovaia ekonomika i mezhdunarodnye otnosheniia* , No. 5 (May 1998): 5–21; No. 6 (June 1998): 5–19. The second part was rife with commentary on NATO.

NATO. Indeed, contemplation of the "Russian Idea" has become increasingly com-
monplace since the fall of Marxism-Leninism. Neo-communist and nationalist
thinkers have used the concept to provide Russians with a sense of uniqueness and
purpose, often explained in anti-Western syllogisms. Extremists quickly turn such
views into xenophobic and messianic diatribe; liberals, such as Arbatov, avoid the
extreme but suggest that Western values and institutions might fit uncomfortably
in the Russian context. In short, the nineteenth-century debate among Russian
thinkers about the relative worth of Russian and Western cultures—Slavophile vs.
Westernizer—is back in Russian intellectual and political circles. For "Westernizer,"
however, one can now read "Pro-American."[266]

The NATO question is peripheral to the philosophizing side of the debate, but
often is seen as a symptom of Western distrust of Russia's character. Commentator
Igor Maksimychev wrote in June that NATO expansion to the east had been the
greatest obstacle in the way of greater Russian integration with Europe. The NATO
question took up so much diplomatic energy that it obscured such important issues
as expanding the mandate of the OSCE, Russian admission to the EU, and even the
notion of any other basis for European security. Calling this phenomenon a "Cold
War by other means," Maksimychev alerted readers that Europe would not have
time to unite before NATO came to dominate it.[267] His opinion was echoed in
Izvestiia by Stanislav Kondrashov, who complained that the United States now acted
very cautiously, even weakly, when faced with regional conflicts, unless there was a
possibility that Russia might become involved. In that case, Kondrashov said, a
"double standard" would immediately apply and the United States would rush into
the fray.[268] According to both tradition and proponents of the newly reformulated
"Russian Idea," a compulsion to isolate Russia had been the natural inclination of
Western powers most often harped upon by Nikolai Danilevskii and the panslavists of the 19th century. Late in 1998 the Communists came up with a strange
new mix for the "Russian Idea." They called for "Spirituality, Justice, Statehood, Peo-

---

[266]For an interesting case in point, one should read carefully the "debate" between
Georgii Mirskii, head researcher at IMEMO, and Aleksei Vasiliev, on Russia, the United
States, and the Iraq crisis: Vasiliev, "Uroki Irakskogo krizisa" [Lessons of the Iraq Crisis],
Nezavisimaia gazeta (25 March 1998); Mirskii, "O postsovetskom antiamerikanizme"
[On Post-Soviet Anti-Americanism], *Nezavisimaia gazeta* (10 April 1998).

[267]Maksimychev, "Uspeet li Evropa stat' edinoi?" [Will Europe Have Enough Time to
Become United?], *Nezavisimaia gazeta* (9 June 1998).

[268]Kondrashov, "Amerika uchitsia skromnosti, no Rossii o etogo ne legche" [America
Learns Modesty, But This Doesn't Make It Easier for Russia], *Izvestiia* (23 June 1998). See
also "Vozmozhen li kompromis?" [Is a Compromise Possible?], *Nezavisimaia gazeta* (22
July 1998), where the United States is again accused of applying "double standards" in international affairs.

ple's Power, and Patriotism" in a Manifesto announced by Zyuganov on 24 November. The new rallying cry for the People's Patriotic Union, a coalition led by the CPRF, included condemnation of the "military-political bloc NATO, standing on guard for the 'gold billionaires,' dooming the rest of the population of the planet to vegetation and poverty."[269]

Searching for a new identity for Russia was one thing; dealing directly with the NATO question was another. By July, Aleksei Arbatov and others already were recommending that Russia's relationship with NATO be thoroughly re-examined.[270] At least one Russian journalist pointed out that the level of her country's military cooperation with NATO was very slight anyway. Quoting SHAPE Commander General Wesley K. Clark's remark in Russia that the relationship "cannot be called strengthened" and Jessie Helm's pleasure at the fact that Russia had no veto over any military decision of NATO, Marina Nesterova suggested that the Founding Act was by no means a guarantee of peace in Europe.[271]

Viacheslav Dashichev had rejoined the discussion in June with a long piece on traditional foundations of Russia's national security, which he thought were being sabotaged. Using the historical context, as Aleksei Arbatov had done, Dashichev worried that Russia's very existence as an independent country was now at risk. Russia must be oriented towards Europe, he said, and resist strenuously America's "absolute weapon," money, or the United States would gain hegemony "without war." NATO was described by Dashichev, using old Soviet style rhetoric, as a "platform" for U.S. rule in Eurasia. In contrast to Soviet-era diatribes against the West, Dashichev found culpable villains within Russia itself: Yeltsin and his government

---

[269]"Manifest NPSP" [Manifesto of the People's Patriotic Union of Russia], *Sovetskaia Rossiia* (24 Nov 1998).

[270]Arbatov, "Pora nachat' 'perenaladku' otnoshenii" [It's Time to Begin the "Re-adjustment" of the Relationship], *Nezavisimaia gazeta* (21 July 1998); see also Yurii Pankov, "Rossiia i zapad poka govoriat na raznykh yazykakh" [Russia and the West Still Speak Different Languages], *Krasnaia zvezda* (10 July 1998); "Vremia sverits pozitsii" [It Is Time to Collate Positions], *Krasnaia zvezda* (14 July 1998); Aleksandr Bovin, "NATO delaet oshibku, rasshiriaias' na vostok" [NATO Makes a Mistake by Expanding to the East], *Izvestiia* (14 July 1998); Vadim Solov'ev, "Opaseniia Moskvy vyzvannye rasshireniem NATO, poniatny" [Moscow's Fear Provoked by NATO Expansion Is Understandable], *Nezavisimaia gazeta* (21 July 1998).

[271]Nesterova, "NATO-Rossiia: Razgovor lukavogo s ubogim" [Conversation of the Cunning with the Miserable], *Nezavisimaia gazeta* (2 July 1998). SHAPE is the NATO School in Oberammergau, Germany. See also Yurii Yershav, "U iubiliarov krysha poekhala?" [Did the Anniversary Celebrants Raise the Roof?], *Rossiiskaia gazeta* (29 July 1998), who ridiculed Solana's celebration of NATO as the guarantor of peace and security in Europe, and called NATO "archaic" and itself a means for conflict in Europe.

for relying so heavily on the United States, and Russia's new financial tycoons for making the economy vulnerable to Western inroads.[272] In this opinion, he concurred with Aleksei Arbatov and Yavlinskii.

At about the same time a new policy thesis was published by Moscow's Council for Foreign and Defense Policy. In the earlier thesis, published in 1994, the Council had warned that Russia's international position would be weakened if a "decision was made to expand NATO that would exclude Russia." In its more recent effort, the Council said little about NATO *per se,* but noted that expansion had consumed too much diplomatic energy. Moscow needed to use its resources more fruitfully, strengthening the CIS, for example, because the PJC was little more than a "discussion club."[273] A military observer also admonished that it was naive to think that NATO and Russia had been drawing closer since the Founding Act. Russia could never fully agree to NATO moving closer to its borders, Vadim Markushin insisted in *Krasnaia zvezda,* because NATO continued to "ignore" Russia's opinions on all questions related to European security. Giving up on military togetherness as futile, another writer advocated, at some length, that Russia concentrate on non-military activities with NATO.[274]

All these opinions had been heard before, many times, but it is worth noting that they were re-surfacing with greater frequency and in greater detail as Russia's economic and political structures teetered on the brink of collapse. The upsurge of calls in Moscow for a revaluation of Russia's relationships with NATO showed what little faith the mainstream press had in reassuring blandishments offered in July by a cross section of European foreign and defense ministers.[275]

---

[272]Dashichev, "Istoriia razrusheniia osnov natsional'noi bezopasnosti strany" [The History of the Destruction of the Basis of the Country's National Security], *Nezavisimaia gazeta* (10 June 1998), *Tsenarii,* No. 6.

[273]"Strategiia Rossii v XXI veke: analiz situatsii i nekotorye predlozheniia (strategiia-3)" [Russian Strategy in the 21st Century: An Analysis of the Situation and Several Recommendations (Strategy-3)], *Nezavisimaia gazeta* (18, 19 June 1998). A translation of the 1994 Strategy (No. 2) can be found in *REDA 1994,* Vol. 1.

[274]Boris Khaloma, "Novaia napravlenie otnoshenii Rossiia-NATO" [New Direction in Russia-NATO Relations], *Nezavisimaia gazeta* (6 Aug 1998); Vadim Markushin, "Rossiia-NATO: Partnerstvo na distantsii" [Russia-NATO: Partners at a Distance], *Krasnaia zvezda* (18 June 1998).

[275]See, e.g., in a series of interviews with defense ministers from Germany, the United Kingdom, and Italy: Vadim Solov'ev, "Opaseniia Rossii neobosnovanny" [Russian Fears are Groundless], (Klaus Kinkel), *Nezavisimaia gazeta* (24 July 1998); Vadim Solov'ev, ""Britanskim i Rossiiskim voennym nuzhno rabotat' vmeste" [British and Russian Troops Need to Work Together], (George Robertson), *Nezavisimaia gazeta* (25 July 1998); Sergei Startsev, "Sudstrategicheskii iadernyi potentsial RF v 20 raz vyshe NATOvskogo" [The Substrategic Nuclear Potential of the RF is 20 Times Higher Than NATO's], (Italian minister of defense), *Nezavisimaia gazeta* (29 July 1998).

Moreover, a very bitterly fought victory for the Italian prime minister, Romano Prodi, who normally relied on communist support for his majority, saw the parliament in Rome approve NATO expansion. Thus a faint hope in Moscow that a NATO country might halt expansion was delivered a final blow in late June. Talk of neutral Austria joining NATO helped raise the level of suspicion in Russia.[276]

All eyes turned to internal affairs in August, as the ruble collapsed and huge foreign and domestic debts threatened to put an end to market reform. On 24 August, Yeltsin dismissed Kiriyenko and his entire cabinet and invited Chernomyrdin back to form a new government. Shortly thereafter Chubais was fired and Nemtsov resigned, as did the head of the Central Bank. The "young reformers" were gone. Yeltsin agreed to transfer some of his powers to Chernomyrdin, but was thwarted when his nominee for prime minister was rejected twice in the Duma. This time, Yeltsin did not risk a third failure and settled on Yevgenii Primakov as a compromise candidate. The State Duma accepted him as prime minister by a 317–63 vote.

The economic situation was such that all political groups in Russia promised, or warned of, social upheaval, so foreign policy issues were moved to the sidelines and the foreign ministry struggled to maintain a bold, "hold the fort" front in international affairs. A familiar confluence of "Russian Idea" and national security was reached when a presidential aide used the term "red line" in reference to an area into which Russia "cannot allow NATO expansion," that is, former Soviet republics (ITAR-TASS, 18 Aug).

That a new day was dawning was clear to ISKRAN's Rogov, who on 1 September again urged that both "sides" be guided by pragmatism and not by emotion.[277] A week or so later, Yeltsin began to relinquish some of the presidential powers to the State Duma, ensuring that anti-NATO viewpoints held greater sway than ever

---

[276]See, e.g., Maksim Turilov, "Idet razmyvanie Avstriiskogo neitraliteta" [Austrian Neutrality Is Being Washed Away], *Nezavisimaia gazeta* (28 July 1998); Yevgenii Grishin, "Shiussel' sobralsia v NATO. A Avstriia tuda ne khochet" [(Wolfgang) Schussel Wishes to Join NATO: But Austria Does Not Want To], *Rossiiskaia gazeta* (5 August 1998).

On Moscow's hope that Italy would reject expansion, see "NATO—von iz Italii!" [NATO, Get Out of Italy!"], *Nezavisimaia gazeta* (6 Feb 1998), and Sergei Startsev, "Rim konfliktuet s soiuznikami" [Rome Argues with its Allies], *Nezavisimaia gazeta* (4 March 1998). For commentary on Italy's decision to ratify, Startsev, "Parlament Italii odobriia rasshirenie NATO" [The Italian Parliament Approves NATO Expansion], *Nezavisimaia gazeta* (25 June 1998).

[277]Sergei Rogov, "Rossiia-SShA. Novaia povestka dnia" [Russia-USA: New Order of the Day], *Nezavisimaia gazeta* (1 Sept 1998).

within government circles. With the ratification of Primakov as prime minister on 11 September, consistent government antagonists of NATO expansion moved up. Igor Ivanov was approved as the new foreign minister and A.A. Avdeev, an especially vocal opponent of NATO expansion to include the Baltic states (see Section 5), was appointed first deputy foreign minister. N.N. Afanas'evskii was posted to Paris as ambassador.[278]

The Kosovo affair served as a rallying point in Moscow. As NATO's repeated threats of air strikes against the Serbs seemed more and more likely to be acted upon in early October, disparate political forces in Russia were thrown together once again. On this issue, Duma committee heads Lukin and Ilyukhin, usually adversaries, spoke as one; the former urged the government to "resolutely resist" NATO's aggression, the latter called for Russian aid to Slobodan Milosevic, even to supplying him with "anti-missile complexes" (Interfax, 5 Oct). The Duma as a whole adopted a resolution calling air strikes against Yugoslavia "illegal" and warned that all existing agreements between Russia and NATO were about to be revisited (Interfax, 2 Oct). A senior defense ministry official told Interfax that the public and the Duma would demand "an immediate severing of relations and the country's withdrawal from the Russia-NATO Founding Act" if Yugoslavia was attacked (Interfax, 2 Oct). Every faction in the Duma supported the resolution and another, similar, motion was approved on 14 October. The Russian government issued an official expression of "profound anxiety" over Kosovo and insisted that military action without UN sanction would be a "crude violation of the UN Charter" (ITAR-TASS, 4 Oct). Ivanov again flew to Belgrade, now as foreign minister, hoping to persuade Milosevic to act more moderately.[279] The press was filled with gloomy forecasts, and talk of a new Cold War grew louder—a "hot" war was foreseen by some.[280] Russia's

---

[278]For a long explication of the new ministry's position on NATO, Kosovo and other world events, see a radio interview with V.O. Rakhmanin, head of the press and information department of the ministry. Radiostantsiia Ekho Moskvy (1 Oct 1998), FBIS-SOV, No. 274. On the Avdeev appointment, see ITAR-TASS (15 Oct 1998).

[279]Yuliia Petrovskaia, "Ivanov vnov' govoril s Milosovichem" [Ivanov Again Spoke to Milosevic], *Nezavisimaia gazeta* (9 Oct 1998); Vladimir Mikheev, "Belgrad vozlagaet nadezhdy na Moskva" [Belgrade Places Its Hopes on Moscow], *Izvestiia* (8 Oct 1998).

[280] Typical was Yuliia Berezovskaia, "Konflikt v Kosovo grozit 'kholodnoi voinoi'" [The Conflict in Kosovo Threatens a Cold War], *Izvestiia* (7 Oct 1998). See also Anatolii Shapovalov, "Serbiia —s mirom, al'ians—s bombami" [Serbia with Peace, Alliance with Bombs], *Rossiiskaia gazeta* (3 Oct 1998), who accused the West of applying "double standards" to Yugoslavia, and quoted Seleznev to the effect that the Duma might "initiate the annulment of the Treaty with the Alliance." Nikolai Paklin, "Zapadnye strategi bespokoiatsia o zhizn' tol'ko svoikh letchikov" [Western Strategists Worried About the Loss of their Own Pilots Only], *Rossiiskaia gazeta* (10 Oct 1998). For much more on this, see Section 2.3.

ambassador and military representative to NATO, Kislyak and Lt. Gen. V. Zavarzin, were recalled to Moscow "for consultations."

Ivanov promptly raised the notion of an inviolable "red line" to near doctrinal status. Speaking to Spanish reporters in Moscow, on 8 October, he said: "There is a red line which we regard as a cardinal change directly related to our security. This line goes along the border of the former Soviet Union, including the Baltic states. If matters come to this, we will have to fully revise our political relations with the North Atlantic alliance, which we do not want to do, because we favor the continuation of cooperation" (Interfax, 8 Oct 1998).

NATO stood down on 13 October after a tenuous agreement was reached between U.S. envoy Richard Holbrooke and Milosevic. Kislyak and Zavarzin returned to Brussels two days later. Moscow, whose part in the settlement passed virtually unnoticed in the West, learned a very grave lesson: its veto power on the UN Security Council could be bypassed by NATO.[281] A contributor to *Nezavisimoe voennoe obozrenie* charged that NATO was fully prepared to intervene in regional conflicts anywhere in the world with or without a mandate from the United Nations.[282] Resentful Russian media commentators showed how fragile the links between Russia and the North Atlantic Alliance had become. They pondered what might happen if the Kremlin cracked down again on separatist movements in Chechnya, or elsewhere in the Russian Federation—would NATO then bomb Russia? Many commentators returned to the argument that Russia was being pushed out of Europe. The possibility that NATO would bomb the territory of any independent state to defend the rights of an ethnic minority was a chilling idea to Russian nationalists.[283]

There were other signals of the seriousness with which Moscow was taking the foreign affairs crisis. On 2 October, the State Duma ratified two military agreements with Belarus and, two weeks later, defense ministers from the two countries strengthened their military ties precisely because of NATO expansion and the threat of military action against Yugoslavia. Several Duma deputies and the defense ministry officials noted above said that air strikes would doom the ratification of START II.

---

[281]A week prior to NATO's decision to use force, the Russia press audience had been told that the UN Security Council had agreed with Moscow that negotiations must be restarted. See, e.g., Yurii Pankov, "SB OON soglasilsia s pozitsiei Rossii" [The UN Security Council Agrees with the Russian Position], *Krasnaia zvezda* (8 Oct 1998).

[282]Igor Korotchenko, "Global'naia zaiavka severoatlanticheskogo al'iansa" [Global Claims by the North Atlantic Alliance], *Nezavisimoe voennoe obozrenie,* No. 40 (23–29 Oct 1998).

[283] See, e.g., Vladimir Mikheev, "NATO bombombit serbov i bez soglasiia OON" [NATO Bombs the Serbs and without the Agreement of the UN], *Izvestiia* (2 Oct 1998), and *Nezavisimaia gazeta* (14 Oct 1998).

Recommendations that Moscow ignore the arms embargo against Yugoslavia and begin shipping weapons to Belgrade were made openly. To some observers the concept of a new Cold War had changed from an angry fantasy to a cold likelihood.

As the sound and fury over Kosovo echoed throughout Russia, Madeleine Albright delivered a speech to the Russian-American Business Cooperation Council, in Chicago, on 2 October. *Nezavisimaia gazeta* published the address verbatim on the 16th and the outcry against America intensified. Her criticisms of Primakov's regulatory anti-crisis measures and her insistence that economic aid be tied to Russia's commitment to market reform and "democratic values" infuriated the communists and their like thinking associates. Some observers connected Primakov's lack of success in negotiating the release of the 4.3 billion (U.S.) promised to the Kiriyenko government by the IMF in June directly to Albright's intervention. The phrase "Doctrine of Interference" came into common use to describe Albright's policy towards Russia and illustrated the degree to which Primakov's Moscow was pulling away from the association with the United States so relied upon by Yeltsin's previous governments.[284]

The foreign ministry's worry about Albright's standpoint was reflected in a long and thoughtful interview granted by Ivanov to *Izvestiia*. Among the burning question for which he said resolution must be found were: the role of the OSCE as an instrument for European security; the limits to NATO expansion (naming the Baltic States and Ukraine as areas to exclude); the role of the UN Security Council in international conflict resolution; and the degree to which Russia could expect to participate in international decision-making.[285]

The American Secretary of State was, in reality, questioning Primakov's hastily adopted anti-crisis measures, which called for a "Russian way" out of the economic mess: increasing government subsidies, printing more money and stiffening controls over banks, all steps that made the IMF reluctant to pour more funds into Russia. During the next few weeks the Russian position hardened up in several directions. Seleznev threatened to lead the Duma into disavowing the Founding Act if force was used against Yugoslavia (Interfax, 14 Oct). Luzhkov

---

[284]V. Tetekin, "Doktrina vmeshatel'stva. Gospozha Olbreit v plenu illiuzii" [Doctrine of Interference: Mrs. Albright in the Grip of Illusions], *Sovetskaia Rossiia* (31 Oct 1998). See also, Safronchuk, "Amerika pouchaet, strashchaet i oskorbliaet. Replika po povodu vystuplenii g-zhi Olbrait" [America Lectures, Threatens and Insults: Rejoinder to Mrs. Albright's remarks], *Sovetskaia Rossiia* (24 Oct 1998). The original Russian version of Albright's speech appeared, in a full page without commentary, as "Zadacha SShA—pravliat' posledstviiami raspada sovetskoi imperii" [The Tasks of the USA Are to Control the Consequences of the Collapse of the Soviet Empire], *Nezavisimaia gazeta* (16 Oct 1998).

[285]"Igor Ivanov" [Igor Ivanov], *Izvestiia* (28 Oct 1998).

warned that a third world war was imminent (ITAR-TASS, 6 Nov), and the Duma again postponed debate on ratifying START II (Interfax, 8 Dec). The popular Mayor of Moscow, openly setting out on a campaign for the Russian presidency, claimed that the West was using Yugoslavia as a training ground for possible "measures" against Russia. Pronouncements such as these were symptomatic of the deep cloud of distrust, apprehension, and confusion that seemed to have settled down over Moscow.[286] Even S.M. Rogov warned, in November, that the connection between the United States and Russia's reform program had broken down, and that there was dangerously little understanding of Russia in Washington.[287]

Late November and early December saw musings in Russia on a wide range of NATO related matters: tentative discussion by the EU, in Rome, of European defense systems without NATO and the United States; Canadian and German suggestions that NATO reconsider its long standing commitment to first strike[288]; further delays in ratification of START II (Interfax, 10 Dec), and admonitions from foreign minister Ivanov that NATO's ambitions for "global power" were "extremely dangerous" (Interfax, 10 Dec).[289] In the latter case, Ivanov was supported by the new head of the Duma's Defense Committee, Roman Popkovich, who told reporters in Washington that if NATO decided to expand its "zone of responsibility," Russia might be prompted to revise its own defense doctrine (ITAR-TASS, 12 Dec). Presumably this warning was greeted in the West as yet another hollow threat from Moscow, but the cumulative weight of such warnings was growing. Russian analysts took comfort at the apparent discord within NATO, especially over the question of first strike and increasing mutterings about a European army and the

---

[286]Luzhkov's charges were especially chilling. He made them after meeting with the leader of the Serbian Radical Party, Vojislav Seselj, in Moscow.

[287]*Segodnia* (12 Nov 1998), excerpts translated for the *Current Digest of Post-Soviet Press* 50, No. 45 (1998): 19–20. See also Rogov's, "Russia and the United States: Test by Crisis," *International Affairs* (Moscow), No. 5 (1998): 1–17.

[288]See, e.g., Nikolai Paklin, "Evropeiskaia oborona. No bez NATO" [European Defense. But Without NATO], *Rossiiskaia gazeta* (1 Dec 1998); "Yadernaia strategiia NATO sokhranit'sia" [NATO's Nuclear Strategy Will Be Preserved], *Krasnaia zvezda* (26 Nov 1998); Yurii Yershov, "Bei pervoi, NATO?" [Be First, NATO?], *Rossiiskaia gazeta* (3 Dec 1998).

[289]See also "NATO tesno v Evrope i Atlantike" [NATO Is Cramped in Europe and the Atlantic], *Izvestiia* (6 Nov 1998); "Rossiia v karantine" [Russia Is in Quarantine], *Izvestiia* (24 Nov 1998).

West European Union.[290] And then came the American and British air strikes against Iraq, an event that, according to even the most neutral observers, raised anti-Americanism in Russia to a level not seen since the height of the Cold War.[291]

The Russian media was filled with such outrage that only a few examples are needed here as illustration. The United States and Britain were referred to as self-styled "Lords of the World," their joint action was termed "barbaric," "savage," and "inhumane." *Komsomol'skaia pravda* (18 Dec) called the bombing campaign an attack on Russia; and *Rossiiskaia gazeta* (18 Dec) claimed that it showed a "lack of respect for Russia." Primakov and the media were very angry that the UN Security Council was not consulted,[292] and disparate individuals such as Yavlinskii, Luzhkov, Seleznev, Lukin, Berezovskii, Zhirinovskii, Zyuganov and, of course, Yeltsin, all vigorously condemned the air strikes. Clinton's problems at home were said by almost every commentator to be the driving force behind Washington's decision to attack.

In a reflective piece published at the end of the year, Vadim Solov'ev called again for a full reevaluation of Russia's place in the world. The "surprise" attack on Iraq was merely another sign that Russia's weakness meant that its opinions would not be considered in world affairs. He mused about Russia's options, finding, for example, that Primakov's recently proposed strategic alignment with India and China (see sections 2, 2.1) lacked promise. Russia would have to accept that "Washington [would] maintain the new world order" and that Moscow's influence on the major Western Powers and NATO was very slight—for the time being.[293]

Russian analysts believed, or claimed to believe, that their country had played by the rules, offering NATO cooperation and joint security programs. But their

---

[290]Nikolai Paklin, "Evropeiskaia oborona, no bez NATO" [European Defense, but without NATO], *Rossiiskaia gazeta* (1 Dec 1998); Igor Maksimychev, "Na kogo natselen pervoi iadernyi udar NATO?" [Against Whom Is NATO's Nuclear First Strike Aimed?], *Nezavisimaia gazeta* (8 Dec 1998); Vadim Markushin, "NATO: pro pokazhet iubileinyi aprel'" [NATO: What Will the April Jubilee Show?], *Krasnaia zvezda* (9 Dec 1998); Yurii pankov, "Transatlanticheskoe edinstvo pod ugrosoi?" [Transatlantic Unity Threatened?], *Krasnaia zvezda* (15 Dec 1998).

[291]Maksim Yusin, "V Rossii nabiraet silu antiamerikanskaia volna" [Anti-American Feeling Gains Strength in Russia], *Izvestiia* (18 Dec 1998).

[292]See, e.g., Grigorii Morozov, "NATO posiagaet na funktsii soveta Bezopasnosti OON" [NATO Encroaches on the Functions of the UN Security Council], *Izvestiia* (5 Dec 1998).

[293]Solov'ev, "Vashington utverzhdaet novyi mirovoi poriadok" [Washington Maintains the New World Order], *Nezavisimaia voennoe obozrenie*, No. 49 (25 Dec 1998–14 Jan 1999).

good faith had, for the most part, been rebuffed or ignored.[294] Solov'ev had articulated what many Russians had come to see as a renewed East-West bipolarity, with Russia and the United States taking opposing positions on far too many issues.[295] Most observers in Moscow attributed the current divergence of Russian and American policy in the world arena to a combination of forces that included American post–Cold War opportunism and Russia's own inability to put its house in order. NATO expansionism is a common denominator in examples used by Russians to corroborate their references to U.S. opportunism; the need to rediscover the "Russian Idea," or "Russian Way," is a common denominator in projections from Russians hoping to resolve Moscow's problems. Furthermore, in 1999 some writers began to characterize Western policy generally as anti-Russian and anti-Slav.[296] Even a cursory glance at agendas offered by a vast majority of social-political-economic organized groupings in Russia makes it clear that the Western formula for "progress," at least in the form espoused by Gorbachev and Yeltsin, has been greatly discredited.

This is a potentially volatile situation, for to date the Russian answer has come mostly in the shape of nationalistic political movements. Zhirinovskii's LDPR, the communist-dominated People's Patriotic Union, Rokhlin's organization in defense of the military and, most recently, Luzhkov's Fatherland movement, are merely the largest and best known of such phenomena. Hopeful Russians, such as the author of an essay for *Rossiiskaia gazeta* who asked "who will rule the world in the 21st century?" and concluded that "Primakov's idea of a multipolar world, which the civilized world is looking at more carefully and with increasing sympathy, will prevail . . . ," were becoming the exception by the end of 1998. The degree to which NATO expansion played a role in bringing us to this dichotomy

---

[294]See, e.g., Vladimir Mikheev, "Russkikh igraiut po pravilam" [Russia Plays by the Rules], *Izvestiia* (10 Dec 1998); Vladimir Yermolin, "Rossiia predlagaet NATO sozdat' edinuiu sistemu PRO" [Russia Suggests to NATO a Single Defense System], *Izvestiia* (17 Dec 1998).

[295]See, e.g., Vladimir Lapskii, "Bagdadskie kuranty otbivaiut gimi Saddamu. Irak rasbombili. Chto dal'she?" [Baghdad Chimes Beat Out a Hymn to Saddam: Iraq Has Been Bombed. What Next?], *Rossiiskaia gazeta* (26 Dec 1998); Vasilii Safronchuk, "God krakha i nadezhda" [Year of Failures and Hopes], *Sovetskaia Rossiia* (31 Dec 1998); and Rogov, "Russia and the United States . . ." *op. cit.* (fn. 78).

[296]See, e.g., Safronchuk, "Daviat na Rossiiu, daviat na slavian" [They Are Oppressing Russia and Oppressing the Slavs], *Sovetskaia Rossiia* (26 Jan 1999), and Sergei Kortunov, "Russia's Way: National Identity and Foreign Policy," *International Affairs* (Moscow), 44, No. 4 (1998): 138–163.

is difficult to quantify precisely, but there is little doubt that as an explanation in Russia for what "needs to be done" it has served as an enormous boon to the groups noted above.[297]

Primakov's attitude lent credence to the nationalist posture. As foreign minister he had insisted that Russia's "size, power, potential, history, and tradition" should guarantee it one of the most important roles in international relations. Most Russian experts on the international scene agreed, but were uncertain about how to regain their traditional place. The fact that they regularly dragged Brzezinski's *Grand Chessboard* out as evidence that Western, mainly American, forces were lining up against them again suggests that the old xenophobia was back.[298]

1.10. 1999: The Anniversary Year

As the year in which NATO's first half century was to be celebrated, and the one in which countries from Eastern Europe finally were admitted as full members, 1999 was not a year looked forward to with much enthusiasm by Moscow's foreign policy elite. Already in January, Russian magazines and papers carried long discourses on NATO's future, its proposed new strategic concept, and its alleged ambition to serve as a global problem fixer. Tensions between Russia and the West over Iraq and Kosovo accelerated throughout January and February, and increasingly radical solutions were offered to the apparently interminable failure of Moscow's negotiating teams. Public statements by Vladimir Volkov, member of the Duma Defense Committee, and Foreign Minister Ivanov, revealed that Moscow's opinions were hardening. In January, Volkov told a press conference that NATO's new strategic concept was a "geostrategic threat to peace," against

---

[297]Vladimir Kuznechevskii, "Kto budet pravit' mirom v XXI veke?" *Rossiiskaia gazeta* (31 Dec 1998). The author took particular exception to Brzezinski's vision of world affairs. For commentary related to the issues raised in this paragraph, see, e.g., Col. Gen. Leonid G. Ivashov, "SShA vnesli razlad v otnosheniia s Rossiei" [The USA Has Sown Seeds of Discord in Relations with Russia], *Nezavisimoe voennoe obozrenie,* No. 49 (24 Dec–14 Jan 1999). Ivashov is chief of the RF Ministry of Defense Main Directorate of International Military Cooperation. See also Aleksandr Batygin, "Eksperiment zakonchen, gospoda khoroshie. Da zdravstvuet eksperiment?!" [The Experiment Is Over, My Fine Fellows: All Hail the Experiment?!], *Rossiiskaia gazeta* (22 Dec 1998), on the Fatherland's founding congress in Moscow. Another writer describes a new Cold War in international trade, e.g., in steel, pitting Russia and the United States against each other. See "Kholodnaia voina iz-za goriachego prokata" [Cold War Because of Hot Rolling Metal], *Rossiiskie vesti* (9–16 Dec 1998).

[298]See, e.g., T.A. Shakleina, "Rossiia v global'noi strategii SShA" [Russia and the U.S. Global Strategy], *SShA,* No. 12 (1998): 71–82; Primakov, "Rossiia i mirovoi politike" [Russia and World Politics], *Mezhdunarodnaia zhizn',* No. 6 (1998): 3–9.

which Russia would have to take "adequate measures." Speaking to reporters after talks with his Finnish counterpart, Ivanov repeated his government's adamant opposition to Baltic accession to the Alliance.[299]

The scale and contradictory nature of the dilemma facing Russian policy makers as NATO prepared for its gala April summit was exposed inadvertently in disconnected but coinciding remarks by public officials on 17 February 1999. The first was an announcement in Warsaw by Poland's minister of national defense, Janusz Onyszkiewicz, who said that after joining NATO his government would speak for Ukrainian interests in Europe. Frankly acknowledging that he did not wish to see Ukraine drawn closer to the CIS and, moreover, that Poland would support the aspirations of the Baltic states for NATO membership, Onyszkiewicz waved a red flag in Moscow's face. More significantly, he said that broadening NATO to include former Soviet republics would "test the credibility of [Russia's] will for cooperation with NATO."[300] From Moscow's perspective this was turning the issue on its head.

But the day wasn't over yet. Almost simultaneously Igor Ivanov informed a news conference in Moscow that Russia would "take any steps it finds necessary to guarantee its national security" if NATO expanded to include the Baltic or any other CIS states (Interfax, 17 Feb). It so happened as well that a PJC session opened in Brussels on that day to discuss, according to delegate Col.-Gen. Valerii Manilov, Russia's military doctrine and NATO's new concept. Manilov told journalists that NATO knew Moscow was apprehensive about the enlarged military infrastructures in East and East Central Europe and was fully aware of its opposition to any NATO "out of zone" military activity not sanctioned by the UN Security Council. The Kremlin hoped that its concerns "could be alleviated at the drafting stage of [NATO's] conceptual documents."[301] In light of position-taking such as these, it would seem that each side expected the other to blink first.

The wind down began formally on 12 March, when Poland, Hungary and the

---

[299]ITAR-TASS (10 Jan 1999); see also Leonid Laakso, "Finny v NATO ne khotiat" [Finns Don't Want to Be in NATO], *Krasnaia zvezda* (12 Jan 1999). For Volkov's statement, ITAR-TASS (14 Jan 1999). See also Yurii Pankov, "Obkhodnye manevry" [Round About Maneuvers], *Krasnaia zvezda* (16 Jan 1999).

[300]PAP (Warsaw), (17 Feb 1999), FBIS-SOV, No. 218. See also Boris Vinogradov, "Pol'sha, Chekhiia i Vengriia vstaiut pod znamena NATP" [Poland, Czechia and Hungary Are Under NATO Banners], Izvestiia (20 Feb 1999).

[301]ITAR-TASS (17 Feb 1999). Ivanov was speaking on the eve of visits to Moscow by Zhu Rongli, China's premier, and Strobe Talbott, with whom he would be discussing the CFE Treaty. See also Aleksandr Kuranov, "NATO rasshiritsia cherez mesiats" [NATO Will Expand in a Month], *Nezavisimaia gazeta* (11 Feb 1999).

Czech Republic joined NATO at a ceremony held in the Alliance's birthplace, Independence, Missouri. In preliminary speeches Secretary General Solana and U.S. Undersecretary of State Talbott spoke enthusiastically of new stability and the end of "dividing lines" in Europe. The door was still open to other candidates, Talbott insisted, but little enthusiasm for further expansion was expressed. Britain's foreign minister, Robin Cook, went so far as to assure Moscow that Washington's gala anniversary event would not be marked by new invitations to candidates for NATO membership. Coinciding with the March ceremony were published reports in the United States and elsewhere suggesting that the Russian public was not much concerned, or even much interested, in NATO's absorption of eastern European countries.[302] The conclusion was drawn that NATO expansion would not be an issue to attract Russian voters to nationalist candidates during the upcoming Russian parliamentary elections.

Such assumptions were myopic. Even though the Moscow government merely repeated its long-standing abhorrence of the Alliance's enlargement plan, NATO and American policies related to Kosovo, Iraq and Iran, increased evidence of Washington's dominance of NATO, and Clinton's request that the ABM Treaty be revised, combined to exacerbate East-West tensions. Russia's helplessness and apparent isolation in world affairs undoubtedly would play a part in election campaigning. It already was in March. The 'unofficial' outcry in Russia around or on 12 March was much more revealing than nonchalant government releases. Some were expected: Zyuganov relied on the adage that NATO expansion was "the biggest mistake in postwar history." Luzhkov said that it was "against Russia's interests." Vladimir Lukin, chair of the Duma's Committee on Foreign Affairs, claimed that "Russia was offended, its view was disregarded," and his deputy Aleksei Podberezkin added that "Russia will have to change its military doctrine" (see section 3.1). The ministry of defense agreed: Col. Gen. Leonid Ivashov proclaimed that the balance of forces had been upset and that "cataclysms" were now possible; Col. Gen. Leontii Shevtsev told journalists that Russia was now short of ground troops and would be unable to defend itself if NATO turned toward Moscow.

Military pundits used the occasion to highlight the failure, for Russia, of the Founding Act and to call again for a general European security system. One reporter quoted Gorbachev's complaint that "the West has betrayed me" and the

---

[302]See, e.g., Michael R. Gordon, "Old Foes Find New Roles on Europe's Rebuilt Stage," *New York Times* (14 March 1999). Gordon cited surveys conducted by Moscow's All-Russian Center for the Study of Public Opinion, which asked 1600 Russians if they felt the recent expansion of NATO was "a threat to the security of Russia." 41 percent of respondees over the age of 40 answered, "yes," 31 percent between the ages of 18–39 agreed. These numbers seem not, in fact, to reflect indifference.

communist press accused Washington of using NATO to gain control of the world's resources. The surprise came from the "liberal" party. Aleksei Arbatov was more acerbic than usual, calling for retaliation against NATO expansion and demanding that Russia prepare treaties to keep nuclear weapons out of the new NATO territories. Leader of Yabloko, Yavlinskii, and the bloc's deputy leader, Sergei Ivanenko, joined Arbatov in the criticism this time. In Yavlinskii's case, this was a marked change in direction, which implied that he was indeed playing the election game.[303]

Well before either the orchestrated or the spontaneous lashing out at NATO died down, the Alliance opened its air campaign against Serbian infrastructure. Although Russia's immediate hostile reaction was expected, it was nonetheless chilling. Primakov cancelled his visit to Washington, ordering his plane to turn around in mid-Atlantic and return to Moscow. His decision was hailed in the Russian media as a "courageous" and patriotic act, even though it may have placed a needed IMF loan in jeopardy.[304] Offical Moscow responses included

---

[303]These statements all appeared in releases issued by ITAR- TASS (12–13 March 1999) and Interfax (12 March 1999), in English. For an earlier suggestion that Russia's anti-missile system be adopted as part of a general European defense mechanism, see Vladimir Ermolin, "Rossiia predlagaet NATO sozdat' edinuiu sistemu PRO" [Russia Proposes to NATO That a Unified Anti-Missile System Be Created], *Izvestiia* (17 Dec 1998).

The official releases were quoted in the Russian (and Western) press often. For a cross-section of Russian responses, e.g., "Net, ne tuda dvinulas' NATO" [NATO Has Moved in the Wrong Direction], *Rossiiskaia gazeta* (13 March 1999); Viacheslav Tetekin, "K itogam parlamentskikh slushanii po rasshirenniiu NATO. Pryzhok k nashim granitsam" [Results of Parliamentary Hearings on NATO Expansion: Leap to Our Borders], *Sovetskaia Rossiia* (13 March 1999); Safronchuk, "Est' li predel rasshireniiu NATO na vostok?" [Is There a Limit to NATO Expansion to the East?], *Sovetskaia Rossiia* (16 March 1999); Vadim Solov'ev, "Raznoskorostnoe sblizhenie s NATO protivorechit interesam evrobezopasnosti" [The Divergent Pace of NATO Growth Contradicts the Interests of European Security], *Nezivisimoe voennoe obozrenie,* No.10 (19–25 March 1999); Yelena Surovtseva, "NATO uzhe u nashikh granits" [NATO Is Already at Our Border], *Krasnaia zvezda* (16 March 1999); Vladimir Katin, "V NATO podniaty flagi novichkov" [Flags of New Members Are Raised in NATO], *Nezavisimaia gazeta* (17 March 1999).

[304]See, e.g., Vladimir Lapskii, "24 marta 16.00 'Tomagavki' ezhe ne vzleteli, a inykh rossiiskikh politikov uzhe kontuzilo" [March 24, 1600 Hours: Tomahawks Not Yet Airborne, But Some Russian Politicians Already Concussed], *Rossiiskaia gazeta* (25 March 1999). Lapskii said that Primakov "behaved as a patriot," because his arrival in Washington at that time would have been "a humiliation for all Russians." Vadim Markushin, "Balkanskii proschet NATO" [NATO's Balkan Miscalculation], *Krasnaia zvezda* (26 March 1999). Editorials in *Komsomol'skaia pravda, Obshchaia gazeta,* and *Nezavisimaia gazeta* carried a similar message.

the recall of its military representative to NATO, Zavarzin, but not ambassador Kizlyak. Cooperation with the PfP was suspended. NATO's military and diplomatic representatives in Moscow, Manfred Diehl of Germany and Alexis Chahtahtinsky of France, were ordered out of Russia until the "aggression" against Yugoslavia had ceased. After some hesitation, and talk of sending as many as seven ships, the Ministry of Defense commanded one intelligence-gathering vessel (the *Liman*) into the Mediterranean from Sevastopol. The ship left port on 2 April, having notified Turkey that it would pass through the Bosporus.

A Russian resolution at the UN Security Council describing the air strikes as a violation of the UN Charter was defeated 12–3. Only China and India supported Russia. Commentators from all political sectors in Russia advised that the UN was in danger of losing whatever credibility it might have as a resolver of regional conflicts.[305] As one might expect, CIS states Belarus, Kazakhstan, Kyrgyzstan, Tajikistan, Moldova, and Armenia rallied around Moscow's position. This time, Ukraine also "regretted" the NATO action and called for the maintenance of Yugoslav territorial integrity. A release from the foreign ministry in Kiev included a statement that the use of "military force against a sovereign state without the sanction of the UN Security Council . . . was unacceptable" (Interfax-Ukraine, 25 March). On 3 April, Ukraine joined with eight of the 10-member CIS Inter-Parliamentary Assembly in condemning the air strikes and warning against the outbreak of a new Cold War (Interfax, 3 April). The coming on-side of Ukraine in opposition to a major NATO initiative was an unexpected, and much welcomed, breakthrough for Russia and the CIS.

Public reaction in Russia was more aggressive than the official one (see section 2.3). Almost overnight it became certain that NATO activities would be an even greater marker in campaigning for the parliamentary elections than previously expected. Support for Yugoslavia and antagonism towards NATO generally and Washington specifically was adopted as a theme by all factions. The communists co-opted nationalism, anti-Americanism, the Hitler analogy, and un-critical support for Slobodan Milosevic all in one long Statement issued by the People's Patriotic Union on 25 March. Calling the air strikes "aggression . . . taking us back to the time of Hitlerism," blaming the United States alone among foreign powers, and labelling Gorbachev and Yeltsin "betrayers" controlled from

---

[305]See, e.g., Safronchuk, "Mozhet li nyneshniaia OON ostanovit' agressiiu NATO?" [Can the Current UN Stop NATO Aggression?], *Sovetskaia Rossiia* (27 March 1999).

overseas, the communists and their allies demanded that Russia send weapons to Yugoslavia.[306]

Primakov telephoned Milosevic on the day of the first strike and flew to Belgrade on the 30th, hoping to negotiate peace. He was strongly encouraged by the French and Italian heads of state, but accomplished little. In fact, the reaction of Russia's officialdom had rather a Keystone Kop atmosphere to it. Primakov's team was preceded in Belgrade by a trio of Russian "liberals," Boris Nemtsov, Yegor Gaydar and Boris Fedorov, who planned also to seek an audience with the Pope and then fly to Washington. Their reception everywhere was either cool or puzzled or both. The State Duma sent a mission of its own to Belgrade. The Federation Council, condemning NATO's action in a rare moment of unanimity, decided not to follow suit.[307] Nevertheless, Federation Council member Lebed went on Moscow TV to claim that Russia had been humiliated by NATO. He recommended that his country send military and technical aid and unilaterally lift the weapons embargo against Yugoslavia.

The significance of Lebed's and other such railing in Russia lies in the fact that the slumbering Russian public opinion bear, treated so casually by Western pundits over the previous years, lurched awake with a thundering growl. Public opinion surveys now showed that up to 90 percent of the "people on the street" believed that NATO had no right to bomb Yugoslavia, and fully 48 percent blamed NATO and Washington for the entire Yugoslav internal conflict (Interfax, 31 March). Strobe Talbott publicly acknowledged this new reality.[308] Others polls showed that the normally positive sentiments felt by Russia's general public towards Americans had practically disappeared. Surveys conducted in May found over 70 percent of Russians interpreting NATO's military operation in Yugoslavia as a direct threat to Russia.[309]

---

[306]"Zaiavlenie Narodno-patriotcheskogo soiuza Rossii. Ostanovit' agresiiu! [Statement by the People's Patriotic Union of Russia: Stop the Aggression!], *Sovetskaia Rossiia* (27 March 1999). The Statement was signed by Zyuganov. See also Yevgenii Popov, "Natovskii kulak nad Yugoslaviei. SShA gotoviat krovaviiu razviazku v Kosovo" [NATO Fist over Yugoslavia: The USA Prepares for a Bloody Settlement in Kosovo], *Sovetskaia Rossiia* (23 March 1999), and many more.

[307]Konstantin Katanyan, "Senatory khochet ostanavit' NATO" [Senators Want to Stop NATO], *Izvestiia* (1 April 1999).

[308]Talbott, "Russia's True Interests," *New York Times* (30 March 1999), and NATO Website. Lebed's long and angry statement was delivered over Moscow's NTV, 31 March 1999, translated for FBIS-SOV, No. 401. See also Michael Wines, "Hostility to U.S. Is Now Popular with the Russians," *New York Times* (12 April 1999), and Yelena Surovtseva, "Rossiiane osupsdaiut agressiiu" [Russians Condemn Aggression], *Krasnaia zvezda* (30 March 1999).

[309]"Polls Show Majority of Russians Afraid of NATO," Interfax (28 May 1999).

There were important exceptions to the collective Russian howl against NATO. Yeltsin's first foreign minister, Andrei Kozyrev, a Duma deputy from Murmansk and member of Gaydar's Russia's Choice bloc, warned his fellow citizens against defending the interests of "bloody dictators" like Milosevic and Hussein. Condemning Russia's media and government for "disinforming" the population, he urged them to take a more balanced position or risk a final isolation from Europe.[310] A week later, when the Duma adopted a resolution to invite Yugoslavia to join the Russia-Belarus Union (293–54, with one abstention), only Yabloko voted against as a bloc. And that negative response came not out of support for NATO, but as a result of worry that Russia might be drawn into war.[311]

Opinions like Kozyrev's, and even Yabloko's, were very rare. Indeed, the crisis in Kosovo triggered name-calling on both sides (Russia and NATO) equal to or even greater than that used during the most strained moments of the Cold War. Charges of ethnic cleansing, genocide, war crimes, and brutal savageries of all sorts flew back and forth across Europe and the Atlantic. Pejorative but otherwise meaningless terms like "henchmen" and "hardliner" were applied liberally by journalists around the globe. "Holocausts" and "concentration camps" were reintroduced to the media lexicon, with very little corroborating evidence. Both "sides" stigmatized their newly found enemies as "fascist" and "Nazi." Leaders were demonized; one side's "terrorists" were the other side's heroes. Rumors that Russia's missiles might be re-targetted towards the United States and Europe were rife, though denied by Defense Minister Sergeev—"for now." An orgy of hyperbole overwhelmed the media, but it was hyperbole that was meant to be taken seriously. The Muse of History was grotesquely abused. None of this was new, but its intensity startled the general public in North America, Europe and Russia, and, among other things, made it clear that the issue of NATO's role in the world had to be defined more carefully.

The caution recommended by Kozyrev had little impact on Moscow's communist media. For weeks, copies of *Sovetskaia Rossiia* devoted two to three of its four pages to screaming headlines demonizing NATO and Washington, Solana and Clinton. The *Drang nach Osten* and Hitler analogies were invoked in almost every issue

---

[310]Kozyrev, "In Step with Milosevich toward Isolation," *Moskovskie novosti* (30 March–5 April 1999), Johnson's Russia List (9 April 1999).

[311]For the Duma vote, see ITAR-TASS (16 April 1999), and "Chtoby ostanovit' agressiiu" [Stopping the Aggression], *Rossiiskaia gazeta* (14 April 1999). See also Melor Sturua, "Priznak slavianskoi antanty slegka napugal Zapad" [The Specter of a Slavic Entente Frightens the West a Little], *Izvestiia* (13 April 1999). For an interview with Aleksei Arbatov, "Soiuz s Yugoslaviei vtianet Rossiiu v voinu" [Union with Yugoslavia Will Drag Russia into War], *Nezavisimoe voennoe obozrenie*, No. 15 (23–29 April 1999).

and cries for Slavic fraternal solidarity with the Serbs abounded.[312] Pictures of protests and demonstrations in Russia and every other country where they took place were carried almost every day. With the Duma election campaigning set to begin officially on 19 August, the predictable anti-NATO and anti-American tone adopted by communists and nationalists had been given a powerful head start.

Moscow's sympathy for Yugoslavia went far deeper than media bluster and self-serving political rhetoric. The Russian spiritual link to Serbia was given special credence when the head of the Russian Orthodox Church, Patriarch Aleksei II, visited Belgrade on 20 April and proclaimed Kosovo a holy ground filled with Orthodox monasteries.

In the midst of this turmoil, the Russian government struggled to find a role for itself. The situation was rife with political, economic and military risk for the Kremlin. Primakov had returned to extraordinarily important negotiations with the IMF; the Duma was moving full speed ahead on impeachment procedures against Yeltsin, paying little heed to warnings against further political destabilization; Yeltsin's popularity rating had hit a new low, and both his health and judgement were widely questioned. Moscow's policy seemed very ad hoc. On 11 April, for example, the Russian envoy to the United Nations brought a draft resolution to the General Assembly asking it to endorse the concept that no individual nation or regional organization may use force against a sovereign state without authorization from the UN Security Council. This seemed a little redundant in light of the UN Charter and current events.

Two days later, a convoy of 68 trucks with aid from Russia arrived in Belgrade. They had been delayed for a few days in Hungary, but were allowed to proceed after several armored vehicles and others carrying fuel were left behind.[313] Budapest was now plainly committed to the "other side." On 15 April, Yeltsin named Chernomyrdin special envoy to Yugoslavia, giving the former prime minister status as negotiator much like that granted to Primakov by Gorbachev during the Gulf War.

---

[312]Typical front-page and large headlines will suffice: "'Kovrovyi' banditizm. SShA i NATO provodiat 'vtoruiu fazu' agressii protiv CRYu" ["Bloody" Banditism: The USA and NATO Introduce the Second Phase of Aggression against Yugoslavia], *Sovetskaia Rossiia* (30 March 1999); A. Cherkalov, "SShA: k mirovomu gospodstvu—cherez genotsid" [The USA: To World Rule through Genocide], *ibid.* (1 April 1999); "Novaia faza genotsida v Yugoslavii. NATO zvereet" [New Phase of Genocide in Yugoslavia: NATO Brutalizes], *ibid.* (15 April 1999).

[313]On 7 April the State Duma had voted, 279–34, with 4 abstentions, to supply Yugoslavia with "weapons, military hardware, and spare parts" (ITAR-TASS, 7 April), but Yeltsin's government rejected this idea.

Chernomyrdin had some limited success, as NATO and Russia both looked for a diplomatic solution to the crisis. Moscow's potential as mediator elevated its profile favorably abroad, but did little to ease the fury that prevailed in the Russian public mood. Whatever indifference Russia's citizenry might have felt towards NATO expansion in the mid-1990s was now gone, replaced by a focussed anger and distrust that is likely to have a long life. Even the Kremlin was charged with appeasement by a wide cross-section of Russia's political elite, media, and public. Primakov faded into the background, suffering from various health problems and from Yeltsin's preference for Chernomyrdin, Luzhkov, and others.

The battle in and over Yugoslavia overshadowed the event that had most concerned the Kremlin for months prior to NATO's air strikes against Yugoslav targets—NATO's anniversary summit in Washington, 22–25 April. Some 1,700 delegates from the 19 member countries and most of the 25 other members of the Euro-Atlantic Partnership Council gathered to celebrate NATO's first half-century and to discuss the Alliance's future. Neither Russia nor Belarus sent representatives.

The atmosphere in Washington was considerably more subdued than had been anticipated and much of the talk focussed on the conduct of war. Few of the big decisions about NATO's new direction were finalized: Russia was relieved that no "second wave" of new invitees was proclaimed, and disappointed that NATO confirmed its intent to settle "out of zone" conflicts. Yet Russia was not entirely isolated from the gathering. Yeltsin telephoned Clinton on the final day of the Washington summit, spoke vaguely of a possible peace accord reached by Chernomyrdin in Belgrade, and agreed to meet with Strobe Talbott in Moscow. On reading the Summit communiqué, Melor Sturua concluded that NATO recognized that Russia shared its desire for stability in the Euro-Atlantic region, granting Moscow a role as "Trojan Horse" in Europe.[314]

Most Russians already believed, however, that a Trojan Horse had been pushed from West to East, bearing arms. Analysts in Moscow treated the Summit as a death knell for the UN, marking a new age in which force applied by NATO would replace diplomacy in international affairs.[315] Sturua's expectations were fleeting anyway. Russia's hopes of being taken more seriously in the international arena were diminished by coinciding dramatic acts in Moscow: on 11 May, the Duma

---

[314]Sturua, "NATO otvodit Rossii rol' Troianskogo konia" [NATO Gives Russia Role of Trojan Horse], *Izvestiia* (27 April 1999).

[315]See, e.g., Yurii Pankov, "NATO primerila mundir" [NATO Put on a Uniform], *Krasnaia zvezda* (27 April 1999); Dmitrii Gornostaev, "Pokhorony OON na sammite NATO" [UN Funeral at NATO Summit], *Nezavisimaia gazeta* (27 April 1999); Vadim Markushin, "NATO: iubilei bez fanfar" [NATO: Jubilee without Fanfare], *Krasnaia zvezda* (23 April 1999).

voted to surge ahead with impeachment proceedings against Yeltsin; the very next day, the president dismissed Primakov and his entire Cabinet. Russia's political, economic, and public infrastructure was poised at the brink of a vortex yet again.

The impeachment effort failed miserably, and a humiliated communist-dominated Duma had little choice but to accept Yeltsin's latest candidate for prime minister, Minister of the Interior Sergei Stepashin. Nothing changed in regards to Russian perception of NATO. In his first speech to the Duma, on 19 May 1999, Stepashin said: "Let's be frank, . . . [NATO's air] strike against Yugoslavia is perhaps not so much against Yugoslavia—as it is a strike against Russia" (ITAR-TASS, 19 May 1999).

This is where we came in.

Section II

Ripple Effects

INTRODUCTION

As NATO moved inexorably eastward, Russia's government and public tended increasingly to evaluate events and leaderships in Europe and the CIS according to their expectations of the Alliance. In an odd twist of fate, NATO became, for the first time since its inception, a real or imagined thorn in all dimensions of Moscow's international activity.

The purpose of this Section is to test the historical tale against Russian thinking about specific regions of the world, and to demonstrate ways in which the NATO question swayed Russian analysts in matters like military reform and strategic planning. Omitted, for the most part, from this list of scenarios are details on the Kremlin's relations with Belarus and the complex Russian negotiations with international economic integrating organizations, such as the EU, GATT, the WTO, the G-7 (G-8), Paris and London Clubs, and so on.

The case of Belarus cannot go altogether unmentioned. Of all the leaders of former USSR republics, Alyaksandr Lukashenka, Belarus president, has been the most consistent supporter of the Russian position on NATO. He raised the question of NATO in a long address to Russia's State Duma in November 1996 and has been harping on it ever since. Passionately supporting the unity of the two countries, Lukashenka complained bitterly about the pressure put on his government by "Westernizers" for the removal of nuclear weapons from Belarus soil. Assuming that NATO would site nuclear weapons in Poland, he questioned the "double standards" of Western advocates of NATO enlargement who protest the Belarus-Russia Union. Because it was left to Belarus to "ensure Russian security in its Western approaches," Minsk and

Moscow have as much reason to unite as former Warsaw Pact countries have to join NATO.[1]

In April 1997, plans were announced for a joint Russian and Belarus Air Force exercise, specifically to prepare contingency plans related to NATO's movement eastward.[2] More to the point were surveys that showed an initially very reluctant Russian public growing more supportive of Russia-Belarus unity as NATO expansion became a hotter subject in the media. A few days before the Founding Act was signed, for example, it was reported that Russian advocacy of union had risen from indifference to "overwhelming" in a matter of a few months.[3] The political "victory" for unionists was complete, and both sides in the debate agreed that the NATO question had been decisive.

The government in Minsk continued to disapprove strongly of NATO expansion eastward after the summit in Madrid. Lukashenka's refrain, "our border with Poland will become a border with NATO," was heard often in one form or the other and the Russian communist press lauded him as the only CIS leader to speak out vigorously against NATO expansion.[4]

In December 1997, the NATO question was cited as the reason for the Russian and Belarusian defense ministers agreeing to an accord on close military cooperation. Shortly thereafter, Lukashenka began to hint that Minsk was reconsidering the wisdom of giving up its nuclear arsenal. The Belarus president raised the matter directly in connection with NATO in late September 1998, telling reporters that the decision by his predecessor to remove such weapons from the country was "a crude mistake, if not a crime" (Interfax-West, 23 Sept).

The Kosovo crisis reverberated within the Belarus-Russian Union, as it did everywhere else in the CIS. On 2 October 1998, in the midst of near hysteria about Kosovo in Moscow, the Russian State Duma ratified two long-delayed Rus-

---

[1]Alyaksandr Lukashenka, "Vystuplenie prezidenta Belorusi v Gosdume Rossii. Na predatel'stve brat'ev schast'ia ne postroit'" [Speech of the President of Belarus in the State Duma of Russia: Betrayal of Brothers Is Not the Way to Build Happiness], *Sovetskaia Rossiia* (14 Nov 1996). The majority communist and nationalist Duma deputies praised the Lukashenka speech; the small Yabloko faction walked out, calling it "buffoonery."

[2]"Rossiia-Belorussiia" [Russia-Belorussia], *Nezavisimoe voennoe obozrenie,* No. 15 (19–25 Apr 1997).

[3]Vladimir Lapkin, "Russia's Way of Union Haste," *Moscow News,* No. 20 (29 May–3 June 1997), 4. For the Russian version, *Moskovskie novosti,* No. 20 (18–25 May 1997). The only reservation held by Russian responders was a dislike for Lukashenka. A poll carried in *Rossiiskaia gazeta* (2 April) put the level of support at 62 percent of the Russian population. Interfax reports set the number at 59 percent in April and 76 percent at mid-May.

[4]Safronchuk, "Obshchestvennost' protiv rasshireniia NATO!" [Society Against NATO Expansion!], *Sovetskaia Rossiia* (28 Oct 1997).

sia-Belarus military treaties (Interfax, 2 Oct). One of them prohibited either side from giving information on their military cooperation to a third party without the other's permission. The second agreement set ground rules for joint control and training of armed forces. In speaking to journalists about these accords, Lukashenka linked them to NATO "insolence" in Europe and once again portrayed Belarus as the front line against an expansionist NATO.

Russian and Belarusian defense ministries declared that they would strengthen military ties further, specifically in response to the threat of air strikes against Yugoslavia (Interfax, 16 Oct). Polish and Lithuanian readiness to participate in NATO operations in Kosovo was clearly a concern in Minsk, as it was in Moscow, and provided still greater reason for closer Russia-Belarus security links. It was Lukashenka who suggested that Yugoslavia be invited to join the Russia-Belarus Union. Seen as frivolous rhetoric in October 1998, this suggestion was taken more seriously six months later when NATO planes began their bombing attacks on Yugoslavia. But even in 1998, *Izvestiia* had proclaimed that Russian and Belarusian generals were forming a defense structure aimed solely against NATO.[5]

Whether it was used as a real reason or an excuse, there can be no doubt that NATO expansion hastened, indeed ensured, the Russian-Belarus Union—in spite of Yeltsin's great reluctance to associate closely with Lukashenka earlier on. Of all the regions in the world where NATO activity shaped Russian political and strategic planning, the Belarus case is the clearest. But Moscow's perception of NATO's aspirations has also had considerable influence on Russian thinking about all other regions in which it has had a traditional interest.

2. GROPING FOR NEW STRATEGIC PARTNERS

The belief that Western European states will circle their wagons to check Russian influence at the European gate has a long history in St. Petersburg and Moscow. Russians who just a few years ago thought that the fall of the USSR would facilitate their integration into Europe now fear that NATO expansion has knocked that goal from their grasp forever.

It is worth remembering as well that the preamble to the Warsaw Treaty Organization, established on 14 May 1955, gave as its main raison d'être "the participation of a remilitarized Western Germany and the integration of the latter in the North-Atlantic bloc." The official reason for the Warsaw Pact in the first place therefore was not the founding of NATO, which took place six years earlier. Instead, it was the movement of NATO eastward on 9 May, the day of West Ger-

---

[5]"Generaly Rossii i Belorussii vystraivanet oboronu protiv NATO" [Russian and Belarusian Generals Construct Defense against NATO], *Izvestiia* (5 Nov 1998).

many's entry, making the alliance appear to the Russians to be on the offensive.[6] The 9th of May 1955 marked as well the 10th anniversary of Stalin's announcement to the people of the USSR that the war with Germany had been won, a point noted with irony in the Soviet press.[7]

The Russian government does not expect to resurrect a defensive bloc resembling the Warsaw Pact. There can be little doubt, however, that the spurt in Russia's relationships with Iran and China, renewed ties with India, and the Belarus-Russian unity charter (draft signed on 2 April, ratified on 22 April 1997) were driven in varying degrees by a perceived need to counter NATO expansion. Extreme nationalists, like Zhirinovskii, have been champions of stronger ties with Iraq, Iran and China for some years. The first LDPR platform, in fact, included such exhortations as "Iraq must be seen as the strategic ally of Russia in the South," "India must remain the largest and most reliable friend of Russia in the Asiatic region," and Russia must "strengthen cooperation with this [China] great nuclear power." It was on this platform that Zhirinovskii ran so successfully in the 1993 parliamentary elections.[8]

Russian authorities were hesitant about making new commitments, and only by late 1996 did they begin to speak seriously of fashioning a new "multipolar" international community in which the United States could not be the single dominant power. This approach was partly rhetorical, in that it helped Yeltsin's team gain a little back from perceived humiliation at the hands of Washington, and it appealed to Russia's nationalists. Nevertheless, advocacy of multipolarism took precedence in the post-Soviet Kremlin. In January 1996, shortly after he was ap-

----

[6]Already in November 1954, at a Soviet-sponsored Conference on European Security meeting in Moscow, the USSR, Poland, Czechoslovakia, the GDR, Hungary, Romania, Bulgaria and Albania condemned the ongoing rearming of Western Germany and warned that new security measures of their own (i.e., Soviet) would have to be taken if West Germany was invited to join NATO. See *Moskovskoe soveshchanie evropeiskikh stran po obespecheniiu mira i bezopasnosti v Evrope* [Conference of European Countries on Safeguarding Peace and Security in Europe] (Moscow, 1954), 145–56.

A Soviet book published between periods of NATO expansions in 1955 and 1997, M. Kukanov, *NATO: ugroza miru* [NATO—Threat to Peace] (Moscow, 1971), was replete with messages similar in tone and content to current opposition to NATO in Moscow.

[7]See, e.g., V. Matveev, "Na opasnom puti" [On a Dangerous Path], *Izvestiia* (6 May 1955), V. Kudriavtsev, "V Varshave nakanune soveshchaniia" [In Warsaw on the Eve of the Meeting], *Izvestiia* (11 May 1955); "Vazhnoe sobytie v zhizni narodov Evropy" [An Important Event in the Life of the People of Europe], *Izvestiia* (13 May 1955); and "Dogovor" [Agreement], *Izvestiia* (15 May 1955).

[8]See "Programma Liberal'no-Demokraticheskoi partii Rossii. Ustav LDPR, Pt. VI," signed by Zhirinovskii and printed by the LDPR in Moscow, 19 April 1992.

pointed foreign minister, Primakov said that NATO expansion would undermine European stability and change the geopolitical status of Russia, perhaps even nullifying the benefits of destroying medium-range missiles. In May that year, Andrei Kokoshin, former policy strategist with ISKRAN and later (briefly in 1998) secretary of the RF Security Council, published a long essay in which he said that NATO expansion forced Russia to reexamine its entire foreign policy and that, among other things, careful negotiations with India and China were mandatory. It was his opinion (quoting Solana) that the threat of nuclear weapons on former Warsaw Pact territory was a real one.[9] The very next day the military paper *Nezavisimoe voennoi obozrenie* said that the United States itself had ensured that START II would not be ratified by the Duma, because NATO expansion eastward skewed the military balance so decisively in favor of the West. And Lebed growled that Americans were trying to draw Russia into military confrontation, and a new round of the arms race, precisely to justify NATO expansion after the fact! Russia must not become the "bogeyman" again, he said. Instead, Moscow should stay calm, reform the army, upgrade its nuclear forces, and let NATO weaken Europe by debilitating its budget on expansion.[10] We recall that in March 1997 Primakov warned journalists in London that under certain conditions Russia might have to look for "partnerships in the East."

As the 27 May 1997 event drew closer, the military press highlighted the possibility of a full Russia-China strategic partnership; tongue-in-cheek, perhaps, but certainly clear that the West should take such possibilities seriously. Zyuganov had made the same point in April during a long report to the IV Congress of the CPRF. Rallying his party under the slogan "Russia will be Great, and Socialistic!", he claimed that when the CPRF achieved power it would counter NATO expansion by forging closer ties with China, India, the Arab states and "other countries on the basis of mutual interests."[11]

---

[9]Kokoshin, "Kazhduiu v Evrope khatu—pod ten' NATO? Tak delo ne poidet" [Shall Each House in Europe be Under the Shadow of NATO? That Is Not the Deal!], *Rossiiskaia gazeta* (15 May 1996). For Primakov's remarks, "Press Conference: Primakov's First Move: The CIS," *Moscow News,* No. 2 (19–25 Jan 1996): 6; the Russian version appeared a little earlier, see *Moskovskie novosti,* No. 2 (14–21 January 1996), 13. See also Alexei Pushkov, "Yevgenii Primakov: Logical Choice for Yeltsin," *Moscow News,* No. 1 (12–18 Jan 1996): 1–2.

[10]Aleksandr Lebed, "Global'naia politicheskaia instsenirovka" [Global Political Bluff], *Nezavisimoe voennoe obozrenie* (NG insert) (16 May 1996); Vladimir Dvorkin, "Narushenie strategicheskogo balansa" [Disruption of the Strategic Balance], *ibid.* (16 May 1996).

[11]Zyuganov, "Rossiia budet velikoi i sotsialisticheskoi!" [Russia Will Be Great and Socialistic!], *Sovetskaia Rossiia* (22 April 1997). Zyuganov said that the CPRF also wanted close relations with the United States and the West, in a multipolar world. For Primakov's remarks, see *Komsomol'skaia pravda* (4 March 1997).

This is not at all to say that Russia preferred then, or now, to deal predominantly with the East. As the "young reformers" lost places in Yeltsin's government, however, it became more common to hear reservations expressed about economic integration with the EU and the WTO. Some analysts, such as Tatiana Parkhalina, continued to see no reasonable alternative to strategic partnership with the West. She suggested in 1997, prior to the blow ups in Iraq and Yugoslavia, that reliance on the likes of Lukashenka (Belarus), Saddam Hussein (Iraq) and Milosevic (Yugoslavia) was futile and risky. But opinions like hers grew less popular in Russia during 1998, at least in print. For a number of reasons, most of them obvious, Russian statesmen long have favored a multipolar world anyway. Indeed, this position was written into a Russian-Kazakhstan treaty of eternal friendship, signed in Moscow, 6 July 1998.[12]

Anxious as Russia's leaders are that their country be recognized as part of Europe, the potential for new strategic directions has its attractions. Aleksei Arbatov made this a central point of a long treatise on Russia's national "Idea" and security, pointing out that "multipolarity . . . is the most advantageous international system for Russia." While he acknowledged that Russia is culturally of the West, Arbatov believed that, if isolated strategically, Moscow had clear and viable options. Arbatov recognized that certain risks accompanied reliance on Iran and China, and that potentially destabilizing forces emanated from Turkey, Pakistan and Afghan-istan. Even the proposed China partnership was important from both the political and economic perspective only temporarily. In the long run balanced relations with Japan would be more helpful. The problem for Russia is that Washington demands loyalty from its allies when it squabbles with Iraq, Iran, Libya, or Cuba. Its willingness to "twist Moscow's arms," and NATO expansion eastward, merely added fuel to Russia's nationalists. Thus, Arbatov concluded, Europe and Asia must be simultaneous objects of concentrated Russian diplomacy.[13]

The urge to find new strategic directions was abetted by important economic considerations. China, India and Iran are very valuable markets for Russian military

---

[12]The treaty committed both sides to close cooperation "under the conditions of the multipolar world that is taking shape to overcome bloc approaches . . . ." See *Rossiiskaia gazeta,* Economic Union supplement (18 July 1998), FBIS-SOV, No. 208. On support for a multipolar world, see, e.g., Andrei Ivanov, "We Will Build Our Own Multi-Polar World," *New Times,* No. 17–18 (4 May 1997). Ivanov said that this trend is not intended to counter NATO, rather it is an essential re-examination of the world arena; and "Evroazi-atskii vystup NATO i Rossiiskii faktor" [The Euro-Asiatic Projection of NATO and the Russian Factor], *Krasnaia zvezda* (4 Nov 1997).

For the Parkhalina comment, see her "O novoi arkhitekture bezopasnosti v Evrope" [On the New Architecture of Security in Europe], *Mirovaia ekonomika i mezhdunarodnye otnosheniia,* No. 12 (December 1997): 14–24.

[13]Arbatov, "Natsional'naia ideia i natsional'naia bezopasnost'" [The National Idea and National Security], *Mirovaia ekonomika i mezhdunarodnye otnosheniia,* No. 6 (June 1998): 5–19.

weapons; India and Iran are consumers of Russian nuclear technology. In October 1997 the deputy director of the Russian Center for Analysis, Strategies and Technologies, Konstantin Makienko, announced that arms cooperation with India and China had been placed on a long-term footing. A 7-year program to sell about $1 billion in arms to India had an unusually reassuring consequence for Russia, he said, because India's growing strength "distracted" China from Russia's border. This, in turn, eased the obvious strategic dilemma raised by Russia's major arms sales to China. Ukraine's deliveries of tanks to Pakistan served to make Russian anti-tank weapons (e.g., KA-50 Black Shark helicopters) attractive to India. Submarines, cruisers and destroyers also were on the negotiation list (Interfax, 8 Oct 1997). Military and technical agreements between India and Russia were finalized during meetings in Moscow, 5–6 October 1997. Western concern for all these arrangements were countered in the Russian media by references to NATO's dramatic growth.

Almost exactly a year later, India and China again ordered war planes from Russia, and Lukin led a delegation from the Duma's Committee on International Affairs to New Delhi, where he told journalists that "Russia must perpetuate and boost the potential of friendly relations with India, and must promote strategic partnership with it" (ITAR-TASS, 14 Sept 1998). Even if one sets aside the characteristic exaggeration of visiting dignitary statements, Lukin's delegation was treated as high priority by India's prime minister and parliamentarians. The next week Moscow announced that it had arranged to sell India booster rockets for satellites.

Given the "provocation" of NATO expansion, Russian nationalists found it easy to drum up new eastern missions. Vladimir N. Volkov, member of the State Duma Defense Committee, made this a public issue on 11 April 1997. In an interview with ITAR-TASS he said that as soon as any Central or Eastern European country joins NATO the "Treaty on Conventional Armed Forces in Europe [CFE] will be rendered meaningless." Summing up, he claimed that Russian security could be ensured only by maintaining "good relations with China, India and other countries of the Asia-Pacific Region."[14] Volkov and other commentators were especially concerned that "certain" Western countries were trying to supplant Russia as the dominant power in the Caucasus and former Soviet Central Asia.[15]

---

[14]ITAR-TASS (11 Apr 1997). The interview was conducted by Anatolii Yurkin, in connection with a conference in Moscow, "Russia-NATO Agreements. Necessity, Possibility, New Approaches."

[15]For the extreme, but alive and well, nationalist perspective, one need only to turn to Zhirinovskii's *O sud'bakh Rossii, Chast II. Poslednii brosok na iug* [On the Fate of Russia. Part II: The Last Dash to the South] (Moscow, 1993), and compare this to N. Ya. Danilevskii's *Russia and Europe,* the "Bible" of Russian panslavism. Danilevskii predicted in 1872 that Slavs, led by Russians, would be victorious in an inevitable clash with Europe and form a new Slavic (Russian) empire with its capital in Constantinople. See section 1.

Russians who demand that their government look for other strategic partnerships made much of agreements signed in 1997 with China, Iran, India, Kazakhstan and the Central Asian states. A flurry of such arrangements, including sweeping agreements with Ukraine, 28–31 May, struck some Russian and foreign observers as part of a major overhaul of Russian foreign policy objectives. An accord with Iran on trade and economic cooperation (14 April), a series of similar deals with China signed on 27–29 June, and even a protocol on exchanging oil for raw sugar with Cuba (3 June), all flew in the face of American preferences.[16]

The agreements were driven by reasons more compelling than NATO expansion: the need for trade; Russia's arms market requirements; Caspian Sea concerns; and so on. But the political class made—and continued to make—use of them in the NATO debate, to the extent that such "partnerships" often became something larger than their original purpose in the public's mind. On 12 May, for example, a few days before the final Primakov-Solana discussion in Moscow about a Russia-NATO accord, *Rossiiskaia gazeta* ran a feature piece that stressed the "commonalities" between Moscow, Beijing and Teheran in respect to NATO's eastward expansion and U.S. policy in Asia. The author was strongly supportive of a new "Asian Entente" with Russia as keynote member.[17] A few days later, two prominent academics in St. Petersburg reacted to the Primakov-Solana announcement by urging their government to look for alliances with Belarus, Iran, Iraq, Syria and Libya. A special alliance between the Slavic and Arab countries would pose a "real counter to the expansion of the West." If Russia does not do this, history professor I. Ya. Frolianov explained, then a "Muslim world, strengthened by the West, will turn against the Slavs."[18] The fact that the Russian government regularly recommended in 1997 and 1998 that sanctions against Iraq be dropped illustrated a consistent difference between the perspectives on the region held in Moscow and NATO's capital cities.

The image of a Russian-Chinese strategic partnership was typified in the military press by a piece that appeared shortly before the 27 May Founding Act signing ceremony. The obvious readiness of the two countries to build a "multipolar world"

---

[16]For the deal with Cuba, *Rossiiskaia gazeta* (25 June 1997); with Iran, *Rossiiskaia gazeta* (24 May 1997); and a description of the accords with China, ITAR-TASS (27 June 1997). More deals were signed with Cuba in May 1999.

[17]See Aleksei Chichkin, "An 'Asian Entente' Could Become a Reality," *Rossiiskaia gazeta* (12 May 1997), FBIS-SOV, No. 091.

[18]Ivanov, "KRESTONATO. Tri pozitsii . . .," *op cit.* (15 May 1997). Professor S.B. Lavrov, president of the Russian Geographical Society, was a strong proponent of union with Belarus as a defensive counter to western "advancement."

with a new "center of gravity" worried the West so much, *Krasnaia zvezda* intoned on 22 May, that it was compelled, via NATO, to put Russia "in its place."[19]

Less than a month after the Founding Act was signed, Russia was, in fact, participating in the G-7 as more than an invited guest, and had full membership in the Paris Club. Yet the practical value of these "openings" remained questionable, at least in so far as a wide range of Russian doubters were concerned. They tended to keep the option of partnerships "to the east" open as part of the rhetorical protest. "Russia is Looking to the East," rang an August headline in *Moscow News*. "It is clear," Andrei Grachev wrote, "that the Atlantic bloc will expand eastward until it comes up against the Russian border." Lack of respect for Russia is endemic in NATO, the EU, and even the G-7, he continued, making a turn to China, the ASEAN countries, and India essential to Russia's economic, and therefore political, well-being. Recognizing the pitfalls of relying on arms sales, especially when there are markets on both sides of a potential conflict (e.g., North and South Korea), Grachev advised that a wise, economics-motivated drive towards the Pacific would lead to more respect from the West.[20]

Grachev was well aware that Western leaders were not going to worry much about Moscow's threat to look elsewhere for strategic partnerships, and mocked Pavel Grachev's promise—when he was defense minister—that "[i]f NATO goes east, we too will go East." Andrei Grachev's point, instead, was that whereas the Russian nationalist vision of an Asian anti-NATO formation was "ill-conceived," it was being heard more and more often in the corridors of power; and NATO expansion provided sub-text for such conversations.

Russians were encouraged to look away from the East by Labour's victory in Britain, especially after foreign secretary Robin Cook told an interviewer in July that relations with Russia were to be a priority of his government.[21] But not for long. The media commented as well that Cook offered no response when asked what he thought of Russia's threat to "abandon" the Founding Act if any of the Baltic states were invited to join NATO.

Many months of active negotiation with India, China and "maverick" Middle Eastern countries reached a crescendo for Russia in December 1997. The first break-through that month, however, came from a NATO member, when a huge,

---

[19]"Gotovnost' Rossii i Kitaia stroit' mnogo-poliarnyi mir ne na shutku obespokoila zapad" [The Willingness of Russia and China to Build a Multi-Polar World Seriously Troubled the West], *Krasnaia zvezda* (22 May 1997).

[20]Grachev, "Russia Is Looking to the East," *Moscow News*, No. 31 (14–20 Aug 1997). It had appeared in *Moskovskie novosti*, No. 31 (3–10 Aug 1997). Signed to press 4 August.

[21]"Rossiia—nash prioritet" [Russia Is Our Priority], *Rossiiskie vesti* (16 July 1997). Cook was in Moscow 13–15 July.

25-year compact to supply Turkey with natural gas was signed in Ankara. The project, which is scheduled to begin in the year 2000 and could be worth billions to Russia, calls for the construction of a pipeline along the bottom of the Black Sea (Interfax, 15 Dec 1997). The labor newspaper *Rabochaia tribuna* claimed that the United States was "actively" opposed to the arrangement. Shortly thereafter, Russian and Indian defense ministers signed a protocol of cooperation in Delhi and, during a celebration in that country of the 30th anniversary of India-Russia cooperation, a contract for delivery of the ninth Russian submarine to India was announced (ITAR-TASS, 22, 24 Dec). Other major agreements with Iran, Iraq, Libya and China (see section 2.1) made December Russia's most successful month in 1997 for working out new or upgraded strategic and economic partnerships.

Strategic re-considerations remained relatively muted in Russia until mid-January 1998. Then the almost simultaneous heating up of a crisis over the UN weapons inspection impasse in Iraq and the signing of a U.S.-Baltic Charter in Washington (16 January) caused a new outburst of anxiety in Russia (see Section 5). Communist leader Zyuganov angrily informed reporters in Strasbourg, where he was attending a session of the Parliamentary Assembly of the Council of Europe, that further NATO inroads were "actively pushing Russia into establishing an alliance relationship in Asia and the Middle East" (ITAR-TASS, 28 Jan). Zyuganov could speak only for his own constituents, but it is worth noting that at the same time Minister of Defense Sergeev told audiences in Germany that Russia was now considering a joint military structure with Belarus, deployed on Belarusian territory to confront a militarily upgraded Poland (Interfax, 29 Jan).[22]

The bottom line came in March 1998 from the Russian Atomic Energy Ministry, which announced that projects involving the construction of nuclear power stations in Iran, India and China had priority because they will earn Russia up to $5 billion (Interfax, 17 March). This economic reality goes a long way towards explaining Russia's reluctance to condemn India, and refusal to contemplate sanctions, for its startling nuclear test in May. Foreign and defense ministry officials made no attempt to hide their belief that India's strained relations with the United States and its continue status as a foil to China made it an ideal partner for Russia. *Rosvooruzhenie,* Russia's government-owned arms export company, announced that it had no intention of cancelling plans to sell two nuclear power plants to India.[23] Explaining

[22]For general commentary, see, e.g., "My za snizhenie voennoi aktivnosti NATO" [We Stand for a Decrease in NATO Military Activity], *Nezavisimaia gazeta* (20 Jan 1998); "U Pol'shi poiavilis' svoi interesy na prostorakh SNG" [Poland Has Its Interests in CIS Space], *Izvestiia* (9 Jan 1998).

[23]See Maksim Yusin, "Moskva ne budet ssorit'sia so svoim souiznikom" [Moscow Will Not Quarrel with Its Ally], *Izvestiia* (13 May 1998).

why his country confirmed the agreement in June—worth up to $3 billion to Moscow's nuclear energy industry—the Russian envoy in New Delhi called India a "strategic partner" of Russia (ITAR-TASS, 20 June). One Russian journalist claimed that the Indian and Pakistani nuclear programs were both created with the secret connivance of NATO countries anyway.[24]

On the other hand, a meeting between French President Chirac, German Chancellor Kohl and Yeltsin in Moscow in late March 1998 was hailed by Yeltsin as the start of a new European partnership. The Russian president acclaimed the talks as the beginning of a "greater European Troika," an "axis of Paris, Bonn and Moscow." Chirac and Kohl would not go that far, and took great care to assure the media that there was nothing anti-American going on. All three heads of state confirmed, however, that one purpose of the session was to prevent NATO expansion from "splitting Europe again."[25] The Russian media was cautious, just as it had been when the meeting was first projected in November 1997, but most commentators treated it as a step towards Russia's full participation in European affairs. The communist press, though, described the "axis" idea as a figment of Yeltsin's imagination.[26]

In March published interviews with defense ministers from the less powerful NATO countries, such as Italy and Greece, and a French diplomat, made NATO

---

[24]Vladimir Sergeev, "Yuzhno Aziatskii vyzov. Deli i Islamabad sozdavali atomnoe oruzhie pri sekretnoi podderzhke stran NATO" [The South Asian Challenge: Delhi and Islamabad Created Atomic Weapons with the Secret Support of NATO Countries], *Nezavisimaia gazeta* (11 June 1998). On the long background to the differences between Moscow and Washington in this matter, see Michael R. Gordon, "Despite Bomb Tests, Russia Is Selling Two Nuclear Plants to India," *New York Times* (23 June 1998).

[25]On this, see, e.g., Igor Maksimychev, "Bol'shaia troika vstretitsia v Podmoskov'e" [Big Three Will Meet Near Moscow], *Rossiiskaia gazeta* (25 March 1998), where German foreign minister Klaus Kinkel was quoted saying that "Russia, Germany, and France together represent a powerful team. Together they could be an engine and stimulus for European and Euro-Atlantic cooperation." Aleksandr Savov said that the "troika" could be a counter to NATO and facilitate some cooperative activity with Iran, see his "Ot Urala do Atlantiki" [From the Urals to the Atlantic], *Rossiiskaia gazeta* (28 March 1998). *Komsomol'skaia pravda* (3 April) called Yeltsin's claims of a new Greater European triad a "fairy tale," but praised the statement that there would be annual meetings between the three leaders; in "Bol'shaia troika tianet Evropu k edineniiu" [Big Three Pulls Europe towards Unity], *Rossiiskaia gazeta* (1 April 1998) Nikolai Paklin noted that Germany and France were strongly committed to NATO but emphasized also the great strategic value of such "Troika Summits." He took comfort in Poland's worry about the meeting.

[26]Vasilii Safronchuk, "'Troika' po geometrii. Tol'ko B.N. Yel'tsin govorit ob 'osi Parizh—Bonn—Moskva'" [A Troika According to Geometry: Only Yeltsin Speaks about an "Axis between Paris, Bonn and Moscow"], *Sovetskaia Rossiia* (28 March 1998).

appear uncertain on what expansion would actually mean for Europe. Each of them expressed a strong wish not to alienate Russia further, yet at the same time proposed that NATO expand to the southeast (Balkans) and even to Central Asia (Transcaucasia).[27] Coupled with NATO exercises in the northwest (see Section 5), these interviews made the spring of 1998 seem to Russian readers as one marked by aggressive NATO expansionism. Perhaps that is why Vladimir Mikheev and Vladimir Kuzar', in *Izvestiia* and *Krasnaia zvezda,* discussed in some detail the possibility that the Western European Union (WEU) might become the seat of a "purely European military organization." Mikheev was encouraged about a "real alternative" to NATO, noting that at a WEU meeting in Greece it was resolved that "without Russia a new European security architecture is impossible." Kuzar' took issue with this viewpoint, asserting that the United States was playing a "dictatorial role" in NATO and would not give up its edge. In the long run, Kuzar' concluded that the WEU was "afraid" to institute a move towards a European security system because the United States would then cut back on economic and infrastructure assistance.[28]

Worry about the growing American presence in Russia's traditional spheres of influence, above all in Transcaucasia and Central Asia (see section 6), began to show up regularly in the Soviet press in the spring of 1998. One common accusation was that the CIA was promoting U.S. oil interests in Central Asia. Others called NATO the main vehicle for an aggressive American strategy in both regions.[29] Russian officials and analysts continued to warn NATO members not to

---

[27]See, e.g., Pavel Anokhin, Mikhail Sevast'ianov, "Piat' neudobnykh voprosov predstaviteliu NATO" [Five Uncomfortable Questions for a NATO Representative], *Rossiiskie vesti* (24 March 1998), an interview with Aleksei Chahtahtinsky, a French diplomat representing the NATO information service, who answered questions about the Russian perception that the United States is aiming for "world supremacy" using NATO as its vehicle; and how NATO might react to a Russian "expansion" towards the west, to include Ukraine and Belarus; Viktor Sokolov, "Predstoit eshche opredelit' filosofiiu NATO" [NATO's Philosophy is Yet to be Determined], *Nezavisimaia gazeta* (31 March 1998), an interview with the Greek minister of defense, who said that NATO might expand to include former Soviet republics in Central Asia; and Sergei Startsev, "NATO sleduet rasshiriat' na yugo-vostok" [NATO Should Expand to the Southeast], *Nezavisimaia gazeta* (21 March 1998), an interview with the Italian minister of defense.

[28]Kuzar, "Zakhochet li Zapadnoevropeiskii soiuz stat' osnovoi 'nezavisimoi oborony' Evropy?" [Will the West European Union Wish to Become the Basis of an "Independent Defense" of Europe?], *Krasnaia zvezda* (2 April 1998); Mikheev, "Dubler NATO priglashaet Rossiiu" [NATO's Understudy Invites Russia], *Izvestiia* (14 May 1998).

[29]See, e.g., Sergei Sokut, Aleksandr Shaburkin, "Shchit dlia tsenta Rossii" [Shield for Central Russia], *Nesavisimoe voennoe obozrenie,* No. 15 (17–23 April 1998), for the CIA essay; and A. Gusher, "On Russian-Iranian Relations," *International Affairs* (Moscow), 43, No. 2 (1997): 38–44.

undermine the United Nations by ignoring its Security Council in regional conflicts. They lobbied consistently for the OSCE as the linchpin of European security.[30] These concerns intensified, culminating on 21 December, shortly after the
first American and British air strikes against Iraq, when Primakov, in New Delhi,
proposed a Moscow-Beijing-Delhi strategic "triangle." His purpose was not a military bloc, the Russian prime minister insisted; rather he hoped for an economic
and diplomatic counterweight to the current "unipolar" situation that enabled the
Americans to act as they wished everywhere in the world.[31] Back in Moscow, Defense Minister Sergeev termed the idea a "stabilizing factor," aimed to create a
more balanced, multipolar world (Interfax, 21 Dec).

NATO's air strikes against Yugoslavia in March 1999 marked the first instance
of Russia, China and India combining in response to an international crisis. They
voted together in a losing resolution to the UN Security Council and subse-
quently announced that they would coordinate their efforts to seek peaceful solutions to the Balkan conflagration. In terms of strategic partnerships, however,
Moscow's bet still lay in a "divide and conquer" policy in Europe. Mixed opinions
among NATO members on nuclear "first strike" was one sign that division could
be exploited. More importantly, Russia could still count on timely support from
France, whose government, newly appointed ambassador N. Afanas'evskii had
said in January, agreed with Russia "on a broad spectrum of international problems," especially on the matter of a European security charter.[32]

From the Russian perspective, by 1999 NATO had moved well beyond the
projections of simple "enlargement" announced in the early 1990s. Three new
members from among Russia's former "allies," a huge base of PfP members, and
an actively pursued "out of zone" policy made NATO far more ascendant than
Moscow had foreseen. Russian thinkers were compelled to come to terms with
their country's lowered international status. Early in March, Irena Zhinkina
asked pointedly, "Is Russia a Great Power?" Concluding that her homeland was

---

[30]See, e.g., Aleksei Liashchenko, "Shturm skandinavii" [The Offensive against Scandi-
navia], *Krasnaia zvezda* (10 Dec 1998); Grigorii Morozov, "NATO posuagaet na funktsii
Soveta bezopasnosti OON" [NATO Encroaches upon the Functions of the UN Security
Council], *Izvestiia* (5 Dec 1998); Yurii Dubov, Yurii Morozov, "S NATO ili bez nego?"
[With or Without NATO?], *Nezavisimoe voennoe obozrenoe,* No. 4 (5–11 Feb 1999).

[31]On this, see Nikolai Paklin, "Treugol'nik Moskva-Pekin-Deli" [Moscow-Beijing-
Delhi Triangle], *Rossiiskaia gazeta* (22 Dec 1998). For an English-language version of the
Russia-India communiqué, see ITAR-TASS (22 Dec 1998); and in Russian, "Rossiisko-
indeiiskoe zaiavlenie," *Rossiiskaia gazeta* (23 Dec 1998). See also, "K strategicheskomu
partnerstvu" [To a Strategic Partnership], *Rossiiskaia gazeta* (23 Dec 1998).

[32]Afanas'evskii, "Parizhskie tainy rossiiskogo posla" [Russian Ambassador's Paris Se-
crets], *Rossiiskaia gazeta* (27 Jan 1999).

no longer influential in the world, with its role in resolving international conflict defined solely by its historical place on the UN Security Council, she warned that the situation was worsening because Washington "with help from NATO expansion" was establishing a new balance of forces in post-Soviet Russian space. In the absence of real allies, a viable military industrial complex and a strong army are Russia's only means to secure its current boundaries. In short, Russia is forced to rearm.[33]

2.1. China

An official visit by Rodionov to China on 14–18 April 1997 resulted, the Russian defense minister said, in a "long-term strategic partnership." At a later press conference, Rodionov remarked that Moscow "appreciates the fact that China shares Russia's concerns over the eastward expansion of NATO." Warming up for Jiang Zemin's official return visit to Russia a week later, Vladimir Lukin spoke for the State Duma's International Affairs Committee when he urged that Russia and China establish a "special relationship of strategic partnership," because the two countries hold the same views on "many issues" (Interfax, 16 April). As one of the three founders (with Yavlinskii and Yurii Boldyrev) of Yabloko, the "liberal" bloc in the Duma, Lukin's voice cannot be set aside as part of the usual Duma opposition to NATO. The normally moderate *Izvestiia* even recommended that Russia support China's position if a conflict broke out on the Korean peninsula, as long as the two countries combined to oppose "American hegemonism."[34] In Russia and China the battle against NATO expansion was now being fought in Cold War language and image making. The actual agreement between Russia and China, signed on 23 April 1997, was termed a new "partnership for the 21st century" in a joint communiqué and the partnership opened with a strongly worded criticism of NATO expansion eastward. All Russian observers portrayed the agreement as a step towards a multipolar world and a positive alternative to a lingering "Cold War syndrome," and many saw it as a direct consequence of NATO expansion eastward.[35]

---

[33]Zhinkina, "Yavliaetsia li Rossiia velikoi derzhavoi?" [Is Russia a Great Power?], *Nezavisimoe voennoe obozrenie*, No. 8 (4–10 March 1999).

[34]Aleksandr Platkovskii, "Rodionov zovet kitaitsev na bor'bu s gegemonizmom" [Rodionov Calls on the Chinese for the Struggle Against Hegemonism], *Izvestiia* (16 April 1997).

[35]See, especially, senior researcher for the Russian Academy of Science's Institute for the Far East, G.A. Bogoliubov, "Rasshirenie NATO na Vostok i rossiisko-kitaiskie otnosheniia" [The Expansion of NATO to the East and Russian-Chinese Relations], *Problemy Dal'nego Vostoka*, No. 6 (1997): 31–41, and Vesevolod Ovchinnikov, "Rossiia i Kitai: mnogopoliarnyi mir, spravedlivyi mezhdunarodnyi poriadok" [Russia and China: A Multipolar World, the Fair International Order], *Rossiiskaia gazeta* (26 April 1997).

It is true that after the Russia-NATO Founding Act was signed, certain elements of China's military elite wondered publicly about Russia's commitment, and claimed that the Kremlin was playing up the idea of "partnership" in the Far East to achieve a favorable *modus vivendi* with the West. The degree to which this charge was correct is difficult to calculate, though it is no secret that Yeltsin's government would prefer a Western association. It is equally clear that the opposition in Russia does not want integration with the West if Russia is made subservient in the association.[36] Chinese leaders do not doubt that Russia could be using their country as a bargaining chip with Europe, but the relationship was no less important for all that, as subsequent events were to demonstrate.

Moscow-Beijing relations flourished. As delegates gathered at the Denver G-8 summit, Boris Nemtsov and a contingent of Russian business representatives were in China to work out a broad spectrum of economic and political arrangements. The program of negotiations was of such significance that Chernomyrdin travelled to Beijing immediately after the Denver meetings, and Security Council member Berezovskii went to China before the end of June. Nemtsov's companion, RF minister for nuclear energy, Viktor Mikhailov (replaced in early 1998), signed a contract to help China construct a nuclear energy plant in Jiangsu province (ITAR-TASS, 24 June). On Chernomyrdin's arrival, a Russia-China Commission was set up to arrange regular meetings between heads of government. Sub-commissions for trade, economic, scientific, and technical cooperation in the area of transport nuclear power engineering were organized as well (ITAR-TASS, 27 June). These agreements represented by far the most extensive Russia-China cooperative planning since the early 1950s. Plans were made for a Yeltsin visit to Beijing.

The role of NATO expansion in this complex new association was indefinite but always there. Declamations on the part of both participants mirrored their perception of a world increasingly dominated by the United States. At least one Russian observer, Andrei Grachev, noted in the *Novoe vremya* that NATO's new "demarcation line" was a sign that Europe had closed ranks on an "unpredictable" Russia, which now might consider building an anti-Western alliance with China.[37] A few days before the Madrid Summit, *Delovoi Mir* carried a long piece on Moscow-Beijing cooperation, the purpose of which was to summarize the consequences of

---

[36]On this, see "Generaly v Pekine raskusili igru Moskvy" [Generals in Pekin Uncovered Moscow's Intrigue], *Izvestiia* (29 May 1997).

[37]Grachev, "The Psychology of Reciprocity," *New Times* (Aug 1997): 41. He did not say that this would happen, rather that it was an option to be taken seriously. The Russian version appeared earlier, in *Novoe vremya*, No. 22 (8 June 1997): 28. See also Andrei Ivanov, "We Will Build Our Multipolar World," *New Times* (June 1997): 38–39.

recent diplomatic activities. The Chernomyrdin visit to China, ending on 28 June, saw an agreement reached on oil and gas cooperation, including the construction of a pipeline to carry Russian oil and gas to China. Dozens of other energy-related projects, plus the possibility of Russia exporting nuclear power plants, cooperating on military technology, and delivering sophisticated military hardware (planes, ships, missile and anti-aircraft systems, and submarines) all were negotiated, it seems, causing "concern" in the United States and Japan.[38]

Increased tensions between the United States and Iran in October/November 1997, connected to a certain extent to the acceleration of Russian and Chinese economic and military cooperation with Iran (see section 2.2), made the timing of a Yeltsin state visit to Beijing in November especially propitious. The visit resulted in a Russian-Chinese joint declaration (ITAR-TASS, 10 Nov) on a number of important issues: they intended to raise the level of cooperation on security and economic matters; they would not pursue "hegemonic or expansionist aims;" they felt that "alliances" and "strategic 'polygons'" were passé; they supported "multipolarity" in relations between major states; and they agreed to make a final demarcation of their mutual borders. Whereas the declaration said twice that Russian-Chinese "unity of opinions" was not aimed at a 3rd party, the inferences about NATO were clear.[39] *Rossiiskaia gazeta* hailed the agreement as a strategic partnership heading into the 21st century.[40]

Final arrangements for the construction of a nuclear energy plant in China, worth up to $5 billion to Moscow, were signed by Russian and Chinese officials on 25 December (Interfax 25 Dec). Just two days before that China's official news service for English-language audiences, *Beijing Xinhua,* carried a piece titled "Yearender on NATO 1997–99," where it was said that NATO had actively promoted expansion eastward but still could not provide any rational reasons for doing so.[41] Almost simultaneously, a Chinese correspondent in Washington attrib-

---

[38]Yurii Paniev, "Moskva i Pekin opredelili novye prioritety budushchego sotrudnichestva" [Moscow and Beijing Have Determined New Priorities for Future Cooperation], *Delovoi Mir* (1 July 1997). The "concern" in the United States and Japan was Paniev's rather pleased claim.

[39]The ITAR-TASS (10 Nov 1997) reference noted in the text is the complete communiqué in translation. The mainstream Russian press hailed the agreement. See, e.g., on 11 November alone, *Rossiiskaia gazeta, Trud, Rossiiskie vesti.*

The border demarcation agreement was signed on 9 November, with the omission of reference to several islands in the Amur (ITAR-TASS, 9 Nov).

[40]"Moskva-Pekin: strategicheskoe partnerstvo, napravlennoe v XXI vek" [Moscow-Beijing: Strategic Partnership Heading for the 21st Century], *Rossiiskaia gazeta* (12 Nov 1997).

[41]*Beijing Hinhua* (22 Dec 197), FBIS-CHI, No. 356. The English-language report was filed by China's correspondent in Brussels.

uted a desire to "re-shape the world" to Secretary of State Albright and described NATO's planned expansion as a means both to strengthen America's place in Europe and to "prevent Russia from staging a comeback."[42]

Almost a year later, a joint "Statement on Relations" issued by Yeltsin and Jiang in Moscow confirmed their strategic partnership. The two presidents added a new emphasis supporting the UN Security Council, of which they are both permanent, veto-wielding members, to their previous call for multipolarity. In this regard they highlighted their mutual opposition to any use of force by NATO in Yugoslavia (ITAR-TASS, 23 Nov 1998). It was clear from this communiqué that Moscow's links with China had been firmed up during 1998 and that NATO's expanding role in regional conflicts had contributed greatly to that advance. During the 2nd session of the Sino-Russian Committee for Friendship, Peace and Development, which met in Moscow on 26 January 1999, Primakov confirmed that China and Russia shared a common front in their insistence on a multipolar world.

Although the fact that Russia and China (and India) took similar positions on the crisis in Yugoslavia took no one by surprise, the extent to which it drew Russian commentators back to the idea of an eastern strategic relationship was startling. Typical of this trend was a long feature by Yevgenii Dezhin, who determined that growing links with China "would diminish Russia's interest in developing relations with the West, especially in the circumstances of NATO aggression against Yugoslavia. . . ."[43]

2.2. Iran-Iraq

a. Iran

When U.S. Secretary of State Albright told NATO foreign ministers in December 1997 that they should adopt a broader strategy for dealing with threats from nuclear, chemical and biological weapons emanating from "the Middle East and Eurasia," she was referring primarily to Iraq, Iran and possibly Libya.[44] Russia was not mentioned, but its foreign ministry vociferously objected to her remarks. As

---

[42]*Renmin Ribao* (17 Dec 1997), FBIS-CHI, No. 356. The report was filed by Li Yunfei, who said also that Albright would provoke Russian nationalism. This Beijing newspaper is the Communist Party of China's *People's Daily.*

[43]Dezhin, "Protivnes sviaziam s NATO im mozhet stat' strategicheskoe partnerstvo Rossii i Kitaia" [A Strategic Partnership between Russia and China Can Be a Foil to Connections with NATO], *Nezavisimoe voennoe obozrenie,* No. 13 (9–15 April 1999). See also Charles Clover, "Dreams of the Eurasian Heartland," *Foreign Affairs* (March/April 1999): 9–13.

[44]See Craig R. Whitney, "Albright, at NATO Meeting, Tells of Peril from 'Eurasia'," *New York Times* (17 Dec 1997).

a matter of fact, the possibility that Russia and Iran were being driven together by American policy had been raised in the spring issue of *Foreign Affairs* by Brzezinski, Brent Scowcraft and Richard Murphy. Caspar Weinberger, former U.S. secretary of defense, had returned to that theme in a *New York Times* OP-ED, 9 May 1997, warning that if the United States did not pay closer attention, Russia and Iran would soon freeze the West out of Caspian Sea energy resources.[45]

Albright's statement accentuated a long standing Kremlin concern for its standing in the Caspian region. As one of the five Caspian Sea countries, with Russia, Kazakhstan, Azerbaijan and Turkmenistan, and a neighbor by land of the two latter countries and Armenia, Iran is extraordinarily important to Russia's strategic considerations. NATO expansion made it even more so. In February 1997, a Russian ministry of foreign affairs publication had outlined thoroughly the advantages of dealing closely with Iran. Both countries are threatened by NATO, A. Gusher wrote, especially as the Partnership for Peace linked Transcaucasia and Central Asia directly to the Alliance. Iran and Russia have similar concerns about separatist forces, Turkish influence in the Black Sea and Transcaucasia, and Western economic penetration. Military-technical contacts are important to both countries, as are trade relations generally. A joint agreement signed in June 1997 to spend millions on building infrastructure in Astrakhan to link that Russian port city with Iranian ports on the Caspian Sea was a testimony to their mutual interests.[46]

Iran's economic isolation began to change in the spring of 1997. Victory by relatively moderate forces in the 23 May Iranian presidential elections and the country's participation (10 percent) in an Azerbaijani consortium to develop offshore oil in the Caspian Sea were both promising events for Russia.[47] The United States

---

[45]Weinberger, Peter Schweizer, "Russia's Oil Grab," *New York Times* (9 May 1997). Brzezinski, Scowcraft, Murphy, "Differentiated Containment," *Foreign Affairs* (May/June 1997): 20–30. The latter study was not on NATO; rather it was on the consequences of the U.S. Administration's "strident" campaign of isolating Iran, and thereby driving it towards Russia.

The Russian Federation's ties with Iran were strengthened further when Tatarstan signed a series of commercial cooperation agreements with Iran in April 1997. A joint coordination committee was put in place for this purpose.

[46]On the Astrakhan-Iran project, ITAR-TASS (3 June 1997). A. Gusher, "On Russian-Iranian Relations," *International Affairs* (Moscow), 43, No. 2 (1997): 38–44.

[47]A few weeks before the election presidential hopeful, speaker of the Iranian parliament Ali Akbar Nategh-Nouri visited Moscow and was treated royally. *Pravda-5* called this meeting part of the restoration of Soviet ties with Iran, Iraq, Syria and Libya and congratulated Primakov for turning Russia "toward the East." Quoted in Robert V. Daniels, "The Danger of NATO Expansion," *The New Leader* (14–28 July 1997): 13.

had forced Iran out of a similar consortium proposal in 1994. Together, Russia and Iran could effectively dominate the Caspian and be in a position jointly to influence a larger region that includes 8 former Soviet republics. They could slow, or even prevent, Turkish inroads in the region, but much depends on decisions about pipeline routes in determining where power lies on the Caspian Basin. There is a sense of urgency in Moscow about association with Iran, to forestall NATO on its southern flank before the United States decides to change its policy of sanctions against that country. Special agreements between Baku and Moscow (see section 6) in June and July 1997 augmented Russia's role in the region. And a series of meetings between Russian deputy foreign minister Viktor Posuvalyuk and his Iranian counterpart in Moscow during the first week of September resulted in a communiqué confirming the two countries' interest in "deepening" their cooperation—particularly on Caspian Sea issues (ITAR-TASS, 2 Sept). Further such meetings were planned.

Yeltsin even found a Western ally in his dealings with Iran in late September 1997, when the president of France paid a state visit to Moscow. Among the several accords signed by Yeltsin and Jacques Chirac the most spectacular was a joint $2 billion natural gas deal with Iran. Niggling rumors since 1995 that Russian scientists had been secretly helping Iran construct a long range missile were heatedly denied by Russian officialdom (e.g., at the S-8 in Denver), but intelligence reports from Israel and Washington contradicted the stand taken by Yeltsin, Chernomyrdin and others. The natural gas deal made Russia's huge monopoly, Gazprom, and France's Total Petroleum major players in Iran, where Russian scientists at Bushehr are openly working on a new civilian nuclear reactor. Al Gore's attempts to dissuade Russia of this relationship when he visited Moscow earlier in September were to no avail because Iran's importance to Russia went further than as a market for arms and nuclear technology: Russia's Iranian policy is a way to demonstrate Yeltsin's independence from the United States.

In August 1997 U.S. officials accused Russia of lying when they were told that if anyone was providing Iran with help in developing the missiles it must be private institutes and companies, not the Russian government. Thus it is not difficult to see why, when the Russia-France-Iran "gas" deal was signed in October, Russian journalists boasted that their country was a clear "winner" in the affair. Moscow was perceived at home to have by-passed America's sanctions against Iran successfully, and in association with a NATO member.

Moscow News carried two long essays on this subject alone, warning that America's "extreme right wingers" were hoping to bring about a dispute between Yeltsin and Clinton by claiming that Russia was arming Iran for an attack on Israel. William Safire of the *New York Times* was singled out as a particular villain in this regard, and Brzezinski was depicted elsewhere as a "diehard Russophobe." The United States was caught in a serious dilemma, in fact, for Gazprom was at the same time raising

$1 billion in the world financial markets, including the United States. If the United States government barred Wall Street from underwriting the Gazprom bond offering, then foreign countries would rush in, as Total Petroleum had done when Clinton forced Conoco Inc. out of a major investment in Iran in 1995.[48]

Politicians on all sides scrambled to make the best of an awkward situation. Public boasting by Iranian military officials and the country's foreign minister about their own missile-manufacturing program, without Russia's help (Agence France-Press, 25 Oct), and Washington's announcement on 4 November that the United States had purchased 21 Soviet-era MIG-29 jets from Moldova so that they would not be sold to Iran gave Russia pause. A few days prior to that, while Jiang Zemin was visiting Washington, the United States agreed to sell nuclear reactors to China if it would agree not to peddle military-nuclear technology to Iran. Threats of sanctions by the U.S. Congress against Russian companies doing business with Iran added to the pressure on Moscow. According to reports in the *New York Times* (12 Nov), on 29 October Clinton telephoned Yeltsin and urged him to take the problem seriously. American influence was effective and, on 11 November, Gazprom postponed a bond offering to raise up to $3 billion for the natural gas project in Iran. The Russian press railed about U.S. interference in their country's affairs.[49]

A month later Gazprom cancelled an agreement with the U.S. Export-Import Bank, which had agreed to guarantee $750 million to finance a purchase of American equipment and services. Gazprom acted in order to avoid threatened embargoes related to its Iranian deal, and decided to look for financing elsewhere. In January 1998 the Russian government retreated further, promising Washington that it would act against Soviet companies and scientists who participate in Iranian ballistic missile programs. This was a very minor concession, for Russia's economic connection with Iran was actually strengthened when Teheran announced that it would open a consulate in Astrakhan, Russia's main port on the Caspian Sea.

In terms of U.S.-Russia relations the question of Iran was made central again

---

[48]Aleksandr Yanov, "Trial Balloon by American Right-Wingers," *Moscow News,* No. 40 (5–12 Oct 1997). The reference was to two acerbic essays by William Safire, directed against Russia and France, in the *New York Times* (28 Sept, 5 Oct 1997); in the same issue of *Moscow News,* Sanobar Shermatova writes of the hypocrisy of the U.S. position, naming Brzezinski; for the "Russophobe" comment on Brzezinski, see Sergei Dukhanov in *Delovoi mir* (8 Oct 1997).

The U.S. Congress passed the Iran and Libya Sanctions Act in 1986, making it possible to impose sanctions against foreign firms that invest more than $20 million in Iran's oil-gas industries.

[49]Not everything had gone smoothly in the Russia-Iran relationship. On 17 November 1997, Russia expelled an Iranian whom it accused of trying to buy missile technology, *New York Times* (18 Nov 1997).

in late May when the U.S. Congress attempted to impose sanctions against Russia for alleged arms dealing with Iran. A Clinton promise to veto the bill did not defuse Russian media anger. *Izvestiia* called the Congress action a "slap in the face" and warned that all it would accomplish would be more public support for communists and nationalists. *Komsomol'skaia pravda* snapped that American legislators "want to stand Russia in the corner" and noted that the Duma was now sure not to ratify START II.[50] The Iran question was tied in all Russian media commentary to NATO expansion.

In 1998, as deepening economic crisis turned in the spring and summer to a political crisis, the relatively secure place of Iran in Russian foreign policy was shaken. Still valuing the country as customer and potential strategic ally, Russian officials began to worry that moderating opinions in the West, and also in Iran, would prompt the lifting of boycotts on Teheran's export of oil. Russian oil exports would therefore become less important on the international market, further diminishing opportunities for economic recovery. Some Russian commentators suggested, subtly, that unless the United States and Iran (and Iraq) remained antagonistic to each other, Russia might be faced with national catastrophe.[51] They had reason to worry. Feelings about Iran had changed in Washington. The recommendations offered by Brzezinski and Scowcroft began to attract more attention than they had when they were published in the spring of 1997. The already nervous Russians now worried more about their place in the Caspian Sea region. Thus, as Seleznev prepared for a visit to Teheran, he told reporters in Moscow that he hoped to encourage more "strategic relations" between Iran and Russia, especially in the Caspian (ITAR-TASS, 19 Sept 1998).

The negotiations set in motion by Seleznev in September culminated in a broad agreement between Russia and Iran for cooperation in the field of gas and oil. Approved by the Russian government on 24 November, the draft accord covered all sides of the energy business, and listed 14 specific joint projects. Together the two countries account for about 40 percent of the world's gas trade, and lead

---

[50] *Komsomol'skaia pravda* (26 May 1998); Vladimir Mikheev, "Amerikanskii kongress vvodit sanktsii protiv Rossii" [American Congress Introduces Sanctions against Russia], *Izvestiia* (26 May 1998). Clinton vetoed the sanction legislation on 24 June, but said at the same time that his Administration still planned to block missile sales to Iran. Russia's foreign ministry applauded Clinton's veto and said that it too was opposed to illegal technology to Iran. See "Clinton Still Aiming to Halt Missile Sales by Russia to Iran," *New York Times* (25 June 1998). Clinton's original veto notwithstanding, 10 Russian companies were finally black listed in the United States in March 1999.

[51] See, e.g., Tatiana Koshareva, Rustan Narzukulov, "Rossiia neposredstvenno stolknulas' s perspektivoi natsional'noi katastrofy" [Russia Is Faced with the Prospects of National Catastrophe], *Nezavisimaia gazeta* (20 June 1998).

the world in reserves. The Russian media could again gloat over Washington's anger, especially as they spoke of bringing Algeria, Iraq and Libya into an international gas-exporting organization led by Moscow and Teheran. Ties with Azerbaijan, Turkmenistan and Uzbekistan also could be tightened by means of a gas-based agency.[52]

The agreement with Iran was driven by a wide range of needs: Russia's financial doldrums, Western special interest (oil) activity in the South Caucasus and the Caspian Basin, and the political and strategic manifestations of an expanding NATO.

b. Iraq

At first sight, Iraq appears less valuable to Russia than Iran, except as a market for arms, yet its significance has increased. As a southern neighbor to Iran and Turkey, and still in the grip of sanctions imposed by the UN Security Council in April 1991, Iraq provides Russia with certain opportunities, made more important by the activities of NATO. Regular discussions between Russian and Iraqi officials in 1996–97 drew repeated requests from Moscow that the sanctions against Iraq be lifted. The opinion represented by these requests was repeated by a Russian State Duma delegation after an official visit to Baghdad on 2 July 1997, and in an earlier Duma resolution that Moscow unilaterally end Russia's participation in the sanctions.

The Duma resolution was, to be sure, rejected by the Federation Council on 4 July, but only because the Russian government did not wish to challenge a decision made by the UN Security Council, of which it is itself a permanent member. The Federation Council agreed with the Duma resolution in general principle. The Duma adopted a similar resolution on Libya, with the same result (ITAR-TASS, 4 July). NATO's advance eastward was an integral part of the deliberations that resulted in these Duma initiatives.

When Saddam Hussein closed Iraq's borders to American members of the UN weapons monitoring team in October 1997, Russia stood at first with the UN, calling the Iraqi action "unacceptable" (ITAR-TASS, 1 Nov). So did China. Russia offered to provide planes for UN monitoring of Iraq. As the threat of military intervention grew, and American officials threatened to go it alone, Russia and

---

[52]"Draft Agreement between the Russian Federation Government and the Government of the Islamic Republic of Iran on Cooperation in the Field of Oil and Gas," *Rossiiskaia gazeta* (5 Dec 1998), FBIS-SOV, No. 344. The copy of this draft agreement was accompanied by a description of the 14 proposed joint projects and a "Commentary" by Aleksei Chichkin, who wrote that "Washington [is] so angry that the U.S. Congress has been conducting hearings on . . . how to punish Russia. . . . "

A. Lebed, "No objections against NATO's expansion eastward,"
Sovetskaia Rossiia" (8 October 1996).

The bait under the NATO helmet is "Partnership for Peace," *Sovetskaia Rossiia*
(12 October 1996).

Sovetskaia Rossiia (6 January 1997).
On front page.

эня?.. Чубайс?!. Гельмут?!! Билл?!! Рис. Глеба ДРИТОВА (Москва).

"Tatiana?. . [Dyachenko, Yeltsin's daughter] Chubais?!. Helmut?!! Bill?!!" *Sovetskaia Rossiia* (18 January 1997).

"Watch your step, idiot!" *Nezavisimaia gazeta* (8 July 1997).
On front page.

Cartoon reprinted from the *Guardian* by *Sovetskaia Rossiia* (17 July 1997).

"We guarantee full security," *Sovetskaia Rossiia* (27 September 1997).
Russia-CIS in mouth.

Drawing accompanying Safronchuk article, "On the Sly . . .,"
Sovetskaia Rossiia (20 January 1998).
Basket holds Estonia, Poland, Hungary, Latvia, Ukraine, and others.

"How far to Russia?" *Sovetskaia Rossiia* (7 April 1998).

"Malbrook is ready to march"—"To Yugoslavia!" *Sovetskaia Rossiia* (13 October 1998).
Solana carrying a bag of bombs marked "New World Order."

"Playboy and Gendarme of the Unipolar World"; on the tablet: "I tell the truth, only the truth, and nothing but the truth"; standing on "Russia," *Sovetskaia Rossiia* (22 December 1998).

"*Drang nach Osten* 60 Years Later," *Sovetskaia Rossiia* (27 March 1999).

"Drang nach Osten," *Sovetskaia Rossiia* (6 April 1999).

China opposed the use of force (Interfax, 10 Nov), just as they were to do later when further crises erupted in the Balkans.[53]

The question of NATO expansion was not central to the Iraq controversy. Yet in that case, as elsewhere, the image of an America demanding to have its way was instrumental in Russian media support for Saddam Hussein. Moreover, Russian companies held contracts valued at up to $8.5 million connected to Iraq's oil industry—and Iraq already owed the Russian government a huge debt. The Russian press, while blaming Iraq for its precipitate actions, tended to hold the United States and Britain responsible for blocking Russian (and also Chinese and French) business activities in the region. *Rossiiskaia gazeta* and *Sovetskaia Rossiia* found a rare point of agreement on this issue. They raised the possibility of a diplomatic consortium with Russian, French and Chinese companies forming the core of a Moscow-Paris-Beijing "pro-Iraqi alliance" to counter the use of force against Baghdad and lobby to have the sanctions lifted.[54] Primakov was credited with "brokering" a solution to the stand-off by 19 November 1997 and the UN monitors returned to their tasks. On the 22nd, Russia, with support from China, asked the UN Special Commission in charge of eliminating such weapons from Iraq to declare Iraq free of nuclear weapons, and nearly free of banned missiles. This request, agreement to which would have made it possible to lift the sanctions, was denied. The Iraq issue raised tensions between the United States and Russia to the extent that, during an interview on NBC, Secretary of State Albright voiced distrust of Russia's motives.

In its turn, the Russian media lectured the U.S. government, calling it hypocritical. Yevgenii Rusakov charged that "the planet's sheriff" supports democracy only for itself. No one disputes the necessity of Iraq following the UN guidelines, he continued in *Rabochaia tribuna,* but force is not the answer. The problem lies with NATO and the United States, who want to control oil prices of the Middle

---

[53]"Gosduma otvergaet silovoe reshenie" [The State Duma Rejects the Use of Force], *Sovetskaia Rossiia* (15 Nov 1997).

[54]Aleksei Baliev, "Sanktsii: ritorika i podopleka. Irakskim dolgam Rossii snova ugrozhaet veto" [Sanctions: Rhetoric and Rationale: Iraq's Debts to Russia Are Again Threatened by Veto], *Rossiiskaia gazeta* (12 Nov 1997); "Irak—na poligon strel'by po zhivym misheniam" [Iraq Is Not a Shooting Ground for Live Targets], *Rossiiskaia gazeta* (15 Nov 1997). The Communist press was still more adamant: see, e.g., Vasilii Safronchuk, "Navis kulak pentagona" [The Looming Fist of the Pentagon], *Sovetskaia Rossiia* (13 Nov 1997); "Gosduma otvergaet silovoe reshenie" [State Duma Rejects Resolution by Force], *Sovetskaia Rossiia* (15 Nov 1997); "Na podstupakh k Iraku" [On the Approaches to Iraq], *Sovetskaia Rossiia* (18 Nov 1997); "K sobytiiam vokrug Iraka" [On the Events Around Iraq], *Sovetskaia Rossiia* (22 Nov 1997).

East by keeping the industry in the hands of friendly states, such as Kuwait and Saudia Arabia. Sanctions against Iran and Libya also came in for heavy criticism, and it was implied that France would soon come over publicly to the Soviet position because of them. The Gazprom deal with France and Iran was cited as evidence that such cooperation was possible.[55]

The Russian moral high ground was undermined somewhat when the radical nationalist Zhirinovskii and communist leader Zyuganov paid separate visits to Baghdad after Primakov returned to Moscow. Both favored lifting UN sanctions from Iraq and blamed Washington for imposing extreme hardships on the Iraqi people. Zyuganov announced that he was certain Iraq had fulfilled the UN's requests in regard to chemical and nuclear weapons, forcing Chernomyrdin into the awkward position of having to disassociate his government from such comments and at the same time advocate lifting the sanctions.

Making a bad situation worse, Zhirinovskii was granted a meeting with Saddam Hussein on 8 December and hailed the Iraqi leader as his "great friend" (ITAR-TASS, 8 Dec 1997). On 25 December, having obtained UN clearance, Zhirinovskii and some 20 members of his LDPR again flew to Iraq, this time with five tons of medical supplies. The plane was the first foreign air craft to land in Baghdad's civilian airport in almost seven years. In its turn, the Russian government continued to oppose force as a solution to Iraq's refusal to allow full international inspections of suspected storage sites for biological and chemical weapons. Primakov made this point "categorically" at the foreign ministers' session of the PJC meeting in Brussels (Interfax, 18 Dec). Vague promises from Iraq about repayment of its huge debt to Russia in return for aid put the government, Zhirinovskii and Zyuganov on the same side for a change.

In January 1998 Russia was the first country to benefit from an Oil-for-Food program approved by the UN, and seven Russian companies purchased some 30 million barrels of oil in return for food airlifts. Through the last few weeks of March and early February, all major Russian papers objected spiritedly to any proposition that the UN use force against Iraq, though even the oppositionist Duma said that Iraq must fulfil its commitments in regards to weapons of mass destruction. The communist press offered scenarios about "who will be next?" if the United States used violence to settle its differences with Iraq. *Izvestiia* warned of the dangers of a chemical disaster as a consequence of bombing Bagh-

---

[55]Yevgenii Rusakov, "The Planet's Sheriff is Angry: U.S. Police Try to Make Russian Diplomats and Gas Officials Live by the Laws of the Wild West," *Rabochaia Tribuna* (3 Dec 1997), FBIS-SOV, No. 337.

dad.[56] Tensions rose enough that even Yeltsin, on 4 February, suggested that Clinton's "actions" could lead to a third world war.

Rhetoric over Iraq began to dominate the Soviet press and create dividing lines in domestic politics, but the divisions were between degrees of opposition to the use of force. A *Rossiiskie vesti* complaint in February that ultimata would not help and that "nobody wishes to become a hostage to U.S. policy" struck a common cord.[57] Russian reviewers began to link NATO expansion with the U.S. stance against Iraq: Vladimir Lapskii told readers of *Rossiiskaia gazeta,* for example, that it was no coincidence that the U.S. Senate began to deliberate the question of new admissions to NATO during the new Gulf crisis. Hungary, Poland, and the Czech Republic all made overtures in support of the United States and British cause. Hungary offered its air space and engineering, medical and chemical protection officers. This was a timely test of their loyalty, Lapskii concluded.[58] It was at this time too that the Russian press spoke of Madeleine Albright's "folly" and accused her of using rhetorical tricks to gain support for her unyielding positions against Iraq and Iran.[59] Estonia's bid to participate in an attack on Iraq generated bitter sarcasm from the Russian press (see section 5).

Diplomatic confrontation over Iraq intensified in April 1998 when the UN Security Council debated whether to lift the sanctions. Russia and the United States stood on opposite sides of the issue, with France hovering in-between. Tensions

---

[56]Sergei Leskov, "Udar po Iraku mozhet obernut'sia khimicheskoi katastrofoi" [A Strike against Iraq Can Cause a Chemical Catastrophe], *Izvestiia* (12 Feb 1998). See also El'mar Guseinov, "Bagdad ot udara spasaiut tol'ko svetlye nochi" [Baghdad Saved from Strikes Only by the Light of Night], *Izvestiia* (13 Feb 1998). For a cross section of remarkably consistent reporting, see, e.g., Primakov's oft-repeated statement that force is an "inadmissable" option, Anatolii Shapovalov, "Ugrozy padaiut kak bomby" [Threats Fall Like Bombs], *Rossiiskaia gazeta* (21 Jan 1998), and "Tropa voiny v persidskom zalive" [Road to War in the Persian Gulf], *Rossiiskie vesti* (4 Feb 1998); Vladimir Lapskii, "Mosty eshche ne sozhzheny no vremeni v obrez" [The Bridges Have Not Been Burnt Yet, But There Is Too Little Time Left], *Rossiiskaia gazeta* (5 Feb 1998); and Safronchuk, "Kto posle Iraka?" [Who Is Next after Iraq?], *Sovetskaia Rossiia* (5 Feb 1998).

For the Duma statement, "Zaiavlenie Gosudarstvennoi Dumy o novom obostrenii situatsii vokrug Respubliki Irak" [Statement of the State Duma on the New Aggravation of the Situation around Irak], *Rossiiskaia gazeta* (6 Feb 1998).

[57]Yurii Nikolaev, "Ul'timatum Saddamu Khuseinu" [Ultimatum to Saddam Hussein], *Rossiiskie vesti* (12 Feb 1998).

[58]Lapskii, "Esli nazval'sia gruzdem . . ." [If You Had Thought of It Before], *Rossiiskaia gazeta* (14 Feb 1998).

[59]"Glupost' Madlen Olbrait" [Madeleine Albright's Folly], *Rossiiskaia gazeta* (26 Feb 1998). For more on this, see section 1.8. See also " 'Irakskaia partiia' Primakova" [The "Iraqi Party" of Primakov], *Nezavisimaia gazeta* (20 Feb 1998).

deepened as bloodshed in Kosovo prompted communists and Russian nationalists to dredge up old Soviet conspiracy theories, attributing world wide hegemonic ambitions to the United States and NATO. Zhirinovskii fed these ideas in Russia when he headed back to Iran on 28 October with a shipment of humanitarian supplies. His visit coincided with a new Iraqi refusal to allow UN weapons inspectors to go about their tasks. As the weeks went by and Hussein grew firmer in his rejection of further inspections and Washington talked more aggressively about air strikes, communists in Russia were joined by Ukrainian colleagues in raging against American and NATO concepts of "new world order." A group of Ukrainian radical left parliament deputies accused Washington of trying to "exterminate" the Iraqi people by starvation and bombs, and lumped Hitler, the Israelis, the United States and NATO into a conspiratorial continuum practicing "genocide" against Iraq, Kurdistan, Lebanon and Yugoslavia. Rather a strange mix![60]

The communist press in Moscow worked hard to keep the issue at the forefront of Russian awareness of the Iraqi dilemma. Blame for the hardships faced by the Iraqi people because of sanctions imposed against their government were attributed not to the actions of Hussein, but to Washington's demand that he submit.[61] Primakov's long-time association with Iraqi leaders ensured that Moscow would not acquiesce easily to American threats against that country. In early December, 1998, he met Tariq Aziz, Iraq's foreign minister, in Moscow and voiced support for lifting the sanctions. Ivanov made the same recommendation, claiming that Baghdad had fulfilled the requirements set out by the Security Council. The events of 16 December showed how futile those gestures had been.

On 16 December, Lukin predicted a strike against Iraq because of U.S. internal problems, warning that the UN Special Commission had left Baghdad "too quickly."[62] Within hours, Clinton authorized American air strikes and the United

---

[60]See, e.g., "Zaiava fraktsii Progresivnoy sotsialistichnoy partiy Ukrayni, Sanktsii SShA proti Iraku ta inshikh krayn—zagroza miru i bezpetsi vsikh narodiv" [Statement by the Ukrainian Progressive Socialist Party parliamentary Faction, the U.S. Sanctions against Iraq and Other States Is a Threat to Peace and Security of Nations], *Holos Ukrayiny* (3 Nov 1998). A cartoon in *Sovetskaia Rossiia* (13 Oct 1998), showed Solana goosestepping towards Yugoslavia, carrying a bag of bombs with the inscription "New World Order." A drawing of Hitler was superimposed in the background. It is worth noting too that in August 1998 a long (340 p.) hagiographic album about Saddam Hussein was published in Moscow: S.I. Zhuravlev, *Saddam Khusein* (Moscow, 1998).

[61]See, e.g., "Beschelovechnye sanktsii protiv Iraka" [Inhuman Sanctions against Iraq], *Sovetskaia Rossiia* (26 Nov 1998).

[62]For Lukin's "prediction," see ITAR-TASS (16 Dec 1997). His conviction that the United States was about to attack Iraq was echoed in the Russian press. See, e.g., Sergei Merinov who wrote in *Rossiiskaia gazeta* (16 Dec 1998) that the Clinton administration shaped the Butler Report for the UN and that a military strike on Iraq was "almost inevitable."

States and Britain began an intensive bombing campaign over Iraq. Russia's government, political parties, and media all reacted with predictable anger. Ambassadors to London and Washington were recalled to Moscow,[63] Sergeev decided not to attend a PJC defense ministers conference set for Brussels (ITAR-TASS, 15 Dec), the Duma aborted all discussion of START II (ITAR-TASS, 17 Dec), and Ivanov spoke of a "slideback" in Russia-U.S. relations (ITAR-TASS, 19 Dec). Russia's missile forces were placed on "permanent military alert" (Interfax, 17 Dec). Eggs were thrown at the American consulate in St. Petersburg; Zhirinovskii and Zyuganov joined picketers in front of the embassy in Moscow.

NATO was harshly indicted. The Duma also adopted a resolution (394-1-2) expressing strong disapproval of American and British behavior, calling it an act of "international terrorism" revealing "the danger for the Russian Federation that is concealed in NATO's eastward expansion and the bloc's desire to act without any legitimate mandate" (ITAR-TASS, 17 Dec). The Federation Council joined the Duma in condemning the assault on Iraq and together the two elected branches of the Federal Assembly called for an increase in their country's defense budget, and threatened themselves to override the UN sanctions against Iraq.

By the end of 1998 no common ground had been found between East and West on this particular issue and the sporadic but nonetheless systematic air strikes against Iraq in 1999 continued to fuel dislike for the United States in Russia. The Iraq question helped reestablish the primacy of suspicion of both the United States and NATO in Russian visions of world affairs.[64] The current Russian media images of a Washington lusting after the entire Middle East were mindful of charges levelled in the Soviet media during the 1960s. Present day suspicions are reflected on the pages of a much freer press, however, a fact that has long term significance for East-West relations. Anger about the air raids over Iraq was sidelined only by still greater outrage over Yugoslavia.

2.3. "Double Standards": Yugoslavia and the Serbs

No one in a position of importance in Russia has suggested that a strategic partnership with Yugoslavia would be helpful. Nevertheless, the long-standing Russian-Serbian connection has led Moscow consistently to support Belgrade in causes very unpopular in the West. The recent and rapidly expanding role of

---

[63]Yurii Fokin resumed his duties in London on 28 December, and Yulii Vorontsov was back in Washington on the 23rd, both still condemning the military strike against Iraq (Interfax, 25 Dec 1998).

[64]See, e.g., Viktor Lapskii, " 'Lisa' snova pokazyvaet klyki" [The "Fox" Bares Its Fangs Again], *Rossiiskaia gazeta* (13 Jan 1999).

NATO in the Balkans, usually in confrontation with the Serb leadership, has created a situation in which Russian and NATO's interests diverge to a much greater
extent than anywhere else.

The question of Bosnia was high on the agenda of discussion between Pri-
makov and Belgian Foreign Minister Erik Derycke in Moscow on 9 September
1997. The meeting was billed as preparatory to the first session of the Russia-
NATO PJC, slated for 26 September, at which Derycke would be present. Chernomyrdin told a press conference that he and his Belgian counterpart agreed that
OSCE should be strengthened and that no particular side should be favored in
Bosnia. In Russia, Bosnian Serb leader and convicted war criminal Radovan
Karadzic continued to receive good press from the communists. Indeed, they had
held to the position that NATO suffered from "anti-Serb hysteria" since 1994.[65]
In contrast, Bilana Plavsic, the favorite of Western powers, was portrayed as a
"rusting lady," supported by NATO and helping to stab patriotic Serbs in the
back.[66] Primakov told reporters in Germany that Russia wanted war criminals put
on trial, but that it was not in the SFOR (UN Stabilization Force) mandate to go
beyond its territorial limitations and arrest people by force.[67]

In October, the Russian government announced that NATO's seizure of Bosnian Serb radio and TV stations was unjustified (Interfax, 2 Oct), and tried a few
weeks later to block parliamentary elections in the Serbian region of Bosnia. Albright had taken the matter up with Primakov in early October, but it wasn't until
17 October that Russia finally agreed at a meeting in Rome of the Contact Group
on Bosnia (i.e., Germany, France, Britain, Italy, the United States, and Russia) that
an election could go ahead on 23 November. The most strongly anti-NATO Russian press continued to denounce NATO's desire to capture Karadzic, and accused
both the U.S. and German military leadership of adopting cavalier attitudes towards

---

[65]See, e.g., Yevgenii Popov, "NATO igraet s bombami" [NATO Plays with Bombs],
Sovetskaia Rossiia (10 Feb 1994), and Karadzhich, "'Ya ne monstr' . . ." ["I Am Not a Mon-
ster"], *Sovetskaia Rossiia* (4 Sept 1997); on the Chernomyrdin-Derycke meeting, Interfax
(9 Sept 1997).

[66]Nikola Zhivkovich, "Rzhaveiushchaia ledi. Pochemu SShA i NATO vdrug vozliubili
Bilanu Plavshich?" [Rusting Lady: Why Did the USA and NATO Fall in Love with Bilana Plavshich?], *Sovetskaia Rossiia* (9 Sept 1997). The author submitted the essay, which
was accompanied by a dark and sombre drawing of Plavshich, from Berlin.

[67]*Bild am Sonntag* (28 Sept 1997). Primakov was interviewed in New York, where the
Russia-NATO Joint Permanent Council was meeting. The mainstream Russian-language
press in Ukraine granted some cautious support for the Russian position; e.g., "Respublika Serbskaia: khochetsia delit'sia, da NATO ne velit" [The Republic of Serbia: Wants to
Divide, but NATO Is Saying No], *Kievskie vedomosti* (12 Sept 1997).

Russian opinion in regards to the Balkans.[68] Part of the reason for the Kremlin's consent to join with NATO in Bosnia, however, was fear of being left out of Balkan negotiations altogether. This possibility was brought home when Russia was not invited to participate in a NATO defense ministers' meeting with PfP representatives from Southeast Europe, held in Sofia on 3 October. Deputy foreign minister Afanas'evskii complained to Russian journalists that the exclusion of Russia when even Poland, the Czech Republic and Hungary attended as observers contradicted Bulgaria's proclaimed desire to develop friendly relations with Russia.[69]

In November and December 1997 the Russian communist press portrayed American and NATO ambitions in the Balkans generally and in Bosnia specifically as part of a larger long-term program of "aggression and occupation." One writer diagnosed the United States as suffering from "globalphobia."[70] In March 1998 the foreign ministry insisted that the Russian component of SFOR would not be placed under NATO command. SFOR's mandate in Bosnia was scheduled to expire in June and, until that time, Russia's units were responsible to a Russian deputy commander of the operation (Interfax, 2 March 1998). The eruption of violence in Kosovo, the Yugoslav province with a mainly ethnic Albanian population, and American calls for forceful interference corroborated a widely held Russian belief that NATO wanted to replace the OSCE and the United Nations as problem solver in the region.[71]

---

[68]See, e.g., Nikola Zhivkovich, "NATO i bundeswer napialivaiut ovech'iu shkuru. A general Naumann blesnul umom . . ." [NATO and the Bundeswehr Pull on Sheep's Clothing: General Naumann Has a Brainwave . . .], *Sovetskaia Rossiia* (18 Oct 1997); Mikhail Georgiev, "Balkanskii uzel. NATO prigrozila Chernogortsam" [The Balkan Knot: NATO Threatens the Chernogorians], *Rossiiskaia gazeta* (12 Nov 1997).

[69]Nikolai Afanas'evskii, "Pro Rossiiu na Balkanakh reshili zabyt'?" [Have the Balkans Decided to "Forget" About Russia?], *Rossiiskaia gazeta* (2 Oct 1997). Other countries sending observers were Albania, Macedonia, Romania, and Slovenia. The Russian foreign ministry sent a "verbal note" to Sofia in protest, saying that the Balkans and Southeast Europe are spheres of "vital interest" to Moscow.

[70]Yevgenii Popov, "Biulleteni . . . so vzlomom. SShA eksperimentiruiut s 'demokratiei Frankenshteina'" [Bulletin . . . with Break-ins: The USA Experiments with a "Frankenstein's Democracy"], *Sovetskaia Rossiia* (25 Nov 1997); Yevgenii Popov, "Stradaiut li SShA globofobiei?! K itogam rozhdestvenskoi poezdki Klintona na Balkany" [Does the USA Suffer from Globalphobia?! Results of Clinton's Christmas Trip to the Balkans], *Sovetskaia Rossiia* (25 Dec 1997).

[71]See, e.g., "Ne dat' podorvat' Balkany" [Don't Let the Balkans Blow Up], *Rossiiskaia gazeta* (4 March 1998), and Feodor Luk'ianov, "NATO ostaetsia v Bosnii" [NATO Remains in Bosnia], *Rossiiskaia gazeta* (5 March 1998); Nikolai Paklin, "Kosovo: istekaet vtoroi srok i terpenie Madlen" [Kosovo: The Second Deadline and Madeleine's Patience Are Running Out], *Rossiiskaia gazeta* (23 Feb 1998).

The fact that ethnic Albanians demonstrated outside an American information center in Pristina, the Kosovo provincial capital, with signs saying, in English, "NATO, where are you?," was all the evidence the communists needed to proclaim a "transparent" U.S. plot.[72] The Russian government and non-communist media also disliked the idea of direct NATO involvement. For example, when the Albanian Foreign Parliamentary Committee presented a draft resolution suggesting that NATO troops be deployed in Kosovo to stop Serb "aggression," the reaction in Moscow was uniformly hostile. Russia remained the member of the international contact group on Kosovo most reluctant to impose economic sanctions against Belgrade, and Russia tended to shift blame for the crisis on to "Kosovo Albanian terrorists."[73]

Even normally moderate papers had been using the Bosnia example to project American-led schemes for control of the oil-rich Persian Gulf and Caspian Sea regions, pointing to NATO-member Turkey's involvement in Azerbaijan and NATO exercises (Tsentrazbat-97) in Central Asia as part of a larger plan for world dominance. Afanas'evskii, for example, said in an otherwise encouraging article, that "NATO's ambition to be not only an important factor in European security but also the main and only factor" was the major hindrance to viable Russia-NATO ties.[74] NATO's approach in this regard is "unacceptable to Russia and also to many other European states," he said. Western reaction to the crisis in Kosovo confirmed the worst fears in the minds of many Russians. Already angered by statements attributed to Ukraine's new foreign minister, Borys Tarasyuk, who told interviewers on 18 April that the current stability in Bosnia showed that NATO was the only security structure able to maintain peace in Europe (see section 4), readers of the communist press readily believed charges of anti-Serb "ethnic cleansing" by Albanians in Kosovo as accurate. "The West is interfering shamelessly in the internal affairs of Yugoslavia and Serbia!" proclaimed *Sovetskaia*

---

[72]See, e.g., Yevgenii Popov, "Koster v Kosovo. SShA i NATO gotoviat novuiu voennuiu avantiuru na Balkanakh, Rossiia snova predaet Serbov" [Bonfire in Kosovo: The USA and NATO Prepare a New Military Venture in the Balkans, Russia Again Betrays the Serbs], *Sovetskaia Rossiia* (12 March 1998).

[73]See Interfax (24 April 1998), where Moscow's general position and the foreign ministry's concern about the "so-called Kosovo Liberation Army" are outlined. For the draft resolution mentioned above, see ATA (10 April 1998), an English-language release from Tirana.

[74]See, e.g., Sergei Putilov, "Bosnian Scenario Projected for Caspian," *Nezavisimoe voennoe obozrenie,* No. 8 (27 Feb–5 March 1998); Afanas'evskii, "NATO-Positions and Ambitions," *Trud* (4 March 1998), FBIS-SOV, No. 064. Communist writers warned also that Central Asia was being targeted by U.S. "monopolies" and NATO, see, e.g., *Pravda* (11 March 1998).

Rossiia, whose Serbian contributor, Nikola Zhivkovich, charged that "NATO tanks are ready to trample . . . the scarlet peonies on Kosovo Field, where our heroic ancestors shed their blood in a life-and-death struggle for Serb statehood."[75] The Russian government and media consistently objected to any new NATO military initiatives against Serbs during the first stages of the Kosovo crisis, though they hedged by suggesting that PfP troops already in the region could be used as peacekeepers.[76] Zhivkovich was back a few weeks later, accusing the United States and NATO of "pushing Kosovo into war" and quoting Radio Beijing's opinion that the United States was using the Kosovo crisis to strengthen its position in the Balkans, undermining Russia's influence there, and expanding NATO's sphere both eastward and to the south.[77] Russian reporting on Kosovo increasingly concentrated on NATO's projected role in the affair, arguing that the UN must lead the way and that American bias against Serbs was undermining the possibility of a diplomatic solution.[78]

---

[75]Nikola Zhivkovich, "Referendum v Serbii: 95 protsentov protiv inostrannogo vmeshatel'stva v kosovskii konflikt. Razdaviat li tanki NATO alye piony?" [Referendum in Serbia: 95 Percent Oppose Foreign Intervention in Kosovo Conflict. Will NATO Tanks Crush Scarlet Peonies?] *Sovetskaia Rossiia* (25 April 1998). See also *Pravda* (21 April 1998), *op. cit.,* where Russian statements against NATO's activities in Bosnia, delivered at a large conference held in Moscow in mid-April, are outlined; Yuliia Petrovskaia, "Referendum v Serbii" [Referendum in Serbia], *Nezavisimaia gazeta* (23 April 1998), and Anatolii Kurganov, "Brosiat li serby perchatku zapadu?" [Will Serbians Challenge the West?], *Rossiiskaia gazeta* (25 April 1998).

[76]See, e.g., Dmitrii Gornostaev, "Rossiia protiv vvoda novykh voisk na Balkany" [Russia Is Opposed to the Introduction of New Troops into the Balkans], *Nezavisimaia gazeta* (7 May 1998).

[77]Zhivkovich, "Mir khrupok, kak freski v dechane . . . . SShA i NATO tolkaiut Kosovo k voine" [Peace Is Fragile, Like a Fresco in Dechani: The USA and NATO Push Kosovo into War], *Sovetskaia Rossiia* (14 May 1998). See also "NATO gotovit varianty" [NATO Prepares Variants], *Sovetskaia Rossiia* (26 May 1998); for a more compromising but also firm editorial from a non-communist medium, see "Primakov—o Latvii i Kosovo" [Primakov on Latvia and Kosovo], *Nezavisimaia gazeta* (6 May 1998). Dechani is the location of an ancient Serbian monastery.

[78]See, e.g., Yuliia Petrovskaia, "NATO aktiviziruetsia na Balkanakh. Al'ians gotovitsia k vvodu voisk v Albaniiu" [NATO Becomes More Active in the Balkans: The Alliance Prepares to Bring Troops into Albania], *Nezavisimaia gazeta* (21 May 1998); Yuliia Petrovskaia, "Kosovo vnov' v tsentre vnimaniia" [Kosovo Is Again the Center of Attention], *Nezavisimaia gazeta* (28 May 1998); Yurii Pankov, "Kosovskii krizis: NATO gotovo predlozhit' svoi uslugi" [The Kosovo Crisis: NATO Is Prepared to Offer Its Services], *Krasnaia zvezda* (29 May 1998).

On 2 June, Primakov laid out Moscow's policy at a news conference in Bern: Kosovo should not secede, for that would lead to war; and international use of force must not be condoned without Yugoslav consent; Kosovo is an internal consideration (ITAR-TASS, 2 June). The Russian press reported Primakov's position and voiced a conviction that Russia's stand would be ignored, or sidestepped.[79] Sergeev, in Bonn with Yeltsin and several Russian cabinet ministers, repeated this message a week later, one day after the United States said that it would support a British resolution in the UN to authorize NATO military intervention in Kosovo (Interfax, 9 June). The Russian defense minister insisted on other occasions that NATO troops not be deployed, and that all military decisions related to Kosovo be made at the UN Security Council level and include permission of the "interested sides."[80]

As a catalyst for a Russia-NATO confrontation, the Kosovo situation slipped out of control. On 15 June Russia recalled its military envoy to NATO, Lt. Gen. Viktor Zavarzin, in protest of what Sergeev called dishonorable behavior by NATO (Interfax, 15 June).[81] Just as Yugoslav President Slobodan Milosevic arrived in Moscow for talks, NATO war planes conducted exercises along the Yugoslav borders with Albania and Macedonia. Russian officials claimed to have been taken by surprise.

Kosovo quickly became the hottest foreign affairs subject in the Russian media, which, almost without exception, portrayed NATO as an aggressor in the

---

[79]See, e.g., Yurii Pankov, " 'Balkanskii dukh' zhenevskoi vstrechi" [The "Balkan Spirit" of the Geneva Meeting], *Krasnaia zvezda* (4 June 1998), and Aleksandr Kuranov, Vladimir Katin, " 'Vtoroi Bosnii' byt' ne dolzhno" [There Must Not Be a "Second Bosnia"], *Nezavisimaia gazeta* (6 June 1998).

[80]For detailed discussion of the Bonn visit, and coinciding discussions between the Russian and German defense ministers, see *Izvestiia* (9 June 1998). On the RF's preference for UN involvement over NATO, see Interfax (3, 9 June 1998) and ITAR-TASS (12 June 1998), and *Nezavisimoe voennoe obozrenie* (29 May–4 June 1998). On the American position, see Steven Erlanger, "U.S. Expresses Support for NATO Action to Halt Serb Attacks," *New York Times* (9 June 1998).

[81]For more details on this see Boris Vinogradov, "Rossiia otzyvaet iz NATO svoego voennogo predstavetilia" [Russia Recalls Its Military Representative from NATO], *Izvestiia* (16 June 1998); Maxim Yusin, "Rossiia pytaetsia spasti serbov ot bombardirovok NATO" [Russia Attempts to Save the Serbs from a NATO Bombardment], *Izvestiia* (17 June 1998).

Balkans.[82] Fed by releases from Yeltsin's government, the Moscow media was convinced that NATO, and the United States, were going to do as they wished no matter the arrangements reached by Russia with Serbian leaders.[83] One writer for *Rossiiskaia gazeta,* for example, accused Western countries of trapping themselves in their own contradictions by encouraging "Albanian terrorists" in the first place.[84] Even the moderate Russian press claimed with great anger that Chechens were being recruited to fight for Albanian separatists.[85]

Crises in Yugoslavia therefore tested the degree to which the Founding Act would provide Russia with a role in NATO decision-making, and found it coming up very short. There were allegations in mid-June that the Russian ministry of defense passed on to Belgrade intelligence information on both the Kosovo Liberation Army and NATO's operational activities in the region. *Nezavisimaia gazeta* hinted that Moscow might help rearm Yugoslavia if a "foreign army" became

---

[82]See, e.g., Vladimir Kuzar', "NATO gotovitsia k agressii v Kosovo?" [Is NATO Preparing for Aggression in Kosovo?], *Krasnaia zvezda* (16 June 1998); Yurii Pankov, "NATO snimaet mundir mirotvortsa" [NATO Takes off the Uniform of Peacemaker], *Krasnaia zvezda* (17 June 1998); Yuliia Petrovskaia, Vladimir Katin, "Spaset li Moskva Miloshevicha?" [Will Moscow Save Milosevic], *Nezavisimaia gazeta* (16 June 1998); Nikolai Paklin, "Vozdushnaia preliudiia k nazemnoi voine?" [Is the Action in the Air a Prelude to a Land War?], *Rossiiskaia gazeta* (17 June 1998); Sergei Startsev, Igor Korotchenko, "Repetitsiia vtorzheniia v Kosovo. Rossiia ne poluchila ot NATO raz'iasnenii otnositel'no uchenii na Balkanakh" [A Rehearsal for the Invasion of Kosovo: Russia Did Not Receive an Explanation from NATO on the Balkan Exercises], *Nezavisimaia gazeta* (17 June 1998).

[83]Yuliia Petrovskaia, Dmitrii Gornostaev, "Yel'tsin ubedil Miloshevicha. Prezident Yugoslavii soglasilsia na peregovory s Kosovskimi Albantsami" [Yeltsin Convinced Milosevic: The President of Yugoslavia Agreed to Negotiate with Kosovo Albanians], *Nezavisimaia gazeta* (17 June 1998).

[84]Yurii Aleshin, "Komy vygodna bol'shaia voina na Balkanakh?" [Who Benefits from a Larger War in the Balkans?], *Rossiiskaia gazeta* (16 June 1998). See also Maksim Yusin, "Ustupki Miloshevicha ne udovletvorili zapad" [Concessions from Milosevic Did Not Satisfy the West], *Izvestiia* (18 June 1998); Vladimir Kuzar', "Po natovskomu stsenariiu gotovy, pokhozhe, pustit' razvitie situatsii vokrug Kosovo zapadnye lidery" [It Seems that Western Leaders Are Prepared to Allow the Kosovo Situation to Develop According to the NATO Scenario], *Krasnaia zvezda* (19 June 1998).

[85]See, e.g., "Gosdepartament SShA soglasilsia s dannymi Rossiiskoi razvedki: Chechenskie boeviki sobiraiutsia voevat' v Kosovo protiv serbov" [The USA State Department Agrees with Reports from Russian Intelligence: Chechen Troops are Planning to Fight in Kosovo against Serbians], *Izvestiia* (19 June 1998); Vladimir Kuznechevskii, "Chechnya v tsentre evropy?" [Is Chechnia in the Center of Europe?], *Rossiiskaia gazeta* (19 June 1998).

directly involved in the Kosovo conflict.[86] Analogies with what the Russians called a "fiasco" in Bosnia abounded.[87]

The situation remained tense, but the Russian position seemed to gain ground when Canada and France insisted that NATO not launch air strikes in Kosovo without a resolution in favor of such action from the UN Security Council. The State Duma published an official Statement on the situation in Kosovo on 20 June, calling on its own government to oppose military intervention.[88] Later in June, Primakov told London's Royal Institute of International Affairs that the use of force in Kosovo was "inconceivable" because it would "change the whole international situation." Referring specifically to the public mood in Russia, he said that such an action would "alienate us" from NATO and undermine the efforts put into making the Founding Act work (ITAR-TASS, 25 June). Primakov resented the American position that UN sanction for military action in Kosovo was unnecessary, believing that Washington merely hoped to avoid facing a Russian veto at the UN.[89] Neither side budged during the summer. The Russian upper house of parliament, the Federation Council, which tends to pay attention mostly to domestic matters, issued an official Statement of its own, calling on "Kosovo Albanian leaders . . . [to] abandon terrorism and separatism." The OSCE, rather

---

[86]Yuliia Petrovskaia, Igor Korotchenko, "Dogovorennosti Yel'tsina i Miloshevicha vospriniaty prokhladno" [Agreements of Yeltsin and Milosevic Were Received Coolly], *Nezavisimaia gazeta* (18 June 1998). The communist press charged NATO and the United States with a strong "anti-Serb" bias and accused Yeltsin of giving in to NATO's interests in order to get further funding for his economic anti-crisis measures. See Yevgenii Popov, "Kosovskii ugol" [Kosovo Corner], *Sovetskaia Rossiia* (16 June 1998) and "Trevogi 'zemli chernykh ptits'" [Worries in the 'Land of Black Birds'], *Sovetskaia Rossiia* (18 June 1998), "Land of Black Birds" is a Serb name for Kosovo, and the title is a play on NATO planes flying over Kosovo.

[87]See, e.g., Aleksandr Kuranov, Vladimir Katin, " 'Vtoroi Bosnii' byt' ne dolzhno" [There Must Not Be a "Second Bosnia"], *op. cit.;* Maksim Yusin, "Vozmozhen li v Kosovo 'Bosniiskii variant'?" [Is a "Bosnian Variant" Possible in Kosovo?], *Izvestiia* (17 June 1998).

[88]"Zaiavlenie Gosudarstvennoi Dumy. O krizisnoi situatsii v Kosovo (Soiuznaia Respublika Yugoslaviia)" [Statement of the State Duma: On the Crisis Situation in Kosovo (Federal Republic of Yugoslavia)], *Rossiiskaia gazeta* (20 June 1998). The Statement was adopted on 17 June.

[89]See, e.g., Paul Koring, "Rift Weakens Threat of Force in Kosovo," Toronto *Globe and Mail* (24 June 1998). ITAR-TASS (12 June 1998) reported that Seleznev rhetorically asked a conference of European parliamentary heads, "Who gives NATO the right to speak about bombing raids on Yugoslavia?", and a very angry article in *Pravda* (16 June 1998) opposed NATO's show of air power in Kosovo. *Rossiiskaia gazeta* (16 June 1998) recommended that Belgrade offer autonomy to Kosovo to end the threat of military force from the West.

than NATO, was the monitoring group to which the Federation Council hoped to see the combatants turn for a peaceful settlement.[90] In August, when NATO announced that it had finalized plans for a possible air operation in Kosovo, Afanas'evskii spoke against military intervention from Pristina.

Russian observers took heart as they perceived some hesitancy among NATO members. Canada, for example, again urged the UN Security Council to take control of the issue, and both France and Italy seemed less committed to military intervention than the United States and Britain.[91] Indeed, as events unfolded in Kosovo, Russians were persuaded that Washington was forcing a hidden agenda on its NATO colleagues.[92] That agenda included war against Yugoslavia.[93]

Even when they were defused somewhat in the early autumn, tensions in the Balkans exemplified rising strains in Russian-American relations. Russian peace-keepers on the ground in the Balkans often were either written off as redundant by the Moscow media or described as a means to monitor the activities of their NATO partners.[94] In a tone reminiscent of the Cold War era, Russian journalists began also to accuse NATO's, and above all Washington's, "special services" of

---

[90]"Zaiavlenie Soveta Federatsii Federal'nogo Sobraniia RF o situatsii v Kosovo (Soiuz-naia Respublika Yugoslaviia)" [Statement by the Russian Federation Federal Assembly Federation Council on the Situation in Kosovo (Federal Republic of Yugoslavia)], *Rossi-iskaia gazeta* (21 July 1998). The Federal Assembly has two elected representatives from each of the 89 components of the Russian Federation, excepting, for now, Chechnya.

[91]Canadian foreign minister Lloyd Axworthy released a statement on 8 August saying that it "is incumbent on the United Nations' Security Council to become fully engaged on the Kosovo issue . . . [beforc] it spirals out of control." See "Russia Rejects NATO Push for Kosovo Military Move," Toronto *Globe and Mail* (8 Aug 1998).

[92]For the striking consistency of Russian anger and suspicion, see, e.g., Nikolai Plot-nikov, "NATOvskii sled v Zheneve" [NATO's Footprints in Geneva], *Nezavisimaia gazeta* (25 June 1998); and Maksim Yusin, "Vashington grozit Belgradu vozdushnymi udarami" [Washington Threatens Belgrade with Air Attacks], *Izvestiia* (24 June 1998).

[93] Yurii Pankov was one of the most consistent proponents of this idea, in regular re-ports for *Krasnaia zvezda*. See, e.g., issues of 11, 14, 18, 20, 22, 28 August 1998. See also Maksim Yusin, "NATO gotova vmeshat'sia v Kosovskii konflikt" [NATO Is Prepared for Intervention in the Kosovo Conflict], *Izvestiia* (5 Aug 1998), and Vladimir Lapskii, "Kosovo: vremia rabotaet protiv vsekh" [Kosovo: Time Works against Everyone], *Rossi-iskaia gazeta* (8 Aug 1998); "NATO gotovitsia k vtorzheniiu v Yugoslaviiu" [NATO Pre-pares for an Invasion of Yugoslavia], *Nezavisimaia gazeta* (13 Aug 1998).

[94]See, e.g., Feodor Luk'ianov, "Kosovo: Podkhod zapada meniaetsia?" [Kosovo: Does the Approach of the West Change?], *Rossiiskaia gazeta* (7 July 1998); Viktor Gavrilov, "Uroki mirotvorcheskikh operatsii" [Lessons of Peacekeeping Operations], *Nezavisimaia gazeta* (16 July 1998); Maksim Yusin, "Operatsii NATO snimaiutsia s povestki dnia" [NATO Operations Are Cancelled], *Izvestiia* (17 July 1998).

using electronic information carriers, such as the internet system, to manipulate and monopolize information about the Balkans, Caucasus and Caspian regions.[95]

The foreign ministry attitude did not change when Primakov moved into the prime ministerial post in September. Indeed, the sound and fury of June returned with a vengeance. Primakov's successor as foreign minister was his former deputy, Igor Ivanov, who had acted as his boss's emissary to Milosevic. On 4 September, Ivanov informed the Yugoslav leader in Belgrade that Russia still regarded the use of force in Kosovo as "unacceptable" (Interfax, 8 Sept). According to Moscow press releases, he confirmed the Russian position on the use of force to Madeleine Albright by telephone (ITAR-TASS, 17 Sept).[96]

The second crisis over Kosovo came to a head in early October, when NATO was poised to conduct an air strike against Serbian positions. All of the usually divergent political groups in Russia rallied together to denounce NATO proposals. The Duma adopted a resolution declaring the use of force in Yugoslavia "illegal" unless sanctioned by the UN Security Council and said that it was ready to revise all existing agreements with the Atlantic Alliance (Interfax, 2 Oct). A senior defense ministry official threatened retaliatory steps, including severing ties with NATO and halting all talk of ratifying START II (Interfax, 2 Oct). The new foreign minister rushed again to Belgrade to negotiate with Milosevic. Individual political leaders who disagree on most other things, such as Zhirinovskii, Zyuganov, Yavlinskii and Lebed, spoke as one on this issue. So did the often competing Duma committee heads, Lukin and Ilyukhin (Interfax, 5 Oct). Public figures, such as Luzhkov, upheld the government in its effort to prevent NATO air strikes against Yugoslavia. The rare burst of unanimity was partly a consequence of historical tradition, and partly a way of demonstrating that Moscow wanted to play an independent role in the world. It was also a signal that Russia's political people were anticipating elections and wanted to be seen on the right side of the NATO issue.

Recalling their ambassador and military representative to NATO for "consultations" in Moscow, on 11 October, the Russia government made a public show

---

[95]See, e.g., Anatolii Yeligarov, Andrei Revunov, "Pochemu Pentagon poliubil internet?" [Why Did the Pentagon Fall in Love with the Internet?], *Rossiiskaia gazeta* (16 July 1998).

[96]As the likelihood of NATO air strikes became stronger and stronger in September–October, Russia's press reporting became more adamant against them, with the Communist press leading the way. See, e.g., Nikola Zhivkovich, "Urok istorii u Aleksintsa" [Lesson of History in Aleksinets], *Sovetskaia Rossiia* (26 Sept 1998). Aleksinets (Aleksinac) refers to a battle in 1876 when Russian volunteers were killed helping Serbs against the Turks. The non-communist press also abhorred the idea of bombing Yugoslavia, see Vladimir Mikheev, "NATO gotovitsia bombit' serbov" [NATO Is Prepared to Bomb the Serbs], *Izvestiia* (25 Sept 1998).

of righteousness (see section 1.9). Russia's media accused NATO of "double standards," asking rhetorically why it was willing to bomb Yugoslavia, but neither Israel nor Northern Ireland, where "exactly" the same arguments to do so could be made. Seleznev summed up the opinion of almost the entire political class, saying that Russia's elected deputies could not look on "with indifference" at NATO's "anti-Serb hysteria."[97]

Opinion surveys taken on 17 October found that nearly 85 percent of Russians claimed to know what was going on in Kosovo, and 70 percent backed Moscow's position. Only 5 percent supported the "Western" position.[98] The American embassy in Moscow was picketed by a group claiming to represent "Russian Youth," some carrying signs saying "Today you bomb Belgrade, tomorrow we'll bomb Washington!" and the communist press charged U.S. congressmen with "pathological hatred against the Serbs," raising again the image of Nazi storm troopers marching on Yugoslavia.[99]

---

[97]For the solidarity of Russia's political class, media, and interested population on this issue see, e.g., Anatolii Shapovalov, "Serbiia—s mirom, al'ians—s bombami" [Serbia — with Peace, the Alliance—with Bombs], *Rossiiskaia gazeta* (3 Oct 1998), *op cit.*, Section 1.9; Yevgenii Popov, "Natovskie 'Tomagavki' uzhe tikaiu" [NATO's Tomahawks Are Already Ticking], *Sovetskaia Rossiia* (3 Oct 1998), on "anti-Serb hysteria"; and Vsevolod Ovchinnikov, "Ne nado, NATO, bombit' ni Izrail', ni Angliiu, ni Serbiiu" [NATO, You Must Bomb Neither Israel, Nor Britain, Nor Serbia], *Rossiiskaia gazeta* (7 Oct 1998); "Net —agressii NATO protiv Yugoslavii!" [No to NATO Aggression Against Yugoslavia!], *Sovetskaia Rossiia* (15 Oct 1998). *Komsomol'skaia pravda* (14 Oct 1998) carried one of the harshest condemnations of NATO's actions, as Sergei Maslov called NATO policy the "public execution of Belgrade" and invoked memories of Vietnam, which some American leaders promised to "bomb back into the Stone Age." See translation in FBIS-SOV, No. 283. *Zavtra* (13 Oct 1998) accused NATO of fostering "anti-Belgrade hysteria" and preparing to be involved in future conflicts within the CIS.

For commentary by Zyuganov, Lukin and Zhirinovskii at a press conference, see Interfax (25 Sept 1998). See also Vladimir Mikheev, "NATO razbombit serbov i bez soglasiia OON" [NATO Bombs the Serbs without the Agreement of the UN], *Izvestiia* (2 Oct 1998), and Konstantin Eggert, "Komandu 'na vzlet' NATO otdast cherez nedeliu" [NATO Will Order 'Let's Fly' in a Week], *Izvestiia* (3 Oct 1998), and Yelena Surovtseva, "Kosovo: poslednie prigotovleniia NATO" [Kosovo: NATO's Latest Preparation], *Krasnaia zvezda* (26 Sept 1998).

[98]ITAR-TASS (30 Oct 1998). 1500 Russians were questioned, in rural and urban settings and in the regions. 54 percent supported Yugoslavia.

[99]See, e.g., Vasilii Belov, "NATO, proch' ruki ot Kosovo!" [NATO, Take Your Dirty Hands Off Kosovo!], *Sovetskaia Rossiia* (13 Oct 1998); Ibragim Usmanov, "Amerikanskoe posol'stvo v kol'tse piketa, v zashchitu Yugoslavii" [American Embassy in a Ring of Pickets, in Defense of Yugoslavia], *Sovetskaia Rossiia* (20 Oct 1998). See also Konstantin Eggert, "Provokatsiia—norma zhizni v Kosovo" [Provocation Is the Way of Life in Kosovo], *Izvestiia* (21 Oct 1998).

As had been the case in the past, tensions grew in Kosovo until Russia was at the brink of severing relationships with NATO. Moscow complained that it was denied a voice in the Balkans.[100] After difficult negotiations, the level of crisis lowered. The OSCE was asked to serve as the umbrella organization for some 2000 unarmed observers to verify Serb compliance with UN resolutions and Serbian withdrawal of troops from Albanian-populated areas in Kosovo. Russia agreed to participate in monitoring operations in a very limited way, as part of verification flights, "Eagle Eye" (ITAR-TASS, 20 Oct). But incidents of violence rose again in mid-November, compelling NATO, Russia, the OSCE, and the UN to anticipate further complications.

The atmosphere remained tense, with conciliatory statements, threats and promises of action flying back and forth until the end of February 1999. By that time, NATO was edging towards military engagement and Russian pundits were more convinced than ever that the Alliance was fully prepared to act outside the mandate provided by the United Nations—and even that Kofi Annan was succumbing to U.S. pressure.[101] Communist leader Zyuganov flew to Belgrade for a 3-day visit on 30 January and hinted that Russia should help Yugoslavia if NATO attacked.[102]

More to the point, however, was a biting attack on NATO policy from the president of the Russian Academy of the Military Sciences. NATO expansion eastward and the lessons of the Balkans "are forcing Russia to revise the main provisions of its military doctrine," General Makhmut Gareev announced on 24 February. Gareev's opinion embodied the new more aggressive approach taken by Russia's military analysts in late 1998 and early 1999. Thinking in the old Soviet tradition of

---

[100]See, e.g., Yuliia Berezovskaia, "NATO otkazyvaet Moskve v prave golosa na Balkanakh" [NATO Denies Moscow the Right to a Voice on the Balkans], *Izvestiia* (10 Oct 1998), and Yel'mar Guseinov, "Kto uchastvuet v 'armade' NATO" [Who Participates in the NATO Armada], *Izvestiia* (14 Oct 1998).

[101]See, e.g., Fedor Lukianov, "Balkanskii uzel: Al'pha minus zdravyi smysl" [Baku Conundrum: Al'ha Minus Common Sense], *Rossiiskaia gazeta* (11 Feb 1999); Nikolai Paklin, "Balkanskii uzel: Peregovory po kosovskomu konfliktu vykhodiat na peredovuiu" [Balkan Conundrum: Talks on Kosovo Conflict Go to the Front Line], *Rossiiskaia gazeta* (16 Feb 1999); Dmitrii Gornostaev, "Kofi Annan soglasen s NATO" [Kofi Annan Agrees with NATO], *Nezavisimaia gazeta* (29 Jan 1999); Maksim Yusin, "NATO i Belgrad govoriat na raznykh iazykakh" [NATO and Belgrade Speak Different Languages], *Izvestiia* (21 Jan 1999); Yulia Petrovskaia, "SShA daviat na soiuznikov" [The USA Puts Pressure on its Allies], *Nezavisimaia gazeta* (22 Jan 1999).

[102]"Zaiavlenie G. Zyuganova v Belgrade—Ugrozy NATO v adres Yugoslavii sovershenno nepriemlemy!" [Zyuganov's Statement in Belgrade—NATO Threats against Yugoslavia are Completely Unacceptable!], *Sovetskaia Rossiia* (30 Jan 1999). See also Yurii Yershov, "Kosovo: voennye aktsii rastut" [Kosovo: Military Actions Escalate], *Rossiiskaia gazeta* (2 Feb 1999).

grand transformations, he enumerated a correlation of forces (NATO's expansion and "out of zone" activities, and the United States' "attempts to withdraw from the ABM Treaty") that compelled Russia now to perfect the military reform and promote greater military cooperation within the CIS. "Balkan lessons" provided him with his rationale (ITAR-TASS, 24 Feb 1999).

During the four month period, December 1998 to March 1999, the most vociferous nationalists and communists in Russia began to use the concept of a Western driven "new world order" to express their hostility towards NATO's activities in the Balkans.[103] In short, media and political proclamations about events in the Balkans confirmed the deep-rooted mistrust that shapes Moscow's perspective on world affairs, and on NATO's ambitions. An essay in the main government paper reviled Clinton's signature on an "Act on the Liberation of Iraq" and ridiculed the OSCE as "assistant" to Washington in punishing Serbs and helping the Kosovo Liberation Army, thereby demonstrating how thin the shell of Moscow's acquiescence in Kosovo was.[104] "Unabated conflicts in the Balkans" are to the U.S. advantage, the author insisted, because they help justify NATO expansion eastward. This opinion gathered momentum in 1999.

By the time NATO initiated its first air strikes against Serbs in late March, the Russian media had already worked itself up to a state of outrage. All of Primakov's predictions about the Russian public mood had come to pass. The West was regularly accused of applying double standards, turning a "blind eye" to Turkish treatment of Kurds while protecting "Albanian terrorists" in Kosovo. Writers even for *Rossiiskaia gazeta* called NATO preparations to attack Yugoslavia part of a "sinister" plan for world supremacy, while communist headlines shrieked, "NATO is an instrument of global tyrany."[105] When the decision to use force was announced, the level of fury directed at NATO and Washington by Russian politicians, the media,

---

[103]See, e.g., Nikola Zhivkovich, "Natovskie 'mirotvortsy' podozhgli fitil' v Kosovo" [NATO's "Peacekeepers" Watch the Wick Burn Down in Kosovo], *Sovetskaia Rossiia* (1 Dec 1998). For an interesting and more balanced Russian view of the great divide in the Balkans, see Viktor Pushkar, " 'El'ba v Bosnii. Vypolniaia obshchuiu zadachu, mirotvortsy NATO i Rossii stremiutsia poniat' drug druga" [The Elba in Bosnia: Fulfilling Their General Tasks, NATO and Russian Peacekeepers Attempt to Understand Each Other], *Nezavisimoe voennoe obozrenie*, No. 46 (4–10 Dec 1998).

[104]Vladimir Lapskii, "Prezident Bill Klinton 'odobril sekretnyi plan sverzheniia rezhina prezidenta Miloshevicha'" [President Bill Klinton "Has Approved Secret Plans to Overthrow Milosevic's Regime"], *Rossiiskaia gazeta* (9 Dec 1998).

[105]See, e.g., "NATO—instrument global'noi tiranii" [NATO Is an Instrument of Global Tyranny], *Sovetskaia Rossiia* (18 March 1999); Igor Rotar', "Kosovo v ozhidanii bol'shoi voiny" [Kosovo in Waiting for a Major War], *Nezavisimoe voennoe obozrenie*, No. 10 (19–25 March 1999); and Valentin Frolov, " 'Orlinyi glaz' NATO" [NATO "Eagle Eye"], *ibid*.

and the public rose higher than at any other time in the post-Soviet era. Outrage was expressed by the usual candidates, Zyuganov, Zhirinovskii, Ilyukhin, Seleznev, Yavlinskii, most Duma committees and patriotic groups. This time they were joined by Federation Council chair, Stroev, and the Orthodox Patriarch. Talk of supporting Yugoslav with arms was widespread, though rejected by the government, as was a rumour that nuclear weapons might be re-sited in Belarus. Zhirinovskii called for volunteers to fight for Yugoslavia; and TV and press interviews of people on the streets revealed near unanimous support for the Serbs. The tension was palpable; the rest is history.

3. NATO AND RUSSIAN NATIONAL SECURITY QUESTIONS: RESURRECTING OLD DEMONS

It is ironic that in the 1980s and during the last years of the USSR Russian military analysts were beginning to believe that the most serious long-term threats to Russia's security no longer lay to the west of Moscow, but rather in the Islamic southern tier and in China. In fact, if it were not for Kaliningrad Oblast, wedged between Poland and Lithuania on the Baltic coast, none of the proposed new NATO members would be neighbors of Russia. At first glance, then, NATO's proposal to include Poland, the Czech Republic and Hungary would seem to have few immediate strategic consequences for Russia.

That first glance would have been deceiving, for NATO expansion caused Russian tacticians to re-evaluate the possibility of danger from the west. A new security concept had been floated before the public already in November 1993, and integral to it were considerations shaped by the possibility of NATO movement eastward. The "Basic Provisions of Russian Federation Military Doctrine," signed into law that month, marked the withdrawal of a long-standing Soviet promise not to use the first-strike with nuclear weapons option. Although it was made plain in the document that Russia regarded nuclear weaponry as a political, not military, means of deterrence, the change in "no first strike policy" was symptomatic of a Russian military that was downsizing and pregnable.[106] NATO, on the other hand, has

---

[106]See "Osnovnye polozheniia voennoi doktriny Rossiiskoi Federatsii" [Fundamental Provisions of the RF Military Doctrine], *Izvestiia* (18 Oct 1993). See also Anatolii Stasovskii, "Voennaia doktrina Rossii: novoe ponimanie bezopasnosti strany" [The Russian Military Doctrine: New Understanding of the Country's Security], *Krasnaia zvezda* (4 Nov 1993).

In December, Russian writers noted that NATO itself was divided on "first strike," with Canada, Spain, and Germany seen as proponents of changing the Alliance's policy; see Yuliia Petrovskaia, Aleksandr Sergeev, "V NATO ne obkhoditsia bez sporov" [In NATO They Cannot Manage without Arguments], *Nezavisimoe voennoe obozrenie,* No. 48 (17–24 Dec 1998).

maintained the option to first use of nuclear weapons for many years, so in 1993 Russia gave up whatever moral high ground it held in this regard.

Local wars, ethnic conflict and even organized crime represented greater danger to Russia than any foreign power at that time. Russia troops had not yet left Latvia or Estonia and others were involved in conflicts in Georgia, Moldova, Azerbaijan, Tajikistan, and Chechnya. The new doctrine, therefore, authorized the army to act on internal matters, but warned that regional conflicts on its borders might draw Russia into unwanted military situations at any time. When, in 1993–94, American statesmen, advisers and pundits began to speak of NATO as the most handy means to avert conflict in East and East Central Europe as the Soviet withdrawal laid bare traditional ethnic and territorial disputes,[107] the attention of Russia's military policymakers was drawn back to Europe.

Yeltsin did not provide good leadership for the military in the NATO affair. In Warsaw, September 1993, he said that his country would not object if Poland joined NATO—and retracted the statement a few weeks later.[108] At that later time, the Russian president said that Poland's admission was acceptable only if Russia too was a member. Yeltsin proposed that Russia be the guarantor of former Warsaw Pact states, a notion immediately seized upon by advocates of expansion as a threat to eastern Europe. By early 1996 NATO expansion was being decried as the "most substantial negative factor" influencing the security of the CIS, or so Russian defense minister Grachev told a CIS Defense Ministers' Council meeting. The Council advocated an all-European security policy, rather than alignment with blocs.[109] Primakov outlined this proposition to the North Atlantic Cooperation Council later in 1996, telling his ministerial colleagues that the OSCE should be the coordinating agency for a new European security system that integrated NATO, the WEU and the CIS.[110] At the same time, he warned

---

[107]See, e.g., Ronald D. Asmus, Richard L. Kugler, F. Stephen Larrabee, "Building a New NATO," *Foreign Affairs* 72, No. 5 (Sept 1993): 28–40; John S. Duffield, "NATO's Functions after the Cold War," *Political Science Quarterly* 109, No. 5 (Winter, 1994/95): 763–787.

[108]Vladimir Lapskii, "Rossiiskii prezident prizyvaet Zapad ne rasshiriat' NATO za schet Vostochnoi Evropy" [The Russian President Calls upon the West Not to Expand NATO at the Expense of Eastern Europe], *Izvestiia* (2 Oct 1993).

[109]V. Berezko, "Integratsiia v voennoi oblast prodolzhaetsia" [Integration Continues in the Military Field], *Krasnaia zvezda* (28 March 1996). Azerbaijan, Georgia, Belarus, Kazakhstan, Kyrgyzstan, and Tajikistan defense ministers were present as full participants, and representatives were sent from the foreign ministries of Armenia, Turkmenistan, Uzbekistan and Ukraine.

[110]"Primakov Intervention," Brussels, NATO HQ (11 Dec 1996), NATO Website (13 Feb 1998).

that the "impulse to expand NATO" was wrong and would merely re-divide Europe. Views of this genre have been supported consistently by the Russian military and strategic complex.

In terms of military preparedness and strategic planning, the South Caucausus became increasingly more important to Russia as NATO's influence grew in the region (see section 6). Russian observers have worried for some time that Georgian and Azerbaijanian membership in NATO's Partnership for Peace program would promote the growing Turkish military presence on the Black Sea. A Turkish-Georgian military agreement of December 1995 had exacerbated that concern.[111] The fact that Russia negotiated an agreement allowing it three military bases in Georgia in September that year did not help much, for the Georgian parliament hesitated many months before ratifying the treaty and, as a quid pro quo, Russia became more directly involved in the Abkhazia crisis. In January 1997, Russia's ambassador to Armenia, Andrei Urnov, was explicit on the importance of the region to Russia in answers to a question about the possibility of Russia withdrawing troops from Transcaucasia. There is no question of Russian withdrawal, he replied; adding that the area is likely to be "exempt" from planned force reductions.[112]

In the spring, Moscow announced that Russia's air defense troops were to be retrained because NATO would add some 400 new eastern airports to its arsenal after expansion. A joint Russian-Belarus air force exercise was planned specifically to counter NATO, and claims were made that the hallowed abolition of medium-range missiles (ABM Treaty, 1972) would now be rendered pointless, since western long-range missiles could be moved much closer to the Russian border. All these activities were signs that Russian blustering represented deeper conviction than many Western pundits had believed.

The communist press harped on Yeltsin's "capitulation" to NATO throughout the spring and summer of 1997, claiming that he had left Russia open to attack in the North (Barents and Baltic Seas), and in the South, where the forces of fundamentalist Islam, the Taliban, were said to be threatening.[113] But the communists were by no means alone in such beliefs. First deputy chief of the Armed Forces General Staff, Pishchev, was unequivocal when he described the nature of the "threat" in late April. Acknowledging that few people believed NATO was planning a large-scale military aggression against Russia, he insisted at the same

---

[111]See, e.g., Mikhail Gerasimov, "Ankara predlagaet Tbilisi tesnoe sotrudnichestvo" [Ankara Offers Tbilisi Closer Cooperation], *Nezavisimaia gazeta* (27 Dec 1995).

[112]*Hayastani Hanrapetutyun* (Yerevan) (25 Jan 1997), FBIS-SOV, No. 041.

[113]See, e.g., Boris Khorev, "Predatel'stvo iskhodit iz Kremlia, vekhi 'rynochnoi' pory" [The Betrayal Comes from the Kremlin, the Landmark of the "Market" Age], *Sovetskaia Rossiia* (17 June 1997).

time the possibility of armed intrusion is something the weaker Russia must con-template. Pishchev pointed out that the modernization of Eastern Europe's mili-tary infrastructure (airfields, ports, arms dumps, lines of communications) will turn those territories into dangerous bridgeheads from which massive air strikes could be launched against Russian targets. Central Europe will now link the NATO northern (Norway) and southern (Turkey) flanks, making the expansion enormously important strategically even if troop contingents from other coun-tries are not stationed in Eastern European countries.[114] In a particularly prophetic evaluation, Pishchev warned that NATO's Allied Armed Forces might become an all-European conflict resolution instrument.

When the U.S. Congress made an important concession by amending the 1990 CFE Treaty to allow Russia more heavy weapons for a longer duration around hot spots in the South, such as Chechnya, it attracted little notice in the Russian press. Much greater attention was paid to the fact that Polish, Czech and Hungarian ad-mission to NATO would alter the military balance dramatically in NATO's favor. The number of tanks, planes, artillery, armored vehicles, and, more importantly, airfields that would fall to NATO was given greater and greater play, making Rus-sia look threatened to readers.[115]

After the Denver Summit closed, Russian strategists (with the exception of the communists) tended to take a longer look at their prospects, setting aside the emo-tional rhetoric driven by the politics of the debate leading up to the Founding Act. A long paper by two experts at Moscow's Center for Military-Strategic Studies of the RF Armed Forces General Staff, Col. Yurii V. Morozov and Lt. Gen. Valerii K. Potemkin, typified this new approach. In analyzing the prospects for a broader system of Euro-Atlantic security, they concluded that there should be a conver-gence of military doctrines within the framework of the OSCE as a "subsystem of the United Nations." The OSCE, which includes neutral and non-aligned states, would itself have to be restructured and given mechanisms (e.g., a security council) enabling it to function more efficiently than it does now. Russia's role would be enhanced as a bridge between East and West, and the United States would also be strengthened as confrontation in the military doctrines of the United States, Russia, NATO and the CIS was eliminated. Whereas these writers

---

[114]Pishchev, "Dal'nii pritsel NATO," *Nezavisimoe voennoe obozrenie* (26 April–16 May 1997), *op. cit.*

[115]Safronchuk's, "Chemu raduetsia ministr RF i chem gorditsia gensek NATO. Illiuziia bezopasnosti" [What Is the RF Minister Happy about and What Is the General Secretary of NATO Proud Of: Illusion of Security], *Sovetskaia Rossiia* (17 May 1997), was but one of many examples of this gun-counting trend.

did not advocate the elimination of NATO, they called for a much broader collective and integrative security system than NATO could possibly offer.[116]

One of the symptoms of Russia's worry that NATO was becoming more than it had been is the consistent rejection by Moscow of calls for more aggressive police action by NATO in Bosnia, Kosovo, and elsewhere. This was evident in the sharp criticism levelled by Russia against NATO's attempt to capture Serbian war criminals in 1977 (Interfax, 31 July). The image of NATO troops serving as a law-enforcement agency for the UN (or the United States) was a disturbing one for Moscow.

Constant admonition that START II ratification would be forestalled in Moscow because of NATO expansion seemed not to be taken seriously by Western pundits before Madrid. Aleksei Arbatov, deputy chair of the Duma's Defense Committee, raised this very issue in Washington during the last week of July. According to a summary of his public statements in the *New York Times,* Arbatov said that there was a "feeling of betrayal among Russia's democrats" because the West was so indifferent to their viewpoint. NATO's expansion into Poland has forced Russia to depend on nuclear deterrence again, leaving START II ratification unlikely, and Russia's defenders of disarmament without support at home. Writing in the *New York Times* himself a month later, Arbatov said that the Madrid meeting "is universally perceived in Russia (by some with grief, by others with malevolence) as a major defeat of Moscow's policy of broad partnership with the West. It is considered a great setback for Russian democrats . . .".[117] Because he is a liberal and a member of Yabloko, Arbatov's observations cannot be disregarded as a voice from the opposition wilderness.

Statements such as those made by Arbatov would have been less worrisome if they were not a reflection of renewed and growing assumptions in Russia that all Western, and especially U.S., motives were suspect. NATO expansion served, in fact, to lift vague suspicions left over from Cold War days back up to the level of conviction. On the one hand, anger and distrust over NATO exercises on the Black Sea are easily understandable, given that Russia and Ukraine have a history of squabbles over the Black Sea Fleet and Crimea. On the other hand, when one of Russia's respected papers complained in September 1997 that a joint military exercise in Central Asia, with Russian, American, Central Asian and Turkish involvement, was part of a broader Pentagon plan to take over the region, one could

---

[116]See Morozov and Potemkin, "'Silovoi karkas' Evropy. Sistema kollektivnoi bezopasnosti dolzhna ob'edinit' voennye potentsialy Rossii i stran-chlenov NATO" [Europe's "Power Frame": A System of Collective Security Should Unite the Military Potentials of Russia and the NATO Countries], *Nezavisimoe voennoe obozrenie,* No. 22 (21–27 June 1997).

[117]See Arbatov, "As NATO Grows, Start 2 Shudders," *New York Times* (26 August 1997). For the earlier commentary, see Thomas L. Friedman, "Clinton's Folly," *New York Times* (31 July 1997).

be excused for suggesting that the old Russian xenophobic vision of the world was re-surfacing.[118] An essay in *Foreign Affairs* by Brzezinski, "A Geostrategy for Eurasia," served to confirm Russian fears. His assertion that the "only real alternative to American leadership [in the world] is international anarchy" was interpreted in Moscow as a claim on unilateral world hegemony. Accompanied as it was with a firm statement in support of a considerably enlarged NATO—to include by at least the year 2003 the Baltic republics, Romania, Bulgaria and, shortly thereafter, Ukraine—the Russian reaction to the essay was one of dismay.[119]

A more systematic Russian explication of the country's geopolitical standing in the world as one determined mostly by rivalries for influence on the territory of former USSR republics came from Col. Sergei Kharlamov.[120] Printed in October 1997, Kharlamov's paper said that there were rivalries between the United States and Western Europe for dominance in the Asia-Pacific region and South Eurasia; between Turkey and Iran in the South; and between China, Korea and Japan in the East. Russia had the longest standing as an influential power in all these regions, but now stood a good chance of losing its lead everywhere. Thus Russia was compelled to advance its interests unceasingly wherever possible in Eurasia.

Russia's minister of defense, Sergeev, confirmed this opinion as one held by his government when he told Belarusian defense ministry officials on 19 December that "NATO's eastward expansion and the United States pursuit of unilateral world leadership pose the main threats to Russia's security from the West" (Interfax, 19 Dec 1997). Sergeev's statement reflected attitudes expressed already in the "National Security Concept" made public under the auspices of the RF Security Council in October (see section 3.1). Early in 1998, the main author of the security concept went one step further and said that, although the Founding Act has diminished threats to Russia, it had by no means eliminated them. Further military integration of the CIS was absolutely essential, Leonid Maiorov said, as the basis of a security system attuned to "the national interests of Russia."[121] The

---

[118]Andrei Krvut, "Amerikanskii desant v Srednei Azii" [An American Landing Force Is in Central Asia], *Nezavisimaia gazeta* (13 Sept 1997). The exercise was named Tsentrazbat-97, i.e., Central Asia Battalion -97.

[119]See, e.g., Karen Butents, "Sverkhderzhavnye iskusheniia" [Great Power Temptations], *Nezavisimaia gazeta* (29 Nov 1997), who saw Brzezinski's essay as a proposal that NATO gain control of Europe and, from there, Eurasia. Brzezinski, "A Geostrategy for Eurasia," *Foreign Affairs*, 76, No. 5 (Sept/Oct 1997): 50–64.

[120]Kharlamov's essay in this regard was published in *Armeiskii sbornik* , No. 10 (Oct 1997), FBIS-SOV, No. 012. Brzezinski had made that point as well.

[121]Maiorov, Dmitrii Afinogenov, "Vazhneishee napravlenie integratsii" [The Most Important Direction of Integration], *Nezavisimaia gazeta* (3 Feb 1998). This full page essay included a large map.

period saw other long essays expressing great distrust over NATO ambitions in North Africa, Poland, and even Latin America. In the case of Poland, a Russian writer on security matters scoffed at Solana's assurances to the parliament in Warsaw that membership in NATO was not going to cost Poland much and that NATO would defend Poland's territory.[122]

During the winter of 1998, the North suddenly emerged as an area of great concern in the strategic debate. A diplomatic crisis between Norway and Russia saw the expulsion from Oslo of several Russian diplomats, allegedly for spying. Norway's potential as spearhead for a renewed NATO "offensive" against Russian dominance in the North was featured by angry Russian commentators. The Duma's Anti-NATO Consultative Council commissioned an investigation of NATO's "expansion" in the North, and concluded in April that the "threat that NATO poses to northern Russia" was serious. In a detailed report, communist journalist V. Tetekin claimed that the extraordinary natural wealth of the mainland of the European North and Siberia, and the Arctic sea shelf, were coveted by the West generally and by the United States specifically. Efforts to turn the northern sea route into an international waterway, and expanded deployment of U.S. nuclear submarines to the Arctic were portrayed as ominous.

In Norway, and perhaps the Baltic States, NATO had ideal surveillance positions. Regular naval exercises provided NATO with the means and tactics to keep the Russian fleet bottled up in the Barents Sea. Moreover, Tetekin charged, Norway was attempting to establish sovereignty over Spitsbergen. Concluding that "NATO members are making deliberate attempts to diminish Russia's role in the Arctic and remove it from Russia's zone of vital interest," he demanded that Russia "rigorously stop other countries from attempting to encroach on our national interests" in the North.[123] One way to safeguard its interests, of course, was for Russia to participate in NATO's Northern war games. On 16 May 1998, it was announced that for the first time a platoon of Baltic Fleet marines would join a NATO exercise in northern Denmark, as part of the PfP program. Russian reporting about this decision was cautious:

---

[122]See, e.g., Sergei Babkin, "Severnaia Afrika v planakh NATO" [North Africa in NATO's Plans], *Krasnaia zvezda* (10 Feb 1998); "Kto samyi vernyi soiuznik SShA" [Who Is the Most Loyal U.S. Ally?], *Krasnaia zvezda* (6 Feb 1998); "Zlye vetry nad Pol'she smeniaiutsia laskovym veianiem NATO" [Angry Winds over Poland Are Changed by Affectionate Breathing of NATO], *Izvestiia* (29 Jan 1998).

[123]Tetekin, " Rossii ugrozhaiut i s Severa . . . Yastreby nad nami" [Russia Also Threatened from the North . . . Hawks above Us], *Sovetskaia Rossiia* (7 April 1998).

generally supportive while still plainly distrustful of NATO operations carried out close to Russia's borders.[124]

None of Moscow's general strategic concerns had been resolved before NATO initiated its bombing campaigns against Iraq and Yugoslavia. By that time, Russia's abiding suspicion of the West's intentions were already greatly exacerbated. NATO's new strategic concept was bitterly and often criticized,[125] Norway's military ambitions were highlighted in the Russian media yet again,[126] and quickly instituted Russian military training exercises were widely discussed as counters to NATO.[127] Other long-lasting post-Soviet strategic considerations, such as the need to rely on nuclear forces and projections of cataclysmic destabilization in Europe, were reformulated in their starkest forms.[128] And Moscow continued to push the OSCE as the most logical vehicle for long term European security.[129] When NATO released the details of its new Strategic Concept, however, expert

[124]Voice of Russia World Service (16 May 1998), FBIS-SOV, No. 136. Correspondent Yuliia Zheglova noted the suspicion, especially about war games that used former Warsaw Pact infrastructure and featured Russia as the villain. At the same time she praised Russian and NATO military personnel and politicians who "are working hard to achieve normal partnership between the Cold War adversaries."

[125]See, e.g., Vyacheslav Krasiukov, "NATO skoro—50" [NATO Soon Will Be 50], *Rossiiskaia gazeta* (4 Feb 1999); "K svedeniiu NATO" [About NATO], *Rossiiskaia gazeta* (9 Feb 1999); Maksim Nadezhdin, "Zapad khochet kupit' nashi vooruzhennye sily" [The West Wants to Buy Our Armed Forces], *Izvestiia* (2 April 1999); Leonid Ivashev, "Gotovitsia obnovlennaia strategicheskaia kontseptsiia dlia evropy" [A New Strategic Concept Is Being Prepared for Europe], *Nezavisimaia gazeta* (25 April 1999).

[126]See, e.g., Dmitrii Elin, "Iz Norvegii potianuiu kholodoi" [Cold Is Drawn from Norway], *Krasnaia vzezda* (4 Feb 1999); "Natovskie ucheniia na severe Norvegii" [NATO Exercises in the North of Norway], *Krasnaia zvezda* (16 Feb 1999).

[127]See, e.g., Dmitrii Danilov, "Voennye perspektivy Evropeiskogo soiuza" [Military Perspectives of the European Union], *Krasnaia zvezda* (5 March 1999); Yurii Golotiuk, "Pokazatel'nyi vystupleniia rossiiskogo VMF" [Demonstration of Force of the Russian Navy], *Izvestiia* (2 April 1999).

[128]See, e.g., Yurii Golotiuk, "Moskva szhimaet svoi iadernyi kulak" [Moscow Squeezes Its Nuclear Fist], *Izvestiia* (23 March 1999); "Balans v evrope budet narushen" [The Balance in Europe Will Be Destabilized], *Krasnaia zvezda* (13 March 1999).

[129]See, e.g., Yurii Dubov, "OBSE neobkhodit ispolnitel'nyi komitet" [The OSCE Needs an Executive Committee], *Krasnaia zvezda* (25 Feb 1999).

opinion in Russia raised the debate to a new level. They were compelled to for-
mulate a new "geopolitical counterbalance."[130]

The security-related debate that was most directly influenced by the Kremlin's
interpretation of NATO policy, however, was military reform.

3.1. Military Reform

On 30 June 1997, at a special ceremony in the Kremlin to honor graduates of
Russia's military academies, Chernomyrdin said that military reform was a priority, given NATO's expansion "to the borders of our country" (ITAR-TASS, 30
June; Interfax, 30 June). Russia's Armed Forces must be streamlined, effective and
mobile, armed with the latest equipment and weapons—within the limits of Russia's constrained budget. "Smoldering coals of military conflicts near Russia's borders" and the approach of NATO military infrastructure, make any delay of reform "inadmissable," he concluded. All this had been said before, most notably
in the 1993 amended military doctrine and subsequent discussion of it. Four years
later, however, the sense of urgency had intensified. In July 1997, Aleksei Arbatov told reporters in Washington that "NATO expansion will figure into every
discussion and paper written on the military reform question."[131] In September,
an expert on military reform in Russia said that his government acted to change
military structure and doctrine only after the "failure of the Chechnya campaign
and the dangerous (above all, due to the economic and political consequences)
expansion of NATO to the East."[132] Even though acidic public comment about
NATO expansion diminished in the second half of 1997, observations such as
these belied the Western media's tendency to assume that the question of NATO
expansion lost its importance in Russia after Madrid.

---

[130] See, e.g., Vadim Solov'ev, Vladimir Mukhin, "NATO zaiavliaet o svoei gotovnosti
k deistviiam vo 'vsemirnykh masshtabakh.' Minoborony RF formiruet geopoliticheskii
protivoves" [NATO Declares Its Readiness for Activities on a "Worldwide Scale." The RF
Ministry of Defense Is Creating a Geopolitical Counterbalance], *Nezavisimoe voennoe
obozrenie,* No. 16 (30 April–6 May 1999). The full text of NATO's Strategic Concept appeared in the same issue. See also Vladimir Abrinov, "NATO otkazyvaetsia ot
oboronitel'noi strategii" [NATO Gives up a Defensive Strategy], *Izvestiia* (23 April 1999).

[131]Quoted in Thomas L. Friedman, "Clinton's Folly," *New York Times* (31 July 1997).
For a detailed Russian perspective on military reform, see A.I. Smirnov, *Rossiia: na puti
professional'noi armii* [Russia: On the Way to a Professional Army], (Moscow, 1998).

[132]Sergei Sokut, "Zachem nuzhna armiia? Ona dolzhna stat' institutom gosudarstva"
[Why Is the Army Needed? It Must Become an Effective Institution of the State], *Nezavisimoe voennoe obozrenie,* No. 33 (5–11 Sept 1997).

As we have seen above, military reform had been in the works for some time. In August 1996, for example, Yurii Deriugin, director of the military-scientific society Security of the Fatherland, wrote that the "threat of NATO advancement to the east finally" forced Russians to recognize that there were new dangers and that the Armed Forces must soon be restructured to counter them.[133] Such exhortations and regular pleas for more funding notwithstanding, little was accomplished in so far as military reform was concerned. Consequently, Minister of Defense Grachev lost his post in the spring of 1997. His replacement, Igor D. Sergeev, came in with a mandate to speed up military re-organization, within the current budget.

Whatever respite this change might have granted the military administration ended abruptly when Lev Rokhlin, chair of the Duma Defense Committee, sent a dramatic public "Appeal" to all servicemen in late June. Blaming Yeltsin for ruining the Armed Forces, he called on senior officers and veterans to "speak out" and unite "in opposition to the destruction of the Army . . . . Otherwise the army is lost."[134] Rokhlin even intimated that Yeltsin's advisers were in the employ of Western intelligence services. Some Russian commentators, and especially government officials, termed this indictment treasonous and a call for a coup d'état; oppositionists saw it as timely intervention. Yet everyone recognized that reform of the military was urgently needed and NATO expansion provided the most compelling reasons for it. Moreover, Sergeev told the Federation Council on 4 July that the possibility of large-scale war could be ruled out only if Russia maintained the combat readiness of its strategic nuclear forces (Interfax, 4 July). NATO expansion confirmed the value of nuclear deterrence in the Russian military mind—dimming the likelihood of START II gaining ratification support.

NATO expansion was a catalyst therefore for the creation, under Rokhlin's leadership and simultaneously with the Madrid Summit, an All-Russia Movement in Support of the Army, Military Science, and Defense Industry. Although Rokhlin himself was a member of Chernomyrdin's NDR, the Movement's membership included Vladimir Kriuchkov, former head of USSR KGB, and General Valentin Varennikov, both participants in the botched coup attempt against Gorbachev in August 1991. A former defense minister, General Igor Rodionov, was elected first deputy chair of the Movement's organizational committee. Hardliner

[133]Deriugin, "Voennaia reforma tonet v melkom podkhode" [The Military Reform Is Sinking in Petty Approaches], *Rossiiskie vesti* (31 Aug 1996).

[134]See, e.g., Rokhlin, "Pravda strashnee bomby. Obrashchenie k Verkhovnomu Glavnokomanduiushchemu Vooruzhennymi Silami Rossiiskoi Federatsii i voennosluzhashchim Rossii" [The Truth Is Scarier Than the Bomb: Appeal to the Commander-in-Chief of the Armed Forces of the Russian Federation and to the Servicemen of Russia], *Sovetskaia Rossiia* (26 June 1997).

opponents of Yeltsin, Generals Albert Makashov and Vladislav Achalov lined up with Rokhlin, along with some 30 armed forces-related organizations, among them the Union of Armed Forces Veterans, the All-Russian Officers Assembly, and the Union of Officers of Russia. Insisting that his movement was not political, Rokhlin was nonetheless surrounded by very political people. The Duma's Anti-NATO Commission's predecessor expressed its formal support for the Movement as well, calling it "timely" and attributing NATO expansion to "the fact that Russia has lost much of its former defense capability"(Interfax, 9 July). It would appear then that a new, and potentially dangerous division, in Russian society appeared to be widening.

To win back the military, Yeltsin and Chernomyrdin scrambled to promise that all wage arrears would be paid to the armed forces by the end of September. On 16 July Yeltsin signed a decree planning cuts of up to 500,000 troops (nearly one-third of the total) by 1 January 1998, eliminate civilian posts in the military, and hold ministry of defense costs to 1 percent of the military budget. The president announced at the same time that conscription would soon be ended and replaced by a volunteer force. Much of this streamlining was driven by budgetary necessity, but NATO's growth was constantly cited among reasons for the re-organization of Russia's land forces, missile units and air force.[135] NATO expansion also was cited by opponents of dramatic cuts in the military as the reason for their objection. One might expect such complaints from Rokhlin's Movement: but they came also from Moscow's mayor, Luzhkov, and Aleksei Arbatov, who at the same time condemned Rokhlin's appeal to the military.[136]

On 7 August, Yeltsin granted official approval to guidelines for military reform, confirming that Armed Forces personnel would be cut to 1.2 million (at that time 1.82 million) by 1 January 1999 (Interfax, 7 Aug). On the same day Sergeev an-

---

[135]As the date of an expected draft military reform law drew nearer, the Russian press was filled with projections and proposals from a wide variety of interest groups. See, e.g., Maj. Gen. (Ret) V.V. Larionov, "Kakaia armiia nuzhna Rossii: Mirazhi i prognozy i zatianuvshemsia spore" [The Type of Armed Forces Russia Needs: Mirages and Forecasts in a Continuing Debate], *Nezavisimoe voennoe obozrenie*, No. 23 (28 June–4 July 1997). Acknowledging that a conflict with NATO was "improbable," Larionov (a professor at the General Staff Military Academy) still insisted that the RF strengthen its "deterrent strategic nuclear forces" and be fully prepared for conflict on the country's periphery. For the announcements, see Interfax (16, 18 July 1997).

[136]For Arbatov's criticism of Rokhlin, see "Vozrozhdenie ofitserskikh sobranii" [The Officer's Assembly Is Revived], *Nezavisimoe voennoe obozrenie*, No. 29 (9–15 Aug 1997). On Luzhkov's objections to the military reforms, see Michael Specter, "Yeltsin's Plans to Cut Military Touches a Nerve," *New York Times* (28 July 1997). Rokhlin chaired the Committee of which Arbatov was deputy chair.

nounced that some 300 places would be cut from the roster of generals (at that time 1,925) by the end of 1997 and that his aim for the future was a total of 1,000 generals.[137] Rokhlin's organization could expect, therefore, to find further support from disgruntled senior officers. Indeed, the Organizing Committee of his Movement soon issued a plea to all citizens of Russia, calling on them to support the impeachment of Yeltsin and his closest advisers. Rejecting "aggressive nationalism" and fascism, Rokhlin urged "all patriots" to join his group to save the Russian economy and its army from further debilitation in the face of pressure from the West. By this time polls showed that Rokhlin had become the most popular political leader in Russia with military officers.[138]

In part to counter the effect of Rokhlin's movement and dire warnings from Lebed to the effect that Russia was poised on the brink of a crisis that would make the conflict in Chechnya seem like "child's play," and in part to get the feel of his new position, Sergeev spent much of the summer touring military bases throughout Russia. He also paid a constructive two-day visit to Kiev during the Sea Breeze-97 exercise (see section 4). In September, he urged the ratification of START II by the Duma, on the grounds that START III—which would end the imbalance in RF–U.S. nuclear potential—could then quickly be prepared. He, Chernomyrdin, and Primakov lobbied the Duma to this end, explaining also that compliance with the 1972 ABM treaty must be one of the conditions of ratification.

Zhirinovskii and Zyuganov immediately issued public statements opposing ratification.[139] They were joined by Rokhlin, still the chair of the Duma's Defense Committee, who told supporters in St. Petersburg that ratification would "complete the ruin of the army." Ratification is needed by NATO, not Russia, he insisted. *Zavtra* called the government's campaign for ratification of START II an attempt to undermine nuclear parity, by catering to Yeltsin's "friend Bill" [Clin-

---

[137]Sergei Pavlenko, "Vostrebovan opyt veteranov" [Veterans' Experience Is in Demand], *Krasnaia zvezda* (8 Aug 1997).

[138]Andrei Korbut, "Lev Rokhlin i ofitserskoe dvizhenie v Rossii. Reiting populiarnosti politicheskikh liderov sredi ofitserov" [Lev Rokhlin and the Officers Movement in Russia: Popularity of Political Leaders with Officers], *Nezavisimoe voennoe obozrenie*, No. 33 (5–11 Sept 1997). Rokhlin, "My skoro poteriaem pravo nazyvat'sia grazhdanami Rossii" [We Will Soon Lose the Right to Call Ourselves Citizens of Russia], *Narodnaia armiia*, special insert in *Sovetskaia Rossiia* (14 Aug 1997).

[139]In a long interview published on 16 September, which was mostly about the social unrest then sweeping over Russia, Zyuganov offered strong support to the Movement in defense of the army, see Zyuganov, "Osen' dyshit protestom" [Protest Is in the Autumn Air], *Sovetskaia Rossiia* (16 Sept 1997). For the Zhirinovskii statement, Interfax (16 Sept).

ton]; a plot on the part of the United States and NATO to replace Russia as the military mediator in the former CIS was the paper's explanation of START II.[140]

On 18 September, Lebed's Honor and Motherland party offered close cooperation with Rokhlin's organization (Interfax, 18 Sept). The Movement's First Congress, which opened in Moscow on 20 September, had Zyuganov and Gen. A. Korzhakov (Yeltsin's disgraced former bodyguard) attending as guests. By resigning his membership in the Our Home is Russia (NDR) Duma faction, Rokhlin jeopardized his position as chair of the Defense Committee, a post unofficially allocated to the NDR. Faction leader Shokhin recommended a replacement, but the Duma itself voted Rokhlin back in place on 26 September.[141] Thus, military reform itself became a subject for heated political debate. The second Congress of Rokhlin's movement met in Moscow on 25 December, this time with 298 delegates from across the country. It again called for Yeltsin's immediate resignation and had continued support from Zyuganov, who served as a keynote speaker (Interfax, 25 Dec 1997).

The military situation was complicated further by former minister of defense under Gorbachev, D.T. Yazov (charged with "betrayal of the Motherland" for his part in the attempted coup in August 1991), who came out strongly against military reform because it had no doctrinal component. He complained that, whereas NATO is an instrument of the national interest of the United States, Britain, and others, Russia seemed unable to think in terms of its own national interest other than merely to say that the army will defend the motherland.[142] So the lines were quickly drawn. Although reform seemed to be going nowhere, the shuffling of senior military personnel continued. Lt. Gen. Viktor Zavarzin, commander of Russia's peacekeeping forces in Tajikistan and First Deputy Chief of Staff in charge of military cooperation in the CIS, was named military envoy to NATO in October,[143] ending rumors that a more political appointment (e.g., Pavel Grachev) might be made. Shortly afterwards, Admiral of the Fleet Feliks Gromov was

---

[140]"Illiuzii mira" [Illusions of Peace], *Zavtra*, No. 38 (September 1997). For Rokhlin's comment, Interfax (17 Sept).

[141]Anna Selezneva, "Kak khorosho byt' generalom" [It Is Good to Be a General], *Rossiiskaia gazeta* (27 Sept 1997).

[142]Dmitrii Yazov, "Ne veriu v takie 'reformy'!" [I Don't Believe in Such "Reforms"!], *Zavtra*, No. 37 (Sept 1997). The Rokhlin Movement's Program Statement was published in *Sovetskaia Rossiia* (27 Sept 1997). On Yazov's earlier activity, see Gen. Leonid G. Ivashov, *Marshal Yazov (Rokovoi avgust 91–90),* (Moscow, 1992).

[143]Vitalii Strugovets, "Voennyi predstavitel' Rossii v NATO" [Russia's Military Representative to NATO], *Krasnaia zvezda* (25 Oct 1997). The appointment was announced on 20 October by ITAR-TASS.

abruptly fired, and dismissed from the military altogether. He was immediately replaced by Admiral Vladimir Kuroedov, who, it was assumed, would speed up the process of reform in the navy.

The month of October also saw the appearance in *Mezhdunarodnaia zhizn'*, journal of the ministry of foreign affairs, of a long explication of the "National Security Concept of Russia," a draft of which was then being widely discussed. Written by Col. Gen. Leonid S. Maiorov, still Deputy Secretary of the Security Council, the essay made official the following security concern:

> In particular, NATO's eastward expansion of NATO and the turning of the bloc into a dominant military-political force is creating a realistic threat splitting up Europe and the possibility of a new stand off spiral.
>
> This radically contravenes Russia's national interests and its policy in the world scene.[144]

Maiorov went on to say that Russia's security concept is now based on "realistic deterrence" and that, while the diplomatic mechanism is the ideal means to resolve dispute, nuclear deterrence, "for the present" is still the most effective way to prevent war. The essay left no doubt that there was a direct link between the formulation of a new security concept in Russia and the movement of NATO eastward. The "Concept" itself was formally adopted by a presidential edict dated 17 December 1997, and published in the government press a week later.[145] It included the statement: "The prospect of NATO expansion to the East is unacceptable to Russia because it represents a threat to its national security."

The worry that drove the Russian military to accelerate reform and modernize the Armed Forces was expressed in a general statement by Chief of the Russian Armed Forces General Staff, First Deputy Defense Minister, Gen. Anatolii Kvashnin, during a visit to Bonn in November. The Founding Act makes it clear that Russia and NATO are no longer enemies, he said, but military professionals cannot help but see NATO as a military bloc: why talk of standardization of armaments, for example, "when there is no enemy?" His attitude to NATO remained

---

[144]L.S. Maiorov, "Russia's Concept of National Security," *International Affairs* (Moscow), No. 6 (1997): 156–166. The Russian version appeared in *Mezhdunarodnaia zhizn'*, No. 10 (October 1997): 18–28.

[145]"Kontseptsiia natsional'noi bezopasnosti Rossiiskoi Federatsii" [Concept of National Security of the Russian Federation], *Rossiiskaia gazeta* (26 Dec 1997).

"negative" (ITAR-TASS, 21 Nov).[146] The Communist press contributed to the discourse by contrasting Russia's declining military forces with increasing American military might. In addition to carrying almost every statement uttered by Rokhlin, *Sovetskaia Rossiia* used its periodic *Narodnaia Armiia* [People's Army] supplement to detail the broadening "threat" posed by the perceived American drive to world domination.[147]

All but the top brass of the military were startled by Yeltsin's address to Sweden's parliament on 3 December 1997, when he promised a reduction by one-third of Russia's nuclear warheads and a 40 percent cut in the infantry and naval groups stationed in the northwest of his country. A simultaneous announcement by the Russian defense ministry at the PJC that Russia's scheduled reductions would include deep cuts in the Kaliningrad special zone, the Leningrad Military District, and in the Northern and Baltic Fleets, apparently caught most military people by surprise.

The fact that the Russian president appeared to have made his statement without consulting his own political advisers merely added uncertainty to debate about arms reduction (especially START II and III) and the Russian commitment to security offers to the Baltic states. In his speech, Yeltsin took another swipe at NATO, indirectly, by emphasizing that "European security is a matter for the Eu-

---

[146]Reliance on nuclear deterrence was a concept not universally held by military commentators in Russia. Yurii Kozhukh wrote in *Flag Rodiny* (19 Nov 1997) that his country spent up to one-fifth of its military budget on nuclear weapons, money that could be better used in some other part of the economy, and added that the very presence of nuclear weapons was immoral. He maintained as well, however, that the enlargement of NATO and the increasing level of U.S. superiority still made a balance of comparable nuclear threats the only way to preserve strategic stability in the world.

[147]See, e.g., A. Verevchenko, "Yesli zavtra v pokhod. Kak my zabotimsia o voennom prevoskhodstve SShA" [If the War Starts Tomorrow: How We Handle the Military Superiority of the USA], *Sovetskaia Rossiia* (27 Nov 1997); Yevgenii Popov, "Verolomnyi 'Zhiraf'" [Treacherous Giraffe], *Sovetskaia Rossiia* (6 Dec 1997).

L. Ya. Rokhlin, "Chego my khotim. Zaiavlenie ispolkoma dvizheniia 'V podderzhku armii, oboronnoi promyshlennosti i voennoi nauki'" [What We Want: Statement of the Executive of the Movement "In Support of the Army, Defense Industry and Military Science"], *Sovetskaia Rossiia* (27 Nov 1997). "Sotvorenie katastrofy. Vystuplenie L'va Rokhlina v Gosudarstvennoi dume 10 dekabria s.g." [The Creation of Catastrophe: Lev Rokhlin's Speech in the State Duma, 10 December 1997], *Sovetskaia Rossiia* (11 Dec 1997).

The communist position on military reform was formulated in 1997 in a 90-page booklet, *Voennaia reforma: Otsenka ugroz natsional'noi bezopasnosti Rossii* [Military Reform: An Evaluation of the Threat to Russia's National Security], (Moscow, 1997).

ropeans themselves" and urging his audience to use the OSCE as the foundation for a continental security system.

Lebed issued a furious rejoinder to Yeltsin, saying that military parity was now gone, and the communist press raged that Russia should be strengthening, not weakening, its Armed Forces, especially in the Northwest with the possibility that the Baltic states might join NATO.[148] At almost the same time, Sergeev reported to the Federation Council that the military was still badly underfunded, pay arrears were still a crucial problem, and the Army's debt had reached a level of approximately 21 trillion rubles.[149] Kvashnin clarified Yeltsin's statements, somewhat, telling a joint conference of the Russia-NATO military committee in Brussels that the nuclear weapons reductions could be carried out within START III, but that this awaited the ratification of START II. He added that none of Yeltsin's proposals implied agreement with the eastward expansion of the NATO military infrastructure, to which Russia still strongly objected.[150]

The State Duma was not mollified and on Rokhlin's initiative adopted a resolution saying that the arms reduction proposals were "inconsistent with Russia's laws" and that Yeltsin, in making them, was "irresponsible . . . given NATO's eastward expansion" (Interfax, 18 Dec). Rokhlin presented the Duma with a draft program on defense, which included his own version of a concept for military reform and military security. He told a news conference that the threat to Russia's security had increased with NATO expansion and that Russia was also challenged from the South and in the Far East as well. Underfunding has prevented maintenance of military hardware and weaponry, he warned, adding that the Duma soon would begin hearings on other proposals offered by his organization (Interfax, 17 Dec).

Kvashnin's resumé of his department's position was echoed, more directly, by Col. Gen. Leonid Ivashov, head of the Main Directorate for International Military Cooperation and leader of the Russian delegation to the first session of the Russia-NATO defense ministry deliberations in Brussels. The only way that Russia might gain from participation with the NATO apparatus would be if NATO

---

[148]See Vasilii Safronchuk, " 'Zhesty pereutomleniia.' Stokgol'mskie siurprizy Rossiiskogo prezidenta" [Gestures of Overstrain: Stockholm Surprise of the Russian President], *Sovetskaia Rossiia* (6 Dec 1997).

[149]Piotr Karapetian, "Kak sokhranit' oboronnyi potentsial Rossii" [How to Preserve the Defensive Potential of Russia], *Krasnaia zvezda* (3 Dec 1997). The text of Yeltsin's speech in Stockholm was printed by ITAR-TASS on 3 December.

[150]Radio Rossii Network (4 Dec 1997), FBIS-SOV, No. 338. For a long treatise on START II, NATO and Russia, which warned that Russia could fall irreparably behind if START II was ratified, see Alla Yaroshinskaia, "NATO i iadernoe oruzhie" [NATO and Nuclear Arms], *Nezavisimaia gazeta* (24 Dec 1997).

became more political and less military, he told an interviewer. At present, however, NATO's purpose is military and even peacekeeping exercises are screens for moving military infrastructures closer to Russia's borders. Talk of establishing a Danish-German-Polish corps within NATO, with its headquarters in Poland (at Szczecin), was of great concern to Russia; as were NATO's efforts to maintain Eastern European (and Baltic) airfields and compel new members to re-equip according to NATO standards.[151]

The question of the Danish-German-Polish NATO corps headquartered in Poland came up again in January 1998, when Sergeev expressed his concern about it during an official visit to Germany (ITAR-TASS, 28 Jan). Speaking to journalists in Bonn after talks with his counterpart, Volker Rühe, Sergeev said that "we do not understand why the North Atlantic alliance is so keen on advancing its armed structures towards Russia's borders." As we have seen above, a diplomatic dispute with Norway brought many of these strategic issues to the forefront in the early spring of 1998, and such concerns were given an added hue when *Izvestiia* raised the possibility of new economic barriers against Kaliningrad as Poland and Baltic states prepared for entry into the EU.[152]

Military reform was brought to the public's attention again in early May, 1998, when Yeltsin told representatives of the military elite that reform was essential because an attack on Russia was still possible. The goal of reform "is to form smaller but efficient Armed Forces, armed with advanced hardware and well-trained personnel," he said, stressing the need to maintain a "potential to deter" (Interfax, 8 May). Sergeev repeated this message to his defense minister NATO counterparts during a June meeting in Belgium.[153] Later in May, Yeltsin himself had been accused by State Duma deputies of contributing to the likelihood of an attack on Russia by "weakening" its military capacity.[154] This charge was levelled by the

---

[151]Mayak Radio Network (3 Dec 1997), FBIS-SOV, No. 337. Sergei Glotov, of the Anti-NATO group in the Duma, also remarked that NATO's eastward expansion was a threat because it would lead to the upgrading of "airfields, bases, barracks, warehouses and communications" on the territories of the new members, ITAR-TASS (24 Dec 1997). See also "Cherez doverie i sotrudnichestvo" [Through Trust and Cooperation], *Krasnaia zvezda* (2 Dec 1997).

[152]"Italiia zazhigaet krasnyi svet na puti Latvii v Evrosoiuz" [Italy Places a Red Light in the Path of Latvia to the EU], *Izvestiia* (9 April 1998).

[153]See, e.g., Oleg Falidev, "Voennuiu silu Rossiia rassmatrivaet kak faktor sderzhivaniia" [Russia Considers Military Strength as a Factor for Restraint], *Krasnaia zvezda* (16 June 1998).

[154]The accusation was contained in a 12-page indictment of Yeltsin that formed part of the Duma's impeachment proceedings against him, supported by 177 of the deputies (Interfax, 20 May 1998).

emi-eulogy: "My ideology is patriotism." A deputy chair of the Duma's De-
Committee, Zhanna Kas'ianenko (Communist), said earlier that she "believes
sia and the future of the army."[158] It was inevitable that the image of NATO
g inexorably towards Russia's borders was to be caught up in rallying cries for
nationally charged campaign to save Russia from disaster.

en the Kosovo crisis brought a further cooling of Russia's already tenuous
nship with NATO, the Kremlin sped up its overhaul of the military. Kalin-
was a particularly vulnerable spot, as it was scheduled to be Russia's neigh-
NATO. Lt. Gen. Nikolai Zlenko voiced the military's main concern in Oc-
noting that NATO forces would increase by large numbers in the
west, whereas Russia's contingents would shrink dramatically.[159] Another
al announced that the tactical plans of Russia's joint defense system with Be-
were being adjusted because of NATO's movement eastward and the Kosovo
(Interfax, 4 Nov). So the ripple effects of NATO's policy in Yugoslavia had
ed Russia's northwest flank.

llover from the Rokhlin Movement was still apparent in Moscow during the
Congress of the Communist-dominated People's Patriotic Union, held dur-
he last week of November. Rokhlin was remembered fondly in most of the
hes, while Yeltsin and the reformers were denigrated for weakening Russia's
ses. Kas'ianenko, for example, spoke for the Congress when she promised
"We [PPU] shall stand beside the Russian soldier and officer while the ene-
of the Fatherland are destroying the army, are prepared to saw up our last
les and submarines, and have opened the way for NATO armies to reach
ensk and Pskov."[160]

he People's Patriotic Union must have been satisfied that it was time to end
ong saga of military reform. On 2 December 1998, they helped the Duma
imously pass the bill "On Military Reform in the Russian Federation." Sub-
ent events in Europe ensured that the issue of changes in Russian armed

---

[8]Kas'ianenko, "Veriu v Rossiiu i ee budushchiiu armiuiu" [I Believe in Russia and Its
re Army], *Sovetskaia Rossiia* (16 July 1998); Rokhlin, " 'Moia ideologiia—patrio-
" [My Ideology Is Patriotism], *Sovetskaia Rossiia* (23 July 1998).

[9]Voice of Russia World Service (19 Oct 1998), FBIS-SOV, No. 292. Zlenko is deputy
of the RF Defense Ministry International Military Cooperation Department.

[0]Kas'ianenko, "Otechestvo, Vera, Pobeda. Pod stiagami patriotizma. Obrashchenie II
a Narodno-patrioticheskogo soiuza Rossii k narodu mnogonatsional'noi Rossii" [Fa-
and, Faith, Victory: Under the Banner of Patriotism—Address from the 2nd Con-
of the People's Patriotic Union of Russia to the People of Multinational Russia],
tskaia Rossiia (24 Nov 1998). Smolensk and Pskov are major Russian cities reached
quickly by German forces in 1941.

communist party as part of its campaign to have the presic
Rokhlin, one of the most dogged impeachment advocates
    Discussion of Russia's defense strategy was stirred up by
Balkans, where it began to appear in Moscow that the Uni
NATO into another foray against Serbians. The military p
picious of NATO's motives throughout the spring and sun
June that a "second Balkan war" was imminent.[155] Rokhli
the military cause a martyr, at least until it was discovered tl
tor Ilyukhin, chair of the Duma's Security Committee, wa
Movement. Makashov, Don Cossack Host leader Nikolai
deputy Igor Bratishchev were chosen deputy leaders. On
leadership to journalists at a press conference, Ilyukhin i
Movement] will not allow Russia to be further disarmed,'
nounced that the Movement had over 150,000 members,
political organizations with collective memberships.[156]
    Rokhlin was eulogized in the communist press and his M
nated. In August, for example, it was able to organize demor
and Vladivostok that forced changes in a joint Russian-Amer
at Vladivostok. Protesting under the slogan "Russia is not
Ground!" for the United States, and "No to NATO on Rus
mostly elderly Russians prompted officials to move the landi
vostok to a closed Russian military harbor.[157]
    As the economic and political crisis worsened, patriotism an
tradition became, if not a last resort, then at least something of t
communist press, using Rokhlin's "last words," emphasized pat.

---

[155]Dashichev, "Istoriia razrusheniia osnov natsional'noi bezopasn
of the Destruction of the Basis of the National Security of the Coun
op. cit.; "Kosovo: napriazhennost' narastaet" [Kosovo: The Tension
zvezda (20 June 1998); Vladimir Kuzar', "NATO gotovitsia k ag
NATO Preparing for Aggression in Kosovo?], *Krasnaia zvezda* (20 Jun
miatina, Nikolai Kalintsev, "Krizis v Kosovo—nachalo 'vtoroi Balka
Crisis in Kosovo the Start of a "Second Balkan War"?], *Krasnaia zve*
Yurii Pankov, "NATO gotovit mezhdunarodnyi pretsedent?" [Is NA7
ternational Precedent?], *Krasnaia zvezda* (26 June 1998).
    [156]"Novyi lider DPA" [New Leader of the DPA], *Sovetskaia Rossii*
    [157]See, e.g., "Na Arbate zvuchit: net desantu Pentagona v Primor'e!"
Hears: No to Pentagon Landing in the Far East!], *Sovetskaia Rossiia* (6
page photo of the demonstration on the Arbat, a famous street in Mosc
women and veterans in uniform carrying pickets.

forces would be a continuing point of contention. By the end of April 1999, military advisers were urging the ministry of defense to deal quickly with weaknesses in the armed forces, and arrange cooperative military-technical programs with Ukraine and Belarus.

The Kremlin took steps of its own. On 19 May, Yeltsin ordered Defense Minister Sergeev to "reconsider" Russia's military doctrine in light of the changing international situation.[161] Thus, the military reform program was fully captured by Moscow's perception of NATO behavior.

4. UKRAINE ENIGMA

Moscow's acute awareness of Ukraine's location—geographic, strategic, and cultural—between Russia and NATO, warrants special investigation. A good place to start this story is in January 1996, when there was much optimism in Russia about Russian-Ukrainian military cooperation. At that time their defense ministers, Pavel Grachev and Valeriy Shmarov, met in Kiev to negotiate 26 agreements signed by them in November 1995. After they were joined by the United States' William Perry, the session became a tripartite discussion on the withdrawal of strategic nuclear forces from Ukrainian territory.[162] Russia was encouraged as well when, on 18 January, Ukrainian president Leonid Kuchma told a press conference that he opposed NATO expansion "categorically" (Interfax, 19 Jan 1996).

Within a few months, however, Moscow had misgivings about "secret" meetings in Kiev between senior Ukrainian officials, including foreign minister Gennadii Udovenko, and Solana. Some Russian reporters were convinced that Ukraine was bartering away its non-aligned status in return for a special partnership with

---

[161] Snark (Yerevan) (20 May 1999), FBIS-SOV, No. 520. Sergeev made this announcement while attending a CIS Defense Ministers' meeting in Armenia. See *Izvestiia* (20 May 1999), and Melor Sturua, "Otvet na agressiiu NATO imeetsia?" [Is There Any Response to NATO Aggression?], *Nezavisimaia gazeta* (28 April 1999).

[162]For the optimistic Russian opinion, see, e.g., Mikhail Shevtsev, "Kommentarii. Mozhno li v 'troike' i v 'dvoike' sotrudnichat' na piaterku? V Kieve otkrylas' pervaia v istorii vstrecha glav voennykh vedomstv Rossii, Ukrainy i SShA" [Is It Possible to Collaborate Effectively in "Threes" and "Two's"? The First Meeting in History Between the Military Chiefs of Russia, Ukraine and the USA Opens in Kiev], *Rossiiskie vesti* (5 Jan 1996).

For a good overview of Ukrainian security concerns and NATO, see Stephen A. Cambone, "NATO Enlargement: Implications for the Military Dimension of Ukraine's Security," *The Harriman Review*, 10, No. 3 (Winter 1997): 8–18.

NATO.[163] In August, Kuchma informed his ministry of foreign affairs that good relations with Russia were still his priority and a precondition to Ukraine's security. Shortly thereafter, in Washington, he proposed a nuclear-free zone in Central and Eastern Europe. On advising reporters of Kuchma's proposal, Udovenko declared that Ukraine was "unequivocally non-aligned," adding that his republic would nonetheless expand cooperation with the Alliance.[164]

At that time the commonly projected new NATO members were Poland, the Czech Republic and Hungary. These countries are neighbors or near neighbors of Ukraine, making it the real buffer zone between Russia and NATO; and this is precisely what Ukraine wished not to be. In this regard, the government in Kiev faced a unique dilemma, and ethnic Russians in Ukraine are blessed with a unique opportunity. Ukraine is the home of 11.4 million ethnic Russians, making up about 20 percent of its total population. It is the largest Russian population outside of Russia. No real ethnic conflict has arisen in Ukraine, but the likelihood of Russian nationalists using their many links in Ukraine for their own political ends is high. Communists in Russia and Ukraine are closely associated, and Ukrainian Communist Party leader, Petro Symonenko, delivered a powerful speech promoting reunification of the two countries at the 4th CPRF Congress in April, 1997. Wide-ranging economic, institutional and cultural associations also make Ukrainian-Russian connections very difficult to sever.

During most of 1996 Ukrainian leaders consistently denied that they wanted to bring their country into NATO and the foreign ministry just as consistently insisted that Ukraine's economic and strategic interests lay in cooperation with Russia. But that once firm stance grew increasingly ambiguous in 1997. Comments by Borys Oliynyk, chair of the parliamentary Commission for Foreign Affairs and Relations with the CIS, set the stage for Russian anxieties. Most members of his Commission, he said in December, now favored joining NATO as the most reliable guarantor of their country's security. Oliynyk's remarks coincided with an OSCE summit on European security, in Lisbon, where Ukrainian delegates supported a resolution in support of NATO expansion, and only Russia dissented.[165] More-

---

[163] See, e.g., a series of essays under the title, "V treugol'nike SShA-Ukraina-Rossiia Vashington vse bol'she ottesniaet Kiev ot Moskvy" [In the USA-Ukraine-Russia Triangle Washington Tries Harder to Push Kiev Away from Moscow], *Nezavisimaia gazeta* (25 March 1996).

[164]Interview with Udovenko, Uniar (2 July 1996), FBIS-SOV, No. 150. See also Tatiana Ivzhenko, "Solana na Ukraine i v pribaltike. Vneblokovyi status stanovitsia predmetom torga" [Solana in Ukraine and the Baltics: Non-Aligned Status Becomes a Bargaining Chip], *Nezavisimaia gazeta* (17 April 1996).

[165]Roman Woronowycz, "Lisbon Summit of OSCE Discusses Future Course for European Security," *The Ukrainian Weekly*, No. 49 (8 Dec 1996): 1, 2. For Oliynyk's observation, see *Holos Ukrayiny* (7 Dec 1996).

over, polls taken in Ukraine (and reported in Russia) demonstrated a growing predilection for NATO in the population, especially among its youth.[166]

Russia's worry about Ukraine's relationship with NATO was closely linked to the Black Sea Fleet question, which had remained unanswered since 1991. *Izvestiia* had carried a story on 6 November 1996 saying that Ukraine already was "secretly" participating in NATO manoeuvres, bringing the Alliance surreptitiously to Russia's borders.[167] A week later, Aman Tuleev, then the Russian minister for cooperation with the CIS, led a delegation to Sevastopol and returned convinced, so he said, that "Ukraine's NATO orientation . . . [may cause] a real threat to the [Black Sea] fleet's combat capability."[168] Ukraine as a tool of NATO's (and Turkey's) policy in the Black Sea was a possibility taken very seriously in Russia by groups opposed to NATO enlargement. A bitter essay by Vladimir Golubov warned in *Rossiiskie vesti* on 1 February 1997 that Ukraine was about to betray Russia on the Black Sea.[169] Russians reacted angrily again a little later when the Ukrainian defense ministry announced plans to set up in Kiev a Center for the Coordination of Ukrainian Participation in NATO's PfP. Information about the Center had been in the public domain for some time, but the fact that the official announcement was delivered in Brussels by Ukrainian Chief of General Staff, Lt. Gen. O. Zatynayko, during talks with NATO Commander (Europe) George Joulwan, bolstered Russian suspicions that the event was orchestrated to coincide with a Solana sweep through CIS countries.

Russian discomfort rose another notch with the publication in the Ukrainian press of an interview with Borys Tarasyuk, Ukrainian ambassador to Benelux (posted in Brussels).[170] Predicting a special relationship between Ukraine and

---

[166]See, e.g., Oleksandr Potekhin, Olena Parakhonska, "Ukraine and NATO: An Elite Poll," and Evhen Golovakha, Ilko Kucheriv, "NATO and Public Opinion in Ukraine," *A Political Portrait of Ukraine. Bulletin,* No. 8 (1997): 20–38, 39–71. This *Bulletin* is published by the Democratic Initiatives Foundation, Kiev. Ukrainian-language versions of the same articles were published in No. 18 (1997): 66–77, 90–121.

[167]Vladimir Skosyrev, "NATO uzhe stoit na nashikh granitsakh" [NATO Is Already at Our Borders], *Izvestiia* (6 Nov 1996).

[168]Tuleev, "Tret'ia osada. ChF—obshchii shit ili yabloko razdora?" [The Third Seige: Black Sea Fleet—Common Shield or Bone of Contention?], *Sovetskaia Rossiia* (12 Nov 1996).

[169]Golubov, "Ukraina, NATO i zapad" [Ukraine, NATO and the West], *Rossiiskie vesti* (1 Feb 1997). He accused Vladimir Horbulin, Secretary of the Ukrainian National Security and Defence Council, of following the advice of Brzezinski and lobbying for admission to NATO by the year 2010.

[170]*Vysokyy zamok* (13 Feb 1997). The interview was conducted by Oleh Pelikhovskyy, with several other Ukrainian journalists present, in Brussels.

NATO and reminding his interviewers of Soviet and Russian actions in Czechoslovakia and Chechnya, Tarasyuk made little effort to hide where his preferences lay.

Kiev officialdom was careful, however, and did not leap on the bandwagon with
Tarasyuk. Oliynyk told a reporter in early March that there was still no official
Ukrainian position on NATO. His own unofficial opinion apparently did not
mirror the collective view of his Commission, for he added that the very existence
of NATO remained a "deep mystery" to him. Not wanting Ukraine to be a buffer
state between East and West Europe, Oliynyk worried especially that the admission of Poland could allow NATO to deploy nuclear weapons in the east. He assumed that mere promises not to do so would not be honored in a war situation,
making Ukraine's position a weakened one. He and other prominent officials in
Kiev much preferred a general European security arrangement in which all states
would be included.[171]

In terms of strategic considerations, the expansion of NATO eastward made
the relationship between the Ukrainian Navy and Russia's Black Sea Fleet more
important than it had been previously. The security of the fleet and the status of
the port at Sevastopol had been bones of contention between the two countries
since the breakup of the USSR.[172] With the announcement in February of a joint
exercise between the NATO and Ukrainian navies on the Black Sea, tensions rose
again very quickly. The exercise, called Sea Breeze-97 and scheduled for August,
was decried in the Russian press as a training drill for trapping the Russian Black
Sea Fleet at Sevastopol.[173]

In March, the Duma's Anti-NATO Association asked Kuchma to "confirm or
deny" reports that Kiev intended to make Sevastopol available to U.S. warships.
There was no reply. *Rossiiskaia gazeta* covered the story and interviewed the commander of Russia's Black Sea Fleet, Admiral Viktor A. Kravchenko. His view of the
overall situation was bleak: no funds, no juridical status, ships being transferred to
Ukraine by politicians, harassment from the Ukraine ministry of foreign affairs,

---

[171]Oliynyk, "Dlia mene problemy rozshireniia NATO ne isnue" [For Me, the Problem
of NATO Expansion Does Not Exist], *Demokratychna Ukrayina* (25 Feb 1997).

[172]On this see statements made by Russia's Black Sea Fleet Commander, Admiral Viktor Kravchenko, in Sevastopol, Interfax-Ukraine (19 Feb 1997). See especially an interview with Leonid Kuchma, "L'Ukraine est un Etat aussi independant que la Russie," *Le
Figaro* (23 Jan 1992).

[173]Andrei Stepanov, "Voenno-politicheskie igry vblizi granits Rossii. Zona strategich-
eskikh interesov strany suzhaetsia" [The Military-Political Games Near Russia's Borders:
The Zone of the Country's Strategic Interests Is Narrowed], *Nezavisimaia gazeta* (1 March
1997). The Russian media said that the exercise was based on the British-French strategy
used during the Crimean War in the mid-19th century! So the historical bells continued
to toll for Russian nationalists.

and so on. Sea Breeze-97 was an especially humiliating event for the Russian navy, he said, portraying NATO as "closing in" on him and his subordinates.[174]

There were Ukrainian stands against NATO. On the very day that Sergei Glotov voiced the Russian Anti-NATO Association's post-Albright aims, a Ukrainian Civil Congress called for the formation of a Ukrainian Anti-NATO political club. Congress leader Aleksandr Bazilyuk said that the club would promote a "military-political alliance with Russia and other CIS countries" and urge the revival of a CIS industrial-military complex (Interfax-Ukraine, 21 Feb). Like their counterparts in Russia, forces opposed to NATO in Ukraine became more active in April, and ethnic Russians picketed the hotel in Sevastopol (Crimea) where NATO officers were posted with strongly worded posters against the military exercise as anti-Russian (Interfax, 17 April). The population living on the Russian side of the Russian-Ukraine border was so worried that Ukraine might join NATO that *Komsomol'skaia pravda* credited the gubernatorial election victory of nationalist Nikolai I. Kondratenko to their apprehensions. Kondratenko was supported in large part by pensioners, the paper said, who were swayed by Soviet-style slogans, such as "NATO Members, Remember Hitler's Fate!"[175] Ukrainian communists were equally consistent and vocal in their hostility to NATO enlargement.

Diplomats seemed to have great difficulty in transmitting an official Ukrainian position to Moscow. In March, Ukrainian ambassador to the United States, Yurii Scherbak, told an audience in Washington that NATO should transform into a broader collective security structure; but, as it moves eastward, all countries that meet the alliance's criteria for membership should have "free access" to it.[176] Comments like these made it easy for Russian observers to believe that Ukraine was considering membership. Almost simultaneously, however, Udovenko informed a news conference in Ottawa that Ukraine "has no intention of joining NATO;" rather it wished to nurture broad cooperation with the alliance.[177] Both officials had high expectations for the special Ukraine-NATO charter then being negotiated.

As the Yeltsin/Clinton meeting loomed and statements emanating from Russia

---

[174]Nikolai Cherkashin, "U matrosov est' voprosy. Chernomorskii flot: proryv v XXI vek" [Sailors Have Questions: The Black Sea Fleet: A Breakthrough into the 21st Century], *Rossiiskaia gazeta* (5 March 1997).

[175]Aleksandr Nikolaev, "No pasaran!" [They Will Not Pass!], *Komsomol'skaia pravda* (4 March 1997). The title is Spanish. Kondratenko was elected from the Krasnodarsk krai.

[176]Interfax-Ukraine (5 March 1997). Scherbak spoke to a seminar on the subject, "NATO after the Summit," sponsored by the Military Academy of the U.S. Defense Department.

[177]ITAR-TASS (6 March 1997). This report by TASS Ottawa correspondent Nikolai Setunskiiy carried the headline, "Udovenko, Canada's Axworthy Hold Similar Views on NATO."

implied that a special arrangement might be reached between NATO and that country, Ukraine began to play trump cards of its own. Knowing full well that one of Yeltsin's requirements from Clinton would be that Ukraine (and the Baltics) not be invited to join the Alliance, Kuchma told journalists on 18 March that Russia was forcing Ukraine, indirectly, into the arms of NATO. The very next day saw the opening first round of talks between Ukrainian leaders (Udovenko and Vladimir Horbulin, head of National Security and Defence Council) and NATO in Brussels. Udovenko told reporters that he did not want his country on the edge of a new dividing line between NATO and the CIS. In response to a specific question, he did not rule out a future membership for Ukraine. Indeed, he now said that Ukraine's "strategic goal" was to join European organizations and alliances, including NATO. This was immediately reported in Russian papers, generating such a furore that the Ukrainian foreign ministry issued a backtracking statement on 25 March.[178]

Yeltsin would have been well aware of these opinions as he sat down with Clinton. Almost immediately after the Russian and American presidents went home, Ukraine's People's Rukh Party declared that Ukraine should apply for NATO membership to protect itself from a "rejuvenated Russian empire" (Interfax, 22 March). A few days later, a formal Rukh statement was published, signed by the movement's leader Vyacheslav Chornovil. Rukh turned the issue into a question of whether or not Ukraine was to become an important part of Europe or remain part of a Russia-dominated eastern backwater. If the latter course prevailed, he said, the communists would return their country to a Soviet-style authoritarian state, "enslaved" by Russia.[179] This was strong stuff, turning the debate about NATO in Ukraine to a pro- or anti-Russia campaign.

As the first major CIS summit for 1997 wound down in Moscow, 29 March, Yeltsin announced that he would visit Kiev in June, before NATO's Madrid meeting, to resolve discord between Russia and Ukraine. He had postponed visits to

---

[178]For a Russian reaction, see, e.g., Yu. K., "Kiev sorevnuetsia s Moskvoi" [Kiev Competes with Moscow], *Nezavisimaia gazeta* (21 Mar 1997). The "backtracking" was issued as an official foreign ministry statement to the effect that Udovenko was placing the matter in the "larger context" and was merely not ruling out any long-term possibilities. At present, however, Ukraine had no "intention" of applying for membership in NATO, *Uryadovy kuryer* (25 Mar 1997).

[179]Chornovil, "Zaiava narodnogo rukhu Ukrayni ta fraktsii Verkhovnoy Radi 'Rukh za narod, za Ukrayni' pro neobkhidnist' vstupu Ukrayni do NATO" [Statement of the People's Rukh of Ukraine and Fraction of the Supreme Rada "Rukh for the People, for Ukraine" about the Necessity for Ukraine to Join NATO], *Holos Ukrayiny* (26 Mar 1997). Chornovil lost his position as Rukh leader in 1999.

Ukraine on six occasions over the previous two years, but this time promised that he would go even if a political treaty was not yet ready for signing. The NATO question evidently was high on the agenda.

Russian observers were very distrustful of Ukraine's designs, and continued to harp on Udovenko's press releases which appeared to make membership in NATO a "strategic aim for Ukraine."[180] Kuchma addressed several of these concerns at the end of April during an interview for Moscow NTV. The occasion of the interview was Kuchma's plan to visit Sevastopol the next day (25 April) and meet with Ukrainian naval officers.

Acknowledging some major differences between the Ukrainian and Russian perspectives on NATO expansion, the Ukrainian president nevertheless said that his country would remain neutral in respect to blocs; that is, it would not join NATO. He said as well that his government shared "the view that on no account should nuclear weapons be deployed on the territory of new NATO members states."[181]

Relieved as they may have been on hearing this, Russian foreign ministry personnel still objected to the Sea Breeze-97 operation, complaining that a maneuver on the Black Sea that included Ukrainian, American and Turkish warships, and others, without consulting Russia was a serious breach of good faith (Interfax, 6 May 1997). On 7 May the NATO Information Bureau was finally opened in Kiev, with Canadian diplomat Roman Lishchynskyi at its head. Solana attended the opening ceremony and delivered a congratulatory speech. About 4,000 people, mostly from ethnic Russian groups, demonstrated against the event, which was greeted with hostility in Russia's mass media.

The Primakov-Solana announcement on 13 May that they had reached a modus vivendi did not ease Russia's anxieties about Ukraine very much, for on the 15th Ivan Zayats, a deputy in Kiev's Supreme Soviet (Council), was quoted in the mass media in favor of an immediate Ukrainian application for NATO membership.[182] Russian qualms about Ukraine's plans were heightened when the Founding Act was made public on 27 May. The absence of any mention whatsoever of Russia's adamant rejection of the idea that any former USSR republic join NATO caused a number of commentators to assume that the way for Ukrainian

---

[180]See, e.g., Nikolai Paklin, "Chem chrevata liubov k NATO" [The Danger of Loving NATO], *Rossiiskaia gazeta* (2 April 1997); Viktor Timoshenko, Dmitrii Gornostaev, "Kiev vse chashche smotrit na zapad" [Kiev Is Looking Towards the West More Often], *Nezavisimaia gazeta* (29 March 1997); Stanislav Kondrashov, "Soglasie o nesoglasii" [Agreement to Disagree], *Izvestiia* (30 March 1997).

[181]Moscow NTV (24 April 1997), FBIS-SOV, No. 080.

[182]Zayats, "Kongresmeni zaproshuiut' Ukraynu v NATO" [Congressmen Invite Ukraine into NATO], *Demokratychna Ukrayina* (15 May 1997).

membership was being smoothed.[183] The fact that Kuchma joined a summit of leaders from the Baltic states and Poland in Estonia on 28 May (see Section 5) lent credence to this opinion.

Almost simultaneously, Ukraine confirmed its own special status with NATO, signing a Charter on a Distinctive Partnership between the North Atlantic Treaty Organization and Ukraine. Initialled by Kuchma on the 29th, the Charter was scheduled for official signing during the NATO summit at Madrid in July. The document located Ukraine's main activity in the Euro-Atlantic Partnership Council (EAPC) and called for a NATO-Ukraine Commission to meet no less than twice a year (NATO Website, 29 May 1997). First deputy foreign minister of Ukraine, Anton Buteyko, delivered a speech at the opening of the ministerial meeting of the North Atlantic Cooperation Council (NACC) and EAPC on the 30th, announcing among other things that Ukraine and Russia were about to sign a dramatic political treaty in Kiev (NATO Website, 30 May). Indeed, three almost simultaneous treaties formalized relations between Kiev and Moscow and appeared to end the long-standing dispute over a division of the Black Sea Fleet. Russia was granted a 20-year lease on its base in Sevastopol, at $135 million per year to be deducted from Ukraine's huge debt (calculated at $3.5 billion, mostly to Gazprom) to Russia.[184] Agreement on the fleet gave Russia a semblance of naval tenure on the Black Sea at a time when Turkey's strategic and economic presence there appeared to be growing at an unprecedented pace.

As the troubled month of May drew to a close, it seemed that after centuries of territorial dispute a treaty basis for normalization in the vast lands shared by Russia, Ukraine, Belarus, and Poland finally had been laid. The Russian government had, in fact, acted against the enduring popular mood in Russia which still tended to see Ukrainian independence as a temporary phenomenon. The treaties guaranteed the integrity of Ukraine's borders and, it was hoped, lessened the need for

---

[183]See, e.g., Nikolai Paklin, "Rossiia-NATO: balans interesov" [Russia and NATO: Balance of Interests], *Rossiiskaia gazeta* (27 May 1997), Aleksandr Shinkin, "V NATO vnemliut Ukrainskoi move" [They Listen to the Ukraine language in NATO], *Rossiiskaia gazeta* (21 May 1997), and "Ameriko-Ukrainskii dialog v Vashingtone" [American-Ukrainian Dialogue in Washington], *Krasnaia zvezda* (17 May 1997).

[184]The *Agreement Between the Russian Federation and Ukraine on the Status and Conditions of the Russian Federation Black Sea Fleet's Stay on Ukrainian Territory* (28 May) was published in *Rossiiskaia gazeta* (7 June 1997); The *Treaty of Friendship, Cooperation, and Partnership between the Russian Federation and Ukraine* (31 May 1997) and the *Russian-Ukrainian Declaration* were printed in English by ITAR-TASS (28, 31 May 1997). The Russian-language versions appeared in *Rossiiskaia gazeta* (5 June 1997). They also can be found in *REDA 1997,* Vols. 1 and 2.

Ukraine to consider membership in NATO. But the optimistic comments to that effect from both governments were uttered too soon.

Already in the first week of June nationalists on both sides found fault with the treaties. Ukrainian journalists complained that the fee for Black Sea porting was far too low and, a few weeks after the event, a Russian-language Ukrainian paper predicted, rightly as it turned out, that the Ukrainian parliament would not ratify the Black Sea agreement. Quoting deputy Yurii Orobets, vice president of the Ukrainian Perspective Fund, the press went so far as to foresee the initiation of impeachment proceedings against Kuchma. The three documents signed with Russia meant, in the opinion of Ukrainian nationalists, that Ukraine had "de facto joined the Russian military bloc."[185] Russia's opposition, on the other hand, interpreted the Black Sea arrangement as a first step in Ukraine's plan to join NATO, for the elimination of the potential for border dispute provided Ukraine with one of the criteria demanded of new NATO members. Ukraine is forming a cordon sanitaire on Russia's border, was Aleksandr Bykovskii's explanation for Kuchma's meeting with Polish and Baltic leaders.[186]

Shortly thereafter, there was bad news and good news for Russia in a written statement by Horbulin, who announced that Ukraine had dropped the notion of non-alignment from its security concept (Interfax-Ukraine, 5 June). Still unprepared to join NATO, Horbulin continued, Ukraine's entry in the Alliance would nonetheless be viewed as part of the country's long-term strategic plan. Here was formal confirmation of the worst case scenario for Russia, ending the confusion caused by Udovenko's earlier equivocation. Deployment of nuclear weapons in the new NATO countries was still "inadmissable," however, and was something that the three NATO nuclear countries should pledge not to do. Russia certainly agreed with Ukraine on that last matter.

The Black Sea agreements had not then been made fully public in Ukraine, so rumors about them abounded. There were suspicions that Sevastopol might itself become a *de facto* part of Russia. Rallies against Sea Breeze-97 in Sevastopol, Kerch, Feodosiia and in the Yevpatoria region of Crimea on 22 June, the anniversary of Hitler's invasion of the USSR, did nothing to mitigate this type of worry. In Simferopol, leaders of the Crimean Union of Soviet Officers told demonstrators that the "motherland" (Russia) was in danger and that NATO ships were really there to counter the Russian Black Sea Fleet (ITAR-TASS, 22 June). Accusations such as these were hotly denied by officers of the Ukrainian Fleet.[187] Ignoring denials,

---

[185] *Vseukrainskie vedomosti* (22 June 1997), FBIS-SOV, No. 122.

[186] *Sel'skaia zhizn'* (3 June 1997), FBIS-SOV, No. 113.

[187] See, e.g., article by Ukrainian Navy Commander of the South Sea Region, Captain Boris Rekuts, in *Flot Ukrayiny* (7 June 1997), FBIS-SOV, No. 122. A NATO exercise off the Bulgarian coast in June also was noted with concern in the Russian press.

184   *Section Two: Ripple Effects*

opponents of NATO expansion in Simferopol protested against Sea Breeze-97 again on 11 July, gathering, they said, 10,000 signatures decrying any landing of NATO forces on Crimean territory (ITAR-TASS, 11 July). The gulf already separating Crimea's largest ethnic minority from Ukraine was clearly exacerbated by the image of NATO spreading inexorably over the Black Sea.

Ukrainian authorities were openly more excited about the NATO summit scheduled for 8 July than Russians were.[188] Among other things, the Charter on a Distinctive Partnership between the North Atlantic Treaty Organization and Ukraine would be signed in Madrid in a special ceremony.[189] Whereas the presidents of Russia and Belarus stayed at home, Ukraine's president attended as a principal participant. Russian nationalists could find solace only in the Communist Party of Ukraine, the central committee of which urged members on 7 July to organize "massive pressure" on the government to stop all forms of military cooperation with NATO (Interfax-Ukraine, 7 July).

During the Madrid Summit, Ukrainian parliamentarians who were opposed to NATO expansion eastward joined their counterparts in Belarus, Russia and Latvia in addressing a statement to parliaments in NATO countries, asking them not to ratify the admission of new members (Interfax-Ukraine, 9 July). They called for a reunification of CIS countries, on the Russia-Belarus model, as a measure against NATO inroads. A draft law banning NATO military exercises on Ukrainian territory introduced by a communist member of the Supreme Council, Anatolii Yurkovskii, resulted in a scuffle in parliament on 15 July (Infobank, 15 July)—but nothing much else.

Russian commentary on the Ukraine-NATO charter revealed the level of concern generated in some circles. To cite but one example, the Charter itself was printed in full in Moscow's *Nezavisimoe voennoe obozrenie,* with a position-taking preamble. Ukraine is being "dragged" into NATO by the Charter, the preamble's author warned, attributing to Kuchma a statement to the effect that the document represents "an intermediate step on the way to a convergence with NATO." This trend "is to the disadvantage of the country's national interests and security," will

---

[188]Read, for example, a long essay on Konstyantyn Morozov's views on Ukrainian relations with NATO. Morozov, former minister of defense, was then the counsellor-envoy of the Ukrainian embassy in Benelux and chief coordinator of cooperation with NATO and the EU in the military sphere: *Molod Ukrayiny* (10 July 1997), FBIS-SOV, No. 225.

[189]The Charter was distributed in English by Interfax-Ukraine, 9 July 1997. It is reprinted in REDA 1997, Vol. 2. For Ukrainian commentary, see "E taka khartiia! Den' Ukrayni u sviti" [There Is Such a Charter! Ukraine Day in the World], *Demokratychna Ukrayna* (10 July 1997).

weaken Ukraine's commitment to the CIS, and put an end to any chance of a CIS unified armed force.[190] These last two projections were soon proven accurate.

Crimean Russians led the way in opposing NATO in Ukraine, and one Sevastopol group even called on Mrs. Kuchma to help stop Sea Breeze-97, as "disruptive" to Russia-Ukraine relations (Interfax, 4 Aug). Later in July a Ukrainian Anti-NATO bloc leader, Tatyana Kurteva, told an interviewer that her group was founded specifically to oppose Sea Breeze-97. The Sevastopol Bastion, as it was called, was joined by 12 other organizations (the city communist branch and veterans groups) and set for itself the tasks of: promoting Ukraine-Russia-Belarus integration; opposing Ukraine joining NATO; and stopping Sea Breeze-97.[191]

Rallies and demonstrations swept Crimea, some of them led by Petro Symonenko, first secretary of the Ukrainian communist central committee, others by Leonid Grach, party chief. Leader of the Russian Duma's Anti-NATO faction, Sergei Glotov, also took part in protests at Crimean sites of the NATO operation. Kurteva claimed that the Bastion had support from 12 parties, organizations and movements, including communists, and a wide cross-section of Russian patriotic and military organizations. They highlighted the many official Moscow statements in opposition to Sea Breeze-97, and blamed the United States and NATO for funding such undertakings. Ukraine is being led into a "mouse-trap" by NATO, one indignant journalist warned.[192] The Sea-Breeze question remained a symbol of NATO's aggressive ambition to Anti-NATO deputies in the State Duma, who again referred to it specifically in a strongly worded open letter to Clinton in mid-October.[193] But the significance of Ukraine to Moscow was encapsulated by Boris

---

[190]"Khartiia ob osobom partnerstve mezhdu Ukrainoi i organizatsiei severoatlanticheskogo dogovora" [Charter of the Distinctive Partnership between Ukraine and the North Atlantic Treaty], *Nezavisimoe voennoe obozrenie,* No. 26 (19–25 July 1997).

[191]See H. Staroverov, "The 'Sevastopol Bastion'" is Operating," *Krymskaia pravda* (26 July 1997), FBIS-SOV, No. 218.

[192]*Ibid.* For Glotov's participation and statements, see ITAR-TASS (25 August 1997); U.S. funding for Sea Breeze-97 was highlighted also in *Uryadovyy kuryer* (19 July 1997), where reference was made to "NATO aggressors" by leftist and Russian nationalist opponents.

[193]"Otkrytoe pis'mo prezidentu SShA Uil'iamu Dzh. Klintonu. NATO rastopchet doverie" [Open Letter to U.S. President William Clinton: NATO Will Trample Trust], *Sovetskaia Rossiia* (16 Oct 1997). There were rumors afloat that Russia had received a million dollars for infrastructure compensation related to Sea Breeze-97, but this was not confirmed. See Nikolai Alekseenko, "Buria v stakane vody. Poluchila li Rossiia za podgotovku 'Si briza-97' million dollarov?" [Storm in a Tea Cup: Did Russia Receive a Million Dollars for the Preparation of Sea Breeze-97?], *Region,* No. 34 (27 September 1997). For more conspiracy thesis writing, see "'Si Briz'—veter peremen?" [Sea Breeze: The Wind of Change?], *Zavtra,* No. 36 (Sept 1997).

Rodionov in July 1997. Lip-service by Clinton and Albright on the importance of maintaining good relations with Russia is conditioned by insistence in the United States that Russia must not re-integrate CIS countries: "It is, of course, a question of Ukraine," he concluded.[194]

Much of the ambiguity in Ukraine's position towards NATO was eliminated in July, when a long interview with Horbulin appeared in the *Uryadovyy kuryer.* Admitting that Ukraine was not yet ready to become a member of NATO, particularly because of the expenditures such membership would entail, Horbulin made it clear that his country's security interests lay with an expanded Atlantic Alliance. He ruled out the OSCE specifically and predicted that difficulties would arise from different interpretations of the Founding Act by Russia and NATO. Fully supportive of Ukrainian participation in Sea Breeze-97, he called on Ukraine's population—meaning its Russians—to stop agitating against it. From the perspective of Russian nationalists Horbulin's commentary represented a sea change in Ukraine's position since 1996.[195]

Russian officials continued to make their position known on Sea Breeze-97, which took place from 25–31 August. Foreign ministry representatives voiced their department's disapproval at press conferences on 14 and 25 August, acknowledging, however, that Ukraine had asked Russia to participate (Interfax, 14 Aug, ITAR-TASS, 25 Aug 1997). Kuchma repeated in late August that Ukraine "is not going to join the NATO bloc," simultaneously rejecting a place for his own country in a CIS defense treaty. The occasion of these latter remarks was a visit to Kiev by Russian defense minister Sergeev and a series of concomitant consultations that appeared to clear the air on a number of disputes, including Sea Breeze-97 (ITAR-TASS, 29 Aug).[196]

---

[194]Rodionov, "Ryvok v 'mirnom nastuplenii' " [Spurt in the "Peace Offensive"], *Rossiiskaia gazeta* (26 July 1997).

[195]Horbulin, "Before and After Madrid," *Uryadovyy kuryer* (26 July 1997), FBIS-SOV, No. 212.

[196]For Russian criticism of Sea Breeze see Tat'iana Ivzhenko, Nataliia Pulina, "Peretiagivanie kanata na Chernomor'e. Ucheniia 'Si briz-97' v Krymu aktivizirovali voenno-politicheskoe sotrudnichestvo Moskvy i Kieva" [Pulling the Rope on the Black Sea: "Sea Breeze-97" Training Exercise Activated Military and Political Cooperation of Moscow and Kiev], *Nezavisimaia gazeta* (28 Aug 1997) and Oleg Falichev, "Peregovory prodolzheny v Sevastopole. Ofitsial'nyi vizit ministra oborony Rossii podkhodit k zaversheniiu" [Negotiations Continue in Sevastopol: The Official Visit of the Russian Minister of Defense Comes to Its Conclusion], *Krasnaia zvezda* (29 Aug 1997). For a Ukrainian defense of the naval exercise, " 'Briz' vlashtovue ne vsikh: dekhto khoche buri" [Not Everyone Likes "Sea Breeze": Someone Wants the Storm Again], *Holos Ukrayiny* (27 Aug 1997).

Apparently Russia's State Duma was not impressed with the flurry of mutual diplomatic appeasements: it issued public statements on Sea Breeze-97 on 2 and 10 September, strongly condemning the participation of Ukraine and Georgia in an "unfriendly act toward Russia," which holds Crimean territory "sacred to every Russian person." The early September statement called the friendship treaty with Ukraine—still not ratified by the Duma—a weakening of Russia's great power status. The Ukrainian Supreme Council (Rada) noted, somewhat redundantly, that such statements "did not help strengthen Ukrainian-Russian relations."[197]

When, on 8 September, Ukrainian troops began participating in peacekeeping exercises at Polish and Latvian military training sites,[198] the Russian Duma lashed out with another official pronouncement. "On the Series of NATO's Military Exercises Close to the Borders of the Russian Federation" blamed the United States directly and called on the Russian government to react to these "hostile" actions. The Ukrainian foreign ministry responded angrily (Interfax, 30 Sept), and the Ukrainian military administration enumerated the benefits of association with NATO: joint exercises in Ukraine were paid for by PfP, proving grounds were equipped, infrastructure built, and personnel training programs were conducted with NATO funds.[199] Tensions at the government level were eased after Yeltsin met with Ukrainian foreign ministry officials in September (Interfax, 16 Sept; ITAR-TASS, 17 Sept), and a joint Russia-Ukraine naval exercise on the Black Sea, designated Peace Fairway 97, was arranged.[200]

In the political arena, however, discussion about the future of Ukraine-NATO relationships heated up again in September–October, as proposed changes in Ukraine's election laws—for a spring 1998 parliamentary election—were debated rancorously in parliament. Political parties began to position themselves in relation

---

[197]"Opiat: dvadtsat' piat'" [Here We Go Again], *Zerkalo nedeli* (13–19 Sept 1997); "Zaiavlenie Gosudarstvennoi Dumy ob ucheniiakh 'Si Briz-97'" [State Duma Statement on Sea Breeze-97 Training Exercises], *Rossiiskaia gazeta* (10 Sept 1997).

[198]"Brave Eagle" at Drawsko Pomorskie, north of Warsaw; "Eagle's Talon" in Poznan, and "Cooperative Effort '97", at Adazi, Latvia, all included U.S. troops. Latvian defense minister, Talavs Juntzis, said that he hoped the latter exercise would bring his country closer to NATO, "Peacekeeping Exercises Open," *Kyev Post* (11–17 September 1997).

[199]"Theses of Speech by Maj Gen Lyudvikh Koberskyy, Deputy Commander of Troops of PrykVO and Chief of the District Administration Education Work: New Tendencies and Prospects in Military Cooperation," *Armiya Ukrayiny* (9 October 1997), FBIS-SOV, No. 319.

[200]For a Russian version of the implications of this joint undertaking, see Oleg Falichev, " 'Farvater mira-97': moriaki dvukh stran deistvovani v edinom poryve" ["The Peace Fairway-97": Sailors of the Two Countries Performed in a Single Wind], *Krasnaia zvezda* (1 Nov 1997).

to NATO, and also to Russia and the CIS. Director of the NATO Information Center, Lishchynskyi, was quoted in *Den'* to the effect that there were no real guarantees that NATO would not place nuclear weapons on the territory of the new members. This resurrected the concern that Ukraine might still be in the "grey" geopolitical zone between Russia and NATO, and made NATO a potential campaign issue.[201] Joint maneuvers like Sea Breeze-97 and Tsentrazbat (in Central Asia) were paraded out by the opposition in Ukraine as examples of American willingness to place Ukraine in the line of fire between Russia and the West.[202]

The Ukrainian political class was, in fact, much more divided on the NATO question than its Russian counterpart. One journalist in Ukraine noted that the Russians seemed to have come to terms with NATO, associating with it and at the same time disapproving of its expansion, whereas the Ukrainian foreign ministry was uncertain about what route it wished to take.[203] Delegates from the Ukrainian Supreme Council attended an Anti-NATO conference in Moscow on 21 October, claiming to represent 205 of the 416 members of that parliamentary body. This fairly even split was echoed in the position taken by Oliynyk, who noted the lack of unanimity among legislators on relations with NATO, but insisted that his country needed further integration into European structures (ITAR-TASS, 27 Oct). The Ukrainian communist party was firm in its antagonism, however. At its 31st Congress, held in October, the CPUk resolved to call for "unity of the struggle for peace and against the expansion of NATO." Symonenko later claimed that his country's "ruling clique's constant flirting with NATO" had cost Ukraine its political independence.[204] Confronted with these sharply conflicting positions, Ukraine's dilemma was obvious.

---

[201]Viktor Zamiatin, "Ukraina mozhet ostat'sia v 'seroi' geopoliticheskoi zone" [Ukraine May Remain in the 'Gray' Geopolitical Zone], *Den'* (25 Sept 1997); Sergei Zguretz, "Nashi vybory dlia NATO ne bezrazlichny" [Our Election Is Not Unimportant for NATO], *Den'* (30 Sept 1997); Grigorii Perepelitsia, "Shliakh do 'siroi zoni' " [Road into the 'Gray' Zone], *Den'* (2 Oct 1997). Mr. Lishchynskyi was killed in a car accident in Ukraine in 1998.

[202]See Perepelitsia, above, and "Skil'ki koshtue 'spokii'?" [What Is the Price of Peace?], *Uryadovyi kuryer* (30 Sept 1997).

[203]Mikhail Sokolovskii, "Maastrikhtskoe randevu" [Maastricht Rendezvous], *Zerkalo nedeli* (4 October 1997). The author was reviewing the results of a 2-day meeting of NATO ministers of defense at Maastricht, and the part played in it by Igor Sergeev. Oksana Bun'kovskaia, "Dlia vstupleniia v NATO zhelaniia strany malo" [The Desire of a Country to Become a NATO Member Is Not Enough], *Holos Ukrainy* (30 Sept 1997). For the Anti-NATO conference in Moscow, see *Sovetskaia Rossiia* (28 October 1997).

[204]Symonenko, "Kolonizatsiia Ukrayni: rik s'omiy" [Colonization of Ukraine: The Seventh Year], *Holos Ukrayiny* (21 Nov 1997); "Ob'edinim usiliia v bor'be za mir, protiv ekspansii NATO. Zaiavlenie III (XXI) s'ezda Kommunisticheskoi partii Ukrainy" [Let Us Unite Our Efforts in the Struggle for Peace, against the Expansion of NATO: Statement of the III (XXXI) Congress of the Communist Party of Ukraine], *Kommunist* (Kiev), No. 43 (October 1997): 2.

The Ukrainian and Russian governments worked hard to facilitate cooperation between their two countries. An informal meeting between Yeltsin and Kuchma in mid-November resulted in an optimistic communiqué about the future of Ukraine-Russia relations, at least at the government-to-government level (ITAR-TASS, 17 Nov). Chummy relations between their presidents failed to mask the confusion at other levels of officialdom: Col. Gen. Anatoliy Lopata, for example, welcomed participation in NATO exercises but pointed out that they had little relation to tasks expected of the Ukrainian military if the country was attacked.[205] He went on to complain about cuts in the military budget of some 20 percent, saying that Ukraine's weaponry would soon be obsolete. At least one other Ukrainian observer took the opposite perspective, looking to the PfP as a means to attract contracts for Ukraine's military-industrial complex. Cooperation with West European enterprises in military equipment manufacturing would lead to greater integration with European structures, and a move away from Eurasia. Valentyna Pysans'ka also raised the question of equipment with regard to NATO's proposed new members, pointing out that they would be saddled with the costs of adding modern weapons to their arsenals.[206] Writing about an upcoming meeting of NATO foreign ministers at Brussels, she inferred that NATO hoped to facilitate improved relations between Ukraine and Russia. NATO could even mediate if differences arose between the two largest Slavic nations, she said—much too optimistically. One Russian investigator urged his own country towards greater economic integration with Ukraine, before the United States turned that country into a strategic opponent of Russia.[207]

In any event, on the very last day of 1997 Udovenko again told a news briefing that Ukraine did not plan to request membership in NATO (ITAR-TASS, 30 Dec). As far as he was concerned, the status quo was quite satisfactory. Udovenko's stance was encouraging to the Russian government and in January 1998 the dis-

[205]*Zerkalo nedeli* (13 Dec 1997), FBIS-SOV, No. 358.

[206]Valentyna Pysans'ka, "NATO khoche vivesti vidnosini Kieva i Moskvi na noviy riven'" [NATO Wants to Bring Relations of Kiev and Moscow to a New Level], *Holos Ukrayiny* (16 Dec 1997). For the observations on the importance of cooperation with NATO for Ukraine's military-industrial complex, see Myroslav Levystkyy in *Vysokyy Zamok* [L'viv], (17 Dec 1997), FBIS-SOV, No. 357. See also "Cherez NATO na Evropeiskii rynok?" [Through NATO to the European Market?], *Holos Ukrayiny* (11 Dec 1997).

[207]Georgii Vel'iaminov, "Moskve sleduet peresmotret' svoiu politiky v otnoshenii Kieva" [Moscow Should Re-examine Its Policy towards Kiev], *Nezavisimaia gazeta* (27 Dec 1997).

parity between the two countries narrowed somewhat. Their foreign ministers met in Moscow on the 13th and signed a consultative pact for the duration of the year, agreeing to confer closely on any problems connected with general European security, the Black Sea, the Sea of Azov, the Straits and the Danube.

Another visit to Moscow by Kuchma, in late February, tightened up the official relationship, as the presidents agreed on cooperation in economic and strategic matters. The importance of mutual arrangements in regards to NATO was stressed. The Russian media was not swayed, mostly agreeing with a communist observation that the "current bourgeois-nationalist regime in Ukraine barely conceals the fact that its ultimate aim is to join NATO."[208] Parts of the Ukrainian press were equally incredulous.[209] A 10-year economic cooperation program, which included a Ukrainian promise not to join NATO, was greeted with great skepticism even by the non-Communist press. A writer for *Moscow News,* for example, said that the promise "can be taken lightly" in light of Ukraine's rush to establish "military-political ties with NATO."[210] The State Duma continued to move very slowly on ratifying the previous year's Russia-Ukraine Treaty, blaming Kiev and NATO for alleged violations of earlier agreements.[211]

The most dynamic opposition to Ukraine's growing association with NATO continued to come from the Ukrainian Communist Party, which made opposition to NATO expansion part of its platform for the March 1998 elections to the Supreme and local Councils. A bloc of seven socialist and peasant parties also wrote opposition to NATO into its collective election platform, promising to "prevent Ukraine turning into a colony and an appendix to

---

[208]Safronchuk, "Chto meshaet sbilizheniiu Ukrainy i Rossii?" [What Prevents Russia and Ukraine from Becoming Closer?], *Sovetskaia Rossiia* (5 March 1998). See also *Trud* and *Izvestiia* (26 Feb 1998).

[209]See, e.g., "A raschety okazalis' drugimi" [The Calculations Turned Out to Be Incorrect], *Holos Ukrayiny* (23 Jan 1998), where it was noted with some puzzlement that NATO officials believed that the cost of expansion to NATO members was far less than American "experts" projected. See also Valentyna Pysans'ka, "Navit' bez natiaki na zagrozu . . ." [Even without Any Hint of a Threat], *Holos Ukrayiny* (19 Feb 1998), who said that the new countries were to be admitted even though they knew there was no threat, and warned that the Baltic states were likely to be next.

[210]Arkady Moshes, "Ukraine: Strange Friend or Quiet Rival?" *Moscow News,* No. 8 (12–18 March 1998): 5.

[211]See, e.g., Sergei Andreev, "Kiev ignoriruet prezhnie dogovorennosti" [Kiev Ignores Prior Agreements], *Nezavisimaia gazeta* (6 Feb 1998).

NATO."[212] The platform of People's Rukh, on the other hand, reiterated Chornovil's statement of the previous year; that is, that Ukraine should strive for "economic, political and military integration with Europe" and demanded that "foreign troops be pulled from Ukrainian territory."[213] Thus, the NATO question was contested, to a certain extent, in the election campaign.

Ukrainian journalists, of course, were well aware of the degree to which their nation was divided over the question of NATO.[214] Pysans'ka described a session that she and fellow journalists attended at the NATO Information Center in Kiev. Openly leery of "propaganda" from Brussels, but by no means opposed to cooperation with NATO, she pondered discrepancies in accounts of the cost to new members of the admittedly necessary upgrade in armaments. She found NATO's insistence that there are no enemies, but that armies are necessary to avoid instability, "interesting." Claims from potential new members that Russia threatens stability in central and eastern European was deemed "odd." She found much to Ukraine's advantage in closer association with NATO, especially in the economic sphere, but at the same time quite understood why "187 people's deputies out of 450 have even initiated a coalition called, 'State Outside NATO'."

Another Ukrainian journalist warned that Russia might be planning to deploy tactical nuclear missiles on ships in the Black Sea Fleet, based in Ukraine's Crimea, if NATO locates nuclear weapons on Polish territory. A new "Berlin Wall" could be erected between Ukraine and Poland, making Ukraine an unwilling "enemy of NATO" if Russia is allowed to ignore Ukraine's nuclear-free status, Anatolyy Skychko wrote in March.[215] The fact that Ukraine's participation in international

---

[212]The seven-party coalition published its platform: "Viborchii blok sotsialisti chnoy partiy Ukrayni ta selians'koy partiy Ukrayni 'Zapravdu, za narod, za Ukraynu!'" [Election Bloc of the Socialist and Peasant Parties of Ukraine, "For the Truth, the People, and Ukraine!"], *Holos Ukrayny* (13 March 1998). The election program of the Ukrainian Communist Party, signed by leader Petro Symonenko, appeared the previous week: Symonenko, "Peredviborna programa Komunistichnoy partiy Ukrayni" [Pre-Election Program of the Communist Party of Ukraine], *Holos Ukrayiny* (5 March 1998). For a translation see FBIS-SOV, No. 075. Among the CPUk charges against the existing government was: "Ukraine . . . is being quickly transformed into a 'banana' republic without any future and into a puppet of NATO and Western financial structures."

[213]Chornovil, "Noviy shliakh Ukrayni. Viborcha platforma narodnogo rukhu Ukrayni" [Ukraine's New Path: Election Platform of People's Rukh of Ukraine], *Holos Ukrayiny* (18 March 1998). The platform was signed by Chornovil as Party chairman.

[214]See, e.g., Valentyna Pysans'ka, "Buti li ne buti v . . . NATO" [To Be or Not to Be in . . . NATO], *Holos Ukrayiny* (11 Feb 1998), and "Khochete znati pro NATO?" [Do You Want to Know about NATO?], *Holos Ukrayiny* (12 Feb 1998).

[215]Anatolyy Skychko, "Just What We Need—Russian Nuclear Warheads," *Vseukrainskiye vedomosti* (26 March 1998), FBIS-SOV, No. 98.

peacekeeping operations had already earned $68 million for the country, and that
Ukraine was scheduled to participate in up to 99 NATO events in 1998, including another round of Sea-Breeze, added significance to such concerns. Developments such as these lent credence to doubts expressed in *Moscow News* about the
significance of Kuchma's "promise" not to join NATO during the lifetime of the
Ukraine-NATO economic treaty.[216]

The resounding success of the Communist Party in the March elections
brought joy to anti-NATO groups in Ukraine and Russia. The Communists won
nearly 25 percent of the votes for eligible parties, whereas People's Rukh, the sec-
ond-place party, gained only slightly over 9 percent. Ukrainian nationalists
promptly reminded citizens of Symonenko's year-old promotion of reunification
with Russia. The same election marked the resignation of Udovenko, who was a
successful candidate for Rukh. In Udovenko's absence, deputy minister Buteyko
told a briefing session in Kiev that a recent workshop in Washington concluded
that Ukraine could join NATO if the Alliance was transformed into part of a
larger European security system—but not until a "transformation" of NATO had
taken place.[217] Russian officials reacted strongly even to that, saying that the comments contradicted Kuchma's Moscow declaration and that Buteyko himself was
soon to be moved out of his position (Interfax, 15 April). The Ukrainian and
Russian media both intimated that Buteyko was positioning himself to replace
Tarasyuk as head of the Ukrainian mission at NATO, and that Tarasyuk was the
most likely replacement for Udovenko. It was assumed by many that the Buteyko-
Tarasyuk team planned to take Ukraine into NATO at the first opportunity.[218]
In fact, Tarasyuk was named foreign minister on 17 April and, almost immedi-
ately, relations with NATO were accelerated.[219]

Russians represented Tarasyuk and Buteyko as part of a strong "pro-NATO"

[216]On this see, Hanna Romantsova, "Mirotvorstvo—golovna tema" [Peacekeeping—
Key Theme], *Holos Ukrayiny* (8 April 1998), and Natalia Filipchuk, "Dumka Polysi ko-
gos' tsikavit'" [Is Anyone Interested in the Thought of Poland?], *Holos Ukrayiny* (13 Feb
1998). For the *Moscow News* (12–18 March 1998) item, see fn. 220, above.

[217]The workshop, on Ukraine-NATO relations, was held in Washington, 8–9 April.
Buteyko headed the Ukrainian delegation. See Interfax-Ukraine (14 April 1998).

[218]See, e.g., Anatoliy Martsynovskyy, "My taki budemo v NATO?" [Will We Be in
NATO Anyway?], *Holos Ukrayiny* (16 April 1998); Volodymyr Prytula, "Operatsiia 'Si . . .',
abo novi prigogy mirotvortsiv" [Operation "Sea . . . ", or the New Adventures of the Peace-
makers], *Holos Ukrayiny* (15 April 1998).

[219]In "Yaki plany u partneriv?" [Are These the Partners Plans?], *Holos Ukrayiny* (24
April 1998), Nadiia Bedrychuk provided a list of Ukraine-NATO upcoming operations,
including the Sea Breeze-98 (see also Prytula, fn. 228).

team in the Ukrainian government.[220] On 18 April the publication in Ukraine of a speech on NATO-Ukraine relations by Klaus Peter Kleiber, political adviser to Solana, confirmed Moscow's suspicions. Kleiber offered a glowing picture of Ukraine-NATO relationships, detailing their multiple facets, praising joint exercises such as Sea Breeze and promising even closer cooperation in the future. The Kleiber speech was accompanied by an interview with Tarasyuk, in which the new foreign minister was quoted saying that NATO was the "only security structure with the ability to maintain peace in Europe." Tarasyuk aggressively chastised critics of the Alliance and pronounced NATO expansion good for everyone. His opinions were repeated almost verbatim by a writer for *Molod Ukrayiny* on 30 April.[221] The Ukrainian connection with NATO was becoming less and less of an enigma and more a point of serious contention for Russian nationalists in both Russia and Ukraine.[222]

As Yeltsin was buffeted in May by a series of crises—Lebed's resounding electoral victory in Krasnoiarsk, the Duma's postponement of a scheduled debate on START II, strikes everywhere, the reopening of impeachment procedures in the Duma, and U.S. Congress attempts to impose sanctions against Russia for alleged arms dealing with Iran—the election of communists in Ukraine took on new significance. It is true that, like its Russian counterpart, Ukraine's parliament has little power in the face of a constitution that supports a powerful presidential office, but Kuchma himself remains sensitive to Russia's concerns. Indeed, as Kiev prepared to welcome Turkish President Demirel, Kuchma made a point of telling journalists that Ukraine's increased cooperation with NATO in no way weakened his country's recognition of "Russia's geopolitical interests" (Interfax-Ukraine, 21 May 1998).

Tarasyuk's opinion was more ambiguous. Rumors that he had informed a seminar on NATO expansion that Ukraine definitely planned to join the Atlantic Alliance caused Primakov to contemplate postponing a scheduled expedition to Kiev, and Seleznev sent a letter to the Ukrainian legislature requesting "clarification" of its standpoint on NATO. The Russian State Duma chairman made it plain, in fact, that the Duma would not consider ratifying the Treaty on Friendship and Cooperation between the two countries until a satisfactory answer was

---

[220]On this, e.g., see Interfax (20 April 1998) which reported former Ukrainian prime minister, Yevhen Marchuk, member of the Social Democratic Party (United), saying that the Tarasyuk appointment would "seriously annoy Russia."

[221]Volodymyr Prytula, "Vigilance: Guarantee of Freedom: NATO—Aggressive Enemy or Reliable Partner," *Molod Ukrayiny* (30 April 19987), FBIS-SOV, No. 147. Tarasyuk and Klaus Peter Kleiber, "Ukraine-NATO: In The Name of Stability on the Continent," *Uryadovyy kuryer* (18 April 1998), FBIS-SOV, No. 114.

[222]See, e.g., "Dialog z NATO" [Dialogue with NATO], *Holos Ukrayiny* (7 May 1998).

in its hands.[223] No such answer was forthcoming. Primakov, who was not accountable to the Duma, did not cancel his visit.

Preparing to greet the Russian foreign minister on 26 May, Tarasyuk took his cue from Kuchma, telling a news conference for foreign reporters that relations with Russia were a foreign policy priority for Ukraine and that joining NATO was not on his agenda. Yet he equivocated, adding that there was nothing constitutional to prevent Ukraine from entering a collective security organization of its own choosing.[224] Comments by Primakov and Tarasyuk after their meeting illustrated the discrepancies in their positions: the Russian called NATO expansion "threatening" and divisive; the Ukrainian emphasized Kiev's desire to integrate with Europe and closely cooperate with NATO (Interfax-Ukraine, 27 May).[225]

The Russian State Duma's refusal (on 22 May) to consider ratifying the Friendship Treaty was driven only partly by the NATO question; it was linked as well to the Ukrainian Supreme Council's own failure to ratify the treaty on the Black Sea Fleet.[226] Neither legislature wanted to make the first move, so the treaties remained a source of discord between the two countries. Thus, the cooperation espoused regularly by Kuchma and Yeltsin had run into serious difficulties in their

---

[223]For details, see Yuliia Mostova, "You May Do as You Please, But Don't Shout," *Zerkalo nedeli* (23 May 1998), FBIS-SOV, No. 152. Tarasyuk was very cautious in an interview for *Uryadovyy kuryer* (14 May 1998), when he said that NATO was not pushing Ukraine to join, but that the door was open to everyone. He noted also that Ukraine would continue to "play a leading role in the CIS," but mainly an economic one. See also Yana Stadil'na, "Podumaemo pro tse zavtra" [Let's Think about It Tomorrow], *Holos Ukrayiny* (2 June 1998), which suggested that Tarasyuk was still keen to join NATO, but not yet.

[224]Moscow NTV (26 May 1998), FBIS-SOV, No. 153. Interestingly, the Russian TV panned over the sign for the NATO Information and Documentation center in Kiev, during this broadcast from Kiev. Tarasyuk spoke in Ukrainian, with Russian superimposed.

[225]Typical Russian skepticism can be seen in the following: Nataliia Larsen, "Poimat' i pereigrat'. Taktika Kieva na peregovorakh s Moskvoi po Chernomorskomu flotu ostaetsia neizmennoi" [To Capture and to Replay: The Tactics of Kiev in Negotiations with Moscow on the Black Sea Fleet Remain Unchanged], *Nezavisimaia gazeta* (26 May 1998); Dmitrii Gornostaev, "Neprostye peregovory v Kieve" [The Complicated Negotiations in Kiev], *Nezavisimaia gazeta* (27 May 1998); Yuliia Petrovskaia, "Vtoroe zasedanie komissii NATO-Ukraina" [The Second Meeting of the NATO-Ukraine Commission], *Nezavisimaia gazeta* (30 May 1998).

[226]The participation of two Ukrainian ships in a 30-vessel training exercise on the Black Sea, 14–27 June 1998, as part of NATO's Cooperative Neighbor '98 war games was an irritant to Moscow as well. See the ITAR-TASS (19 June 1998) summary of Russian defense ministry commentary.

respective parliaments, both dominated by communists. A visit to Kiev by Zbigniew Brzezinski in early June with a message to the effect that Ukraine should be preparing to join NATO by 2010 brought the situation back to its starting point for many Russians.[227]

Solana arrived in Kiev a few weeks after Brzezinski to negotiate a NATO military mission in that city. The event was preceded by a flood of government press releases, newspaper articles and TV broadcasts that left no doubt that Horbulin planned to expand Ukraine's involvement with NATO. He appeared indifferent to Russia's concerns, when asked about it specifically, and hinted that Brzezinski's prediction of the year 2010 as the entry date could be moved up. Interestingly, notwithstanding the increased NATO publicity campaign in Ukraine, opinion polls showed in June that Ukrainian public support for admission to NATO remained stuck at about 25 percent.[228]

The first anniversary of the Charter on a Distinctive Partnership between NATO and Ukraine was celebrated enthusiastically by Ukrainian officialdom. Horbulin prepared a statement glorifying Ukraine's achievements in the international relations field and called for expanded NATO involvement in resolving conflict in Europe.[229] Although Horbulin also said that Ukraine was "not necessarily seeking to join the Alliance," the Ukrainian media began to take it for granted in the spring and summer that membership was inevitable. Coinciding, as it did, with a new emerging crisis in Yugoslavia, this perceived trend in Ukraine greatly frustrated Russians—and many Ukrainians.

Journalists for the moderately pro-Russian *Holos Ukrayiny* asked what had hap-

[227]See, e.g., Viktor Tomoshenko, "Bzhezinskii vnov' posetil Kiev. Po ego mneniiu Ukraina v 2010 godu mozhet byt' priniata v NATO" [Brzezinski Again Visits Kiev: In His Opinion Ukraine Can Join NATO in 2010], *Nezavisimaia gazeta* (4 June 1998). Brzezinski was critical of Ukraine, in fact, and many Ukrainians resented his commentary.

[228]See Interfax-Ukraine (26 June 1998) and Ukrainian TV, same date, translated by FBIS-SOV, No. 177. Both stories stressed Horbulin's desire for a NATO military mission in Kiev and represented reporting on preliminary talks between him and Klaus Kleiber. See also Olena Zvarych, "Ukraine-NATO: Life in Virtual Reality Accompanied by Lasting Storms of Applause," *Ukrayina Moloda* (8 July 1998), FBIS-SOV, No. 190. The data on Ukrainian public desire to join NATO comes from Zvarych, who described in detail what she called a NATO propaganda campaign to sway Ukrainian politicians.

[229]NATO is the most "reliable and capable pillar of European security," Volodymyr Horbulin said in "Ukraine's Contribution to Security and Stability in Europe," *NATO Review*, No. 3 (Autumn 1998): 9–12.

pened to Ukraine's "neutrality,"[230] and insisted that Ukraine had more important matters to attend to than further integration with NATO.[231] But the fact that sentiment in Ukraine against joining NATO, or at least further association with NATO, had clearly diminished, was recognized by Russian observers.[232] A wish to appease Moscow may have been the reason why, in August, Kuchma again submitted the treaty on the Black Sea Fleet to Ukraine's Supreme Council. Much of the Ukrainian media reacted in protest, calling the treaty blackmail (in relation to the Ukrainian debt to Russia) and a blow to Ukrainian sovereignty.[233]

Russian writers began to vilify Ukrainians who at first opposed NATO expansion and were now strongly supporting it. Visions of access to oil and gas from Turkmenistan and Azerbaijan via pipelines sponsored by Western countries were among the reasons why Ukrainians were now being accused of opportunism by parts of the Russian media.[234] Talks between Tarasyuk and Polish foreign minister Bronislaw Gieremek in September strengthened the Russian conviction that Ukraine was poised to apply for membership in NATO. In a post-meeting press conference, the foreign ministers agreed that Poland and Ukraine would expand their military-technical cooperation, the Polish-Ukrainian Battalion, and a program for cooperation in military and defense industries.

---

[230]See, e.g., ""My za NATO, a vi . . . " [We Are for NATO, and You . . .], *Holos Ukrayiny* (3 July 1998); "Neitralitet vidkhodit' u minule?" [Does Neutrality Go to the Past?], *Holos Ukrayiny* (3 July 1998); Borys Oliynyk, "Shche raz pro podviini standarti" [Yet Another Time about Double Standards], *Holos Ukrayiny* (17 July 1998); "Pid odnim evropeis'kim dakhom" [Under One European Roof], *Holos Ukrayiny* (18 July 1998); Khristina Nazarchuk, "Bezneka i bez NATO bezneka" [Security and, without NATO, Security], *Holos Ukrayiny* (23 July 1998); Tamara Molina, "Spivrobitnitstvo z NATO i neitralitet ne superechat' odne odnomu" [Cooperation with NATO and Neutrality Do Not Contradict Each Other], *Holos Ukrayiny* (24 July 1998).

[231]See, e.g., "Spochatku dobrobut, a potim uzhe NATO" [The First Thing Is Welfare, and Then NATO], *Holos Ukrayiny* (11 July 1998).

[232]See "Khav'er Solana posetil Ukrainu" [Javier Solana Visited Ukraine], *Nezavisimaia gazeta* (11 July 1998); "Dveri vidkrito . . ." [The Door Is Opened . . .], *Holos Ukrayiny* (27 July 1998); Nadiya Bedrichuk, "Instrumenti mira—u nashikh rukakh" [The Instruments of Peace Are in Our Hands], *Holos Ukrayiny* (20 July 1998).

[233]See, e.g, "Black Sea Fleet Means Someone Else's Fleet," *Vechirniy Kyyiv* (13 Aug 1998), FBIS-SOV, No. 254. Ethnic Russians in Crimea protested vigorously when the flagship of the U.S. 6th Fleet, representing NATO, visited Sevastopol in September. See *Izvestiia* (14 Sept 1998).

[234]See, e.g., Kirill Viatkin, "Staraia Ukraina trebuet novoi politiki so storony Rossii" [The Old Ukraine Requires New Politics on the Part of Russia], *Nezavisimaia gazeta* (22 July 1998), carried in a special supplement on the CIS.

Gieremek, who was then serving a term as chairman of the OSCE, overplayed his hand by inviting Ukraine to play a greater role in resolving regional conflicts, including some where Russia now dominates: Nagorno-Karabakh, Transdiestr, and Abkhazia.[235] Pacifying communiqués released after talks between Kuchma and Yeltsin in Moscow, 18–19 September, generated little enthusiasm in either country. The extremist Ukrainian Progressive Socialist Party demonstrated the level of its concern in its new platform, where it was said that the economic crisis was leading to financial catastrophe, "after which the colonization of Ukraine will be completed by the hobnailed boots of NATO troops."[236] In that way, the *Drang nach Osten* analogy was raised in Ukraine.

Already testy, Ukrainian-Russian relations were inflamed in late September when Seleznev led a parliamentary delegation to Kiev. Representing, indirectly, the new Primakov government, Seleznev addressed the Ukrainian parliament and infuriated nationalists by suggesting that Ukraine join the Russia-Belarus Union and complaining that the Russian language was not being treated well in Crimea and elsewhere. The Russian embassy in Kiev, picketed by demonstrators, lodged a formal complaint about alleged "insults" to Seleznev on the occasion of his visit. Among the pickets outside the embassy was at least one saying, "Ukraine, join NATO!" (Interfax, 29 Sept). Tarasyuk, who advised the Russian delegation that the NATO issue was a "fabricated" problem (ITAR-TASS, 28 Sept), condemned Seleznev's actions.[237] Rukh's Bohdan Boyko termed the Duma speaker "a cheat who intended to deceive everyone." Right-wing parliamentarians accused the Russian of "interfering" in Ukrainian domestic affairs. Ironically, the distance between perspectives was such that, on his return to Moscow, Seleznev called the visit a success, as did communist participants who claimed to have noticed a wellspring

---

[235]See Interfax-Ukraine (16 Sept 1998), and Oleksandr Bittner, "Polish Bridge to Europe," *Uryadovyy Kuryer* (19 Sept 1998), FBIS-SOV, No. 267.

[236]Natalya Vitrenko, Volodomyr Marchenko, "Sotsialistichna opozitsiia: sut' i prichini stvorennia" [The Socialist Opposition: Its Nature and the Reasons for Its Formation], *Holos Ukrayiny* (18 Sept 1998), FBIS-SOV, No. 280. Vitrenko is head of the PSPU; Marchenko leads the party in parliament. The PSPU earned slightly over 4 percent of the bloc votes, and 14 of the 225 bloc seats in parliament.

[237]Interfax (29 Sept 1998). Tarasyuk expanded upon his criticism of Seleznev a few days later in an interview for *Ukrayina Moloda* (6 Oct 1998), FBIS-SOV, No. 282. In that interview he also made it clear that he expected few changes from the Ivanov foreign ministry in Moscow. He rejected the idea of a Slavic union and reemphasized Ukraine's desire to be integrated with Europe, especially via the EU.

of support for Slavic unity in Kiev.[238] Other Russian papers called the visit a disaster and a scandal.

In so far as NATO was concerned, however, the Russian press appeared almost fatalistic about Ukraine's rapidly expanding integration into the Alliance's programs. In comparison to the outcry against Sea Breeze-97, the 1998 version of the naval training exercise went smoothly. This time Russia participated and, as one Russian commentator noted, the protest against Sea Breeze-98 seemed like child's play compared to the fury expressed over Kosovo.[239] The essay was accompanied by two photos: one of a participating Russian war ship, the other of a group of protesters in Crimea carrying a sign saying "NATO, Go Home!" in English. Another Russian commentator spoke of Ukraine as NATO's "largest firing range," objecting that Ukraine was allowing itself to become a training ground for armies of Western countries, "and especially the USA," while Russia sits back and does nothing.[240]

Ukrainian communists echoed their Russian colleagues' vituperation against the Alliance's activities in Yugoslavia. In addition to the harsh statement issued by the Progressive Socialist Party (see section 2.2), in early November, communist members of the Ukrainian Supreme Council printed an Appeal that made even *Zavtra* editorials sound moderate. Calling NATO the agent of the "American jackboot regime in the Balkans," Ukrainian communists accused Washington of attempting to transform the world into "slaves" of U.S. capital. Like their Russian comrades, they demanded that the government in Kiev rescind all agreements with NATO if Yugoslavia was bombed.[241]

A speech delivered by Tarasyuk at the RF foreign ministry's Diplomatic Academy in late November failed to clear the air. Acknowledging the multiple and necessary

---

[238]Yurii Nikiforenko, "Lichnye vpechatleniia o parlamentskom vizite v Kiev. Iz bedy vykhodit' vmeste" [Personal Impressions of the Parliamentary Visit to Kiev], *Sovetskaia Rossiia* (6 Oct 1998). Nikiforenko is a member of the CPRF and also deputy director of the Duma Committee on geopolitics. The non-communist Russian media, for the most part, termed the Seleznev visit a "failure" and a "scandal." See *Nezavisimaia gazeta* (30 Sept 1998) and *Kommersant* (30 Sept 1998). Ukrainian officials also complained that Russia had levied import duties against their agricultural products and had not yet ratified the Friendship Treaty. On Boyko's comment, see *Ukrayina Moloda* (3 Oct 1998), FBIS-SOV, No. 282.

[239]See, e.g., Aleksandr Shaburkin, "V 'primorskoi respublike' bushuet stikhiia" [The Storm Has Abated in the "Maritime Republic"], *Nezavisimoe voennoe obozrenie,* No. 40 (23–29 Oct 1998).

[240]See, e.g., Liubov' Golubeva, Vladimir Georgiev, "Bol'shoi poligon NATO" [NATO's Largest Firing Range], *Nezavisimoe voennoe obozrenie,* No. 41 (30 Oct–5 Nov 1998).

[241]"Zvernennia chleniv fraktsiy Komunistichnoy partiy Ukrayni" [Appeal by Members of the Communist Party of Ukraine Faction], *Holos Ukrayiny* (27 Oct 1998). The Appeal was signed by A. Domanskyy, V. Moiseyenko, and A. Strohanov.

links between Moscow and Kiev, he pointed out that Russia still had not ratified the fundamental political treaty signed by the two presidents in May 1997 and approved by Ukrainian parliamentarians in January 1998; that many economic agreements did not work; and that the Black Sea Fleet issue was not fully resolved. Tarasyuk made it clear that, while Russia would remain very important to Ukraine, Kiev was heading towards far greater integration with Western Europe.[242]

The wind was taken out of Tarasyuk's sails, to a certain extent, when the Treaty of Friendship was finally ratified by Russia's State Duma on 25 December. The Duma voting undoubtedly was swayed by a speech it heard from the speaker of Kiev's parliament, Oleksandr Tkachenko, on 18 December. Tkachenko advocated much closer cooperation between the two countries, supported economic union, and even called for greater Ukrainian participation in the CIS. What is more, he urged the Duma and Kiev's Supreme Council to coordinate their NATO policies (ITAR-TASS, 18 Dec).

Russian nationalists, including the LDPR faction, were appeased by his criticism of the U.S./UK bombing of Iraq and a reference to widespread opposition in Ukraine's "Supreme Council and society" to NATO expansion. Seleznev took advantage of the combination of Tkachenko's speech, which was broadcast on Russian TV, and the Duma vote, to exult that Ukraine now would not join NATO and that Russia and Ukraine were "eternal allies" (ITAR-TASS, 29 Dec). He chose to ignore the fact that Kuchma strongly criticized Tkachenko, as did Ukrainian nationalists,[243] and that the Friendship Treaty still had to pass through the Russian Federal Assembly's upper house, the Federation Council.

Thus, Seleznev's political rhetoric notwithstanding, optimism of the type expressed by Russians about Ukrainians in 1996 and early 1997 had all but disappeared by the end of 1998. During January and February 1999, ratification was in fact postponed in the Federation Council, where Luzhkov lobbied aggressively against it.[244] When the Council finally approved the Treaty, in mid-February, it

[242]*Zerkalo nedeli* (21–27 Nov 1998), FBIS-SOV, No. 331.

[243]For Kuchma's remarks, in which he took particular exception to Tkachenko's call for a joint defensive doctrine with Russia, see *Ukrayiny Moloda* (24 Dec 1998), FBIS-SOV, No. 363. For an example of general Ukrainian criticism, see the piece by Oleh Medvedev, "Oleksandr Tkachenko Told Duma about Seven Terrible Years," *Kievskie vedomosti* (19 Dec 1998), FBIS-SOV, No. 364.

[244]Oleh Oliynyk wrote angrily against Luzhkov (a member of the Federation Council as Mayor of Moscow) and the Council's hesitation to ratify the Treaty. "The subject of NATO," which he said drove the Russian nationalist position, "is a constant propagandist bugaboo" for politicians in Moscow. See Oliynyk, "Taking into Consideration Political Reality," *Uryadovyy Kuryer* (20 Jan 1999), FBIS-SOV, No. 025.

(and Primakov) dampened Kuchma's enthusiasm by insisting that the accord not be considered operable until after the parliament in Kiev ratified the three outstanding agreements on the Black Sea Fleet.[245] In the meantime, Ukraine pushed for integration with European structures, NATO significantly among them. Ivan Zayats, first deputy chair of the Ukrainian Parliamentary Committee for Foreign Affairs and CIS Relations, was one of the strong public voices in support of NATO.[246]

The intensification of ties between Ukraine and Poland, whose presidents met six times in 1998, also was watched with concern in Moscow. In February, shortly before Defense Minister Janusz Onyszkiewicz announced that Poland would serve as Ukraine's patron in NATO (see section 1.9), Premier Aleksandr Kwasniewski visited Kiev to arrange the implementation of agreements signed in 1998. Much was made in that city and in Warsaw about Poland as Ukraine's conduit to Europe.[247] Ukraine's nationalist press described the Onyzskiewicz visit as a sign that Ukraine and Poland would be "strategic partners for decades." Military cooperation with Poland was portrayed as a means for Ukraine to be drawn into European security structures and the Ukrainian-Polish peacekeeping battalion (created in 1995) was depicted frankly as the vehicle by which Ukraine could "enter into cooperation with NATO 'through the back door'."[248]

Still more grief came Russia's way when NATO announced a plan to make use of the Yavoriv Testing Ground in Western Ukraine, a former Warsaw Pact facility. Russian military personnel growled that Yavoriv was an ideal "bridgehead for a massive tank assault against the East." While not suggesting that such an attack was an actual NATO ambition, a spokesman for the Russian ministry of defense pointed out that the training grounds were ideally suited for combat operations

---

[245]See "Zaiavlenie Soveta Federatsii v sviazi s ratifikatsiei Dogovora o druzhbe, sotrudnichestve i partnerstve mezhdu Rossiiskoi Federatsiei i Ukrainoi" [Statement of the Federation Council in Connection with the Ratification of the Treaty on Friendship, Cooperation and Partnership between the Russian Federation and Ukraine], *Rossiiskaia gazeta* (2 March 1999).

[246]Zayats, "Slig zatespechiti real'nu integratsiiu do NATO" [Real Integration with NATO Should Be Achieved], *Holos Ukrayiny* (13 Jan 1999).

[247]See a long interview with Tarasyuk, "Zovnishnia popitika mae buti vivazhena i peredbachuvana, a diplomatiia—profesiyna" [Foreign Policy Should Be Balanced and Predictable, and Diplomacy Should Be Professional], *Holos Ukrayiny* (3 Feb 1999).

[248]See Ihor Melnychuk, "Polish Week in Review," *Ukrayina Molody* (12 Feb 1999), FBIS-SOV, No. 220; "O sammite NATO" [On the NATO Summit], *Krasnaia zvezda* (12 Feb 1999). One Russian note of optimism came from Tatiana Ivzhenko, "Ukraina ne vstupit v NATO v blizhaishie 10 let" [Ukraine Will Not Join NATO within the Next 10 Years], *Nezavisimaia gazeta* (11 Feb 1999).

against the Balkans.[249] More apropos, however, was the fact that NATO use of Yavoriv complicated Russian-Ukrainian relations at an awkward time. Several well-placed Ukrainian parliamentarians, such as the heads of the committees for defense and foreign affairs—Georgiy Kryuchkov and Borys Oliynyk—publicly opposed NATO exercises in Ukraine and demanded that these matters be discussed by parliament. Protests such as these notwithstanding, the Ukrainian slide towards NATO and Europe seemed inexorable.[250]

The slide was put to the test, however, when NATO began its bombing runs against Yugoslavia, and even Tarasyuk was compelled to condemn NATO's decision. Blaming Milosevic for the escalated crisis in Kosovo, the Ukrainian foreign minister insisted that an attack against a sovereign country without a mandate from the UN was "unacceptable" (ITAR-TASS, 26 March). He and Ukraine's defense minister flew to Belgrade on the 26th, before Primakov arrived, but with little success. A few days later, Ukraine joined the CIS Inter-Parliamentary Assembly and signed, with seven other members, an urgent call on NATO's parliamentarians to halt the air strikes.

On 6 April the parliament in Kiev rejected a resolution that all joint military exercises with NATO on Ukrainian soil be banned, and unratified agreements with the Alliance be cancelled. The vote was close. Needing 226 yeas, the resolution received 191 from the 334 deputies attending the session. Only 53 opposed (Interfax, 6 April). Speaker Tkachenko was a strong advocate of the resolution, so some might interpret the vote as a blow to his presidential aspirations. Yet the public discussion would suggest that Ukrainian politicians were now more anxious than before to guard their country's neutrality. Friendly association with the United States was still very important to Ukrainian analysts, but NATO had become decidedly less attractive. Kuchma warned on 15 April that the air strikes posed a threat to all of Europe.[251]

His trip to Washington a week later to attend the NATO anniversary fête was

---

[249]See "Natovskie smotriny Yavorskogo poligona" [NATO Examines the Yavoriv Testing Grounds], *Krasnaia zvezda* (13 Feb 1999).

[250]For two long and detailed explications of the "NATO debate" in Ukraine, see Oleksiy Havrylenko, "Political Accounting—Calculations or Settling of Accounts?" *Zerkalo nedeli* (20–26 Feb 1999), FBIS-SOV, No. 308; and Ivan Zayats, "The Left Is Greatly Opposed to Seeing Ukraine as a Full Member of the European Family," *Nezavisimost* (10 March 1999), FBIS-SOV, No. 315. Both published in Russian.

[251]On this, see esp. Oleksiy Havrylenko, "Albright and Solana in the Role of NATO's Susanin," *Zerkalo nedeli* (3–9 April 1999), FBIS-SOV, No. 409, and, on the parliamentary resolution, *Ukrayina Moloda* (7 April 1999), FBIS-SOV, No. 412. On Kuchma's statement, ITAR-TASS (15 April 1999).

treated as an act of outright cynicism by the Russian media, who saw Kiev being "bought out" by NATO.[252] While Kuchma was out of the country Kiev's Supreme Council finally adopted a resolution condemning the "aggressive nature" of NATO's new doctrine and calling for a re-examination of Ukraine's relationship with the Alliance.[253] The Ukrainian place between NATO and Russia remained an enigma in Moscow.

5. THE BALTIC STATES: DRAWING A "RED LINE" IN THE SAND

If one takes Russian commentary on NATO expansion eastward at face value, the question of former USSR republic membership in the Alliance generally, and the admission of Baltic republics particularly, are the points at which Moscow has drawn its final "line in the sand." The degree to which Moscow's position on this issue is taken seriously in the West, furthermore, may well determine the success or failure of NATO's enlargement enterprise.

The expectation among Russians that the Baltic states would campaign vigorously to join NATO, largely by employing fear of the "Russian threat" as their most persuasive vehicle for that access, also has a long history. A prominent Russian journalist, Aleksandr Tsipko, predicted as much in September 1991, a few weeks after the failed coup against Gorbachev and resulting Baltic declarations of independence from the USSR. Until recently, in fact, Moscow comfortably thought of the Baltic Sea as its own, and still regards the Baltic states as within its sphere of influence.[254] But Russia now has only two remaining bases for its Baltic Fleet, Kronstadt, near St. Petersburg, and Baltiisk in Kaliningrad. The determination with which the Kremlin would react to Baltic membership in NATO was expressed clearly in the joint report issued by the U.S. Atlantic Council and

---

[252]Ivanna Gorina, "Ukraine ne zhit' bez NATO?" [Can't Ukraine Live without NATO?], *Rossiiskaia gazeta* (20 April 1999).

[253]"Shchodo vidnosin Ukrayni i Organizatsiy Pivnichnoatlantichnogo dogovoru (NATO)" [Resolution by the Ukrainian Supreme Council on Ukrainian-NATO Relations Adopted on 23 April 1999 in Kiev], *Holos Ukraying* (27 April 1999). The Resolution is translated in FBIS-SOV, No. 505.

[254]For early commentary on this, see Saulius Girnius, "Relations Between the Baltic States and Russia," *RFE/RL Research Report* 3, No. 33 (1994): 29–33. For the Tsipko prediction, see *Moscow News*, No. 37 (15–22 Sept 1991): 5. This section is in part a summary, with update, of my "Russia and NATO Expansion Eastward: Red-lining the Baltic States," *International Journal* 54, No. 2 (Spring 1999): 249–266.

IMEMO scholars in November 1997.[255] By 1998 Russian foreign policy analysts spoke of the absorption of the Baltic states by NATO as Moscow's "most acute issue" and predicted that Russia's position on the Baltics would be ignored by Western leaders.[256]

Throughout 1997, the three Baltic states actively lobbied for membership in the EU and NATO at a time when only Lithuania could be said to have normalized relations with Russia. Moscow's sense of vulnerability was reinforced when the three countries were formally accepted among 12 candidates for NATO. Early in that year, it was the possibility of Estonian entry that was most troublesome and prompted the first explicit words of warning from Yeltsin and his government. The large Russian population in that country claimed that it was being discriminated against.[257] On 20 February 1997, in spite of assertions by Estonian President Lennart Meri to Russian interviewers that his country's aspirations were not anti-Russian, Moscow's diplomats in Tallinn threatened Estonia with economic sanctions if it persisted in its efforts to join NATO. Russia, they said, would deal only with a non-aligned Estonia.[258]

Primakov made Russia's position clearer on 26 February when he told journalists in Copenhagen that "it is unacceptable to Russia for the Baltic countries to

---

[255]See the joint statement, "Rossiisko-amerikanskie otnosheniia na poroge novogo veka" [Russian-American Relations on the Threshold of a New Century], *Mirovaia ekonomika i mezhdunarodnye otnosheniia,* No. 5 (May 1998): 109–115.

[256]See V. Shustov, "Russia and Security Problems in the Baltics," *International Affairs* (Moscow), 44, No. 1 (1998): 39–44, and "Baltiiskie strany stanut chlenami NATO" [The Baltic Countries will become Members of NATO], *Nezavisimaia gazeta* (23 June 1998). See also Tatiana Ivzhenko, "Solana na Ukraine i v pribaltike" [Solana in Ukraine and the Baltics], *Nezavisimaia gazeta* (17 April 1996), where the NATO general secretary was accused of attempting to persuade Ukraine and the Baltics to work actively towards association with NATO.

[257]At the time of renewed independence, August 1991, the Russian population was distributed in the Baltic states as follows: Estonia, 28 percent; Latvia, 33 percent; Lithuania, 8.6 percent.

[258]Tallinn ETA (20 Feb 1997), FBIS-SOV, No. 034, summarizes statements made in Tallinn by Andrei Yakushev and Mikhail Gavrilin, Attaché and First Secretary at the Russian Embassy in that city. For the interview with President Meri, see Aleksandr Bangerskii, "Estoniia ne khochet vstupat' v NATO obraztsa vremen kholodnoi voiny" [Estonia Does Not Want to Be Part of a NATO Shaped in the Time of Cold War], *Nezavisimaia gazeta* (15 Feb 1997).

join NATO." He had no objections to adherence of the Baltic states to the European Union, but their bringing of a military infrastructure created by Russians into NATO would undermine Russia's "relations with NATO as a whole" (ITAR-TASS, 26 Feb). Delivered a week after the breakthrough conversation with U.S. Secretary of State Albright in Moscow, Primakov's hard line position appeared to have met with success.

Baltic leaders put on a bold front. Vytautas Landsbergis, speaker of the Lithuanian parliament, ridiculed Russia's complaints and on 24 February called for immediate NATO enlargement (Interfax, 24 Feb). He insisted that no concessions be made to Russia at Baltic expense. On 28 February, the Latvian foreign minister, Valdis Birkavs, told a German correspondent in Munich that his country wanted NATO membership precisely to guarantee its security against Russia.[259] One day before Yeltsin and Clinton met in Helsinki, Lithuanian foreign minister Algirdas Saudargas asked the NATO Council to grant Lithuania's application serious consideration. In contrast to the other Baltic applicants, he said, Lithuania had neither border disputes with its neighbors, nor a problem with a Russian-speaking population (ITAR-TASS, 20 March).

Yeltsin's several offers to guarantee the security of the Baltic republics notwithstanding, the summit in Helsinki failed to achieve the hoped-for agreement about limiting future NATO expansion.[260] Baltic leaders therefore acted swiftly to have their cases heard. Birkavs told the press (Interfax, 24 March) that Latvia wanted to be accepted by NATO in July and cited Russia's recent warnings against Baltic membership. Estonian prime minister, Mart Siimann, took a more conciliatory tack, announcing that his country was anxious to normalize relations with Russia, but also wanted to be part of the larger European political, economic and security systems, including NATO (Interfax, 24 March). The Russian media responded quickly by accusing Estonia of being "anti-Russian."[261] Three

---

[259] *Süddeutsche Zeitung* (28 Feb 1997).

[260] Antoninia Yefremova, "Vstrecha v verkhakh: positivnyi kompromiss" [Summit Meeting: Positive Compromise], *Rossiiskaia gazeta* (25 March 1997). For far less optimistic views than Yefremova's, see "Komu nuzhna vtoraia 'kholodnaia voina'" [Who Needs a Second "Cold War"], *Rossiiskie vesti* (21 March 1997), and the even harsher "NATO prët kak tank" [NATO Pushes Like a Tank], *Zavtra*, No. 10 (March 1997).

[261] Typical was a piece by Lev Dorogushin and Arnold Pork, "A byvalo, moskvichi 'katali' na vykhodnye v Tallinn" [And in the Past Muscovites Used to Go to Tallinn for the Weekend], *Rossiiskaia gazeta* (22 March 1997), who linked Estonia's request to join NATO with the crushing of Russian-language rights in the country.

days later Lennart Meri told a news conference in Tallinn that, in light of Yeltsin's "demands" at Helsinki, NATO represented the only true security open to his country (Interfax, 27 March). Speaking the same day on the Helsinki summit, Yeltsin's foreign policy adviser, Dmitrii Ryurikov, warned that Russia would "revise" its position if NATO admitted any of the "neighboring countries."[262]

The American government added to Russia's unease on 28 March, when a spokesman for the Clinton administration announced that the United States was interested in "defining and codifying" security relations with the Baltic states. A security agreement would not preclude Baltic membership in NATO.[263] In response, *Rossiiskaia gazeta* thundered that Baltic leaders were duping the West into admitting them by raising the specter of Russian military aggression and equating Helsinki with Munich (1938) and the policy of appeasement.[264]

The Anti-NATO group of deputies took aim at the Baltic states, suggesting they wished to be part of an "anti-Russian alliance." Marina Kuchinskaia of the Russian Institute of Strategic Studies went so far as to predict a series of orchestrated crises, part of an "anti-Russian" campaign by American and Baltic officials, designed to persuade NATO to admit Baltic states.[265] More significantly, it was made plain to Russian observers that if the Baltic states joined NATO and later

---

[262]Ryurikov, "Nikakikh illiuzii . . . ," *Moskovskii komsomolets* (27 Mar 1997), *op. cit.* Ryurikov, who said that the atmosphere of the Yeltsin-Clinton meeting had been very tense and that an invitation from NATO to former Soviet republics would jeopardize START II ratification and sharply divide Russian society, lost his position as adviser in April 1997. See also Boris Fedorov, "Rossiia dolzhna vstupit' v NATO?" [Should Russia Become a Member of NATO?], *Moskovskie vesti* (26 March 1997).

[263]"U.S. Considers New Link with 3 Baltic Nations," *New York Times* (29 March 1997). The spokesman was Michael D. McCurry.

[264] See Igor Maksimychev, "Privedët li dvoinaia moral' pribaltiiskikh politikov v NATO?" [Will the Double Standards of Baltic Politicians Get Them into NATO?], *Rossiiskaia gazeta* (29 March 1997), and Nikolai Paklin, "Chem chrevata liubov k NATO" [The Danger of Loving NATO], (1 April 1997), *op cit.*

[265]Kuchinskaia, "Ochered' v NATO" [Queue into NATO], *Nezavisimoe voennoe obozrenie,* No. 12 (29 March–4 April 1997). For the Anti-NATO group's statement, see ITAR-TASS (2 April 1997).

were asked if NATO troops and nuclear weapons could be deployed on their territories, the answer would be in the affirmative.[266]

When Primakov and Solana announced, on 14 May, that a "tentative" Russian-NATO agreement had been reached, the Baltic States did not react with the enthusiasm typical of much of the Western press. Although Russia was not given a veto over any NATO decisions, the role it might now play in NATO committees posed a dilemma for Baltic candidates. Lithuania's Landsbergis raised the stakes by demanding the withdrawal of Russian troops from Kaliningrad (ITAR-TASS, 19 May). A Russian foreign ministry official responded by telling reporters that Yeltsin would immediately "revise" the still unsigned agreement with NATO if the Baltic states were admitted (Interfax, 20 May). Presidential aide Yastrzhembskii reiterated this stance two days later, as Baltic leaders vigorously rejected Yeltsin's implicit threats. The extremist communist paper, *Zavtra,* accused Baltic leadership of playing a very dangerous game by attempting to restructure Northern Europe and cut off Russia from the Baltic Sea.[267] The Russian State Duma adopted a draft statement repeating that the admission to NATO of former Soviet republics, with specific reference to the Baltic states, was "unacceptable" (Interfax, 23 May). The point was made clearly before the Founding Act was signed.

Reacting to the Founding Act, the three Baltic presidents held a summit in Otepaa, Estonia, at which they called again for early admission to NATO. They were joined the next day by the presidents of Ukraine and Poland, prompting yet another RF foreign ministry official, Gennadii Tarasov, head of the Information and Press Department, to confirm that any precipitate action by NATO would cause the "sharpest of reactions" in Russia (ITAR-TASS, 28 May). Tarasov's warning was not offered casually, and it had the support of an increasingly surly Russian public. The Baltic meetings, in fact, ensured that the cautiously optimistic attitude with which the Russian media greeted the Founding Act would dissipate very quickly. Mainstream papers, such as *Izvestiia* and *Rossiiskie vesti,* changed their

---

[266]There were Russians who still believed that Albright had promised not to move nuclear weaponry to the eastern NATO territories. See, e.g., Dmitrii Gornostaev, "RF i NATO podpisali plan sovmestnykh deistvii" [The RF and NATO Have Signed a Plan for Joint Activities], *Nezavisimaia gazeta* (18 Dec 1997). The opinion that nuclear arms would be moved to the Baltics if need be came from a member of the State Duma Defense Committee and of the CPRF, Vladimir N. Volkov, who claimed to have asked the question of Baltic participants in a seminar, December 1996 (ITAR-TASS, 11 April 1997).

Even the opening of a bar called the NATO Cafe in Vilnius had evoked a sarcastic response from the Russian mass media, see M. Aleksandrov, "V 'NATO' i otdokhnem," *Rossiiskaia gazeta* (1 Nov 1996).

[267]Ye. Kriukov, "Baltiiskaia igra" [Baltic Game], *Zavtra,* No. 20 (May 1997).

first opinions of the Act and began to express serious doubts about its value. A writer for *Rossiiskaia gazeta* summed up the new mood, complaining that one "gets the impression that the United States and its allies took no notice of the Russian president's statement that if NATO admits [former USSR republics] Russia will review its relations with the Alliance."[268] The perception that NATO was ignoring Russian interests grew perceptibly, and Russian national consciousness began to crystallize around alleged slights inflicted by NATO and the Baltic republics.

Turkish President Demirel made matters worse by promising in Tallinn (3 June) that his country would support early Estonian membership. Already worried about the rise of Turkish influence on the Black Sea, Russian observers found this intervention especially irksome.[269] At about that time, a group of Russian journalists travelled to The Netherlands and Belgium to interview NATO Deputy Secretary General Gebhardt von Moltke at length. They returned convinced that no Baltic State would soon be admitted because they did not meet requirements set out in the Washington Treaty. The issue continued to crop up in the Western press, they believed, only as a provocation to "set Moscow's nerves on edge." According to one of the touring journalists the Founding Act, though forced on Russia, gave Moscow a chance to precede the Baltic countries and other former USSR republics as a presence in NATO.[270] He urged, naively, that Russia take advantage of this situation to impose its own views on NATO.

Undaunted, Baltic leaders continued to say openly and regularly that they were preparing to have their countries included in a promised second wave of new NATO members. In their turn, Russian officials and commentators continued to draw the line at Baltic entry: Gennadii Seleznev told journalists that Baltic

---

[268]See Paklin, "Rossiia-NATO: balans interesov" [Russia-NATO: Balance of Interests], *Rossiiskaia gazeta* (27 May 1997); "Zachem sobralas' piaterka v Talline" [Why the Five Met in Tallinn], *Rossiiskie vesti* (30 May 1998); "V Talline sozdaetsia 'Baltiisko-Chernomorskii' Blok" [A "Baltic–Black Sea" Bloc Is Created in Tallinn], *Izvestiia* (28 May 1998).

[269]For Demirel's statement, see FBIS-SOV, No. 154.

[270]Vladimir Kuznechevskii, "People at NATO Learn Russian: Balts Trying All Their Might to Join Alliance May Find the One Thing They are Fleeing—Russia—in All Military Structures There], *Rossiiskaia gazeta* (21 June 1997), FBIS-SOV, No. 121. See also Interfax (23 June 1997). The predominant opinion that the Baltic republics must be excluded from NATO was expressed forcefully by Vladimir Churkin in Prague, where he headed a Russian delegation at an international seminar called "The New NATO Bloc: A Path into the Future" (ITAR-TASS, 24 June 1997).

One of the offending articles was a piece by William Safire, who called for the immediate entry of all three Baltic states, see Safire, "Clinton's Good Deed," *New York Times* (7 May 1997).

admission to NATO would cause his country to "review" its attitude towards the Founding Act (ITAR-TASS, 9 July). Tarasov repeated this position on Moscow's Mayak Radio Network; and Yeltsin impressed it upon Finland's President Martti Ahtisaari at a July meeting in Karelia.[271]

The next day, in Vilnius, Madeleine Albright said that she could not guarantee that Baltic states would be invited to join NATO in 1999 (ELTA [Vilnius], 13 July). A U.S.-Baltic Charter was in the making, she added, but nothing of substance was revealed about its nature. Albright's subsequent swing through the other Baltic capitals drew much comment from the Russian media, prompting Yeltsin to term the idea that NATO might even be considering Baltic members as a "dangerous" one.[272] Andrei Fedorov, member of the Collegium of Directors, Council on Foreign and Defense Policy, accused the Baltic leadership of waging an "anti-Russian campaign," falsely portraying Russia as an enemy so as to gain the West's sympathy. He charged Estonia and Latvia with conducting "soft" ethnic cleansing for the purpose of evoking harsh reactions from nationalists in Russia.[273] His central point was that NATO must be absolutely aware of what the admission of a Baltic country would signal to Russia.

There was no let up in Russian diplomatic pressure against the idea of Baltic entry into NATO. Nemtsov warned Solana, who travelled to Moscow for a "personal visit" in August, that Russia "would not tolerate the possible admission of the Baltic republics into NATO" (Interfax, 4 Aug). Chernomyrdin repeated these opinions on 3 September as he set out for Vilnius to participate in an OSCE summit. If any Baltic state was invited to join NATO, "mistrust and suspicion" would ensue. The Russian prime minister voiced Moscow's continued "alarm" at references to the Baltic region in the Madrid Declaration and cautioned the West not to attempt any revision of international agreements on the status of Kaliningrad (Interfax, 3 Sept).

In his opening address at a conference of Central and Eastern European leaders in Vilnius, on 5 September, Chernomyrdin confirmed Russia's attitude towards Baltic efforts at integration with NATO and again called the Alliance's

---

[271]For Yeltsin's comment to Ahtisaari, ITAR-TASS (13 July 1997); for the Tarasov interview, Mayak Radio Network (9 July 1997), FBIS-SOV, No. 190. Reference to the Baltic region in the Madrid Declaration put Russia "on our guard," Tarasov said.

[272]On Yeltsin's comments after his discussion with the Finnish president, see Boris Rodionov, "Rybok v 'mirnom nastuplenii'" [Spurt in the "Peace Offensive"], *Rossiiskaia gazeta* (26 July 1997).

[273]Fedorov, "Rossiia i Pribaltika: chto v perspektive?" [Russia and the Baltics: What Are the Prospects?], *Rossiiskaia gazeta* (15 July 1997). See also Sergei Alekhin, "Pochemu bolit golova u russikh v Estonii" [Why Russians Have Headaches in Estonia], *Rossiiskaia gazeta* (25 June 1997).

eastern expansion the "biggest strategic mistake made so far in world politics since the end of the Cold War."[274] Offering to guarantee security in the region and to facilitate military cooperation between Russia's armed forces in Kaliningrad and the Baltic armed forces, he asked, in return, that the Baltic countries join no military bloc. The Russian propaganda counter-attack continued through the first two weeks of October: Chernomyrdin, Sergeev, Primakov, and the chair of the Duma Committee for International Affairs, Vladimir Lukin, all made the point that Baltic republic adherence to NATO would cause Russia to reconsider its relationship with that organization. They spoke, respectively, at The Hague, Moscow, Ottawa, and the United Nations (ITAR-TASS, 1, 2, 15 Oct).

After the Vilnius Conference concluded, Baltic leaders jointly rejected Chernomyrdin's position, but Russia's leadership was not deterred in the least. In an interview related to preparations for the first session of the Russia-NATO Permanent Joint Council, First Deputy Foreign Minister Igor Frolov told reporters that the admission of former Soviet republics (he named only the Baltics) was "categorically unacceptable" (Interfax, 17 Sept). Shortly after the Council's inaugural session, Primakov answered unequivocally a German journalist's question about the possibility of NATO's membership talks with the Baltic states: "[it] would endanger Russia's good relations with NATO."[275] On 3 October, in the context of a scheduled visit to Moscow by President A. Brazauskas, the Russian Duma's Anti-NATO Association demanded that Yeltsin pursue a tougher line with Lithuania.[276]

There was an immediate context for this hard line. Just prior to this action, *Sovetskaia Rossiia* carried a long feature accusing the United States of isolating Russia with its military manoeuvres in Ukraine, Poland, Estonia and the Baltic Sea, naming Landsbergis as especially culpable.[277] Positioning himself for another campaign for the Russian presidency, Lebed told reporters in Berlin that NATO expansion was not a threat to Russia "at the present time," adding that "it is another matter if the expansion of the alliance crosses into the zone of Russia's geopolitical interests—if there are attempts to extend it to the Baltic countries and

---

[274]Radio Riga Network (5 Sept 1997), FBIS-SOV, No. 248. Eleven countries participated in the conference.

[275]*Bild am Sonntag* (28 Sept 1997). Primakov was then still in New York.

[276]Radio Mayak Network, Moscow (3 Oct 1997), FBIS-SOV, No. 276.

[277]Mikhail Postol, "Krivoe vereteno" [The Crooked Spindle], *Sovetskaia Rossiia* (27 Sept 1997).

Ukraine." If such became the case, Russia's people and leadership would unify against it, leading perhaps to "uncontrollable conflict."[278]

On 24 October, Yeltsin offered security guarantees to the Baltic countries, presenting them as a "unilateral obligation" (ITAR-TASS, 24 Oct), with the anticipation that legally based mutual agreements would follow and make Baltic membership in NATO unnecessary. The initiative appeared successful initially when Lithuania's Brazauskas came to Moscow to discuss borders. Communist commentators took umbrage, however and called Russia's new (24 October) border treaty with Lithuania capitulation and "cowardice." Contacts between Brussels and the Baltic countries were intensifying, Vasilii Safronchuk wrote, and Washington's support for a quick Lithuanian membership would be strengthened with the signing of the treaty. Ceding ownership of Memel (Klaipeda), which Safronchuk claimed had been Soviet, not Lithuanian territory, to Lithuania was yet another blow to Russia's territorial integrity.[279]

Safronchuk's concerns were borne out when, within a week of signing the border agreement, the Lithuanian government was the first to reject Yeltsin's security proposition, delivering a message to the Russian embassy in Vilnius that it preferred integration into the EU and NATO (ELTA, 30 Oct). Lithuania had, in fact, gained more than a border agreement: the elimination of the potential for frontier disputes raised its eligibility for NATO membership to a higher level. Estonia rejected Russia's offer on 2 November, saying that it much preferred NATO membership. The Latvian foreign ministry followed suit two days later.[280] Russia's proffer of security guarantees therefore seemed to have backfired completely.

---

[278]Lebed was interviewed for *Die Welt,* Internet version (7 Oct 1997), FBIS-SOV, No. 280. He was in Berlin for a conference on "Russian Foreign Policy and Security Policy in Connection with the NATO Expansion," sponsored by the Aspen Foundation. The Berlin speech was printed in *Moskovskie novosti,* No. 40 (5–12 Oct 1997), and *Moscow News* ("Alexander Lebed Gives a Speech . . . ," No. 40 [16–22 Oct 1998]: 3), so it had a very wide Russian and English-language audience.

[279]Safronchuk, "Spory v Severoatlanticheskom al'ianse i vokrug nego" [Arguments in the North Atlantic Alliance and Around It], *Sovetskaia Rossiia* (21 Oct 1997). Memel was part of a tiny coastal territory, called Memelland, stripped from Germany in 1919 and placed under a French High Commissioner. Lithuania seized it in 1923, but in March 1939 Hitler coerced that country to return it to Germany. The Russians therefore claimed it as part of the spoils from their WWII victory over Germany.

[280]ITAR-TASS (6 November 1997). See also Yevgenii Vostrukhov, "A nel'zia li v NATO po snizhennomu tarifu?" [And Can One Get into NATO at a Sale Price?], *Rossiiskaia gazeta* (13 Nov 1997), where the Baltic republics are accused of setting their economic agendas against Russia so as to appeal to NATO and Western Europe.

On 8 November, the Baltic Assembly adopted a resolution asking NATO for immediate accession talks[281] and on the 10th the three Baltic presidents issued a communiqué jointly rejecting Russia's blandishments (Interfax, 10 Nov).

Russian Duma members reacted predictably. Speaker Seleznev reiterated the Duma's (and the government's) long-standing position, "If the Baltic countries join NATO, we will revise the treaty with this organization." Aleksei Mitrofanov, LDPR deputy and chair of the Geopolitics Committee, called for tougher action against the Baltic Republics and criticized the border agreement with Lithuania. Yabloko deputy Sergei Ivanenko called Russia's offer an "error" in the first place, saying that the government must have known that it would be turned down (Interfax, 11 Nov). The cranky reaction from the communist press was to be expected, but the usually conservative *Delovoi mir* [Business World] also went on the attack, pointing out that Yeltsin had handed Lithuania a winning card in its application to NATO and warning that the Baltic states were prepared to put themselves forward to NATO as a package—rather than individually.[282]

Baltic state membership in NATO was a prevailing subtext during a Russian security-seeking mission in Scandinavia, which began with meetings between Sergeev and his Norwegian counterpart Dag Jostein Fjaervoll in Oslo, on 26 November. A program for military-to-military cooperation for 1998, mostly in the Arctic, was signed. While discussing these measures at a press conference, Sergeev noted that the Norwegian defense minister shared his opinion that Russia's concerns should be taken into account when security terms for the Baltic states were determined. Russia's position was clear: Baltic entry into NATO would cause a strategic imbalance and have a "negative" impact on Russia's security (ITAR-TASS, 26 Nov).

In Stockholm, President Yeltsin surprised his hosts with a proposal to reduce Russia's military personnel in the northwest (see section 3.1), hoping that Sweden would in turn help persuade the Baltic states to participate in a "Baltic region confidence-building regime [to be] set up in the border zone and in the Baltic Sea" (ITAR-TASS, 3 Dec). But simultaneous statements from Moscow to the effect that border treaties with Latvia and Estonia depended entirely on the way in which those countries resolved problems faced by their Russian-speaking minorities (ITAR-TASS, 2, 3 Dec) ensured that Yeltsin's Stockholm speech would have

[281]Radio Tallinn Network (8 Nov 1997), FBIS-SOV, No. 313. See also "NATO Baltii blizhe" [NATO Is Closer to the Baltics], *Krasnaia zvezda* (1 Nov 1997).

[282]Vladimir Skripov, "Litva—pervaia v ocheredi v NATO" [Lithuania Is First in Line to Join NATO], *Delovoi mir* (12 Nov 1997). The Russian-Lithuania border demarcation treaty, although signed by Yeltsin, still had not been ratified by the State Duma as of April 1999.

little effect.[283] The cuts proposed by Yeltsin angered Russian nationalists, who rushed to point out how greatly weakened their country already had become in the region.[284] The Baltic question loomed larger for Russian strategists as they began to perceive a renewed NATO focus on the North. With Baltic membership in NATO, the communist press complained in April 1998, Russia's entire northwest salient would be open to attack from sea-launched missiles and more stringent NATO surveillance. Norway's role as NATO member for the North was highlighted in this regard.[285]

Yeltsin's diplomatic offensive in the Baltic region suffered more setbacks early in 1998. On 5 January a long-time resident of the United States, 71-year old Valdas Adamkus, was elected Lithuanian president; and on the 16th U.S. president Clinton and the three Baltic presidents signed a Charter of Partnership which explicitly supported eventual Baltic entry into NATO. The purpose of the Charter, Clinton said, was to "further America's commitment to help Estonia, Lithuania and Latvia to deepen their integration and prepare for memberships in the European Union and NATO." Russia's media either ridiculed or abhorred both developments.[286] The communist press was angry, calling the Charter another stage in

---

[283]Safronchuk and the Communist press saw the whole affair as another stage in the undermining of Russia's security; see " 'Zhesty pereutomleniia.' Stokgol'mskie siuprizy Rossiiskogo prezidenta" [The Gestures of Overwork: The Stockholm Surprise of the Russian President], *Sovetskaia Rossiia* (6 Dec 1997).

[284]See, esp., Yuliia Zheglova, "Baltiiskaia dilemma Rossii i severnoi Evropy" [The Baltic Dilemma of Russia and Northern Europe], *Nezavisimoe voennoe obozrenie,* No. 45 (5–18 Dec 1997). In 1994 Kaliningrad was given the status of Kaliningrad Special Defensive Area and placed under the command of the Baltic Fleet. Russia's Northern Fleet has been much reduced, making SLBM's the country's only real defense in the North.

[285]See V. Tetekin, "Rossii ugrozhaiut i s Severa . . . yastreby nad nami" [Russia Also Threatened from the North . . . Hawks above Us], *Sovetskaia Rossiia* (7 April 1998).

[286]The communist press treated the Adamkus election as both a U.S. plot and a patently naive decision by the Lithuanian electorate. see, e.g., "Valdas Adamkus—prezident Litvy" [Valdas Adamkus Is President of Lithuania], *Sovetskaia Rossiia* (6 Jan 1998); Yevgenii Popov, "Prezident Litvy—'amerikanskii ekolog' Valdas Adamkus. Strannyi vsadnik na belom kone" [The President of Lithuania, the American Ecologist Valdas Adamkus: A Strange Rider on a White Horse], *Sovetskaia Rossiia* (9 Jan 1998). The non-communist press also was puzzled and concerned over the election of Adamkus; see, e.g., "Novyi prezident Litvy Valdas Adamkus obeshchaet 'ochen' aktivny' kurs' " [The New President of Lithuania, Valdas Adamkus, Promises a "Very Active" Course], *Nezavisimaia gazeta* (13 Jan 1998). A long piece by Yevgenii Vostrukhov, "Bez garantii bezopasnosti" [Without Guarantees of Safety], *Rossiiskaia gazeta* (14 Jan 1998) cast few stones but criticized the Baltic presidents for almost frenzied attempts to gain U.S. guarantees for their security and NATO membership.

the "rejection" of Russia.[287] The non-communist press demonstrated puzzlement, concern and some anger. No one was indifferent, all charging the United States with unilaterally ensuring that the Baltic republics would enter NATO over Russia's objections. The ministry of defense's main newspaper, *Krasnaia zvezda,* led the way this time in criticizing American policy in the Baltics.[288]

On the other hand, American officials were cited as saying that the official response from Moscow was "surprisingly low-key."[289] The United States did not attach much significance to a Russian foreign ministry statement that, "with absolute certainty," Russia will revise its relationship with the Alliance after Baltic admission to NATO (Interfax, 20 Jan 1998). For several weeks after the signing ceremony in Washington, the Russian press continued to reflect dismay and distrust over the U.S.-Baltic agreement, both in relation to NATO and the obvious increase of U.S. influence in the region.[290] The Duma's Anti-NATO Commission expressed its "deep concern" and doubt in the "effectiveness" of the Founding Act, urging Yeltsin to develop a national program against NATO expansion (Interfax, 15 Jan). On 23 January, the Duma adopted a resolution demonstrating its collective concern about the question. The resolution, prepared by Chairman of the Committee on International Affairs Lukin and committee member Aleksandr Shabanov, concluded: "Until such time when NATO is no longer a military bloc, the further expansion of the alliance to the east, especially if it includes states who were once part of the USSR in its orbit, is incompatible with the Founding Act . . . between the RF and NATO" (RIA Novosti, 23 Jan). Russian nationalists even reopened the Pandora's Box of Soviet annexation of the region in 1940, saying that Baltic references to that event as justification for admission to NATO were anachronistic and an abuse of history (Interfax, 21 Jan). Antagonistic and anxious press, radio and television commentary on the U.S.-Baltic Charter continued well

---

[287]Safronchuk, "Tikhoi sapoi. Khartiia 'SShA-Baltiia' —ocherednoi etap 'otbrasyvaniia' Rossii" [On the Sly: The USA-Baltic Charter—the Next Step in the "Rejection" of Russia], *Sovetskaia Rossiia* (20 Jan 1998).

[288]See, e.g., "SShA podpishut khartiiu s pribaltami" [The USA Will Sign a Charter with the Baltics], *Krasnaia zvezda* (14 Jan 1998); V. Sturua, "Vashington priotkryvaet Baltii dver' v NATO" [Washington Partially Opens the Door in NATO for the Baltics], *Izvestiia* (14 Jan 1998); "Amerika gotovit strany Baltii k vstupleniiu v NATO" [America Prepares the Baltic Countries for Entry into NATO], *Nezavisimaia gazeta* (16 Jan 1998).

[289]See Steve Erlanger, "Clinton and 3 Baltic Leaders Sign Charter," *New York Times* (17 Jan 1998).

[290]See, e.g., "Vashingtonskii veksel' dlia pribaltov" [A Washington Promissory Note for the Baltics], *Krasnaia zvezda* (20 Jan 1998); "Amerikanskoe vliianie v Baltii rastët" [American Influence in the Baltics Grows], *Nezavisimaia gazeta* (22 Jan 1998).

into February, associated with Yeltsin's restatement of Russia's strong opposition to Baltic membership in NATO during a state visit to Italy.[291] Tallinn's offer in February to help impose obedience on Saddam Hussein by force evoked real anger at Estonia's "blatant opportunism" from Russia's media and officialdom. Only in April did Russian commentators began to ease up on their sarcasm about Estonian "posturing," and that was attributable in part to a new focus on Latvia.[292]

Senior foreign ministry strategists in Moscow began printing studies showing how "vital" the Baltic region was to their security and how likely the West was to act without considering Russia. Their consistent refrain was that the Founding Act would be "undermined" the moment a Baltic country entered NATO.[293] The importance of the Baltic area to Russian national security was outlined at great length in an interview with a senior member of the Russian ministry of foreign affairs, A.A. Avdeev, on 18 February. From the Russian perspective, still undemarcated borders and the large Russian populations in Latvia and Estonia remained grave points of contention. But the question of NATO loomed most large: Avdeev described in detail the proposals tendered for Baltic security by the Russian government, and repeated the long-standing messages about NATO and the Baltic Republics. NATO is "dragging [Russia] by its coat tails backwards, into the nuclear confrontation of the 1960s and 1970s," he contended, blaming the United States in particular.[294] Less than a year later, Avdeev would become the number two man in the foreign ministry.

---

[291]See, e.g., Yurii Pospelev commentary on Voice of Russia World Service, in English, (11 Feb 1998).

[292]On Estonia's position on Iraq, Igor Teterin, "Berechis', Saddam Khusein, goriachie Estonskie parni idut!" [Beware, Saddam Hussein, the Estonian Hotshots Are Coming!], *Rossiiskaia gazeta* (24 Feb 1998). For later commentary on Estonia's new "realism," see Igor Kluev, "Estoniia: vo vneshniuiu politiku—bol'she real'nosti" [Estonia: More Realism in Foreign Policy], *Krasnaia zvezda* (30 April 1998).

The situation of Russians in Latvia had, of course, long been a matter of concern for the Russian government and media. See, e.g., Aleksandr Shinkin, "U liuda 'vtorogo sorta' v Latvii obshchii priznak—russkie" [For the "Second Class" People of Latvia There Is a Common Symbol—Russian], *Rossiiskaia gazeta* (18 Jan 1998).

[293]See, e.g., Shustov, "Russia and Security Measures in the Baltics," *op. cit.,* and, in the same issue, B. Kazantsev, "NATO Moving East: The Aftermath," 32–38; and a more recent piece, Viktor Sokolov, "Dialog Moskvy i Vil'nusa. On oslozhnilsia lish' stremleniem Litvy v NATO" [Dialogue between Moscow and Vilnius: It Was Complicated Only by Lithuania's Attempts to Join NATO], *Nezavisimaia gazeta* (16 June 1998).

[294]Avdeev, "Region Baltii—zona nashikh natsional'nykh interesov" [The Baltic Region Is a Zone of Our National Interests], *Rossiiskie vesti* (18 Feb 1998). At that time Avdeev was deputy head in charge of the Western Europe section in the ministry of foreign affairs.

Moscow's concerns were replenished by specific incidents related to ethnic Russians living in Latvia, and that country replaced Estonia in the Russian media as the greatest Baltic villain. When a Russian war memorial in Liepaja was vandalized in early March, instant and angry protests were issued by the Russian government and media. Before that outcry died down the televised image of Latvian police disrupting a demonstration by mostly Russian pensioners in Riga further strained Russian-Latvian relations. The Duma adopted a Statement equating the action of "young thugs in uniform" with fascist behavior during the 1930s and demanded that the Russian government not sign a border agreement with Latvia. The Statement included another promise that Russia's security arrangement and relations with the Alliance would have to be reviewed if NATO changed its stance towards the Baltic countries, especially Latvia. More outrage was elicited when Latvian authorities granted permission to veterans of the Latvian voluntary SS Legion to celebrate its 55th anniversary (Interfax, 16 March).[295]

A later "provocation" against a Russian war memorial, in the Latvian city of Dobele, evoked more charges of neo-Nazism from Russian communists and nationalists. Releases from the Russian foreign ministry referred to the event as "an insult to our memory."[296] The communist press saw a deeper conspiracy in these events, describing them as part of a larger scheme to bully ethnic Russians into emigrating or preventing them from getting citizenship.[297] Avdeev had already told NTV "Hero of the Day" viewers that all these anti-Russian episodes were "stage-

---

[295]"Zaiavlenie Gosudarstvennoi Dumy, Ob otnosheniiakh mezhdu Rossiiskoi Federatsiei i Latviiskoi Respublikoi" [Statement of the State Duma, on Relations between the Russian Federation and the Latvian Republic], *Rossiiskaia gazeta* (21 March 1998); the Statement was issued on 6 March. See also, e.g., "Latviia: Posle raspravy—vandalizm" [Latvia: After the Violence—Vandalism], *Sovetskaia Rossiia* (10 March 1998); *Izvestiia* (11 March 1998). The harshest outcries against the SS anniversary can be found in the Communist papers, e.g., "Marsh legionerov SS po ulitsam opozorennoi bespraviem Rigi" [The March of SS Legionnaires along the Streets of Riga Disgraceful by Lawlessness], *Sovetskaia Rossiia* (19 March 1998), and *Pravda* (17 March 1998), but the RF foreign ministry also issued a formal protest. Protests against the SS event were raised from the general Latvian population as well.

[296]"Oskorblenie nashei pamiati" [An Insult to Our Memory], *Rossiiskaia gazeta* (8 May 1998), Yevgenii Vostrukhov, "Latyshkie natsisty ne unimaiutsia" [Latvian Nazis Won't Stop], *Rossiiskie vesti* (6 May 1998), and "Primakov—o Latvii i Kosovo" [Primakov on Latvia and Kosovo], *Nezavisimaia gazeta* (6 May 1998). See also Interfax (5 May 1998).

[297]See, e.g., Viacheslav Altukhov, "Zhdat' ili deistvovat'? Pis'mo iz Rigi o problemakh grazhdanstva v Latvii" [To Wait or to Act? Letter from Riga on the Problems of Citizenship in Latvia], *Sovetskaia Rossiia* (5 May 1998). Failure to achieve citizenship also would mean that they could not vote against NATO if the occasion arose.

managed" by a 3rd party, who remained nameless but hardly hidden. Polls taken in Russia in March showed that a majority of citizens wanted their government to levy sanctions against Latvia (Interfax, 18 March), an attitude that was hardened by the events in May. Economic sanctions were, indeed, imposed as of 1 July.

Conspiracy theorists looked back to March, when Norway's government declared five Russian diplomats *persona non grata* for spying, postponing its prime minister's planned visit to Moscow (Interfax, 13 March). The Russian government retaliated by expelling only two Norwegian diplomats (17 March), which suggests that it did not wish to make too much of the matter. Yet the fact that Russia's earlier proposals, in Stockholm, of a northern security system had been summarily dismissed by Sweden and the Baltic states made the unexpected breach in relations with Norway more serious than it might otherwise have been. Some Russian commentators linked the expulsion to the fact that a large scale NATO military exercise (Strong Resolve-98), the venue of which was Norway, the North Sea and the Norwegian Sea, was scheduled to take place at that same time.[298]

Government-to-government relations with Norway were patched up in April/May, as defense and foreign policy officials met and discussed their differences. A return to the cordial diplomatic relations notwithstanding, members of the Duma Anti-NATO Commission continued to voice suspicion of Norway's motives in the North. Communists at a huge international conference on the "New Security Architecture of Europe and NATO" in April accused Norway of "insidious" motives and, usually in the same breath, angrily protested the possibility of Baltic admission to NATO. Chairman of the Commission, Baburin, opened the conference with an exhortation that a "red line" be drawn forbidding any Baltic country from joining NATO. Primakov also used the term, saying that there was already a "red line" which Russia could not allow NATO to cross, and it enclosed the Baltic Republics.[299]

---

[298]First deputy Chief of the RF Armed Forces General Staff, Col. Gen. Valerii Manilov, complained bitterly about these exercises, saying that they flew in the face of the purpose of the Founding Act (Interfax, 13 March 1998). See Section 1.8, above. In "Naskol'ko zhe sil'no 'sil'noe reshenie?" [How Strong Is the "Strong Resolve"?], *Krasnaia zvezda* (18 March 1998), Vadim Markushin linked the expulsion of Russian diplomats from Norway directly to the war games. See also Konstantin Eggert, "NATO gotovitsia k oborone" [NATO Prepares for Defense], *Izvestiia* (31 March 1998).

[299]For Primakov's remarks, see S. Glotov, "Evropa sama sebia obezopasit" [Europe Will Take Care of Its Own Security], *Rossiiskaia gazeta* (12 May 1998); on Baburin, see Viktoriia Ivanova, "Rasshirenie NATO bylo i ostaetsia nepriemlemym" [NATO Expansion Was and Remains Unacceptable], *Nezavisimaia gazeta* (14 May 1998), Vladimir Gerasimov in *Pravda* (21 April 1998), *op. cit.* For similar comments by Oleg Mironov, another Anti-NATO Commission deputy, see "Novaia arkhitektura bezopasnosti Evropy i NATO" [A New Architecture of Security in Europe and NATO], *Krasnaia zvezda* (17 April 1998).

Hard line comments such as these compelled Baltic leaders to lobby even more aggressively for admission to NATO. In Lithuania's case, however, the rhetoric was toned down. In May, Adamkus informed a Russian interviewer that Lithuania's aspiration to join NATO should not be viewed as opposition to Russia. He went on to predict that Russia itself would eventually join "NATO as the all-European security system."[300] Solana told a Russian NTV audience on 26 May that whereas "every country has the right to choose which security structures in which it wants to participate," NATO will "take Russia's opinion [about Baltic entry] into account."[301] In June, he went so far as to moot Russian membership and spoke tentatively, while visiting the Baltic capitals, of the possibility of a separate security scheme for the Baltic region to include Russia. This concept, even though very speculative, cheered some Russian observers.[302] Russia itself was encouraged to play a greater role in NATO activities, a fact evidenced by an agreement that a platoon of Baltic Fleet marines would join a military exercise in Northern Denmark in late May; and that Russia would send observers to the Baltic Challenge 98, a NATO maneuver scheduled for Lithuania in July.[303] Not assuaged, Seleznev lectured a delegation of French parliamentarians on 8 June,

---

[300]In the long interview, carried in *Obshchaia gazeta*, No. 18 (7–13 May 1998), Adamkus made it clear that there was no likelihood of situations arising in Lithuania like those taking place then in Latvia and that productive relations with Russia were important to his country. The interview is translated for FBIS-SOV, No. 148 (1 June 1998). The Estonian foreign minister, on the other hand, told a Canadian interviewer that Russians "are a pain in the ass. They've never gotten over their post-colonial stress syndrome." The minister, Toomas Ilves, was raised in the United States, see Charles Enman, "Selling Estonia to the West," *Ottawa Citizen* (8 June 1998), B4.

[301]Moscow NTV interview with Solana conducted by Svetlana Sorokhina, on 26 May, FBIS-SOV, No. 146. Sorokhina asked if NATO, knowing that Russia has said it would "re-examine its relations with NATO" if Baltic countries were admitted, would "hold consultations on this issue with Russia?" A long essay on the Baltic Fleet's historic importance to Russia kept the issue of Russia's vulnerability alive, see Valerii Gromak, "Baltiiskii flot: 295 let na sluzhbe Rossii" [The Baltic Fleet: 295 Years of Service to Russia], *Krasnaia zvezda* (19 May 1998).

[302]See, e.g., Nikolai Laskevich, "Solana razocharoval pribaltov" [Solana Disappoints Balts], *Izvestiia* (19 June 1998). A Crimean Russian nationalist paper treated the entire discussion as a Polish-Lithuanian plot to get Russian forces out of Kaliningrad. See *Flag Rodiny* (22 April 1998), FBIS-SOV, No. 190.

[303]ELTA, Vilnius (9 June 1998), and Voice of Russia World Service, Moscow (16 May 1998), both in the English-language. See also Boris Vinogradov, " 'NATOvskaia prem'era' Rossiiskoi morskoi pekhoty" [The "NATO Premiere" of Russian Marines], *Izvestiia* (20 May 1998).

two days before the French National Assembly met to endorse the first wave of NATO expansion, telling them that "in the event of Baltic countries joining NATO, our revision of relations with NATO will be inevitable."[304]

He was right to be cautious. In June, the speaker of Lithuanian parliament, Landsbergis, took a much harder line than Adamkus, saying that his country could not accept Moscow's security guarantees in lieu of NATO because it was not clear that Russia would remain democratic (Interfax, 3 June). Landsbergis proved to be wise in his caution as well, as Moscow's evolution toward democracy took several steps backward during the second half of 1998. A State Duma delegation to Vilnius demonstrated Russian intransigence well enough, telling their Lithuanian counterparts that they would not ratify the border treaty signed by Yeltsin and Brazauskas the previous October without some guarantees on access to Kaliningrad. In the meantime, the Russian media made it clear that the chief obstacle to ratification was Lithuania's continued aspirations for NATO membership.[305]

As the summer wore on and Russia's economic and political crisis deepened, Moscow's stance on a "red line" hardened. Russian commentators had little reason to believe Solana's conciliatory approach and continued to assume that their country's point of view would not be considered in the West. Albright's remarks earlier in the spring to the effect that Russians were indifferent to NATO expansion, an opinion that was typified neatly in the *New York Times* as recently as 2 May 1998, demonstrated the resilience of notions espoused by Brzezinski in 1996.[306]

Accommodations such as participation in a Baltic Sea NATO exercise represented only minor adjustments in what is a very difficult strategic, political and psychological issue for Russia. When, on 23 June, the Danish foreign minister was quoted at a meeting in Copenhagen of representatives of the 11-member Council of Baltic Sea States that the Baltic countries would, in fact, join NATO, the Russian press was outraged. *Krasnaia zvezda* was especially testy, warning that Russia's "adequate measures" were more than enough for air defense in the Baltic region and reiterating Primakov's well-worn statement to the Council that further

---

[304]ITAR-TASS (8 June 1998). The occasion was the 4th meeting of the Grand Russo-French Inter-Parliamentary Commission. Speaker of the National Assembly, Laurent Fabius, led the French delegation.

[305]See, e.g., Viktor Sokolov, "Dialog Moskvy i Vil'nusa . . .," *Nezavisimaia gazeta* (16 June 1998), *op. cit.*

[306]Michael R. Gordon's, "NATO Is Inching Closer, But Russians Don't Blink," *New York Times* (2 May 1998) was challenged aggressively by Melor Sturua, veteran Soviet journalist, in "Molchalivoe pronatovskoe lobbi Rossii" [The Silent Pro-NATO Lobby of Russia], *Nezavisimaia gazeta* (14 May 1998).

military integration of the Baltic countries with NATO was unacceptable.[307]
Russian pundits pointed out as well that the Baltic countries would be expected
to pay their own way in NATO, unnecessarily placing further strains on their already weakened economies.[308]

A few weeks later a flurry of unfavorable and suspicious commentary greeted
Strobe Talbott's participation in the first session of the Commission for Partnership Between the United States and the Baltic Countries, held in July. Talbott endorsed a communiqué which implied that the Baltic countries were being prepared for entry into NATO. The Russian response was predictable, yet unusually
universal: a promise implicit in the Founding Act was being broken, the United
States intended to establish a bridgehead on the Baltic Sea, and the region itself
will be included in NATO's "sphere of influence as soon as possible." Further
charges flowed that the United States was ignoring Russia's hopes for a "blocless"
European security system. A large-scale NATO exercise near Kleipeda was being
projected and NATO's plans to set up a corps headquarters in Poland's Szczecin
were ominous. Spokesmen for the Russian military claimed that the new corps
represented a direct violation of Article IV of the Founding Act.[309]

---

[307]See, e.g., Vladimir Kuzar', "Stremiashchimsia v 'atlanticheskii rai' bylo by polezno znat'
ob adekvatnykh merakh Rossii" [Those Who Wish to Rush into the "Atlantic Paradise" Need
to Know of Russia's Adequate Measures], *Krasnaia zvezda* (25 June 1998). On the Danish
foreign minister's statement, see "Baltiiskie strany stanut chlenami NATO" [The Baltic
Countries Will Become Members of NATO], *Nezavisimaia gazeta* (23 June 1998).

[308]See, e.g., Yevgenii Vostrukhov, "'Besplatnykh zavtrakov ni dlia kogo ne budet'—
govoriat rukovoditeli NATO, namekaia na to chto dlia vstupleniia pribaltiiskikh stran v
Severoatlanticheskii soiuz im nuzhno raskoshelit'sia" ["No One Will Get Free Break-
fasts"—NATO Leaders Say, Making Baltic Countries Understand That They Will Have
to Pay to Join the North Atlantic Union], *Rossiiskaia gazeta* (25 June 1998).

[309]See, e.g., Igor Korotchenko, "Al'ians ukrepliaet pozitsii na Baltike. Formirovanie
datsko-pol'sko-germanskogo korpusa pereshlo v zavershaiushchuiu fazu" [The Alliance
Strengthens Its Position on the Baltic: The Formation of a Danish-Polish-German Corps
Moves towards Completion], *Nezavisimoe voennoe obozrenie*, No. 48 (17–24 Dec 1998);
Aleksei Baliev, "Protiv kogo druzhat Amerika s Baltiei?" [Against Whom Did America Become Friendly with the Baltics?], *Rossiiskaia gazeta* (17 July 1998); Il'ya Nikiforov, Yev-
genii Grigor'ev, "Yavlenie Klaisa Kinkelia pribaltam" [The Appearance of Klaus Kinkel in
the Baltics], *Nezavisimaia gazeta* (17 July 1998); Nikolai Lashkevich, "NATO uzhe pod
Klaipedoi" [NATO Already Is Near Klaipeda], *Izvestiia* (10 July 1998); Vladimir Kuzar',
"Partnery poka ne gotovy" [The Partners Are Not Yet Prepared], *Krasnaia zvezda* (14 July
1998); Vladimir Dmitrichenkov, "A poutru oni prosnulis' . . ." [They Woke Up in the
Morning . . .], *Krasnaia zvezda* (14 July 1998).

None of this was helped by reports that Landsbergis had persuaded Talbott that the demilitarization of Kaliningrad was an important goal for all of Europe (ELTA, 8 July). A month later, Landsbergis told a conference in Vilnius, attended by the presidents of Poland and Latvia plus representatives from NATO and the EU, that the Baltic republics might still be a victim of a modern "Munich" if they were not admitted to NATO.[310] These old but recurring themes took on a new intensity after the Copenhagen meetings. It is not surprising, therefore, that the concept of an inviolate "red line" was given official status by presidential aide Sergei Prikhodko on 18 August, during a briefing session about the upcoming Yeltsin-Clinton meetings in Moscow. Asked if NATO enlargement would be a matter for discussion at the summit, he promised that Russia would revise its relations with NATO if the Alliance crossed the "red line" and admitted any former Soviet republic (ITAR-TASS, 18 Aug). The policy was confirmed by the new foreign minister, Igor Ivanov, as the crisis in Kosovo reached a boiling point in October.[311] In February 1999, Deputy Chief of Staff Prikhodko was assigned further duties as head of the presidential foreign policy department, augmenting the anti-NATO expansion forces in the government.

The growing unease in Moscow about Russia's strategic and political place on the Baltic came to a head of sorts in December, when Igor Ivanov paid his first visit to Stockholm and Oslo as foreign minister. The trip was preceded by an announcement that the military cuts promised in December 1997 would be completed by 1 January 1999. Russia's northern complement of troops was decreased by 40 percent, and armed forces personnel in Kaliningrad were cut by almost 60 percent (see section 3.1). Concerned that NATO's Norway was supplementing its forces in the region, Ivanov hoped that his example would evoke some reciprocal gesture from Russia's Scandinavian neighbors (Interfax, 1 Dec). Failing to gain even a vague emulation of his example, Ivanov had to fall back on the standard Kremlin statement against NATO expansion, threatening again to revise the nature of Russia's relations with the Alliance (Interfax, 4 Dec).

Russian media, politicians and public were enraged at, and cynical about, the Baltic countries' quick support of NATO air strikes against Yugoslavia. Moscow's officials were therefore pleased when they were quietly reassured that no immediate second wave of invitations to join NATO would be announced at the Wash-

---

[310]Konstantin Eggert, "Baltii predlozheno ne toropit'sia NATO" [Baltic States Told Not to Be in a Rush by NATO], *Izvestiia* (12 Sept 1998).

[311]The Baltic states ranked high in Ivanov's statement about NATO expansion to Spanish reporters visiting Moscow: "There is a red line . . . [which] goes along the border of the former Soviet Union, including the Baltic states" (Interfax, 8 Oct).

ington summit. By that time the Russian government had so often and so consistently promised retaliatory action if any Baltic state joined NATO, that the question of a "second wave" had become a question of just how far Moscow could be pushed. Already pushed to the point of giving up hopes for a constructive association with NATO, Moscow appears to have drawn its line in the sand at the Baltic borders. NATO now must calculate precisely the risk it would be taking by crossing that "red line."[312]

6. THE COMMONWEALTH OF INDEPENDENT STATES: RETURN OF THE "GREAT GAME"?

The day on which Primakov and Solana announced their agreement on a Russia-NATO document, 14 May 1997, also marked the fifth anniversary of the Commonwealth of Independent States' (CIS) Collective Security Pact.[313] The ministry of defense newspaper was alone in highlighting the irony of the situation, noting that the CIS was in no way a counter to NATO.[314] In 1992 the internal debate about military integration within the CIS had been linked to NATO expansion

---

[312]Nikolai Lashkevich, "Stran Baltii podderzhivaiut deistviia NATO" [The Baltic Countries Support NATO Actions (in Yugoslavia])], *Izvestiia* (30 March 1999). For the continued relevance of the Baltic question for Russia, see Aleksei Lyashchenko, "Strany Baltii speshat v NATO" [Baltic Countries Rush to NATO], *Krasnaia zvezda* (23 Feb 1999); Sergei Putilov, "Kaliningrad karta ee razygryvaiut strany Baltii stremias' prisoedinit'sia k NATO" [The Kaliningrad Card Is Played at the Baltic Countries Trying to Join NATO], *Nezavisimoe voennoe obozrenie*, No. 9 (6–12 March 1999).

[313]Although 10 members of the CIS agreed to joint peacekeeping at a summit in Kiev in March, 1992, only 6 members signed the CIS Collective Security Pact on 15 May 1992 (Russia, Armenia, Kazakhstan, Kyrgyzstan, Tajikistan, and Uzbekistan). The Pact was confirmed, however, in "Section III. Collective Security and Military-Political Cooperation," Articles 11–15, of the CIS Charter, signed in Minsk, 22 January 1993, by the six states noted above, plus Belarus. Georgia came on board in 1994. See "Ustav Sodruzhestva Nezavisimykh Gosudarsta" [Charter of the CIS], *Rossiiskaia gazeta* (12 Feb 1993), and "Reshenie Soveta glav gosudarstva Sodruzhestva Nezavisimykh Gosudarstv" [Decision of the Council of the Heads of the CIS States], *Rossiiskaia gazeta* (12 Feb 1993). The 5-year Pact was not fully ratified until 1994, when the Kazakhstan parliament approved it. Thus 1999 is the year when the pact came up for renewal.

[314]"NATO-Rossiia: eshche odna popytka k 'proryvu'" [NATO-Russia: One More Attempt at "Break Through"], *Krasnaia zvezda* (14 May 1997).

eastward only loosely.[315] Five years later the connection was inextricable, and some supporters of integration for economic reasons began speaking of the CIS's added value as an agency for defense against the United States and Europe.

A rising concern that NATO expansion was synonymous with diminishing Russian influence in the CIS was illustrated in essays carried by *Rossiiskie vesti, Nezavisimaia gazeta* and elsewhere during the autumn of 1997. The first coincided with the 9th meeting between Al Gore and Chernomyrdin, this time in Moscow; the second appeared almost simultaneously with Primakov's trip to New York for the opening session of the PJC. But it was Yeltsin who told Gore bluntly that attempts by "certain circles" in the United States to declare regions of the CIS zones of special interest to the United States was unacceptable. Russian foreign affairs analysts were looking over their shoulders by late 1997, worrying that their influence within the CIS might seep away into a U.S.-NATO vortex if they were not vigilant. The Caucasus was named often as the particular focus for American attention.[316] In November, Aleksei Pushkov warned readers that the United States was hoping to become a major player in the Central Asian components of the CIS.[317] A few months afterwards, Yevgenii Kozhokin, director of Moscow's Strategic Studies Institute, pointed out that no CIS country, including Russia, was truly capable of protecting its own territorial integrity. The only solution to glaring individual weaknesses was a much strengthened Russian military force, for the good of "everybody" in the CIS.[318]

Apprehensions such as these are of fairly recent vintage. Two full years before Kozhokin proffered his uniquely Russian answer to centrifugal tendencies in the CIS, a quite different perspective on the fate of the CIS could still be found. In

---

[315]At that time, S.M. Rogov wrote in support of the CIS Joint Strategic Armed Forces and lobbied for the CIS Collective Security Treaty in March 1992, arguing that it should have a juridically-based political structure patterned on the NATO model. See his "Nyzhna li Rossii svoia politika natsional'noi bezopasnosti?" [Does Russia Need Its Own National Security Policy], *Nezavisimaia gazeta* (6 March 1992).

[316]"Rossiiu v strankh SNG nichem ne zamenish'" [Russia Cannot Be Replaced in the CIS], *Rossiiskie vesti* (25 Sept 1997). On the expanding American interest in the Caucasus, see Ian Bremmer, "Rethinking U.S. Policy in the Caucasus," *ACE: Analysis of Current Events* 9, no. 10 (October 1997): 7–8.

[317]Pushkov, "Amerika—novaia sverkhderzhava evrazii" [America, the New Super Power in Eurasia], *Nezavisimaia gazeta* (14 Nov 1997). For an especially hostile view in this regard, see "Oni uzhe Rossiiu podelili" [They Already Have Divided Russia], *Zavtra*, No. 46 (Nov 1997).

[318]Kozhokin, "Sil'naia Rossiia nuzhna vsem" [Everybody Needs a Strong Russia], *Nezavisimaia gazeta* (6 March 1998).

March 1996, at a session of the CIS Council of Defense Ministers, for example, the possibility that NATO expansion might even drive some CIS member states toward further integration seemed realistic. Russia, Belarus, Kazakhstan and Kyrgyzstan expressed an interest in expanding their cooperation in air defense, military-technical matters, and even the legalization of a collective security system (ITAR-TASS, 26 March 1996). The RF defense minister at that time, Pavel Grachev, called NATO expansion the "most substantial negative factor" influencing CIS security considerations.[319] It may be that the infamous Solana tour of Transcaucasia in February 1997 attracted attention less because it was truly threatening to Russia than because it could be so easily characterized as a NATO plot to forestall the reintegration of former Soviet republics. This is precisely what presidential spokesman Yastrzhembskii termed it (Interfax, 12 Feb), as did the Russian ministry of foreign affairs in response to Solana's protestations.[320] As early as December 1995, in fact, Russian observers had warned that NATO member Turkey was mounting a concerted effort to increase cooperation with Georgia, its neighbor on the Black Sea, and suggested that a Turkish military presence in Georgia was possible. Thus, as Georgian President Shevardnadze pointed out in a radio interview broadcast in Tbilisi on 17 February 1997, an "acute reaction" to Solana's tour was expected from Russia.[321]

By the summer of 1997 supporters of further integration within the CIS had grown pessimistic about their chances. Musing on the future of the CIS in

---

[319]Vladimir Berezko, "Integratsiia v voennoi oblasti prodolzhaetsia" [Integration in the Military Field Continues], *Krasnaia zvezda* (28 March 1996). See also Boris Vinogradov, "'Effekt matreshki' v SNG—ne pomekha dlia integratsii" [The "Matreshki Effect" in the CIS Is Not an Obstacle to Integration], *Izvestiia* (13 April 1996).

[320]Vadim Lukov, head of the foreign policy planning directorate at the RF Ministry of Foreign Affairs, said on Moscow radio that the timing of Solana's visits was insensitive to Russia's interests at that important moment in the Russia-NATO dialogue: "I therefore believe that the signal sent from the Kremlin [Yastrzhembskii] . . . will be correctly understood . . ." Radiostantsiia Ekho Moskvy (13 February 1998), FBIS-SOV-97, No. 030. "Gensek NATO v stolitsakh SNG" [General Secretary of NATO in the CIS], *Nezavisimaia gazeta* (11 Feb 1997); Yuliia Petrovskaia, in a "debate" with Aleksandr Kurganov, said that Solana's trip was "anti-Moscow"; see "NATO mozhet ogranichit'sia odnim kandidatom" [NATO May Limit Itself to One Candidate], *Nezavisimaia gazeta* (13 Feb 1997). It was left to the radical left to find conspiracy, "Auktsion na Kavkaze" [Auction in the Caucasus], *Zavtra*, No. 16 (April 1997).

[321]Tbilisi Radio Tbilisi Network, FBIS-SOV, No. 033. For the earlier Russian concern, see Mikhail Gerasimov, "Ankara predlagaet Tbilisi tesnoe sotrudnichestvo" [Ankara Proposes Closer Cooperation with Tbilisi], *Nezavisimaia gazeta* (27 December 1995).

Moskovskie novosti at the end of July, Sanobas Shermatova foresaw the organization splitting into "pro-West" and "pro-Russia" blocs. Oil was the honey attract-
ing the Western bees, mainly the United States, to Transcaucasia and Central Asia;
strategic considerations persuaded them of the importance of Ukraine and the
Baltics. Placing only Belarus and Tajikistan firmly in the Russian camp, Shermatova gave proponents of further CIS integration little hope in the face of Western
economic pressure.[322] Separate trips to Washington by the presidents of Kyrgyzstan, Georgia, and Azerbaijan that same month, and the establishment of customs
and border control by Belarus on the Ukrainian border added credence to the
trends described by Shermatova. Early in 1998, Russian pundits began musing
also about U.S. competition for influence in Moldova, suggesting that as soon as
Russian troops fully withdrew from that area it would quickly become a NATO
sphere of influence.[323]

Less than eight months later, as Primakov struggled with the daunting tasks of
his new post as prime minister, another tour of Transcaucasian capital cities by
Solana raised the hackles of Moscow's international affairs pundits.[324] The image
of foreign investors flocking to the Caspian to reap benefits from huge unex-
ploited sources of oil and gas made pipeline diplomacy more crucial to Russia's
interests in the region than military concerns. Solana's trip evoked vague suspicions among Russia's nationalists that there might be a link between fresh anti-
Russian acts in Chechnya, where a Russian envoy was murdered, and NATO's apparent readiness to support a "separatist" movement in Kosovo. No one in
Moscow blamed these particular events directly on Solana, even after he told journalists in Tbilisi that the South Caucasus was a "priority" for NATO. Nevertheless, Georgian parliamentary chairman Zurab Zhvania showed Moscow how the
new "Great Game" was to be played. He requested that the international community, and NATO, counter Russian "incitement" of Abkhazian separatists.

Many Russian observers find it difficult to trust the Georgian president when
it comes to NATO expansion and consistently cast him in the role of villain. They
recalled that it was he who, as Gorbachev's foreign minister, concurred with Ger-

---

[322]Shermatova, in *Moskovskie novosti,* No. 29 (20–27 July 1997). See also Shermatova
interview with Boris Agapov, Security Council deputy chief in charge of Caucasus affairs,
Moscow News, No. 34 (4–10 Sept 1997).

[323]See, e.g., Natal'ia Prikhodko, "NATO aktiviziruetsia. Moskva tozhe. Rezul'taty poka
raznye" [NATO Becomes More Active, Russia Too: The Results Are Still Different], *Nezavisimaia gazeta* (25 Feb 1998). Prikhodko advocated a greater Russian economic involvement in Moldova.

[324]See comment by Gaiaz Alimov, "Gensek NATO proinspektiroval Kavkaz" [NATO
General Secretary Inspected the Caucasus], *Izvestiia* (1 Oct 1998).

man reunification. Because they "allowed" the new Germany to join NATO, She-vardnadze and Gorbachev often are held responsible for a policy that, as one correspondent put it in February 1997, "paved the way east for NATO, something that the military bloc intends to achieve without firing a single shot."[325] Even a Shevardnadze visit to Kiev was viewed suspiciously by Russian observers, some of whom also connected the Solana trip to Madeleine Albright's talks in Moscow, scheduled for a few weeks later.[326] No one spoke of these events as coincidence.

The linkages here may seem whimsical to some, paranoic to others. The reality is that one should not expect Russia to view the sequence of events in Transcaucasia any other way. The well-established notion that the "West," and above all the United States, was working against CIS integration in the South was merely given wider credibility in Russian nationalist circles by Solana's various travels. Moscow was especially angered when Solana remarked in Moldova on 10 February that the Russian 14th Army should be withdrawn from the Transdniestr, in compliance with an OSCE recommendation. The very next day, Yurii Baturin (Defense Council), also in Chisinau, responded that the Army would withdraw only when the conflict was resolved, not when NATO demanded it.[327]

A long report by Aman Tuleev, at that time RF Minister for CIS Cooperation and later Governor of the Kemerovskaia Oblast, laid bare the conviction that the CIS, so long ignored in Europe and North America as irrelevant, was now perceived in the West as a vehicle for renewed Russian expansionism. Published in the widely-read *Rossiiskaia gazeta,* Tuleev's treatise opened with a call for closer economic cooperation within the CIS, but concentrated on what he believed was the ill-treatment of Russians and Russian culture in the "Near Abroad." Without

---

[325]Sergei Maslov, "Javier Solana on the Trail of 'Cold Peace,'" *Komsomol'skaia pravda* (13 Feb 1997), FBIS-SOV, No. 034. See also "Ivan Rybkin vzvolnoval shar zemnoi" [Ivan Rybkin Shakes up the Globe], *Rossiiskaia gazeta* (13 Feb 1997), and Aleksandr Rybkin, "Chem nedovolen Shevardnadze" [What Dissatisfies Shevardnadze], *Rossiiskaia gazeta* (25 March 1997).

[326]See, e.g., "Zavershilsia vizit Shevardnadze v Kiev" [Shevardnadze's Visit to Kiev Is Over], *Nezavisimaia gazeta* (15 Feb 1997); "Moskva kak magnit pritiagivaet zarubezhenykh viziterov" [Moscow, Like a Magnet, Attracts Foreign Visitors], *Nezavisimaia gazeta* (19 Feb 1997); Aleksandr Krasulin, "Madlen Olbreit priblizhaetsia k granitsam Rossii. I NATO . . . tozhe?" [Madeleine Albright Approaches the Russian Border: And NATO as Well?], *Rossiiskaia gazeta* (20 Feb 1997); Edgar Cheporov, "Vo chto oboidetsia SShA rasshirenie NATO" [How Much Will the U.S. Spend on NATO Enlargement], *Rossiiskaia gazeta* (26 Feb 1997).

[327]Baturin was quoted on Radio Romania, Bucharest (12 February 1997), FBIS-SOV, No. 029.

ever mentioning NATO, he argued that "Clinton's second term is marked by the desire to prevent the integration of the CIS countries." Washington especially disliked the idea of East Slavic unity, that is, Russia, Ukraine and Belarus. Moreover, whereas a few Russian writers were encouraged by Ankara's early reluctance to support NATO expansion, Tuleev sided with the majority by accusing Turkey of doing all it could "to prevent Russia's integration with the Central Asian States."[328] This seige mentality was important because it was given voice by a central figure in Yeltsin's liaison mechanism with CIS.

NATO's hand was seen everywhere. For example, on 1 March Anatolii Kurganov harked back to the Solana tour of the Caucausus and Moldova, angrily denouncing it as a "reconnaissance" and an attempt to intimidate Russia. NATO is hinting that the "door is open" to membership even for former Soviet republics and is setting the stage for further "anti-Russia" political campaigning in the former Soviet Central Asian region, Kurganov complained.[329] Apparent differences in the level of reception given NATO visitors by Armenia and Azerbaijan were seized upon by Russian journalists as signs of the degree to which either country might be expected to stay in CIS.[330] As the Russia-NATO agreement approached, more commentary was heard about regional security systems and the value of a CIS "zone" of its own.

The tenuousness of Russia's links to Transcaucasia through the CIS and bilateral agreements was revealed in another interview granted by Shevardnadze, shortly after the Founding Act was signed. Speaking to a radio audience on 2 June, Shevardnadze noted first how greatly his country's economic recovery depended on the World Bank and the EBRD. Acknowledging that Georgia still needed Russia's help with Abkhazia, he was nevertheless skeptical of the ability of either

---

[328]For the Tuleev report, *Rossiiskaia gazeta* (15 Feb 1997), FBIS-SOV, No. 033. See also "Turtsiia vystupila protiv rasshireniia NATO" [Turkey Speaks out Against NATO Expansion], *Nezavisimaia gazeta* (30 Jan 1997), and Sergei Putilov, "Politicheskaia nestabil'nost' v Ankare" [The Political Instability in Ankara], *Nezavisimaia gazeta* (12 Feb 1997). For a glowing Russian report on its "peacekeeping" activities in the CIS, see Sergei V. Lavrov, RF ambassador to the UN, "Peacekeeping and Conflict Settlement in the Region of the Commonwealth of Independent States," *ACE: Analysis of Current Events* 10, No. 3–4 (1998): 3–4.

[329]Anatolii Kurganov, "Solana Goes to CIS on Reconnaissance: On the Outcome of the recent Lightning Visit by NATO Secretary General Javier Solana to Chisinau, Tbilisi, Yerevan, and Baku], *Rossiiskaia gazeta* (1 March 1997), FBIS-SOV, No. 062.

[330]See, e.g., "Yerevan ne budet prosit'sia v NATO" [Yerevan Will Not Ask for Admission to NATO], *Nezavisimaia gazeta* (14 Feb 1997), and "Aliev' za tesnoe sotrudnichestvo s al'iansom" [Aliev Supports Closer Cooperation with the Alliance], *Nezavisimaia gazeta* (15 Feb 1997).

Russia or the CIS to resolve that conflict. Shevardnadze welcomed the treaty between Russia and Ukraine and the Russia-NATO Founding Act, but noted that the division of the Black Sea Fleet, by ignoring Georgia's claim, "is injustice on Russia's part." A later Tbilisi news release announced that when Shevardnadze arrived in Madrid for the NATO Summit he would attempt to persuade NATO to get more involved in the Abkhazia conflict, perhaps even usurping the OSCE and Russia's peacekeeping operations there. It was clear that the Georgian president now saw membership in the CIS as a matter of expediency, and NATO was a more appealing association. This too was a matter of great concern for Russia.[331]

As a Black Sea nation and land link between Russia and Turkey, Georgia holds the key to Russia's relations with NATO in the South. The long-lasting crisis in Abkhazia, where Russian "peace-keeping" troops maintain a semblance of order, is a symptom of that relationship. The area contains a large and important piece of the Black Sea shoreline and provides Russia with access to the Transcaucasian interior. When talks over the future of Abkhazia moved to Geneva in July 1997, Shevardnadze urged that the United Nations serve as the umbrella agency for finding solutions to the situation in Abkhazia. Abkhazian leaders objected to a UN presence and Russia (23 July) extended the period of its peacekeepers' tour of duty. The Russian press fretted that a UN role would mean NATO troops in Georgia, and Moscow officials said that if any such proposal went forward Russia would veto it in the UN Security Council. As the crisis in Abkhazia intensified, with new bursts of violence in 1998, Russian observers accused Shevardnadze of intriguing to call in NATO troops.[332]

---

[331] For the interview with Shevardnadze, Radio Tbilisi Network (2 June 1997), FBIS-SOV, No. 107. Georgia joined the CIS at a Heads of State summit in Ashgabat, December 1993; Azerbaijan rejoined, having withdrawn in 1992 to observer status, at the same meeting. The Russian rationale for excluding Georgia from any discussion on dividing the Black Sea Fleet was that a Protocol on this matter was adopted at a CIS summit in January, 1992. Azerbaijan, which was then a member, received a few ships from the Caspian Flotilla. See *REDA 1992*, Vol. 2.

In August Georgia officially gave up its claims to part of the Black Sea Fleet (Interfax, 23 Aug 1997). For an irate Russian commentary, see Albert Kochetkov, "Gruzinskie vitiazi v lis'ei shkure" [Georgian Heroes Wear Fox Pelts], *Rossiiskaia gazeta* (6 May 1997).

[332] See, e.g., Sergei Samuylov, "Perspektivy kollektivnoi bezopasnosti v SNG" [Perspectives on Collective Security in the CIS], *Nezavisimaia gazeta* (14 April 1998), Igor Maksimychev, "Otkrytyi iuzhnyi flang kontinenta" [The Open Southern Flank of the Continent], *Nezavisimaia gazeta* (14 April 1998). A full year later, Russian border guards began to withdraw from Abkhazia; but regular "peacekeeping" Russian forces remained.

At least one gaping hole in Russia's Transcaucasia network was patched, temporarily, when Yeltsin and the president of Azerbaijan, Heydar Aliev, signed a Treaty of Friendship, Cooperation and Security, on 3 July 1997. Long-standing complications in the relationship between the two countries were smoothed out and Yeltsin agreed to make a solution of the Nagorno-Karabakh conflict a priority. Mutual aid in the event of an outside threat to either side was a vital part of the agreement, and both countries condemned separatism. This Treaty, and an announcement a few days later that the oil pipeline connecting Baku to Novorossisk via Groznyy (Chechnya) would be operable by the autumn, were the result of intensive negotiations, accelerated, insiders said, by the specter of NATO countries challenging Russia's influence in Transcaucasia.[333]

Negotiations faltered on several occasions during the summer and the pipeline project was only finally confirmed by the first week of September. So there was nothing certain for Russia where Chechnya and Azerbaijan were concerned, and visits by Chechen leaders to both Baku and Tbilisi upset Moscow. The atmosphere in Transcaucasia was charged up in late August when Levon Ter-Petrosyan, then the Armenian president, and Yeltsin signed a treaty like that signed between Moscow and Baku. But Russia's accord with Armenia had a substantial military cooperative content, which was absent in Moscow's deal with Azerbaijan. Moscow and Yerevan agreed to immediate consultation if either side was threatened by a third party, guaranteed a common defense, and set the stage for general military cooperation.[334]

Although the truce between Armenia and Azerbaijan over Nagorno-Karabakh and the peace in Abkhazia continued to hold, Russia found itself standing on the sidelines as the three Transcaucasian republics followed diverging diplomatic paths. Opinion surveys taken in Armenia during the late summer 1997 suggested that up to a million citizens would consider joining the union between Russia and Belarus, prompting nervous Armenian officials to reject a call for a referendum on the matter. On the other hand, Turkish influence in Azerbaijan was drawing that country further into the NATO orbit. Indeed, foreign ministers from Turkey and Azerbaijan issued a joint statement on 9 September in which the former

---

[333]A synopsis of the treaty was printed by ITAR-TASS (3 July 1997), and the entire Treaty was published the next day. The pipeline agreement, which was briefly interrupted by Chechen demands that it have equal participation with Russia and Azerbaijan, was announced by Interfax (7 July 1997); the three-way treaty was printed by Turan (Baku), on 14 July.

[334]For the Armenian president's evaluation of this treaty and growing Armenia-Russia ties, see *Moskovskie novosti,* No. 35 (31 Aug–7 Sept 1997). The accord was printed by Interfax (29 Aug 1997).

country promised to help "expand Azerbaijan's ties with NATO countries."[335] Both censured Armenia for occupying Azerbaijan territory and refused to restore political, economic, or commercial relations with Yerevan until the conflict was settled. Plans to implement a project linking an oil pipeline between Baku and the Turkish terminal at Ceyhan were confirmed. Thus, through Turkey, NATO's direct involvement in the Black Sea continued to grow.

In October a Russian-language newspaper published in Baku noted a striking difference in the tone of dealings between individual Transcaucasian countries and NATO. Armenia seemed to pay little attention to a regional tour by Robert Hunter, head of the U.S. mission at NATO, while Georgia and Azerbaijan made much of his visit. The Georgian foreign minister spoke of expanding contacts with NATO; and the Azeri president praised NATO expansion to the East. It was only in Azerbaijan that Hunter met with a defense minister. The article turned the question of Transcaucasian interest in NATO into a discussion on whether NATO was likely to get involved in conflicts in the region. Pointing to the Sea Breeze-97 exercise, President Aliev's answer was "yes," and he left readers with the vague impression that a "separatist" crisis in Crimea might even lead to a collective NATO response on Ukraine's behalf. The dilemma faced by Russia in the Transcaucasus remained troublesome and in early 1998 the perceived threat to Russia's interests in the Caspian region was such that it became a subject of concern in leading academic journals.[336]

Russia's presence in the South Caucasus was challenged in the spring of 1998 as Georgia again made noises about seeking NATO help in Abkhazia, where a truce was broken by Abkhazian attacks on Georgians in Gali and elsewhere. Although the tense peace was restored, Russians remained wary of Shevardnadze's intentions. The appointment of David Tevzadze, former head of the military inspectorate and a graduate of NATO training courses, as the new Georgian defense minister in late April gave Moscow pause.

As Georgian parliamentarians lobbied American congressmen to become more involved in the region, mostly to counter the predominance of Russia and Iran, Aleksei Gromyko resurrected the term "Great Game" for the diplomatic and economic competition in the region separating the Black and Caspian Seas. A long time observer of the international scene from Moscow, Gromyko warned that

---

[335] *Turan* (Baku) (9 Sept 1997), FBIS-SOV, No. 253.

[336]See, e.g., S. Kolchin, "Neft' i gaz Kaspiia: strategicheskie interesy Rossii" [Oil and Gas of the Caspian: Russia's Strategic Interests], *Mirovaia ekonomika i mezhdunarodnye otnosheniia,* No. 3 (February 1998): 97–103; for Aliev and the remarks on the Hunter visits, see *Baku Zerkalo,* No. 42 (25 Oct 1997), FBIS-SOV, No. 318.

Russia could not afford to lose influence in this, its "zone of vital interests."[337] He was worried above all about American "encroachments" and foresaw Washington going so far as to mitigate its animosity towards Iran in exchange for greater influence in the Caspian Sea basin.

Gromyko's admonitions served as a follow-up to a bitter essay by Vladimir Mukhin, who reproached Azerbaijan for campaigning against the "completely legal" Russian-Armenian links, and for catering to nascent antagonisms against Moscow in the United States, Turkey, Kazakhstan and Uzbekistan. Ukraine also was a target of angry Russian accusations of pandering to NATO in return for access to pipelines from Azerbaijan and Turkmenistan routed through Georgia to the Black Sea.[338]

In addition to its obvious geographic edge, Russia does have a few political cards to play in the competition for influence in the territory of the former USSR. One of these is the presence of large ethnic Russian populations in many of the new countries. Another is the fact that communist parties in what Russians call the "Near Abroad" share Moscow's misgivings about the Atlantic Alliance. In July 1997, for example, Moldovan communists demonstrated against NATO expansion and anti-NATO parliamentarians in Ukraine, Belarus, and Latvia issued a joint statement (with their Russian counterparts) to parliamentarians and peoples of NATO countries, urging them not to ratify the decisions made at Madrid. That communist solidarity remained important was confirmed by an agreement reached at an informal meeting between leaders of the Russian, Armenian, Belarusian, Moldovan and Ukrainian CP's in October 1998. A joint press release declared their intent to step up cooperation in a wide variety of activities, among them their use of the mass media and political slogans to have their views heard. Even the most moderate mainstream Russian observers exhorted readers that Americans had a messianic urge to control the oil-rich Caspian Basin.[339]

---

[337]Gromyko, "Novaia 'velikaia igra' " [The New "Great Game"], *Nezavisimaia gazeta* (20 Aug 1998). This piece, with map, took up an entire page. On the Georgian lobbying, see Revaz Adamia (Georgian parliamentarian), "Uncle Sam in the Southern Caucasus: Global Policeman and Hegemon, or Troubleshooter and Partner?" *ACE: Analysis of Current Events*, 10, No. 7–8 (July/Aug 1998): 16–17.

[338]Kirill Viatkin, "Starina Ukraina trebuet novoi politiki so storony Rossii" [The Old Ukraine Demands a New Policy on the Part of Russia], *Nezavisimaia gazeta* (22 July 1998); Mukhin, "Prichiny anti-Rossiiskoi pozitsii riada gosudarstv SNG" [The Cause of Anti-Russian Positions in Several CIS States], *Nezavisimaia gazeta* (24 July 1998). See also a Ukrainian commentary, Yana Stafil'na, "Chi prinese NATO mir na Kavkaz?" [Will NATO Bring Peace to the Caucasus], *Holos Ukrainy* (8 July 1998).

[339]See, e.g., Gaiaz Alimov, "SShA pribiraiut Kaspii k rukam" [The USA Takes the Caspian in Hand], *Izvestiia* (16 Sept 1998). For the communist press release, see ITAR-TASS (20 Oct 1998).

The large Russian population and communists in Kazakhstan, which has a large share of the Caspian shoreline, also took up the NATO issue as that country pondered its own relationships with Russia. Solana arrived in Almaty in the Spring of 1997 to arrange Kazakhstan's participation in a joint NATO-Central Asiatic military exercise planned for the following September. At that time some Russian military commentators were sharply critical of what they believed to be a Kazakh attempt to "blackmail" Russia.[340] The problem was compounded for Russian nationalists on 10 September when the prime ministers of Kazakhstan and Turkey signed a wide-ranging trade, economic, and technical cooperation agreement in Almaty. It seemed to some at the time that Russia's only strong "fall back" in the region was Iran, a country that supported Russia and Turkmenistan against Azerbaijan and Kazakhstan in the dispute over the way in which Caspian Sea oil should be divided.

At any rate, it is extremely unlikely that Kazakhstan will be swayed from an enduring association with Russia. Kazakh president, Nursultan Nazarbaev, has been a strong supporter of the CIS since its inception in December 1991, and has consistently recommended that it be strengthened. Moreover, a Declaration of Eternal Friendship and Allied Relations signed by him and Yeltsin on 6 July 1998 confirmed the unusual closeness of the two countries. Agreeing to act jointly if either state was threatened, the two presidents agreed to cooperate in "the multi-polar world that is taking shape to overcome bloc approaches and avoid the drawing of new dividing lines in international relations." Active participation in the PfP notwithstanding, this pronouncement mirrored Kazakhstan's distaste for the single bloc potential that NATO represents.[341] A similar position was taken by Umirserik Kasenov, whose long two-part essay on Kazakhstan's national security was printed in Almaty in September, 1998. His central point echoed Kozhokin's earlier analysis; that is, Kazakhstan cannot defend its huge borders without the help of a major power, necessarily Russia. Kasenov judged that NATO expansion was not a threat to Kazakhstan and recommended that his country not join any military bloc opposed to NATO. Implicit in his observations was a greater concern, in the long run, about China.[342]

---

[340]See Andrei Grozin, Vitalii Khliupin, "Armiia Kazakhstana" [Army of Kazakhstan], *Nezavisimoe voennoe obozrenie*, No. 23 (28 June–4 July 1997). See also Aleksei Pushkov, "Amerika—novaia sverkhderzhava Evrazii" (14 Nov 1997), *op. cit.*

[341]*Rossiiskaia gazeta* (*Ekonomicheskii Soiuz* Supplement) (18 July 1998), FBIS-SOV, No. 208. See also "Zachem Nazarbaev priezzhal v Moskvu?" [Why Did Nazarbaev Come to Moscow?], *Nezavisimaia gazeta* (22 Jan 1998).

[342]*Delovaia nedelia* [Almaty] (11 Sept 1998), FBIS-SOV, No. 292. Kasenov died before this essay, and its second part, appeared. For another view of Russia-Kazakhstan relations, on the closeness of their economies, see Tagzhan Kasenova, "Rossiiskii krisis opasen dlia Kazakhstana" [The Russian Crisis Is Dangerous for Kazakhstan], *Delovaia nedelia* (3 July 1998).

Announcements of an Azerbaijan protocol and accord with NATO, and of NATO military training sessions in Uzbekistan and Kyrgyzstan (Interfax, 19 Jan), gave Russian nationalists further reason to feel that the Alliance was "closing in" on them.[343] Coupled with the near frenzied international competition for access to, and control of, Caspian Sea oil exploration and development, these war games fuelled Russian anxieties about the vulnerability of its southern flank. The long Black Sea coastline of Abkhazia suddenly took on greater strategic significance for Moscow, and Azerbaijan's and Georgia's flirting with NATO became more ominous.

Russian unease about American designs in the Caspian Sea area was set out clearly by Sergei Putilov, who claimed that the Pentagon recently had decided to create a mechanism for protecting U.S. oil and gas interests in Azerbaijan, Kazakhstan and Turkmenistan. Quoting the *U.S. News and World Report,* Putilov charged that NATO was a vehicle for incorporating the Caspian region into an American "sphere of military-political influence." The communist press followed up on his theme aggressively.[344]

Even though the Caspian Sea region is in great danger of destabilization and a consequent U.S./NATO presence, one Russian observer noted fatalistically, his country still had a few cards to play. Neither NATO nor the United States have the means to provide security to the former USSR regions that border on China. As these areas grow in importance, Russia's role must be appreciated. Russia and Kazakhstan, also worried about its own long border with China, finally agreed on the division of the Caspian seabed at the end of April, putting an end to at least some of their shared uncertainties. The agreement called for the demilitarization of the sea itself, leaving only the seabed to be divided up into national sectors. Russian journalists interpreted the Russia-Kazakhstan accord as a way to forestall a larger U.S.-NATO presence on the Caspian.[345]

---

[343]See, e.g., "Novye ucheniia v Uzbekistane" [New (Military) Studies in Uzbekistan], *Nezavisimaia gazeta* (23 Jan 1998).

[344]Zyuganov, "Ne igrat' sud'boi Rossii" [Don't Play with the Future of Russia], *Sovet-skaia Rossiia* (27 Feb 1997), Safronchuk, "Kto zhe pobedit vo 'vtorom raunde?" [Who Will Win in the Second Round?], *Sovetskaia Rossiia* (27 Feb 1997), and "Koshmar rasshireniia NATO" [The Nightmare of NATO Expansion], *Sovetskaia Rossiia* (25 Feb 1997). Putilov, "Bosniiskii stsenarii proetsiruetsia na Kaspii" [A Bosnian Scenario Is Projected for the Caspian], *Nezavisimoe voennoe obozrenie*, No. 8 (27 Feb–5 Mar 1998). Putilov pointed to NATO-member Turkey's military instructors in Azerbaijan and the participation of American and Turkish troops in the Tsentrazbat-97 military exercises in Central Asia.

[345]Aleksei Baliev, "Kaspii—obshchee dostoianie" [The Caspian Is a Common Asset], *Rossiiskaia gazeta* (15 Apr 1998). On the general premonition of trouble in the Caspian, see Maksimychev, "Otkrytyi iuzhnyi flang kontinenta," *op. cit.,* and Samuylov, "Perspektivy kollektivnoi bezopasnosti v SNG," *op. cit.*

On the other hand, PfP activities in Central Asia grew noticeably. In June, NATO Military Committee Chairman Klaus Naumann met with parliamentarians in Astana, Kazakhstan's new capital city, and told them that an enlarged NATO would need closer ties with Central Asia, and with Russia. The Central Asian Battalion-98 (Tsentrazbat) exercise in Kazakhstan, Uzbekistan and Kyrgyzstan was confirmed for September (Interfax-Kazakhstan, 29 June).[346]

Crises in the Balkans, above all in Kosovo, the START II ratification debate, and increased tensions in the Baltic drew Russian media attention away from Transcaucasia and Central Asia in the spring of 1998—but never completely. In early June, for example, a writer for *Pravda* predicted a "large new Caucasus commotion" that would serve as a "springboard" for NATO absorption of Georgia and Azerbaijan.[347] Turkey would be a central player in drawing these two countries further into the NATO orbit, creating a three-way strategic alliance and diminishing Russia's influence in the region. The Russian military press, in its turn, described Turkey's growing military strength as "very dangerous," for it gave that country the means to "dictate its will" on "small" neighboring countries.[348]

In addition to imputations about Turkey's resurgent expansionism, the U.S. Congress was accused of supporting new NATO momentum in the South Caucasus. Shevardnadze and Tevzadze were deprecated as leading individual facilitators of United Nations-NATO activities designed to turn the Abkhazian conflict into a "Bosnian scenario." By the end of the year, Tevzadze was calling for new military treaties with Russia "to replace outdated ones" (Interfax, 24 Dec). He made it plain that his ministry was not much interested in coalition CIS armed forces and that Russia's military bases in Georgia were to come under close scrutiny. Tevzade's remarks struck a very sensitive chord in Moscow. They followed by only a few days a CIS Defense Ministers' Council meeting at which Igor

---

[346]For caustic Russian commentary on this NATO exercise, see Madina Abdulaeva, "Sovmestnye ucheniia v Uzbekistane" [Joint Training in Uzbekistan], *Nezavisimaia gazeta* (9 June 1998). See also an earlier piece, "Tsentral'no Aziatskii Soiuz prevrashchaetsia v voennyi blok" [Central Asian Union Is being Transformed into a Military Bloc], *Nezavisimaia gazeta* (20 Dec 1997).

[347]Mariia Mamikonyan, "Everything Is Only Just beginning: The Specter of NATO in the Caucasus Could Materialize," *Pravda* (6 June 1998), FBIS-SOV, No. 167.

[348]See Yurii Pankov, "Turtsiia narashchivaet voennuiu moshch'" [Turkey Increases Its Military Power], *Krasnaia zvezda* (9 July 1998).

Sergeev called for a common CIS defense policy, in light of "the unpredictable policy of the United States" (ITAR-TASS, 21 Dec).[349]

In late 1998, Moscow's alarm about centrifugal forces in the CIS and perceived NATO and U.S. inroads in Transcaucasia and Central Asia were mirrored in two significant studies. The first was prepared by G.A. Trofimenko, doctor of the historical sciences and the top "scientific associate" at ISKRAN. Trofimenko's detailed study targetted U.S. policy in the former Soviet Central Asia (Uzbekistan, Kyrgyzstan, Tajikistan, Turkmenistan), and Kazakhstan, CIS states in which an "active battle for influence" was underway. The battle was being waged to a certain extent, he contended, "against Russia," mostly for control of the region's considerable oil and gas resources. Brzezinski's infamous (in Russia) "A Geostrategy for Eurasia" came under attack once more as a proposal dictated by an "anti-Sovietism" now turned into an urge to "beat Russia" by any means. The PfP again was taken to task as an agent of American interests in the region, and Strobe Talbott was blamed for turning the Central Asian countries into pawns of a "propaganda campaign of the United States and its allies in an anti-Russian coalition"—whose purpose it was to diminish Russia's influence within the CIS. According to the author of the second paper, "American Methods of Expanding its Sphere of Influence," Georgia, Armenia and Kazakhstan are objectives of heightened diplomatic and economic pressure from the United States. Control of the Caspian Sea Basin is Washington's ultimate goal, Dmitrii Nikolaev concluded. A similar opinion was expressed in the ministry of foreign affairs journal, where S. Cherniavskii warned that NATO hoped to extend its sphere of influence to the Caucasus by using Turkey as its forward line.[350] Thus, all levels of expertise in Russia had restored the southern flank to its pride of place as the country's most vulnerable point.

---

[349]The Defense Ministers' Council meeting was held in Moscow, 21–22 December 1988, and the bombing of Iraq was very much on Sergeev's mind. Ten countries were represented, with only Moldova and Kyrgyzstan absent. For an unhappy Russian piece on Georgia's movement towards NATO, see "A Tbilisi aktivizruet sotrudnichestvo" [But Tbilisi Activates Collaboration], *Krasnaia zvezda* (20 Nov 1988).

[350]Cherniavskii, "Southern Caucasus in NATO Plans," *International Affairs* (Moscow), No. 6 (1998): 145–151; Nikolaev, "Amerikanskie metody rasshireniia sfer vliianiia. Vashington vytesniaet Rossiiu s Kavkaza i iz Tsentral'noi Azii" [American Methods of Expanding Its Influence: Washington Squeezes Russia out of the Caucasus and Central Asia], *Nezavisimoe voennoe obozrenie,* No. 46 (4–10 Dec 1998). See also "Mirotvorcheskaia agressiia NATO" [Peacekeeping Aggression of NATO], *ibid.,* No. 42, *op. cit.,* where Yurii Morozov and Igor Nekipelyi described NATO's actions in Kosovo as a model for a planned invasion of the North Caucasus (section 1.7, fn 10). Trofimenko, "Tsentral'noaziatskii region: politika i problemy neftegazovogo eksporta" [The Central Asian Region: U.S. Policy and Problems with Oil and Gas Exports], *SShA,* No. 11 (Nov 1998), 21–36.

The initial bombing of Iraq and subsequent strikes on specific targets high-lighted some of the sharpest divisions in the CIS. For example, Uzbekistan's gov-ernment said that the air strikes were justified (Interfax, 17 Dec), whereas Tajik-istan and Belarus condemned them. A body-blow was delivered to Russian policy in the CIS when, in early January 1999, Vafa Guludze, foreign policy adviser to Azerbaijan's president, made an informal proposal that Turkey, the United States, or NATO set up military bases in his country. Defense Minister Sefer Epiev spoke as well about the need for a military alliance between Azerbaijan, Turkey and the United States, to counter "policies pursued by Moscow." These observations were rendered while Azerbaijan's president, Aliev, was hospitalized in Turkey, but ob-viously were delivered as part of Azeri anger about Russian arms deliveries to Ar-menia. Repeated denials from Baku that these were anything but idle musings were not believed in Moscow, where the specter of an American or NATO pres-ence in the South Caucasus was taken very seriously.[351] The Kosovo crisis accen-tuated Russia's worry. Azerbaijan was one of the few CIS states not to condemn NATO's air strikes, prompting Russian analysts to wonder if Baku was preparing to host planes for attacks on the Balkans.[352] From Moscow's perspective, the ad-monitions from Nikolaev and Cherniavskii were gaining credence.

The main test, however, was scheduled for 1999 when the CIS Collective Se-curity Pact came up for renewal after its first five-year term. Early in the year, Uzbekistan announced that it would not participate. Azerbaijan followed suit, but with less certainty. By mid-February, Kazakhstan, Kyrgyzstan, Armenia, Belarus and Russia were advocating renewal and Russian emissaries travelled to Tashkent and Baku to discuss the matter with Karimov and Aliev—with little success.[353]

---

[351]There were many very angry articles, e.g., "Zachem ofitsial'nye litsa delaiut neofit-sial'nye zaiavleniia. Segodnia vopros o natovskoi voennoi baze pod Baku ne stoit. A zav-tra?" [Why Officials Make Unofficial Statements: The Question of a NATO Military Base Near Baku Not on the Agenda Today—But Tomorrow?], *Rossiiskaia gazeta* (30 Jan 1999), Boris Talov, "Ne nyzhen nam natovskii voin" [We Don't Need NATO Troops], *Rossiiskaia gazeta* (29 Jan 1999), "Baku gotov priniat' bazy NATO" [Baku Is Prepared to Accept NATO Bases], *Nezavisimoe voennoe obozrenie,* No. 3 (29 Jan–4 Feb 1999), Asya Gadzhizade, "Azerbaidzhan stoit na svoei" [Azerbaijan Stands Its Ground], *Nezavisimaia gazeta* (2 Feb 1999), and *Rossiiskaia gazeta* (27 Jan 1999).

[352]See, e.g., Nurani, "Budet li a Azerbaidzhane voennye bazy NATO?" [Will NATO Military Bases Appear in Azerbaijan?], *Rossiiskie vesti,* No. 10 (10–17 March 1999); Yurii Nikolaev, "Vzgliad iz Moskvy" [View from Moscow], *ibid.*

[353]On this, see "Mir i Rossiia. Nel'zia razdeliat' gosudarstva" [Russia and the World: States Must Not Be Divided], *Rossiiskaia gazeta* (12 Feb 1999), for an account of the dis-cussion of the issue between Karimov and Seleznev; and Vitalii Strugovets, "Proshchai brat-stvo po oruzhiiu?" [Goodbye to Military Brotherhood?], *Krasnaia zvezda* (5 Feb 1999).

Of the former USSR republics, Kazakhstan, Kyrgyzstan, Tajikistan, Armenia, Moldova and Belarus stood firmly behind Russia's position on Kosovo in March. The CIS Defense Ministers Council unanimously opposed NATO's action, calling it "inhumane" and illegal because it was not sanctioned by the UN.[354] Georgia's response was ambiguous, but Shevardnadze did not condemn NATO policy. Ukraine hedged and, while not agreeing with Russia directly, at first voiced concern over the Alliance's attack on a sovereign state without a clear mandate from the UN Security Council. On the 26th, however, Foreign Minister Tarasyuk called the air strikes "unacceptable" (see section 4). The governments of Azerbaijan, Latvia and Estonia, however, approved the NATO strikes against the Serbs and Baku even offered to send a token number of soldiers to participate alongside Turkish troops if land forces were used (Interfax, 25 March). In the meantime, Russian journalists continued to insist that the entire Transcaucasian region was a target for oil-greedy governments and imply that the military buildup there was part of a much larger "Western" scheme. NATO was being wielded as Washington's "iron fist," one journalist concluded.[355] The United States, Turkey and NATO were portrayed as seducers enticing Georgia and Azerbaijan into their parlors with visions of strength and prosperity.[356] Typical of this growing vision was an analysis offered in May by Aleksandr Ruzskii, who gave notice that NATO's actions in the Balkans marked a prelude to encroachments against Russian interests in the CIS. Dredging up the 1941 analogy, Ruzskii reminded readers that Hitler delayed his attack on Russia so as to pacify Yugoslavia first. He concluded

---

[354]ITAR-TASS (25 March 1999). This report did not say who attended the meeting, held in Moscow; only that it was chaired by Sergeev. See also Vladimir Yermolin, "Ministerstvo oborony stran SNG ogranichilis' sovmestnyi zaiavleniei" [CIS Ministers of Defense Make Only a Joint Statement], *Izvestiia* (26 March 1999).

[355]Vladimir Kuznechevskii, "NATO—zheleznyi kulak Ameriki" [NATO Is America's Iron Fist], *Rossiiskaia gazeta* (27 March 1999).

[356]See, e.g., Andrei Korbut, "Gde neft', tam i konflikty" [Where There Is Oil, There Are Conflicts], *Nezavisimoe voennoe obozrenie,* No. 8 (4–10 March 1999); Safronchuk, "Est' li predel rasshireniiu NATO na vostok?" [Is There a Limit to NATO Expansion Eastward?], *Sovetskaia Rossiia* (16 March 1999), who saw expansion as part of a U.S. plan to control oil and gas resources in the Caucasus and Central Asia. For broader explanation and warning: Vladimir Vedernikov, "NATO khochet otvechat' za Blizhnii vostok" [NATO Wants to Be Responsible for the Middle East], *Izvestiia* (4 March 1999), and Natal'ia Itrapetova, "Urok dlia vsekh stran SNG" [A Lesson for All CIS Countries], *Nezavisimaia gazeta* (1 April 1999).

that CIS territory (Moldova, Azerbaijan, and perhaps even Crimea) were next in NATO's "grand scheme" for a new world order.[357]

Thus, from the point of view of Russian analysts, the Great Game was being played intensely in Transcaucasia and Central Asia, with powerful Washington-led NATO players closing in on a weakening Moscow-led CIS team.

CONCLUSIONS

The foregoing history of Moscow's reactions to NATO expansion and its "ripple effects" sheds light on the intuitive preferences that have and will shape the decision-making process in Russia. Having said that, one cannot avoid the implications for Moscow of the rapidly changing international circumstances in late 1998 and early 1999. In the mind's eye of the Russian government, and increasingly the general population, a new world order is emerging while their country stands by as helpless observer. Even the most outspoken nationalists were caught off guard as their mostly rhetorical prognostications actually appear to be coming true. A new world order characterized by a United Nations diminishing in influence and NATO behaving as the world's policeman forces Russian policy planners to re-think their place in the world. The UN Security Council had provided Russia stature as a player in world affairs, but Moscow's veto may now have lost much of its value. The Founding Act has not been a substitute, because NATO, the JPC notwithstanding, is an organization where Russian opinion counts for little. At least this is how Russia's media sees it.[358]

Until recently, few Russians believed that NATO's post-Soviet eastern relationships posed an immediate military threat to them, but expansion was nonetheless a threatening phenomenon. Political and military leaders in Moscow, including Yeltsin and Primakov, regularly said that (undefined) "threats" to Russian security still existed. Until 1999, the government in Moscow was more concerned about the possibility of isolation from Europe than it was of any military danger. Previous outbursts of anger and feelings of helplessness generated by spe-

---

[357]Ruzskii, "Preliuda k novomu pokhodu na vostok. NATO gotovit pochvu dlia perenosa balkanskogo stsenariia na territoriiu SNG" [Prelude to a New Campaign in the East: NATO Is Preparing the Means to Shift the Balkan Scenario to CIS Territory], *Nezavisimoe voennoe obozrenie*, No. 18 (14–20 May 1999).

[358]This opinion is expressed clearly in Nadezhda Arbatova, "Samyi tiagostnyi urok poslednego vremeni" [The Most Depressing Lesson of Modern Times], *Nezavisimaia gazeta* (6 April 1999).

cific Western action in the Balkans and against Iraq had been fleeting, when such actions were mandated by the United Nations. A real sense of danger emerged after NATO began acting "out of zone" and behaving, according to many Russian observers, as "vigilantes" outside the framework of international law and the strictures of the UN Security Council. The truth of such charges may be moot; but the fact that both Russia's political leaders and its general population have come to believe them is significant. Among other things, the widespread notion that only Russia's foreign policy elite was concerned about NATO expansion surely can be set aside now as dead wrong.

The publicity generated by proponents of NATO enlargement over the last few years unwittingly has revealed the nature of the dilemma faced by Russia. Panels, conferences, symposia, and dinner speeches on the subject of enlargement were common fare in NATO countries well before the actual admission of three new members. These proceedings tended to be dominated by generals, admirals, senior bureaucrats, academics, and advisers to government agencies, many of whom had vested interests in the enhancement of NATO. There was astonishingly little public debate in the West on the subject of NATO *per se,* although the very reason for its founding had gone the way of the "Soviet threat." Even the Alliance's new Strategic Concept, calling for "out of zone" activities, was greeted in the West with thundering silence. The Kosovo crisis hauled NATO out into the Western public eye, but the contentious points are vastly different than they would have been a mere year ago.

During the limited discussion of expansion itself, NATO was portrayed by advocates as the sole safeguard of European and North American security, leaving little room for serious discussion of alternative security arrangements. Enlargement was defended, when necessary, in historical terms: bringing East and East Central European peoples back into Europe; in political terms: to ensure democratic development and European stability; in economic terms: wider markets; and in strategic terms: to put an end to "dividing lines" in Europe. In short, bringing light into darkness. But few of the explanations stand up very well under the Russian gaze.

Assuming that the "reasons" are sincerely held to be true and worth acting upon for the most altruistic reasons, they still leave room for striking contradiction even to Western observers. To name but a few: new dividing lines are, in fact, being created in Europe, and the potential of such agencies as the OSCE, the WEU, and perhaps even the UN as security-providers is on the wane as NATO's profile grows. Most importantly, the "reasons" for expansion are driven directly and indirectly by NATO's attitude towards Russia.

Russians in their turn ask why NATO continues to endure at all if the reason for its creation—a Stalinist USSR—no longer exists. Russian strategists believe that the world is in danger of becoming unipolar, with NATO acting as an instrument of American global hegemony. [359] They much prefer a multipolar world in which the prerogatives for international intervention lie with the UN or, in Europe, with the OSCE. Russian international policy itself has not moved very far away from the concepts of "spheres of influence" and nuclear deterrence.

Moreover, Moscow's self-proclaimed sphere of influence is precisely what NATO appears now to be challenging. Peering out at the arguments for NATO expansion from behind the Kremlin wall, it is not hard to see why Russian analysts and nationalists worry that their country's influence on the Baltic and the Black Seas, in the Caspian basin, in the South Caucasus and even Central Asia might soon be greatly curtailed, even to the point of exclusion. It is not difficult to understand why some Russians interpret their rejection by the EU and the WTO as part of a larger process; nor can they help but interpret NATO expansion as a specific American attempt to keep them "in their place." Shrugging off such sentiments, no matter if their premises are false, may well be the greatest strategic mistake made by the West in the post–World War II years.

There is an important pyschological factor at play here. One cannot discount historical consciousness in any strategic debate. The rhetoric of conflict in former Yugoslavia is evidence enough of that. Russian philosophers and historians have pondered their country's place in Europe for centuries, many of them concluding from events of the Napoleonic era, the mid-century Crimean War, and the famous "Eastern Question," that Russia must expect rejection from a combined Europe. Tsarist ideologies laid a firm basis for a "them versus us" approach to the world long before the Marxist-Leninists gave the idea a singularly official stamp. The explanation that NATO's growth is a continuation of an historical contest between East and West may not be a correct one, but to humiliated Russians it rings true.

The collapse of the USSR left Russians scrambling to resurrect their organic history from the dustbin into which the CPSU had cast it. Evidence that a slavophile vision lurked beneath the surface of even the most openly "westernizing" groups emerged when the least aggressive opponent of expansion among Russia's major political leaders, Yavlinskii, warned that NATO's plans represent a psychological "rejection" of Russia. Yavlinskii drew a parallel with Germany in

---

[359]The communist media is, of course, filled with this type of analysis. For representative expressions from the Russian government press, see, e.g., Vladimir Kuznechevskii, "Plany NATO—na polimira" [NATO Plans Include Half the World], *Rossiiskaia gazeta* (16 April 1999), and "Svobodu—po ul'timatumu: SShA ob'iavili XXI vek epokhoi amerikanskikh standartov dlia vsego mira" [Freedom by Ultimatum. The USA Has Proclaimed the 21st Century as an Epoch of American Standards for the Entire World . . .], *Rossiiskaia gazeta* (7 May 1999). See also Grigorii Vanin, Aleksandr Zhilin, "Utogi voiny na Balkanakh iasny dazhe segodnia" [The Results of the War in the Balkans Are Clear Even Today], *Nezavisimaia gazeta* (10 April 1999).

1919, as did Gorbachev. For obvious reasons, the image of a new version of *Drang nach Osten* comes quickly and readily to the Russian mind.[360] One should not forget, indeed, that present day Russian politicians and journalists are almost all themselves products of the USSR. A mistrust of Western, and especially American, motivation was inculcated in them during their childhood school days and in their early professional careers. The stereotypes learned from the Soviet system of upbringing (*vospitanie*) cannot be discounted fully unless there are compelling reasons to cast them aside.

Russia's current state of severe economic crisis, political stalemate, and national humiliation makes scapegoating inevitable, and exponentially linked to the degree of chaos in Russia. The perception that NATO is at best indifferent to Russia's troubles, at worst delighting in them, is a psychological variable that has enormous implications for European security, and warrants far more careful analysis than it has received to date.

There have been political and economic consequences of NATO expansion in Russia as well. The prediction by Yavlinskii that NATO expansion would compel (or allow) the Russian industrial-military complex to demand more subsidies, and persuade the General Staff to keep the "threat from Europe" a priority held true until the end of May 1997. Yeltsin's dismissal of Rodionov and Samsonov ended the public squabbling over funds and the apparent confusion in the senior ranks, for awhile. The adoption of new military concepts, which gave priority to nuclear deterrence and even an acceptance of the principle of first nuclear strike, was plainly a result of Moscow's inability to fund anything else. But the new concepts were justified to the public in part by the radically altered balance of power caused by NATO's expansion eastward. Even the final approval of Russia's new military doctrine, in December 1998, was thrown to the wind when NATO attacked Yugoslavia. In May 1999, the RF military doctrine was placed under review once more.

Rokhlin's movement in support of Russia's Armed Forces was also a byproduct of economic and social problems faced by the military, but it too was shaped by the expansion of NATO. The movement's close ties to the Duma's Anti-NATO Commission and its prominent role in impeachment campaigns against Yeltsin, helped draw together wide ranging organizational opposition to the government.

---

[360]See, e.g., Maj.-Gen. Vagif A. Guseinov, "The "Renewal" of NATO and Russia's Security: The Cold War Era Is Being Replaced by an Era of Domination by the West," *Nezavisimoe voennoe obozrenie*, No. 14 (16–22 April 1999), FBIS-SOV, No. 505. Guseinov is a member of the Foreign and Defense Policy Council. For the nearly hysterical communist view, see Safronchuk, "Fashistov NATO—k sudu!" [Take the NATO Fascists to Court!], *Sovetskaia Rossiia* (5 May 1999).

Luzhkov's Fatherland and other nationalist parties and organizations have used NATO's growing strengh as a symbol of what they believe is wrong with Russia. And even the NDR, the largest mainstream party generally supportive of the government, included opposition to NATO expansion in its political platform. So has the "liberal" Yabloko.

It is from the Communist Party of Russia and its affiliates in the People's Patriotic Union that the most powerfully organized antipathy to NATO comes. It is they who, with Communist and Anti-NATO movements in Ukraine and Belarus, ensure that the question of NATO expansion is kept close to the forefront of the Russian political scene. The NATO question will be one of the few subjects on which all parties competing in the next State Duma (December 1999) and presidential (2000) elections will agree. Candidates will try to outdo each other in their patriotism.

Moreover, the Russian government is forced to oppose NATO expansion itself so as not to lose credibility with the voting public. In 1997 and 1998, the Kremlin found it difficult to defend itself from the CPRF's strident charges that Yeltsin, Chernomyrdin, Kiriyenko and phoenix-like Chubais were toadying to the IMF and Yeltsin's "friend Bill." Primakov replaced Kozyrev as foreign minister in part to dispel that image. Later, as prime minister, he made it absolutely clear that he was searching for a specific "Russian way" out of the country's doldrums. In addition, Primakov's new foreign minister, Ivanov, and several senior members of the newly promoted foreign policy team had long records of targeting NATO. Primakov's dismissal in the midst of the Kosovo crisis was not likely to generate much change in the Kremlin's vision of NATO. Whether they actually believe it or not, the entire Russian political spectrum now treats NATO expansion as a plot against Russia.

In so far as the West is concerned, Moscow has acted as a "spoiler" in the international arena. It stands in the way of NATO and American policies in the Balkans and the Middle East, refuses to condemn India for its nuclear test, pursues closer relations with China, and continues to sell both arms and nuclear technology to governments disliked in the West. These reflect traditional Soviet and Russian practices, to be sure, but current Russian intransigence is shaped also by its perception of NATO. One need mention only the continued failure of the State Duma to ratify (or even debate) START II to find an international manifestation in Russia of NATO expansion.

The "ripple effect" consequences referred to in this study were all predicted long ago by a wide cross-section of Russia's politicians and journalists, and by many observers in the West. It was expected that Russia would struggle to maintain and strengthen the CIS, and construct contingency partnerships with China, India, and Iran. It was pointed out regularly that Russia's military reform, and the military-industrial program, would be influenced by NATO decisions. No one doubted that NATO expansion eastward would have a powerful impact on the

Russian political arena and on Moscow's political elite. In short, NATO's decisions about enlargement and "out of zone" policing activities were made in full knowledge that the Russian government would be unpersuaded and angered. The degree to which anti-NATO and anti-American feelings would well up in Russia's public domain, however, was unexpected at both the government and pundit level in NATO countries. NATO's failure in this regard is inexplicable.

Furthermore, it is ironic that the old Soviet image of a rapacious West has resurfaced on Russian streets, and this time the sentiment is more spontaneous than orchestrated. NATO policy is by no means responsible for the overwhelming economic and political disarray that drives Russian grievance. Yet, as a result of its startling inability to understand Russian resentment of expansion, NATO has provided a convenient backboard against which angry Russians of all strata can vent their spleen.

The formal admission of Poland, the Czech Republic and Hungary is now history. The next round of additional memberships in NATO will be of far greater importance to Russia than the current one, for it will bring the Alliance still closer to Russia's borders and could include former Soviet republics. The renewed debate will likely be conducted in Russia under a new government and probably a new president. Moscow recognizes that NATO has the right to admit any legitimate candidate, and that all legitimate candidates have the right to apply for admission. It may be, however, that a considered delay would benefit all concerned parties.

The United Nations' Security Council will be one of the stakeholders in any future discussion about NATO enlargement, for the UN's credibility as a forum in which international conflicts can be resolved has been weakened by a stronger NATO. The future of the OSCE must be weighed into the bargain. An alternative to adding more members to NATO would be the regeneration of the PfP and the integration of Russia more fully into its undertakings. Eventually the PfP could serve as a basis for a new, all-European and North American security system. NATO as we now know it, dividing lines in Europe, and the final vestiges of the Cold War, might then finally fade away. A truly appropriate "geostrategy for Eurasia" could finally be found.

At any rate, for reasons that need not be explained further, it is incumbent upon NATO to comprehend fully the Russian understanding of NATO expansion eastward.

Russian Newspapers, News Agencies, and Other Sources

RUSSIAN NEWSPAPERS

The information listed here includes newspapers' titles, print runs, nominal owners, and general attitude in 1996–97. The information in this section was drawn in part from a "Daily Report Supplement," FBIS-SOV, No. 233-s (5 December 1995), and from later source descriptions by FBIS. Citations were made from other newspapers as well, but the papers themselves were not searched to the same extent as the ones listed here.

Dom i Otechestvo: a regular supplement to *Rossiiskaia gazeta* (see below), and organ of the party, Our Home is Russia (NDR).

Izvestiia: 600,000; Izvestiia Journalists Collective; daily; anti-communist; mixed on Yeltsin.

Komsomol'skaia pravda: 1.5 million; Journalists Collective; daily; supports economic reform; mixed on Yeltsin; often critical of the West; sensationalist.

Krasnaia zvezda: 110,000; Ministry of Defense; daily; military interest group paper.

Nezavisimaia gazeta: 55,000; Editorial Collective; 3 issues/week; pro-reform; financed by a consortium headed by tycoon Boris Berezovskii, former executive secretary of the CIS for whom an arrest warrant was issued in April 1999 (for money laundering).

Nezavisimoe voennoi obozrenie: a weekly published by *Nezavisimaia gazeta* (see above).

Novoe vremya: 25,000; Journalists Collective; weekly; pro-reform, emphasis on foreign policy; English version: *New Times.*

Pravda Rossii: CPRF; weekly supplement to both *Pravda* (when it is published) and *Sovetskaia Rossiia;* not published in 1998.

Rossiiskaia gazeta: 500,520; RF Council of Ministers; daily; prints government laws, decrees and edicts, and point of view.

Rossiiskie vesti: 130,000; Presidential Staff and RV Editorial Collective; daily; government paper.

Sovetskaia Rossiia: 250,000; "Independent People's" daily; the leading communist paper.

Zavtra: 100,000; private sponsorship; strongly communist and hostile to Yeltsin; anti-semitic; extremist.

NEWS AGENCIES, COLLECTIONS, AND INTERNET SOURCES

ITAR-TASS: the official state news agency, sponsored by the Russian Council of Ministers; its representative attends meetings of the Council of Ministers and its Presidium. Supportive of the Yeltsin government.

Interfax: an independent news agency, supportive usually of reform; has branch offices in Ukraine and Kazakhstan. According to FBIS the Interfax director serves with the presidential administration.

FBIS-SOV: Foreign Broadcast Information Service. Daily U.S. government translation service (Russian newspapers, TV, radio), carried on Internet via World News Connection.

REDA: J.L. Black, ed. *Russia and Eurasia Documents Annual* [REDA] (formerly *USSR Documents Annual*). Gulf Breeze, FL: Academic International Press. Two annual volumes of translated documents from the USSR and Russia, and statements by political, military and economic leaders, published annually since 1987. The collections include laws and policy pronouncements.

Further Reading

Afanas'evskii, Nikolai. "Osnovopolagaiushchii akt Rossiia-NATO" [The Russia-NATO Founding Act]. *Mezhdunarodnaia zhizn'*, No. 6 (1997): 8–12.

Arbatov, Alexei. "As NATO Grows, Start 2 Shudders." *New York Times* OP-ED (26 August 1997).

———. "Natsional'naia ideia i natsional'naia bezopasnost'" [The National Idea and National Security] *Mirovaia ekonomika i mezhdunarodnye otnosheniia*, No. 5 (May 1998): 5–21; No. 6 (June 1998): 5–19.

Armstrong, G.P. *Russia, the South Caucasus and the Caspian: A Handbook.* Ottawa: Directorate of Strategic Analysis Policy Group, Department of National Defence, D Strat A Research Note 98/05 (August 1998).

"Asmus, Ronald D., Richard L. Kugler, and F. Stephen Larrabee. "Building a New NATO." *Foreign Affairs* (September 1993): 28–40.

———. "NATO Expansion: The Next Steps." *Survival* 37, no. 1 (Spring 1995).

———. "What Will NATO Enlargement Cost?" *Survival* 38, no. 3 (Autumn 1996): 5–26.

Baker, Howard, Jr., Sam Nunn, Brent Scowcroft, and Alton Frye. "NATO: A Debate Recast." *New York Times* OP-ED (4 February 1998).

Bailes, Alyson J.K. "NATO Enlargement: The General Case." *ACE: Analysis of Current Events* 9, no. 5 (May 1997): 7–8.

Barry, C., ed. *Reforging The Transatlantic Relationship.* Washington, DC: Notre Dame Press, 1997.

Bebler, Anton. "A Double Standard for NATO." *Transitions* 4, no. 5 (July 1997): 75–79.

Belkin, Alexander. "The Evolution of Russian Foreign Policy." *National Strategy Reporter* (Spring 1997).

Birkavs, Valdes [Latvian Minister of Foreign Affairs], "Future European Security: Latvia and NATO." *ACE: Analysis of Current Events* 9, no. 5 (May 1997): 1, 4–5.

Black, J.L. "Russia and NATO Expansion Eastward: Red-lining the Baltic States," *International Journal* 54, No. 2 (Spring 1999): 49–66.

Blank, Stephen. "The Baltic States and Russia: The Strategic and Ethnic Contexts," *The Harriman Review* 10, No. 4 (1998): 15–32.

Bogoliubov, G. "Rasshirenie NATO na Vostok i rossiisko-kitaiskie otnosheniia" [NATO

Expansion to the East and Russian-Chinese Relations]. *Problemy Dal'nego Vostoka*, No. 6 (1997): 31–41.

Borovoi, Konstantin. "NATO Is Coming!" *New Times* (March 1997): 50.

Brzezinski, Zbigniew. "A Plan for Europe." *Foreign Affairs* 74, No. 1 (Jan/Feb 1995): 26–42.

———. "A Geostrategy for Eurasia." *Foreign Affairs* 76, no. 5 (Sept/Oct 1997): 50–64.

———. "On to Russia." *Washington Post* (5 March 1998).

Brzezinski, Zbigniew, and Anthony Lake. "For a New World, a New NATO." *New York Times* OP-ED (30 June 1997).

Cambone, Stephen A. "NATO Enlargement: Implications for the Military Dimension of Ukraine's Security." *The Harriman Review* 10, no. 3 (Winter 1997): 8–18.

Carpenter, Ted Galen, ed. *The Future of NATO*. London: Frank Cass, 1995.

Chernomorskii flot, gorod Sevastopol' i nekotorye problemy rossiisko-ukrainskikh otnoshenii: Khronika, dokumenty, analiz, mneniia (1991–1997 gg.) [The Black Sea Fleet, the City of Sevastopol and Some Problems in Russian-Ukrainian Relations]. Moscow: Nezavisimaia gazeta, 1997.

Cornish, Paul. *Partnership in Crisis: The U.S., Europe and the Fall and Rise of NATO*. London: RIIA, 1997.

Crow, Suzanne. "Russian Views in an Eastward Expansion of NATO." RFE/RL *Research Report* 2, No. 41 (1993): 21–24.

———. "Russia Asserts Its Strategic Agenda." RFE/RL *Research Report* 2, No. 50 (1993): 1–8.

The Costs of Expanding the NATO Alliance. CBO Papers, Congressional Budget Office (March 1996).

Daniels, Robert V. "Another Cold War? The Danger of NATO Expansion." *The New Leader* (14–28 July 1997): 11–13.

Dashichev, V.I. *Natsional'naia bezopasnost' Rossii i ekspansiia NATO* [Russian National Security and the Expansion of NATO]. Moscow: IMERI RAN, 1996.

David, Charles-Philippe, and Jacques Levesque, eds. *The Future of NATO: Enlargement, Russia and European Security*. Montréal: McGill-Queen's UP, 1999.

Davidov, Yu.P. "Rossiia i NATO: 'posle bala' " [Russia and NATO: "After the Ball"]. *SShA*, No. 1 (January 1998): 3–18.

Duffield, John S. "NATO's Functions after the Cold War." *Political Science Quarterly* 109, No. 5 (Winter 1994/95): 763–787.

Dutkiewicz, Piotr, and R. Jackson, eds. *NATO Looks East*. New York: Praeger, 1998.

Eisenhower, Susan. "The Bear at Bay." *The Spectator* (12 July 1997).

——— "NATO Expansion Fallout." *ACE: Analysis of Current Events* 10, No. 7/8 (July/Aug 1998): 10, 12.

The Enlargement of NATO: Why Adding Poland, Hungary and the Czech Republic to NATO Strengthens American National Security. U.S. Department of State, Public Information Series (February 1998).

Falkenrath, Richard A. *Shaping Europe's Military Order: The Origin and Consequences of the CFE Treaty*. Cambridge, MA: MIT Press, 1995.

Friedman, Thomas L. "Russia's NATO Fix." *New York Times* (24 July 1996).

———. "Europe's Wild Ride." *New York Times* (16 February 1997).

———. "Held Hostage." *New York Times* (28 April 1997).

Gaddis, John Lewis. "The Senate Should Halt NATO Expansion." *Washington Post* (29 January 1998).

———. "History, Grand Strategy, and NATO." *Survival*, No. 40 (1998): 145–151.

Galeotti, Mark. *The Age of Anxiety: Security and Politics in Soviet and Post-Soviet Russia.* London, 1995.

Gareev, M. "NATO's Expansion: Security Aspects. "*International Affairs* (Moscow), 42, No. 3 (1996): 141–148.

Garnett, Sherman. "Russia's Illusory Ambitions." *Foreign Affairs* 76, no. 2 (March/April 1997): 61–76.

General Accounting Office (GAO). *NATO Enlargement: Cost Estimates Developed to Date are Notional.* Washington, DC: August 1997.

Girnius, Saulius. "Relations between the Baltic States and Russia." RFE/RL *Research Report* 3, No. 33 (1994): 29–33.

Golan, Galia. "Russia and Iran: A Strategic Partnership?" RIIA Paper (December 1997).

Goldgeier, James. "NATO Expansion: The Anatomy of a Decision." *Washington Quarterly* 21(1998): 85–102.

Gorbachev, M.S. *Memoirs.* London: Doubleday, 1996.

Gordon, Philip. "Recasting the Atlantic Alliance." *Survival* 38, No. 1 (Spring 1996): 32–57.

———, ed. *NATO's Transformation—The Changing Shape of the Atlantic Alliance.* Lanham, MD: Rowman & Littlefield, 1997.

Hagland, David, ed. *Will NATO Go East? The Debate over Enlarging the Atlantic Alliance.* Kingston: Queen's University Center for International Affairs, 1996.

Hamos, Laszlo. "NATO Expansion and Human Rights." *ACE: Analysis of Current Events* 10, No. 6 (June 1998): 8–9.

Haslam, Jonathan. "Russia's Seat at the Table: A Place Denied or a Place Delayed?" *International Affairs* (London) 74, No. 1 (January 1998): 119–30. See Odom, below.

Havel, Vaclav. "The Charms of NATO." *New York Review of Books* (15 January 1998): 24. See also Steel, below.

Hopf, Ted. "Russia and the U.S.: Growing Cooperation?" *Great Decisions 1977.* New York: Foreign Policy Association, 1977, 27–36.

Huntington, S.P. "The Clash of Civilizations." *Foreign Affairs* 72, No. 3 (Summer 1993): 22–49.

Ivashov, L. "Russia-NATO: Matters of Cooperation." *International Affairs* (Moscow), No. 6 (1998): 110–119.

Judt, Tony. "New Germany, Old NATO." *New York Review of Books* (29 May 1997): 38, 40–45.

Kamoff-Nicolsky, George. "Russia—The Issue of NATO Enlargement." *National Network News* 4, No.2 (July 1997): 8–11.

Karaganov, Sergei A., et al. "View from Russia: Russia and NATO," *Comparative Strategy,* No. 15 (January–March 1996): 91–99.

Kartchner, Kerry M. *Negotiating START: Strategic Arms Reduction Talks and the Quest for Strategic Stability.* New Brunswick, NJ: Transaction, 1992.

Kazantsev, Boris. "First Steps towards Russia's Partnership with NATO." *International Affairs* (Moscow), No.12 (1994): 17–23.

———. "Posledstviia rasshirenie NATO" [The Consequences of NATO Expansion], *Mezhdunarodnaia zhizn'*. No. 11/12 (1997): 20–26.

———. "NATO Moving East: The Aftertaste." *International Affairs* (Moscow), 44, No. 1 (1998): 32–38.

Kelley, Charles T., Jr. *Admitting New Members: Can NATO Afford the Costs.* Santa Monica, CA: RAND Corporation, 1996. Paper No. P-7903.

Keohane, Robert O., and Stanley Hoffman, eds. *The New European Community: Decision Making and Institutional Change.* Boulder, CO: Westview, 1991.

Kolchin, S. "Neft' o gaz Kaspiia: strategicheskie interesy Rossii" [Oil and Gas of the Caspian: Russia's Strategic Interests], *Mirovaia ekonomika i mezhdunarodnye otnosheniia,* No. 3 (February 1998): 97–103.

Korolev, N. "Natovskii stsenarii dlia Rossii" [NATO's Scenario for Russia]. *Dialog,* No. 10 (1997): 73–77.

Kortunov, Sergei. "Russia's Way: National Identity and Foreign Policy." *International Affairs* (Moscow), 44, No. 4 (1998): 138–163.

Kozyrev, Andrei, "A Treaty of Cooperation and Partnership with NATO Is Needed." *New Times* (March 1997): 44–45.

Kremenyuk, V.A. "Rossiisko-amerikanskie otnosheniia: novoe nachalo?" [Russian-American Relations: A New Beginning?]. *SShA,* No. 11 (November 1997).

Kross, Sheril. "Vopros o rasshirenii NATO: v poiskakh optimal'nogo resheniia." *SShA,* No. 9 (September 1996): 47–57. A translation of Sheryl Cross, "The Question of NATO Expansion: Searching for the Optimal Solution," *Mediterranean Quarterly* 7, No. 1 (Winter 1996): 44–64.

Kuchin, N., and Yu. Rusanova. "Russia and America Yielded, But Did Not Retreat. Russia Yielded More," *New Times* (Novoe vremia) (30 March 1997).

Kugler, Richard, and Marianna V. Kozintseva. *Enlarging NATO: The Russian Factor.* Santa Monica, CA: RAND Corporation, 1996.

Kupchan, Charles A. "Reviving the West." *Foreign Affairs* (May/June 1996): 92–104.

Kuzio, Taras. "Why Ukraine and Russia Will Not Sign an Inter-State Treaty." *ACE: Analysis of Current Events* 9, No. 4 (1997): 9–10.

Lebed, Aleksandr. *Za derzhavu obidno. . . .* Moscow: Moskovskaia Pravda, 1995.

Legault, Albert, and Allen Sens. "Canada and NATO Enlargement: Interests and Options." *Canadian Foreign Policy* 4, No. 2 (Fall 1966): 88–93.

Lewis, Flora. "Why NATO—Not the United States—Frightens Russia." *Transition* (23 Feb 1996): 50–51.

Lockwood, J.S., and K. O'B. Lockwood. *The Russian View of U.S. Strategy: Its Past, Its Future.* New Brunswick, NJ: Transaction, 1993.

Mandelbaum, Michael. "Preserving the New Peace: The Case Against NATO Expansion." *Foreign Affairs* 74, No. 3 (May/June 1995): 9–13.

Mandelbaum, Michael. *The Dawn of Peace in Europe.* New York: Twentieth Century Fund, 1996.

Matlock, Jack F., Jr. *Autopsy of an Empire.* New York, 1995.

———. "The One Place NATO Could Turn for Help" [Russia], *New York Times* OP-ED

(20 April 1999).

Mihalka, Michael. "European-Russian Security and NATO's Partnership for Peace." RFE/RL *Research Report* 3, No. 2 (1994): 34–45.

———. "Continued Resistance to NATO Expansion." *Transition* 1, No. 14 (August 1995): 36–41.

Mlechen, Leonid. *Yevgenii Primakov: istoriia odnoi kar'ery* [Yevgenii Primakov: History of a Career]. Moscow: Tsentrpoligraf, 1999.

Molochkov, S.F. "Kanada, NATO i Rossiia. Nekotoriye rassuzhdeniia" [Canada, NATO and Russia: Several Considerations]. *SShA,* No. 2 (1998): 87–93.

Morrison, James. *NATO Expansion and Alternative Future Security Alignments.* Washington, DC: Institute for National Security Studies, National Defense University, 1995(McNair Paper 40).

Moynihan, Daniel Patrick. "NATO Expansion and Nuclear War." *ACE: Analysis of Current Events* 10, No. 7/8 (July/August 1998): 5–6.

"The NATO Enlargement Process: News from the Front." *Update.* The Atlantic Council of the United States, No. 4 (20 February 1998).

"NATO Rationalizes Its Eastward Enlargement." *Transition,* 1, No. 23 (December 1995): 19–26.

Nekotorye problemy demarkatsii rossiisko-kitaiskoi granitsy, 1991–1997 gg. Sbornik statei i dokumentov. [Some Problems in the Demarcation of the Russia-China Borders]. Moscow: Nezavisimaia gazeta, 1997.

Odom, William E. "Russia's Several Places at the Table." *International Affairs* (London), 74, No. 4 (October 1998): 809–822. Response to Haslam, above.

Oldberg, Ingmar, ed. *Priorities in Russian Foreign Policy: West, South or East?* (Proceedings of a Conference in Stockholm, 3 June 1996).

Osipov, G.V., et al. *Rossiia u kriticheskoi cherty: Vozrozhdenie ili katastrophe* [Russia at the Critical Line: Revival or Catastrophe]. Moscow: Respublika, 1997. On security and NATO expansion, pp. 262–287.

Parkhalina, Tatiana. "Of Myths and Illusions: Russian Perceptions of NATO Enlargement." *NATO Review* (Web edition), 45, No. 3 (May–June 1997): 11–15.

———. "O novoi arkhitekture bezopasnosti v Evrope" [On the New Security Architecture of Europe]. *Mirovaia ekonomika i mezhdunarodnye otnosheniia,* No. 12 (December 1997): 14–24.

Pellerin, Alain. *NATO Enlargement—Where We Came From and Where It Leaves Us.* Ottawa: Canadian Council for International Peace and Security. (Aurora Papers, 29) (30 May 1997).

Perlmutter, Amos, and Ted G. Carpenter. "NATO's Expensive Trip East." *Foreign Affairs* 77, No. 1 (Jan/Feb 1998): 2–6.

Pierre, J. Andrew, and Dmitrii Trenin. "Developing NATO-Russian Relations." *Survival* 39, No. 1 (Spring 1997): 5–42.

Primakov (interview on NATO expansion). *Novoe vremya,* No.15 (20 April 1997): 24–26.

Pushkov, A. "A Compromise with NATO?" *International Affairs* (Moscow), 43, No. 3 (1997): 13–22.

Rakhmaninov, Yu.N. "Nekotorye soobrazheniia o rasshirenii NATO" [Some Reflections on the Expansion of NATO]. *SShA,* No. 2 (January 1997): 56–60.

Ratifikatsiia dogovora SNV-2: Resheniia, problemy, perspecktivy (*Prilozhenie k zhurnalu "Obozrevatel'-Observer"*) [Ratification of the START-2 Treaty: Decisions, Problems, Prospects]. Moscow: Agentstvo Obozrevatel', 1996.

Rasshirenie NATO v Vostok: k miru ili voine [NATO Expansion to the East: Towards Peace or War]. Moscow: Klub "Realisty," 1998. Information Bulletin, No. 36.

Razvitie integratsionnykh protesssov v Evrope i Rossii: Problemno-tematicheskii sbornik [The Growth of the Integrative Process in Europe and Russia]. Moscow: INION RAN, 1997.

Rogov, S.M. "Rossiia i NATO" [Russia and NATO]. *SShA,* No. 10 (October 1996): 3–8.

"Rossiisko-amerikanskie otnosheniia na poroge novogo veka" [Russian-American Relations on the Threshhold of a New Century]. *Mirovaia ekonomika i mezhdunarodnye otnosheniia,* No. 5 (May 1998): 109–115.

Royen, Ch. [Germany], "Why Does Russia Object to NATO's Eastward Expansion?" *New Times* (Novoe vremya) (April 1996): 50–51.

Rubinstein, Alvin Z. "The Unheard Case Against NATO Enlargement." *Problems of Post-Communism* (May–June 1997): 52–55.

———. "NATO Enlargement vs. American Interests." *Orbis,* No. 1 (1998): 37–48.

Ruggie, John Gerard. *Winning the Peace.* New York: Columbia University Press, 1996.

Sedykh, Igor. "A Gateway to the East: Russian Delegation in Davos Continues Its Strange War against NATO's Eastward Expansion." *New Times,* No. 5 (9 February 1997): 24–25.

Sergeev, Marshal Igor. "We Are Not Adversaries, We Are Partners." *NATO Review,* No. 1 (Spring 1998): 15–18.

Shearman, Peter. "NATO Expansion and the Russian Question." In *Security after the Cold War,* edited by Robert Patman. New York: Macmillan, 1998.

Shustov, J. "Russia and Security Problems in the Baltics." *International Affairs* (Moscow), 44, No. 1 (1998): 39–44.

Siumon, Jeffrey, ed. *NATO: The Challenge of Change.* Washington, DC: National Defense University Press, 1993.

Sloan, S. "U.S. Perspectives on NATO's Future." *International Affairs* 7, No. 12 (April 1995): 217–231.

Solana, Javier. "NATO in Transition." *Perceptions: Journal of International Affairs* 1, No. 1 (1996).

Spechler, Martin. "To Expand beyond Enlargement." *ACE: Analysis of Current Events* 9, No. 12 (December 1997): 5, 8–9.

Steel, Ronald. "Instead of NATO." *The New York Review of Books* (15 January 1998): 21–24. See also Havel, above.

Talbott, Strobe. "Why NATO Should Grow." *The New York Review of Books* (10 August 1995): 27–30.

———. "Russia Has Nothing to Fear." *New York Times* Op-Ed (18 February 1997).

———. "A NATO Expansion Architect Makes His Case." *Christian Science Monitor* (27 October 1997).

Valasek, Tomas. "NATO: Creating Its Own Demons." *ACE: Analysis of Current Events* 9, No. 5 (May 1997): 6, 9–10.

Volkov, Vladimir. "NATO's Eastward Expansion: A Russian View." *Problems of Post-Communism* (May–June 1997): 61.

Winrow, Gareth. "NATO and Out-of-Area: A Post–Cold War Challenge," *European Security* 3/4 (Winter 1994): 617–38.

Yavlinskii, Grigorii. "The NATO Distraction." *Transition* 3, No. 5 (21 March 1997): 32–34.

————. "Shortsighted: By Supporting the Yeltsin Government You are Alienating the Average Russian." *New York Times Magazine* (8 June 1997): 66.

Zyuganov, G.A., general editor. *Voennaia reforma: Otsenka ugroz natsional'noi bezopasnosti Rossii* [Military Reform: Estimate of the Threat to Russian National Security]. Moscow: Narodno-patrioticheskii Soiuz Rossii, 1997. Publishers are the People's Patriotic Union of Russia and the movement Dukhovnoe nasledie [Spiritual Heritage].

SPECIAL ISSUES OF MAGAZINES AND PERIODICALS

ACE: Analysis of Current Events 9, No. 5 (May 1997). Special issue on NATO expansion.

"NATO-Russia Relations: A Key Feature of European Security." *NATO Review*, No. 3 (May/June 1997).

"NATO's Partnerships." *NATO Review*, Vol. 3 (Autumn 1998).

A Political Portrait of Ukraine. Bulletin of the Democratic Initiatives Foundation. Kiev, Nos. 3, 18 (1997), articles on Ukraine and NATO.

"Russia-NATO." Special section, *New Times* (Novoe vremya) (November 1996).

"Toward NATO Enlargement." *NATO Review*, No. 1 (January 1996).

MAGAZINES AND INFORMATION BULLETINS

NATO: fakty i kommentarii [NATO: Facts and Commentary]. Moscow: NATO Documentation Center for Questions of European Security. A bulletin edited by Tatiana Parkhalina.

NATO Review. Brussels.

NATO Weekly Review of the Ukrainian Press. Prepared by the Democratic Initiatives Foundation, Kyiv, for the NATO Information Center.

Novini NATO [NATO News]. Bulletin published in Brussels for the NATO Centre for Information and Documentation, Kyiv.

Name Index

Names of journalists are listed only when they appear in the main text. The most prominent individuals (e.g., Yeltsin) and phenomena (e.g., NATO, United States, Russia) are mentioned throughout, but indexed only for specific reference.

Achalov, Gen. Vladislav, 166
Adamkus, Valdas, 212, 217, 218
Afanas'evskii, Nikolai N., 29n, 52n, 59, 62, 100, 129, 145, 146, 151
Agapov, Boris, 224n
Ahtisaari, Martti, 208
Albright, Madeleine, 25, 27, 29, 30, 32, 43n, 45, 46, 51, 55, 56, 62, 63, 70, 79, 82, 84, 89, 102, 133, 139, 141, 152, 186, 204, 206n, 208, 218, 225
Aleksei II, Patriarch, 113, 156
Aliev, Heydar, 228, 235
Alksnis, Viktor, 7n, 9
Annan, Kofi, 48, 154
Arbatov, Aleksei, 2–3, 29, 34, 83, 88, 95ff, 97, 98, 109, 122, 160, 164, 166
Arbatov, Georgii, 61, 94–95
Avdeev, A.A., 100, 214, 215
Axworthy, Lloyd, 151n
Aziz, Tariq, 142

Baburin, Sergei N., 26, 43, 51, 66, 67, 73, 77, 87, 89, 216
Baturin, Yurii, 20, 225
Bazilyuk, Aleksandr, 179
Belonogov, Aleksandr, 60

Berezovskii, Boris A., 19, 104, 131
Birkavs, Valdis, 204
Boldyrev, Yurii, 130
Borovoi, Konstantin, 28, 34, 43
Boskholov, Sergei, 86
Bovkin, Ye., 40
Boyko, Bohdan, 197
Bratishchev, Igor, 173
Brazauskas, A., 209, 210, 218
Brzezinski, Zbigniew, 2, 3, 11, 18, 28, 44, 45, 56, 106, 134, 137, 161, 195, 218, 234
Buteyko, Anton, 182, 192
Bykovskii, Aleksandr, 183

Chahtahtinsky, Alexis, 110, 128
Charlemagne, 17
Cherniavskii, S., 234, 235
Chernomyrdin, Viktor, 12, 21, 26, 29, 30, 34, 44, 76, 77, 99, 113–14, 131f, 135, 140, 164, 167, 208f, 222, 241,
Chernov, Vladislav, 11
Chichkin, Aleksandr, 64
Chirac, Jacques, 21, 30n, 76, 79, 127, 135
Chornovil, V., 180, 191

Christopher, Warren, 12
Chubais, Anatolii, 24, 26, 29, 45, 57, 66,
    99, 241
Clark, Gen. Wesley K., 42–43, 97
Clinton, Bill, 12, 27, 31, 36, 38, 43,
    49–50, 53, 55–6, 68, 75, 82, 90–91,
    108, 112, 114, 135, 137n, 141, 142,
    155, 167, 179–80, 185, 186, 204,
    212, 226, 241
Cohen, William, 56, 85
Cook, Robin, 125

Danilevskii, Nikolai, 5, 6, 49, 96,
    123n
Davidov, YuP., 80
Dashichev, V.I., 19–20, 31, 41, 64, 97
Dean, Jonathan, 71
Demin, V.A., 57n
Demirel, Suleman, 193, 207
Deriugin, Yurii, 165
Derycke, Erik, 144
Diehl, Manfred, 110
Dezhin, Yevgenii, 133
Dini, Lamberti, 29–30
Dukhov, Col. Gen. Boris, 43n

Eggert, Konstantin, 60
Eisenhower, Susan, 69n
Epiev, Sefer, 235

Fabius, Laurent, 218
Fedorov, Andrei, 208
Fedorov, Boris, 111
Filatov, Gen. Viktor, 64–65
Fjaervoll, Dag Jostein, 211
Friedman, Thomas L., 70, 84
Frolianov, I.Ya., 48, 124
Frolov, Igor, 209

Gareev, Gen. Makhmut, 154
Gavrilin, Mikhail, 203
Gaydar, Yegor, 111, 112
Gerasimov, Vladimir, 57
Gieremek, Bronislaw, 74, 197
Gingrich, Newt, 41n

Glotov, Sergei A., 26, 32, 89, 172n, 179,
    185
Golubov, Vladimir, 177
Gorbachev, M.S., 2, 6, 7, 15, 19, 22, 39,
    41, 42, 105, 108, 110, 113, 165, 202,
    224–25, 240
Gore, Al, 12, 45, 135, 222
Gornostaev, Dmitrii, 12, 25
Grach, Leonid, 185
Grachev, Andrei, 55, 125, 131
Grachev, Pavel, 125, 157, 165, 168, 175,
    223
Greshnevikov, Anatolii, 82
Gromov, Adm. Feliks, 19, 168
Gromyko, Aleksei, 229–30
Guludze, Vafa, 235
Gusher, G., 134

Havel, Vlacav, 53
Helms, Jesse, 70, 97
Hitler, Adolph, 53, 64, 66–67, 110, 112,
    142n, 153, 179, 183, 210n, 236
Holbrooke, Richard, 101
Horbulin, Vladimir, 177n, 180, 183,
    186, 195
Hunter, Robert, 229
Hussein, Saddam, 80, 12, 138ff, 142,
    214

Ilves, Toomas, 217n
Ilyukhin, Viktor I., 34, 49, 51, 100, 152,
    156, 173
Ivanenko, Sergei, 109, 211
Ivanov, Igor, 75, 100, 101, 102, 103,
    106, 142, 143, 152, 220, 241
Ivanov, Sergei, 48, 50
Ivashov, Col. Gen. Leonid, 29n, 50, 78,
    93–94, 108, 171

Jiang, Zemin, 130
Joulwan, Gen. George, 14, 43, 177
Juntzis, Talavs, 187n

Kachanovskii, Yurii, 63
Karadzic, Radovan, 14, 144

Karaganov, Sergei, 84n
Karimov, Islam, 235
Kasenov, Umirserik, 231
Kas'ianenko, Zhanna, 174
Kennan, George, 30, 61, 71
Khrushchev, Nikita, 6
Kharlamov, Col. Sergei, 161
Khudolea, K.K., 48
Kikilo, V., 31
Kinkel, Klaus, 29, 38
Kirichev, Vladimir, 46
Kiriyenko, Sergei V., 87, 88, 99, 102, 241
Kisfalvi, Janos, 73
Kislyak, Sergei, 84, 100, 101, 110
Kissinger, Henry, 46
Kleiber, Klaus Peter, 193
Kohl, Helmut, 6, 17, 22, 25, 42, 66, 79, 127
Kokoshin, Andrei, 84, 121
Kondratenko, Nikolai I., 96, 179
Korolev, Oleg, 61
Korzhakov, Gen. A., 168
Kovacs, Lazlo, 73
Kovalev, Sergei, 34
Kozhokhin, Yevgenii, 47, 222, 231
Kozitsin, Nikolai, 173
Kozyrev, Andrei, 8, 9, 10, 11, 12, 14, 28, 61, 112, 241
Kramer, Franklin D., 72
Kravchenko, Adm. Viktor, 178
Kremenyuk, V.A., 53, 78
Kriuchkov, Vladimir, 165
Kryuchkov, Georgiy, 201
Kuchinskaia, Marina, 205
Kuchma, Leonid, 62, 175–76, 178, 180, 181, 182, 183, 184, 186, 189, 190, 192, 194, 196, 197, 199, 200, 201–2
Kuchma, Mrs., 185
Kurganov, Aleksandr, 223n
Kurganov, Anatolii, 226
Kuroedov, Adm. V., 169
Kurteva, Tatyana, 185
Kuvaldin, Viktor, 25
Kuzar', Vladimir, 128

Kvashnin, Gen. V., 75, 77, 169, 171
Kwasniewski, Aleksandr, 200

Landsbergis, Vytautas, 204, 206, 209, 218, 220
Lapskii, Vladimir, 141
Larionov, Sergei, 52
Lavrov, S.B., 48, 49, 124
Lavrov, S.V., 226n
Lebed, Aleksandr, 14, 35, 39, 40, 47, 49, 54, 56, 59, 63, 111, 121, 152, 167, 171, 193, 209, 210n
Lenin, V.I., 6, 32 *See also* Leninism.
Lenskii, V., 34
Likhachev, Vasilii, 85
Lima, Viktor, 77
Lishchynskyi, Roman, 181, 188
Lopata, Col. Gen. Anatolii, 189
Lough, John, 84
Lukashenka, Alyaksandr, 33, 59, 117f, 122
Lukianov, A., 69
Lukin, Vladimir, 1, 29, 49, 77, 100, 104, 108, 123, 130, 142, 152, 209, 213
Lukov, Vladimir, 223n
Lunev, Sergei, 65–66, 70
Luzhkov, Yurii, 56, 102–3, 104, 105, 108, 114, 152, 166, 199, 241

Maiorov, Col. Gen. Leonid S., 29, 161, 169
Major, John, 44
Makashov, Gen. Albert, 67, 90, 166, 173
Makienko, Konstantin, 123
Maksimychev, Igor, 96
Mandelbaum, Michael, 30
Manilov, Col. Gen. Valerii, 37, 85, 107, 216n
Marchuk, Yevhen, 193n
Markushin, V., 98
Matlock, Jack F., Jr., 22, 31, 61, 71
Matutes, Abel, 46
McConnell, Donald, 87
McCurry, Michael D., 205n
McFaul, Michael, 63

Meri, Lennart, 203, 205
Migranyan, Andranik, 54
Mikhailov, Viktor, 131
Mikheev, Vladimir, 128
Milosevic, Slobodan, 100, 101, 110, 111, 121, 148, 152, 201
Mironov, Oleg, 87
Mitterand, François, 20
Mitrofanov, Aleksei, 211
Mladich, Ratko, 14
Moltke, Gebhardt von, 207
Moroz, Oleg, 28, 34
Morozov, Col. Yurii, 159
Moynihan, Daniel Patrick, 71
Mukhin, Vladimir, 230
Murphy, Richard, 134

Napoleon, 5
Naumann, Gen. Klaus, 235
Nazarbaev, Nursultan, 231
Nemtsov, Boris Y., 45, 56, 57, 99, 111, 131, 208
Nesterova, Marina, 97
Nevskii, Aleksandr, 17
Nikolaev, Dmitrii, 34, 234, 235

Oliynyk, Borys, 176, 178, 188, 201
Onyszkiewica, Janusz, 107, 200
Orobets, Yurii, 183
Ovinnikov, Richard, 58, 58

Paklin, Nikolai, 52,
Parkhalina, Tatiana, 80
Perry, William, 175
Piadyshov, Boris, 20, 60
Pishchev, Col. Gen. Nikolai, 40, 41, 46, 158, 159
Plavsic, Bilana, 144
Pliaus, Jakov, 11
Podberezkin, A.I., 51, 83, 108
Popkovich, Roman, 103
Popov, Yevgenii, 23
Postal, Mikhail, 65
Posuvalyuk, Viktor, 135
Potemkin, V.K., 159

Prikhodko, Sergei, 220
Primakov, Yevgenii, 4, 9, 14, 15, 16, 21, 23, 25, 27, 29, 30, 32f, 38f, 40, 42, 44, 45f, 48, 51, 60, 75–76, 78, 79f, 87, 99f, 102, 104f, 109, 111, 113, 121, 124, 139f, 142, 144, 148, 150, 152, 155, 157, 167, 193f, 197, 200, 201, 203f, 209, 216, 218, 222, 224, 237, 241
Prodi, Romano, 99
Pushkov, Aleksei, 75, 222
Putilov, Sergei, 232
Puzanovskii, A., 35
Pysans'ka, Valentyna, 189, 191

Rakhmaninov, Yu. N., 31
Razuvaev, Vladimir, 26
Roberts, Peter M., 3
Rodionov, Boris, 186
Rodionov, Gen. Igor, 22, 30n, 47, 48, 57, 130, 165, 240
Rogov, S.M., 18, 28, 31, 53, 99, 103, 222n
Rokhlin, Gen. Lev, 27, 63, 90, 165–74 *passim,* 240
Romashkin, Col. P.B., 83
Rühe, Volker, 172
Rusakov, Yevgenii,139
Ruzskii, Aleksandr, 236
Rybkin, I.P., 57, 84
Ryurikov, Dmitrii, 38, 205
Ryzhkov, Nikolai, 13, 32

Safire, William, 135, 207n
Safronchuk, Vasilii, 54, 57, 61, 66, 70, 210
Samsonov, Gen. Viktor, 22, 240
Saudargas, Algirdas, 204
Scherbak, Yurii, 179
Scowcraft, Brent, 134, 137
Seleznev, G.N., 37, 61, 87, 90n, 91, 102, 104, 137, 150n, 153, 156, 193, 197, 199, 211, 217
Sergeev, Gen. Igor, 48, 76, 82, 83, 87, 112, 126, 143, 148, 161, 165, 166ff,

171f, 175, 186, 188n, 207, 209, 211, 234
Serov, Valerii, 59, 62
Sheiman, Viktor, 59
Shermatova, Sanobas, 224
Shevardnadze, Eduard, 223, 225, 226–27, 229, 236, 233
Shevtsev, Col. Gen. Leontii, 14, 108
Shmarov, Valeriy, 175
Shokhin, A.N., 26, 60, 168
Siimann, Mart, 204
Simonov, Vladimir, 31
Skychko, Anatolyy, 191
Solana, Javier, 16, 23, 25, 34, 40, 46, 47, 64, 92, 108, 121, 124, 162, 175, 177, 181, 183, 195, 208, 217, 218, 223, 224, 225, 226, 231
Solov'ev, Vadim, 86, 92, 104–5
Sorokin, Eduard, 82
Sorokina, Svetlana, 217n
Stalin, J.V., 120, 239
Stepashin, Sergei, 115
Stoliarov, Nikolai, 23
Stroev, Yegor, 34, 156
Sturua, Melor, 54, 89, 114
Surikov, A.V., 83
Symonenko, Petro, 175, 185, 188, 192

Talbott, Strobe, 7, 32, 64, 108, 111, 114, 219, 234
Tarasov, Gennadii, 61, 206
Tarasyuk, Borys, 88, 146, 177–78, 192f, 194, 196, 197, 198–99, 201, 236
Ter-Petrosyan, Levon, 229
Tetekin, V., 162
Tevzadze, David, 229, 233
Tkachenko, Oleksandr, 199, 201
Trenin, Dmitrii, 3, 24n, 27, 34

Trofimenko, G.A., 234
Tsipko, Aleksandr, 202
Tuleev, Aman, 177, 225–26

Udovenko, Gennadii, 175, 176, 179, 180, 181, 183, 189, 192
Urnov, Andrei, 158

Varennikov, V., 69, 165
Volkov, Vladimir N., 106, 123, 206n
Voronin, Lt. Gen. Aleksandr, 92

Weinberger, Caspar, 134

Yakushev, Andrei, 203n
Yastrzhembskii, Sergei, 50, 206, 223
Yavlinskii, Grigorii, 21, 23f, 36, 40, 56, 95, 98, 104, 109, 130, 152, 156, 240
Yazov, Gen. D.T., 168
Yeltsin, Boris, *passim*
Yurkovskii, Anatolii, 184

Zatynayko, Lt. Gen. O., 177
Zavarzin, Lt. Gen. Viktor, 100, 101, 110, 148, 168
Zayats, Ivan, 181, 200
Zheglova, Yuliia, 163
Zhinkina, Irena, 55, 129
Zhirinovskii, Vladimir, 10, 18, 34, 23, 51, 90, 104, 105, 120, 121n, 140, 142, 143, 152, 156, 167
Zhivkovich, Nikola, 46, 147
Zhvania, Zurab, 224
Zlenko, Lt. Gen. Nikolai, 174
Zyuganov, Gennadii, 9, 13, 14, 18, 31, 55, 66, 69, 83, 87, 90, 97, 104, 108, 121, 126, 140, 143, 152, 154, 156, 167, 168

Subject and Place Index

Abkhazia, 158, 197, 224, 226, 227, 229, 231, 233
ABM Treaty, 78, 108, 154, 156, 167. *See also* Nuclear Deterrence/Arms
Afghanistan, 122
Agrarian Party, 27, 43
Albanians, 146
Algeria, 138
Anti-NATO Commission (Association), 27, 32, 39, 43, 51, 66, 77, 82, 85, 89, 93, 163, 166, 178–79, 185, 192, 205, 209, 213, 216, 230, 241
Anti-NATO Club (Ukraine), 77, 185, 188, 191, 192
Armed Forces, Russian, 37n, 43, 63, 78, 79, 98, 101, 108, 156f, 158–59, 164–75, 211–12, 217
Armenia, 100, 134, 226, 229–30, 236, 234–45
Arms Race, 83, 170f
Arms Sales, Russian, 125–26, 132f, 136, 193
ASEAN, 125
Austria, 99
Azerbaijan, 50, 71, 134, 138, 146, 157, 158, 196, 224, 226, 227n, 228- 30, 231, 235–36

Balkans, 127, 143–56; Bosnia, 53, 63, 144–45, 146; Kosovo, 66–67, 81, 93, 100ff, 118, 142, 145–56, 198, 201, 235–56, 238; Yugoslavia, 46, 67, 100ff, 109–15, 143–56, 195, 198, 201f, 230f, 236, 240
Baltic Challenge 98, 217
Baltic Charter, 82, 126, 205, 208, 212–14, 219
Baltic Sea, 158
Baltic States, 39, 53, 55, 61, 62, 71, 77, 86, 93, 107, 161, 162, 190n, 202–21. *See also individual Baltic countries*
Belarus, 13, 59, 77, 83, 101, 110, 117–19, 223, 224, 230, 235, 236
Belarus-Russia Charter. *See* Slavic Union
Black Sea Fleet,177f, 181, 182, 183f, 186, 191, 194, 196, 199, 200, 227
Black Sea Region, 158, 160, 207, 227
Bosnia. *See* Balkans
Bulgaria, 145, 161

Canada, 60, 103, 150, 151
Caspian Sea Region, 134–35, 137–38, 146, 152, 229, 230, 231f, 234
Cato Institute, 27n, 68
Coalition Against the Expansion of NATO, 71
Chechnya, 57, 101, 149, 157, 159, 164, 167, 178, 224, 229
China, 17, 37n, 38, 83, 88, 104, 110,

120, 122f, 130–33, 136, 139, 156, 231, 232, 241–42

Club of Realists, 39

Cold War, 95ff

Cominform, 57

Committee of [Russian] War Veterans, 64

Commonwealth of Independent States (CIS), 65, 80, 98, 107, 110, 155, 157, 161, 179, 180, 184, 195, 186, 194, 199, 221–37; Collective Security Pact, 186, 221f, 223, 241; Council of Defence Ministers, 223, 233–34, 235–56; Inter-Parliamentary Assembly, 201

Communist Party of the Russian Federation (CPRF), 9, 13, 27, 56, 67, 90, 96–97, 170, 241 (*see also* Zyuganov); IV Congress (1997), 44, 121

Concept of National Security, Russian, 80, 161f, 169, 173

Conference on Security and Copperation in Europe (CSCE). *See* OSCE

Conventional Armed Forces in Europe (CFE), 18, 78, 123, 159

Cooperative Neighbor 98, 194

Council of Baltic Sea States, 218

Council of Europe, 76–77, 83

Council for Foreign and Defence Policy, Russian, 12, 34, 98, 208

Crimea, 183–84, 185, 191, 197, 198

Croatia, 46

Cuba, 80, 122, 124; Missile Crisis (1962), 31

Czech Republic, 9, 53, 59, 72f, 108

Danish-German-Polish Corps, 172, 219

Denmark, 172, 218

Drang nach Osten, 48, 52, 58, 63, 64–68, 112, 197, 153, 240

Duma. *See* State Duma

Estonia, 84, 141, 157, 202–21 *passim,* 236

Euroatlantic Council. *See* NATO

European Union (EU), 10, 96, 103, 117, 125, 210, 220, 239

Fatherland Party, 105, 241

For Atlantic Dialogue, 43

Foreign Intelligence Service (FIS), 8–9, 15, 16

Founding Act (1997), 38ff, 48ff, 52–54f, 56, 59, 61, 64, 78, 80, 84, 87, 92f, 97, 102, 124–25, 149, 150, 159, 169, 181, 186, 206, 207, 213f, 219, 237

France, 30, 39, 88, 93, 135, 139–40, 150, 151

G-7 (G-8), 17, 52, 58, 59, 89, 117, 125, 131

Gas/Oil. *See* Oil

Gazprom, 135–36, 140, 182

Germany, 2, 7, 19f, 29, 39, 48, 59, 64f, 103, 119f, 127, 240; German Reunification, 6, 22 28, 95, 119–20, 225,

Georgia, 50, 157, 158, 187, 223, 223f, 226–27, 229, 230, 231, 234, 236

Government, Russian, *passim;* Federal Assembly, 9, 12, 32, 143; Federation Council, 34, 82, 111, 143, 150, 1541, 156, 199–200; State Duma. *See* State Duma

Great Britain, 88, 143, 151

Greece, 127–28

Helsinki Summit, 33, 36–38, 180

Hungary, 9, 30, 57, 59, 72f, 107

Impeachment, Russia, 90, 113, 172–73, 193, 241; Ukraine, 183

India, 104, 110, 123, 126–27, 241, 242

Institute for the World Economy and International Affairs (IMEMO), 15, 70, 102

Institute for USA & Canada (ISKRAN), 18, 31, 53. *See* also Rogov

International Monetary Fund (IMF), 45, 109, 241

Iran, 3, 80, 122, 133–38, 142, 230, 231, 242

Iraq, 80, 82, 84, 104f, 120, 122, 133, 138–43, 199, 235, 238

Israel, 67

Italy, 29, 99, 127, 151

Japan, 59, 132

Joint Permanent Committee (JPC). *See* NATO

Kaliningrad, 43, 74, 156, 170, 172, 174, 202, 206, 208, 212n, 218, 220

Kazakhstan, 13, 17, 85, 110, 134, 223, 231–32, 233–36

Kosovo. *See* Balkans

Kyrgyzstan, 17, 110, 223, 224, 231, 235, 236

Latin America, 162

Latvia, 55, 157, 187, 202–21 *passim,* 230, 236

Leninism. *See* Marxism-Leninism

Liberal Democratic Party of Russia (LDRP), 18, 43n, 105, 120, 199. *See also* Zhirinovskii

Libya, 122, 124, 133, 138, 140

Liman, 110

Lithuania, 85, 202–21 *passim*

London Club, 117

Madrid Declaration, 208, 230

Madrid Summit (1997), 59–64, 131, 160, 165

Marshall Plan, 53, 55, 56, 57

Marxism-Leninism, 6, 55, 65, 96, 239

Memel, 210

Military Doctrine, Russian, 40, 156–57, 159, 160f, 240. *See also* Nuclear Deterrence

military reform, Russia, 164–75, 211; United States, 159

Moldova, 9, 27, 77, 110, 136, 157, 224, 225, 230, 236

Movement in Support of the Army, 165 ff; Rokhlin, Gen., 27, 63, 90, 165–74, *passim,* 240

Nagorno-Karabakh, 197, 229

NATO, *passim;* Euro-Atlantic Partnership Council (EAPC), 59, 114, 182; European Security and Defense Identity (ESDI), 21; North Atlantic Cooperation Council (NACC), 8, 9, 182; Partnership for Peace (PfP), 10–11, 12, 75, 79, 86, 110, 134, 145, 146, 158, 162, 177, 187, 231, 242, 234; Permanent Joint Council (PJC), 53, 76, 85, 93, 98, 170, 237, 222; Rome Summit, 8; IFOR, 14; SFOR, 144, 145; Strategic Concept, 8, 103f, 114, 157, 163, 164, 237, 238

National Security Concept, Russia. *See* concept of National Security, Russian

Norway, 30, 86, 162, 163, 172, 211–12, 216, 220

Nuclear Deterrence/Arms, 18, 83, 103, 123, 126, 156–57, 170, 206, 240. *See also* ABM, military doctrine

Organization for Security and Cooperation in Europe (OSCE), 8, 12, 18, 21, 25, 41, 44, 52, 53, 61–62, 790, 82, 89, 96, 102, 129, 145, 150, 154, 157, 159, 163, 171, 176, 186, 227, 238, 239, 242

Our Home is Russia (NDR), 44, 168, 241

Oil/Gas, 135–38, 139–40, 196, 224, 229, 230f, 236

Pakistan, 122, 123

Pamiat, 6, 7, 19

Paris Club, 45, 52, 59, 117, 125

Peace Fairway 97, 187

Peaceful Coexistence, 6

People's Patriotic Union, 27, 97, 105, 110, 174

Poland, 9, 37, 43, 59, 55, 72f, 74,

107–8, 157, 162, 172, 178, 191, 196f, 200, 206, 219

Power to the People!, 13, 27

Public Opinion, 2–3, 27, 86–87, 106ff, 111f, 114–15, 143, 153, 155, 177, 190, 195, 216, 218, 228, 238, 242

"Red line" *See* spheres of influence

Romania, 9, 62, 161

Rukh, People's, 180, 191

Russia, relations with; Baltic States. (*See* Baltic States); Azerbaijan; Belarus, 24, 33, 41, 83, 117–19, 124, 126; China, 17, 38, 95, 120, 121, 1234ff, 130–33; Czech republic, 58; France, 127; Germany, 25, 127; Hungary, 58; India, 38, 95, 120, 121, 123ff, 1267; Iran, 3, 37, 95, 120, 124, 133–38; Iraq, 37n, 124, 138–43; Kazakhstan, 122f, 231f; Poland, 58; Syria, 124; Turkey, 126; Ukraine, 12, Section 4, *passim;* United States, 2, 27, 65, 103, 105f, 135–37, 151–52, 222ff. *See also separate entries*

Russian Way (idea), 95ff, 99, 102, 105

Russia's Choice, 112

Sea Breeze, 97, 98, 178–79, 181, 183–84, 185, 186ff, 192, 198, 229

Sevastopol Battalion, 185f

SFOR. *See* NATO

Slavic Union, 24, 77, 101, 112, 113, 116, 117–18, 120, 182, 185, 197, 226

Slavophiles, 5, 96, 239

Slovakia, 9, 30

Slovenia, 62

Soyuz, 6, 7

Spheres of Influence ("Red line"), 38, 53, 54, 101, 216, 218, 219, 220, 239

START, II, III, 27, 68, 69, 77, 80, 82–83, 88, 90, 91, 95, 101, 103, 121, 137, 143, 152, 160, 165, 167, 170, 171, 193, 241

State Duma, 2, 8, 13–14, 32, 34, 99, 138, 143, 150, 152, 168, 187, 190, 194, 199, 215; Defence Committee, 27, 49, 103; Committee on Economic Policy, 35; International Affairs Committee, 11, 51, 77; Security Committee, 49

Strong Resolve, 98, 85, 216

Tajikistan, 17, 110, 157, 235, 236

Taliban, 158

Transcaucasia, 27, 50, 127, 158, 222f, 226, 229, 233, 236

Transdniestr, 197, 225

Tsentrasbat, 86, 146, 160, 161n, 188, 232n, 233

Turkey, 33, 37n, 122, 134–35, 138, 146, 155, 158, 182, 223, 226, 228–29, 231, 233–34, 236

Turkmenistan, 134, 138, 196, 230, 231

Ukraine, 12, 13, 33, 37, 55, 62, 75, 74, 77, 85, 107, 110, 123, 124, 142, 146, 161, 175–202, 206, 229, 230, 236; Charter with NATO, 62, 175–76, 179, 192, 184f, 195; Treaties with Russia, 182–83, 187, 190, 193–94, 196, 199–200

Ukrainian Communist Party, 67, 184, 188, 190–91, 198

Ukrainian Progressive Socialist Party, 67, 142, 197, 198

Union of Russian Officers, 57

United Nations, 8, 13, 41, 52, 82, 89, 100f, 113, 145, 146, 201, 227, 237, 233, 238, 239, 242; Security Council, 8, 101, 102, 104, 110, 113, 130, 138f, 141, 150, 151n, 152, 227, 237–38

United States, 11, 39, 64, 145, 151, 155, 187, 198, 201, 207, 213, 222f, 236; Congress, 42, 70, 136–37, 159, 193, 233; Senate, 88–89, 141

Unity and Accord Party, 60n

Uzbekistan, 50, 138, 230, 231, 233, 235

Visegrad Group, 9, 31, 58

Warsaw Treaty Organization, 2, 6, 8, 18, 43, 119, 239
West European Union, 128, 157, 238
Westernizers, 96, 239
World Bank, 226

World Economic Forum (Davos), 26
World Trade Organization, 45, 52, 59, 117
World War I, 2
World War II, 43, 65, 66

Yabloko, 11, 21, 40, 43, 109, 112, 130, 241
Yavoriv Testing Ground, 200–1
Yugoslavia. *See* Balkans

About the Author

Born in Sackville, New Brunswick, Canada, and educated at Mount Allison University (Sackville), Boston University, and McGill University (Montreal), J. L. Black has been a Professor of History at Carleton University (Ottawa) since 1976. He was Director of the Institute of Soviet & East European Studies from 1982 to 1990 and has been the director of the Centre for Research on Canadian-Russian Relations (CRCR) since 1990.

The recipient of seven university and provincial research honors and two teaching awards, he has just completed a two-year term (1997–99) as a NATO Research Fellow. Black has written or edited more than twenty books on Soviet and Russian history, foreign policy, and education, the most recent of which is *Canada in the Soviet Mirror: Ideology and Perception in Soviet Foreign Affairs, (1917–1991)* (1998).